PRAISE FOR *HELL AND OTHER DESTINATIONS*

"This richly detailed memoir by the former secretary of state covers the period since her departure from government in 2001. With clarity and wisdom, Albright recounts moments of pride, like receiving the Presidential Medal of Freedom in 2012, and acknowledges recent criticisms of her record, including those concerning the human cost of the sanctions that the Clinton administration imposed on Iraq. Ultimately, the book presents an intricate portrait of a diplomat, and her ardent belief in democratic values and human rights, transatlantic partnerships and arms control, and open economies and sturdy institutions."   —*The New Yorker*

"By turns poignant and hilarious."   —*New York Times*

"In a blunt and revealing memoir, the former secretary of state reflects on the final stages of her career, working productively in her later decades and the state of the world since she left office in 2001."
—*USA Today*

"The book reflects the energy and churn of her post-State Department life.... What resonated with me most were the human moments...her successes and her failures. The changes she's witnessed and the glass ceilings that remain."   —*NPR*

"A humorous, self-deprecating account of her past two decades as a professor, businesswoman, mother, and grandmother."
—*Wall Street Journal*

"This passionately told account of Albright's 'afterlife' will inspire readers to become involved in the issues meaningful to them. Recommended for all interested in politics, leadership, and women's studies." —*Library Journal* (starred review)

"Former Secretary of State Albright weaves geopolitics with her own life story in this intelligent and personable memoir. . . . She proves to be a capacious storyteller, willing to share personal disappointments, such as the dissolution of her marriage, as well as professional accomplishments. This appealing memoir will charm readers interested in contemporary politics and women's issues." —*Publishers Weekly*

"Dishy, as policy-wonkish memoirs go, and a pleasure for readers interested in the art of negotiation." —*Kirkus Reviews*

HELL AND OTHER
DESTINATIONS

HELL AND OTHER DESTINATIONS

A 21st-Century Memoir

MADELEINE ALBRIGHT

WITH BILL WOODWARD

HARPER PERENNIAL

NEW YORK • LONDON • TORONTO • SYDNEY • NEW DELHI • AUCKLAND

HARPER PERENNIAL

HarperCollins books may be purchased for educational, business,
or sales promotional use. For information, please email the Special
Markets Department at SPsales@harpercollins.com.

FIRST HARPER PERENNIAL EDITION PUBLISHED 2022.

Designed by Fritz Metsch

Library of Congress Cataloging-in-Publication Data
has been applied for.

ISBN 978-0-06-280227-9 (pbk.)

22 23 24 25 26   LSC   10 9 8 7 6 5 4 3 2 1

To Life

What I love about the theater are arrivals, departures, and returns, entrances and exits, from the wings to the stage, and from the stage to the wings. It's like going from one world into another. And on stage, I love gates, fences, walls, windows, and, of course, doors. They are the borders between different worlds, cross-sections of space and time that carry information about their contours, their beginnings, and their ends. Every wall and every door tells us that there is something on the other side of it, and thus they remind us that beyond every "other side" there is yet another "side" beyond that one. Indirectly, they ask what lies beyond the final "beyond" and thus broach the theme of the mystery of the universe and of Being itself. At least I think they do.

—VÁCLAV HAVEL, from *Leaving*, a play (2008)

Contents

PREFACE ix

ONE: Afterlife 1

TWO: Voice Lessons 9

THREE: From the Ground Up 17

FOUR: "Do Not Be Angry" 28

FIVE: Quicksand 39

SIX: Clubbing 49

SEVEN: Professor Maddy 60

EIGHT: Bulls 70

NINE: Democrats with a Small *d* 80

TEN: A Foothold 93

ELEVEN: Things Unseen 102

TWELVE: Advise and Dissent 115

THIRTEEN: Companions 124

FOURTEEN: Digging Out 134

FIFTEEN: Making of the President 2008 142

SIXTEEN: First Light 154

SEVENTEEN: Thought and Purpose 163

EIGHTEEN: The Serpent's Tale 173

NINETEEN: Muscles in Brussels 182

TWENTY: A Bigger Sea 194

TWENTY-ONE: Puzzles 201

TWENTY-TWO: Inferno 211

TWENTY-THREE: R-E-S-P-E-C-T 222

TWENTY-FOUR: "You Are Just Like Your Grandmother" . . 230

TWENTY-FIVE: Leaving. 242

TWENTY-SIX: Cradle of Civilization 255

TWENTY-SEVEN: Breathless 266

TWENTY-EIGHT: Midnight 278

TWENTY-NINE: A Warning 288

THIRTY: Unhinged 296

THIRTY-ONE: Renewal 306

THIRTY-TWO: Shadows and Light 314

JOURNAL OF RŮŽENA SPIEGLOVÁ 325

AFTERWORD 335

ACKNOWLEDGMENTS 355

NOTES 359

INDEX 377

Preface

SINCE ANCIENT TIMES, we humans have had much to say about Hell. Hercules' twelfth labor was to subdue the multiheaded hound that guards its gates. Dante used the inferno as the starting point for one of literature's epic journeys. Mark Twain advised us to go to paradise for the climate but to the other place for more interesting company. In slang, we use the H-word to describe something that can be given or raised, or that can zoom about on wheels. It is also the name of a town in Michigan that, on occasion, actually does freeze over. More to the point, I have so often said, "There's a special place in Hell for women who don't help other women," that Starbucks put the declaration on a coffee cup—hence the title of this book.

Although we are inescapably mortal, not every destination is final. We fill our days with projects big and small that are, at any moment, in various stages of completion. The fact that we pursue them on borrowed time only heightens our desire to move ahead quickly. We yearn to accomplish much that is pleasing and praiseworthy, and from the hour our primeval ancestors began painting images on cave walls, our instinct has been to leave behind a record of what we think, do, and feel.

In a 2003 memoir, *Madam Secretary*, I write about my middle years, especially my career as a diplomat representing the United States as UN ambassador and secretary of state. In the more recent *Prague Winter*, I delve into my European childhood and the tests that my parents' generation confronted amid war and the Holocaust. In *Hell and Other Destinations*, I will look back on the experiences that have accompanied my attempt to navigate life's third act—and steal a glance forward as well.

Early in 2001, as I neared the end of my tenure at the State Department, I directed a favorite question at myself: What's next? I was but sixty-three years old; not ready for the rocking chair. When interviewers asked how I wished to be remembered, I replied that I didn't want to be remembered. I was still here and had plenty more I intended to do. The first step, clearly, was to draw up a list of priorities, but I am the sort of person who hates to rule anything out. So, as I prepared for what I have called my post-government "afterlife," I ruled everything *in*—with results I describe in pages to come.

There are many prescriptions for how best to spend our allotted time on Earth. Various expert authors counsel us to be assertive, to meditate, to avoid fatty foods, to not sweat the small stuff, and never to leave home without a gun. This book, though, isn't of the self-help type. Instead, it is a collection of stories based on the premise that, although we can learn constantly from one another, we also have unique characteristics and cannot be perfect models. My own motor, as you will see, is revved to a high gear; I am most always busy. That formula might work for you, but it may not. We each have to chart our own course. Be forewarned, though, that the tales I have to tell are products of memory, and therefore untamed; they leap from one subject to the next, dip back and forth in time, and veer sharply between episodes of delight and sadness. There is a reason the ancient Greeks employed two masks— those of tragedy and comedy—to reflect the human drama.

Our ambitions flow naturally from our interests, in my case an abiding preoccupation with world affairs. In the years that furnish this book's focus, we witnessed the horror of 9/11, the U.S. invasion of Iraq, a debilitating financial breakdown, the leadership of three very different American presidents, and the revival of antidemocratic tendencies in many countries, including the United States. Such events supply a backdrop for the narratives that follow, some of which take place beneath a global lamp while others are more intimate—and a few, embarrassing.

Several years ago, at the end of a long overnight flight, I was tired and having trouble clearing British customs. Pulled out of line, I was made to wait, then instructed by a guard using a clipped imperial accent to open my suitcases and each of the smaller bags within. I care as much as anyone about security, but I was also nearly eighty years old, blessed with a benign, albeit wrinkled countenance, and late for a meeting. Under my breath, I muttered, "Why me?" More minutes elapsed with the guards just standing around and onlookers whispering among themselves, pointing, and imagining what I must have done to deserve such treatment. Made shameless by frustration, I finally confronted my officious tormenters by pulling rank: "Do you know who I am?" *There*, I thought, *that should do it.* "No," came the sympathetic reply, "but we have doctors here who can help you to figure that out."

HELL AND OTHER
DESTINATIONS

ONE

Afterlife

JANUARY 2001 MARKED the beginning of a new century and the conclusion of my service as America's sixty-fourth secretary of state. I rarely admit to feeling tired, but I was by then a little over-cooked. Years of rushed plane trips, not enough exercise, too many official dinners, and bowls of taco salad when flying home had taken a toll on the contours of my Central European body. I was growing the way a mature tree does: out not up. A Washington columnist, trying to be funny, compared me to an igloo.

Although I realized that I could benefit from a less rigorous schedule, I didn't want my job to end. I loved every frenetic minute, the nonstop parade of questions, the ever-shifting mix of people with whom to share ideas, and above all the conviction that what I said and did had significance beyond my own personal fence lines. An exciting position replenishes the energy it consumes. Each morning, a brain alive with plans drew me from my slumber. Gulping coffee, I placed phone calls, jotted notes, and inhaled the narcotic aroma of breaking news. To awaken to an unfolding international clash or opportunity and know that you might have a say in its outcome is addictive—and addicts, when deprived of their regular fix, search for a new buzz.

Per the U.S. Constitution, as amended, January 20 was Inaugura-tion Day. At noon, the new president would swear to faithfully exe-cute the duties of his office, after which members of his team would expect us to be gone. As the hour of departure approached, I found solace in knowing that I had never been more comfortable handling the demands of my job. Eight years in the State Department had given me the best education in international affairs one could conceive. I felt as if I were a graduate student whose long nights of study had prepared her to begin a career, not a grizzled actor about to take her final bow. While in office, I had developed skills as a negotiator, become more adept in dealing with the press, learned much about what the world looks like from vantage points abroad, and thought unceasingly about how to address global problems. Every morning, when I strode from the elevator and headed for my desk, dynamic colleagues were poised to join with me in doing vital work.

I wanted more. Despite my exhaustion, I wished that time would move at a more languid pace so that I might make the most of every hour and meeting. In the White House, President Clinton told foreign leaders whose terms would outlast his that he envied them. He, too, wanted to pack in as much productive activity as possible. Still, the rosy-fingered dawns kept coming, then turning all too quickly to twilight and darkness.

With the finish line drawing near, images of the recent past were on my mind—the foreign ministers of Hungary, Poland, and the Czech Republic rejoicing at their countries' entry into NATO; civilians from Kosovo thanking us for rescuing their homeland from ethnic cleansing and terror; the king of Jordan, gaunt and dying of lymphoma, pleading with Israeli and Palestinian negotiators not to squander a chance to make peace between their peoples; women clad in saris, burkas, and other traditional robes pressing the case for gender equality and beginning at last to be heard; and a July 4 ceremony on Monticello's front steps, where I handed naturalization certificates to new citizens with such all-American names as Martínez, Kim, Yang, Thieu, Hassan, Kabila, Waleski, O'Malley, Stern, Garcia, and Marconi. Later, I heard one man exclaim to his family, "Can you believe that I came to the United States as a refugee, and I've just received my citizenship papers from the secretary of state?" I went up to him and, referring to my Czechoslovak heritage, said "Can you believe a refugee *is* the secretary of state?"

When the clock struck twelve, I would have no choice but to exit the ball. The rules were plain, enshrined in documents cherished by all small-*d* democrats. My gratitude to President Clinton for the trust he had placed in me was beyond expression. Even in those moments when it felt as though the world had gone crazy, I thrilled to the challenge. That final morning, sitting at my desk, I plucked a piece of stationery from the top drawer and wrote a note to my successor, Colin Powell:

> *Dear Colin,*
> *We have been working hard and hope when you arrive in the*
> *office it is clean. It will, however, still be filled with the spirit of*
> *our predecessors, all of whom felt representing the United States*
> *to be the greatest honor. So I turn over to you the best job in the*
> *world. Good luck and best wishes.*
>
> > *Madeleine*

AS WE GROW older and the past lengthens, we recall our life in stages: mewling infant, whining child, sighing lover, multitasking parent, ladder-climbing breadwinner, and so on. We learn by experience that moving from one role to the next can be wrenching. I was sure that leaving the State Department would change both how I felt about myself and what others thought of me.

This time, at least, I was prepared for the transition. Two decades earlier, I had not been. On a snowy morning in January 1982, my husband, Joe Albright, ushered me into the living room. "Our marriage is dead," he informed me, "and I am in love with someone else." Just a single sentence, a dozen words spoken quietly, with a weight that nearly crushed me. We had been married for twenty-three years. In that span, my every thought had been colored by the expectation that we would remain together 'til death parted us. Like most marriages, ours had not always been a fairy tale, but I had a scrapbook full of memories and little inkling that Joe's aspirations were diverging so sharply from my own. I had no major complaints about him as a husband or father to our three daughters; I felt terribly let down that he had found someone he preferred to me.

The irony is that had we not divorced, I doubt very much that I would ever have become secretary of state. It's true that six years earlier, at thirty-nine, I had taken my first Washington job, as chief legislative assistant to a U.S. senator. I went from there to the staff of the National Security Council under President Jimmy Carter. I was intent on having a vocation, but I was also supportive of Joe's aspirations as a journalist. I thought of myself as an accomplished researcher or second in command, not as someone with a strong and independent voice. Due to my late start, I was also older than most who were at a comparable stage in their careers. In the time I had left, I could not expect to rise very high. The divorce and all it signified came as a massive blow to my already limited confidence.

For a while, I could neither see myself clearly nor identify the right direction in which to set out. I didn't know how it would feel to be an unattached adult woman because I had never been one. Joe and I had wed just three days following my graduation from Wellesley. Now, after more than two decades of being one half of a couple, there was suddenly no "us" to think about, no "we" to make plans for.

Then something happened that I had not anticipated: the word *I* began to assume a deeper, richer shape. The transformation was gradual, for it takes months at least for the habits of years to fade. Eventually I began to sample a flavor of freedom I had not tasted before. No longer did I have to coordinate my schedule, shop, cook, or arrange my mood in line with a husband's preferences. Over time I liberated myself from the need to look to another person for validation. Buttressed by help from family and friends, I shed the feelings of inadequacy that had dampened my spirit. I developed my own yardstick to measure what I could and should do.

With children nearly grown and Joe consigned to my past, I plunged guilt-free into activities that now seemed perfect for me. Soon I was teaching at Georgetown University and advising Democratic candidates for national office. In 1984, I became vice chair of the board of the newly created National Democratic Institute and, several years later, president of a think tank. In 1993, following the election of Bill Clinton, I moved back into government as U.S. ambassador to the United Nations; then, four years further on, became secretary of state. In January 2001, upon leaving office, I arrived at the threshold of another transition; I had to find a new line of work.

Amid the uncertainties, one thing was sure: it had taken me a long time to find my voice; having done so, I had no intention of shutting up. But how best to be heard? What is there for a former secretary of state to do?

IN AMERICA'S EARLY years, the position of chief diplomat had been a springboard to the White House. Beginning with Thomas Jefferson, five of the first ten secretaries were later elected president, but then the springboard lost its bounce. Between the 1830s and 2000, only one former secretary (James Buchanan) made the jump, and he, a pro-slavery Pennsylvanian, performed dismally. Half a dozen others tried to reach the Oval Office but fell short. One (Edward Everett) ran for vice president, losing to the ticket headed by Abraham Lincoln. Three years later, the scholarly Everett preceded Lincoln in delivering an address at the Civil War battlefield in Gettysburg, where he said less in two hours than Honest Abe would say in two minutes.

Like Henry Kissinger before me, I was foreign-born and therefore constitutionally ineligible to run for chief executive, at least of the United States. Václav Havel suggested that I reverse my childhood voyage across the Atlantic and succeed him as president of the Czech Republic. I was flattered, and the idea of living in the famed castle overlooking Prague was tantalizing, but I couldn't believe that the Czech people would want me. Besides, I had long since become an American.

There were, of course, options other than the presidency. William Jennings Bryan enjoyed a lively second career as a publisher, lecturer, and promoter of real estate bargains in Florida. As a prosecutor, he faced off against famed attorney Clarence Darrow, who was defending a man (John T. Scopes) accused of violating Tennessee law by teaching evolution. In this widely publicized 1925 showdown between science and Presbyterian fundamentalism, Bryan won a conviction but, to show there were no hard feelings, offered to assist in paying the defendant's $100 fine.

Notable, as well, were the crowdfunding efforts of William Maxwell Evarts, secretary of state from 1877 to 1881, who chaired a campaign to raise money for the pedestal of the Statue of Liberty. When contributions from the wealthy proved insufficient, Evarts and the newspaper mogul Joseph Pulitzer turned to the public. They noted that the statue itself had been financed in France "by the working men, the tradesmen, the shop girls, the artisans . . . It is not a gift from the millionaires of France to the millionaires of America, but a gift from the whole people of France to the whole people of America." In response to this appeal, more than 125,000 citizens, including many schoolchildren, sent in their pennies and dimes, saving a project that, had it failed, would have deprived the world of its most compelling symbol of freedom.

ON JANUARY 21, 2001, I was out of office and ready to follow—or not—the examples of my predecessors. It's true that I was eligible for Social Security benefits and qualified for a senior's discount when purchasing movie tickets, but I was healthy and resolved to get in better shape. My hair had retained its natural hue, albeit by unnatural means; beyond that, however, I wasn't interested in extraordinary measures. When, at a party, a woman (half socialite, half journalist) told me how "brave" she thought I had been for not getting a facelift, I was tempted to comment on the courage she had shown in dealing with the results of hers.

I am a practical person; the description of myself that I like best is that of problem-solver, or doer. Each morning, my eyes scamper through newspapers looking for items of interest and finding one on nearly every page. To me, much of life consists of trying to figure stuff out, and the kind of puzzles that held my attention as secretary of state always will. Sometimes, I come across people who complain that every day seems identical to the next. Probably, you have heard the same gripe, but this is not a feeling I share. Even when nothing dramatic is going on, there is always a slight twist of the kaleidoscope. How can one be bored in a world where a billion examples of human ingenuity, peculiarity, pigheadedness, and compassion are on regular view? Retreat to the sidelines? No way. In my dictionary, circa 2001, *retirement* was a four-letter word.

Still, I was in a hurry. It's not that I brooded about mortality. In fact, when the subject came up, I was often chided for saying "*if* I die" not "*when*." But I was aware of biological principles and could count. I didn't know whether the adventures I would have in my "afterlife" would last for three years, or five, or ten, or perhaps longer. I did know that the sooner I started and the faster I went, the more I could do.

In thinking about next steps, I did have concerns. I wanted to strive for the same goals I had while in government, including the promotion of democracy and the empowerment of women. I also hoped to live up, as best I could, to the kind words many had said about me. I wished to gratify, not disappoint. Whether this desire to please was a symptom on my part of natural amiability or chronic insecurity, I leave for others to judge.

When in office, I developed the sense that I had somehow acquired a twin—a look-alike who had pilfered my name, and whose words and actions meant something to people I had never met. This other Madeleine Albright wasn't the familiar one I had seen in the mirror every morning of my life; she was a separate being who shared my body and got invited to give commencement speeches, lend her name to worthy causes, and accept awards just for showing up. This was the high-minded doppelgänger people talked about when introducing me at an event, a me that in quieter moments I didn't always recognize. The more public Madeleine would not, for example, ever admit to having enjoyed quail hunting in her twenties or, in her thirties, wearing a fur coat.

As I laid plans, I was determined to find room for both identities: to enjoy the restoration of privacy and to try, at the same time, to make myself useful.

LUCKILY, FROM MY perspective, that January I was not the only one preparing to make a fresh start. Many members of the team that I had assembled during my years in government were as well. These were men and women whose skills and friendships I valued and didn't want to lose. I hoped to find a way to keep us together—and that meant devising projects that would test their talents and generate enough income to prevent them from going elsewhere. I had also formed a connection to many fellow diplomats overseas and wished to maintain my ties to them.

What were some options? I assumed I could give speeches and fully intended to write a memoir. I could return to teaching. I discussed with some colleagues the idea of starting a small consulting firm, run primarily by women. Freed from the duties of public office, I could become active again in politics, supporting the candidates of my choice. I already had requests to testify before Congress on national security issues, and when unforeseen events happened, the networks would surely recruit me as a talking head. I had acquaintances in academia and at think tanks who wondered if I might help them with specific projects. I looked forward to getting together more with old friends and with the family I had been neglecting—sister Kathy; brother John, his wife, Pam, and their two sons; my daughters Anne, Alice, and Katie; and five (soon to be six) grandchildren. I also had a farm in rural Virginia with a herd of cows that required my attention.

It was an exhausting list. Common sense, and actuarial tables, suggested that I limit the demands on my schedule. However, I was intent on making the next stage of my life even more exciting than the last. I said "Hell, yes" to everything.

TWO

Voice Lessons

THE WEEK AFTER leaving office, I vacationed at a health spa in the Baja California region of Mexico with two longtime friends. We stayed in a small adobe villa and, during group exercise sessions, called on our creaky bodies to hop, stretch, and lift. We ate green vegetables, drank herbal tea, and paid close attention on hikes when Noah, our guide, pointed out unusual geological formations and coyote scat. We were there for only a few days, but I took the opportunity to clear my head except for random thoughts about the new president, U.S.-Mexico policy, and regrets over never having learned Spanish.

I returned to Washington a little unwound, if not fully refreshed, and eager to commence my new life. Joined by fellow alumni from the State Department, I set up a temporary office in a law firm. At first the pace was slow. My days no longer began with CIA briefings or extensive lists of phone calls to return. Instead of presiding at a senior staff meeting from one end of a huge oval table, I sat at a small square desk flanked by a couple of (usually empty) chairs. We had planning sessions, but these were leisurely; there was no need to rush to the next appointment. The tempo would soon accelerate, but at the beginning, we all went out for lunch each day and headed home, even in February, before dark.

For the first time since 1993, I drove myself to and from the office. Gas stations had long since ceased to be full service, so I pumped my own. After those first months, I was also on my own with respect to security. Though I had not become bulletproof, the agents who had for eight years accompanied me with guns at their hips and wires in their ears were assigned elsewhere. Now that I was a former somebody, the Diplomatic Security Service had higher priorities than the protection of "Pathfinder" (my code name). As much as I treasured the restored privacy, I also felt a little like an egg without a shell as I made my way solo down city sidewalks. I didn't know whether the next person I encountered would smile, do a double take, mutter ominously, or (as most did) stride by with eyes straight ahead. This uncertainty about being recognized produced a bit of tension that accompanies my travels to this day. Most times, I can stroll unnoticed wherever I want; on other occasions, it is impossible to avoid a scene even when buying an electric toothbrush at Costco.

EARLY ON, I reached an agreement with the Washington Speakers Bureau (WSB) to deliver speeches to various groups, ordinarily at annual conferences or as part of a lecture series. This seemed a logical undertaking, but as I began to prepare, I grew nervous. Imagine being asked to stand in front of thousands of strangers and tell stories about yourself for an extended period, then reply to questions for just as long. When in government, I spoke publicly all the time—but my remarks concerned foreign policy and the job I was doing, not reflections on my life. The issue that bothered me was neither shyness nor modesty, for I am unburdened by those qualities. It's just that I am not given to public confession. I had been conditioned since childhood to direct conversation toward the health and activities of those with whom I am talking. This approach feels natural to me and was an aid to my career as a diplomat. If pressed, I could engage in repartee with a potato; but now I was supposed to go before large paying audiences and enthrall them with tales of Madeleine. Though hardly petrified, I was also far from at ease. I asked the Speakers Bureau for advice.

To give me an idea of what was expected, the WSB sent along a video featuring one of its most popular clients, Colin Powell. I inserted the disc, pushed the appropriate buttons, and concluded almost immediately, *This isn't going to help*. From start to finish, Powell had the crowd entranced. Speaking casually and without notes, he told the uplifting saga of his childhood in the South Bronx, career in the army, and role as chairman of the Joint Chiefs of Staff during Operation Desert Storm and the end of the Cold War. Throughout, he spoke about the demands of leadership and offered motivational advice. Coming from him, the words sounded on target but made me anxious: I had never excelled at formulating rules for self-improvement. Every time I tried, I found myself adrift in a sea of clichés or sounding like Polonius ("neither a borrower nor a lender be") before Hamlet stabs him. Also, Powell is tall and looks like the military commander he was. In terms of height, I identify more with Bashful, Doc, and Sneezy.

Still, backing out was not a realistic option. To settle the butterflies in my stomach, I thought much about what to say and in what manner I could best deliver my message. In the process, I tried to put myself in the shoes of attendees. What would matter most to them? What words could I find that might cause them to laugh, cry, think, and cheer, preferably in that order? A speechmaker's gravest sin is to leave the listener indifferent. I was determined not to be dull.

MY MAIDEN VOYAGE was in San Diego on March 24, 2001, at the annual conference of the National School Boards Association. The event was well attended; in fact, there were enough school board members sitting elbow-to-elbow to fill an auditorium commonly used for basketball games and rock concerts. As I waited backstage, I remembered the first rule for every public speaker: to establish a personal connection with attendees, metaphorically to "shake hands." In that spirit, I began by citing my academic credentials as a student, parent, grandmother, and professor. I also mentioned the many times I had visited classrooms, bringing with me a globe to twirl around and show where I had traveled as secretary of state. The sphere inevitably prompted younger students to ask such questions as: "Did you ever visit Santa Claus at the North Pole?" and "Do people in Australia have to walk upside down?"

In other appearances and in later years, my attempt to forge a link with listeners was aided by coincidence. The week before addressing a cohort of lawyers, I was called to jury duty. A few days prior to an event with dentists, I had a root canal. And about a month before my speech to an insurance industry convention, one of the cows at my farm in Virginia was hit by lightning. The incident provided a diverting topic for my remarks, but sadly the cow didn't live, and the insurers didn't pay.

The speech in San Diego marked the first time I had told my life story, albeit highly abridged. I was born in Prague shortly before World War II. My parents and I were forced to flee when the Nazis invaded. During the war years, we were in London, weathering the Battle of Britain and joining other expatriates in supporting the Allied effort to wrench Europe free from Hitler's grasp. Following the German surrender in 1945, we returned to Czechoslovakia but soon decamped to Belgrade where my father served as ambassador to Yugoslavia. Three years later, when Communists seized control of our native country, we were pushed into exile again. We found refuge in the United States, starting on Long Island and then moving to Denver. My ambition at the time was straightforward: to become a typical American teenager.

I adored my parents, but they tended to be serious and formal—very "old Europe"—and no help in the fitting-in department. When I went out on a date, my ever-vigilant father followed in the family car and later invited the poor boy in for milk and cookies. For a while I didn't have many second dates. My mother liked to tell fortunes by reading palms or coffee grounds and didn't hesitate to predict to men whose wives were sitting next to them that they would soon meet a beautiful and mysterious woman. In her way, my mother was even more protective than my father. When he decided to be strict, it was often a reaction to her fretting. As I would discover, she had much cause for grief but hid her feelings and did all she could to make the lives of her children seem normal. Like most women of her time, she lacked a university degree, but she was warm and loving, a shrewd judge of character, and had little time for fools.

When I enrolled in college, it was at Wellesley, a women's school in Massachusetts where incoming students had to be photographed topless to show whether we had "an understanding of good body alignment and the ability to stand well." The school graded the pictures and made us do exercises if we flunked. We never knew what happened to the photos until someone came across them years later in a vault—at Yale.

Having explained to the audience in San Diego where I had come from and why I believed what I did, I went on to describe the highs and lows of my years in government and to praise schoolboard members for their commitment to public education. Though I may not have been in the same league as Colin Powell, the speech went over well; people clapped and made generous comments. It was just one event, but I left San Diego thinking that I might thrive on the speakers' circuit after all. In high spirits, I headed to the airport for the return flight to Washington.

As I sat in the departure lounge reading a newspaper, a well-dressed, gray-haired man came in and surveyed the room. There were many empty seats, but he marched right over and plopped down next to me, setting his briefcase atop my foot. Then, as I feared he might, he spoke:

"You're Madeleine Albright."

"Yes, I am."

"I just saw a documentary about you."

"Oh."

"According to Michael Douglas, you like to flirt."

"Not everybody is Michael Douglas."

"You've lost your job and all your power; you must feel awful."

"This is America, it's how the system works. I feel fine."

"No, no, no. I used to work for Republicans in the White House, and when we lost our jobs, we felt awful. You must feel awful."

So much for my good mood. I decided, after liberating my foot, to wait in the ladies' room.

SINCE THAT INAUGURAL outing, I have spoken at hundreds of events for WSB. It has been a pleasure working with Harry Rhoads, Christine Farrell, Kate Salter, and others at the bureau. Along the way, I have traded ideas with teachers, accountants, travel agents, pharmacists, factory workers, grocery store owners, bankers, appliance salespersons, scrap recyclers, hospital employees, members of the Junior

League of Toledo, and representatives of the fertilizer industry—with whom I had yet another chance to talk about cows.

I consider all this to be part of my continuing education. I learn by traveling to cities where I would not otherwise go and by having conversations with men and women whose backgrounds and views differ widely from my own. The give-and-take is important to me. Even today, when I read about an international crisis, I reflexively insert my name in place of the current secretary of state's and think about what I might do were I in his or her shoes. The opportunity to speak in public gives me a means to share those thoughts and to remind people that I exist.

SOME BELIEVE IT is wrong for a former public official to accept money to speak, and I understand that. People hear that so-and-so is getting paid to make an appearance and assume that the recipient is motivated solely by cash. For some, that may be true; I can't say. In my case, however, and I suspect for many others, the fees are swallowed up by the cost of leasing office space and paying a salary and benefits to a communications aide, a personal assistant, a writer, and one or two staffers to handle correspondence and projects. An ex-president receives a federal stipend to support his work; an ex-cabinet official does not. Without the WSB engagements, I wouldn't be able to respond to more than a small fraction of the thousands of letters and requests I receive each year; nor could I find time to prepare the many speeches I give for free to public interest groups of every description. No one is going to pay me to sing or play golf, so the WSB events are why I can often say yes to good people asking for a share of my time.

Paid or not, I love giving speeches and interacting with those who attend them. There are, however, some practical issues associated with such events that I have had to work my way through.

One is time. The WSB told me that the usual practice for a speaker is to deliver an opening presentation of at least forty-five minutes, then answer a few questions. I tried this, but soon decided that three quarters of an hour is too long. I know from teaching that attention spans are limited. Hence the maxim: "the mind can absorb only what the seat can endure." In U.S. history, the best-remembered speeches have been short. Nearly every line in John Kennedy's inaugural address could have been expanded into a paragraph or even a full page, but the added detail would have lessened the impact without enhancing the meaning. Also, the briefer my remarks, the more minutes I will have to answer questions. I enjoy that more now than when I was in government, because back then I had to weigh each reply carefully for fear of misspeaking and thus getting fired or, worse, starting a war. Now, I just vent.

Even when speaking my mind, however, I can only have a fruitful conversation with people whom I can see and who can see me. Because of my height (barely five feet), I would be all but lost behind many a lectern were it not for the three-inch-tall wooden block on which I customarily perch. In Washington, we lug such a platform with us; on the road, we ask that one be provided. Sometimes we are given a crate with slats that invite calamity for a person wearing high heels. On other occasions, the block is too thick, thin, or wobbly. Usually I manage, even if it means having to maintain a white-knuckled grip on the sides of the rostrum to keep from tumbling over backward.

There are days when, instead of giving a speech, I participate in an open-ended conversation with an interviewer. The arrangement works well if the moderator is well-informed and charming. It also helps if the chairs are not so big that I get lost in them and the stage lights are not so intense that I feel like a criminal being given the third degree. It's hard to establish a bond with someone whose questions are coming to you out of a bright white blur.

The location of a speech can be another complication. I voice the same opinions wherever I go, but my emphasis may be different in a deeply conservative area as opposed to a more liberal one. I don't duck fights, but as a guest, I think it courteous to avoid starting them.

I also learned while secretary of state that it can be as important to know *what not* to say to an audience as it is to know *what* to say. This is especially true when addressing a group overseas. In Arab countries, for example, one is well advised to refer to the Persian Gulf as the

"Arabian Gulf." What Americans call the South China Sea has separate and distinct appellations in China, Indonesia, Vietnam, and the Philippines (none of which translates as "South China Sea"). When describing distances, every listener except those in America, Liberia, and Burma will think in terms of kilometers, not miles, and the people of Burma will explain that their homeland's name is actually Myanmar. In Muslim states, it may be thought offensive for a non-Muslim (no matter how well-intentioned) to quote extensively from the Quran or to presume to interpret Islamic tenets. In Egypt, one might be tempted to flatter the memory of former president and martyr for peace, Anwar Sadat, but the man has long since been without honor in his own nation—he is unpopular in Egypt as are, in Russia, ex-leaders Mikhail Gorbachev and Boris Yeltsin. When speaking anywhere in the Western Hemisphere, U.S. diplomats are asked to remember that theirs is not the only country that considers itself "American;" all do, whether of the North, Central, or South American variety.

Finally, as much as I enjoy meeting and talking with people, I can't stay in one place forever, and it is sometimes difficult to find a graceful way to leave. When the time comes for me to depart, my communications director, Liza Romanow, will point to her watch and declare (truthfully) that I have a plane I must catch. Such an announcement can be in vain should I still have to wade through a crowd of friendly, eager-to-chat, people to reach the front door. That's why we always try to have an alternative exit strategy. Over the years, I have passed through many a hotel kitchen en route to an alleyway complete with Dumpsters, garbage cans, and urban wildlife. After two decades of speeches, I feel as if I have made more getaways than Bonnie and Clyde.

THREE

From the Ground Up

I AM NOT SURE who came up with the notion that I should start a consulting firm. It might have been Wendy Sherman, the State Department counselor during my tenure as secretary who had excelled in many positions in public life and the private sector and would later lead successful negotiations to curtail Iran's nuclear program. A second possibility is Jim O'Brien, a lawyer blessed with both wit and wits who had worked closely with me as special presidential envoy for the Balkans. Another candidate is Suzy George, the State Department's deputy chief of staff, whom I had known since her graduation from law school and who had a gift for running an organization. It might also have been some random friend; none of us remembers for certain. We do know that the idea emerged gradually from conversations we were all having about what we might do when our days in government ended.

Venturing into the business world was an exciting prospect that became more so as I considered and rejected other possibilities. At my request, Wendy journeyed to Texas to visit Rice University's James A. Baker III Institute for Public Policy. Named for the sixty-first secretary of state, the institute is a magnet for scholars of politics and world affairs. I had delivered speeches there. The thought of establishing something similar held appeal for us but would require a ton of money to implement. The same drawback applied to starting a foundation dedicated to one or another of my pet causes. Bill Clinton was in the process of creating a body that would surely dwarf any organization we could forge and likely compete for the same funds.

Early on, I received several invitations to join a corporate board. I quickly decided, however, that I didn't want to be identified closely with companies over which I would have little control. Also, a board membership would do nothing to satisfy my desire to keep a congenial set of coworkers together, engaged in projects about which we were enthusiastic.

Within weeks, the thought of forming a business began to take hold. What I liked most was the chance to attempt something I had never before done. A person who is learning has less time to think about growing old. I also enjoy surprising people, and this seemed a sure way to do it. How could a group that consisted primarily of women with scant business experience create a viable international consulting firm? The odds were stacked against it. Aside from a company headed by former U.S. trade representative Carla Hills, I was aware of no such entity led by a woman. There seemed to be about a million run by men.

FOR INSPIRATION, WE might have looked to the past: one of the first and most prestigious consultants was a woman—the Pythia, or Oracle of Delphi. In return for gold and other gifts, the Greek high priestess offered insights into the future from her vantage point at what contemporaries held to be the center of the world. The women who succeeded to the position must have been skillful, for beginning no later than the eighth century BC, they remained in business for more than a thousand years. Chroniclers testify that they were well paid, took winters off, and shared their advice in dactylic hexameter. They were also influential—Cicero wrote that for a long time no major military expeditions were begun without input from the Oracle. Like consultants of today, the priestesses were careful not to claim too much; they offered guidance, not guarantees. Where they differed from the current generation was in their pre-work routine: each morning when on duty, they drank holy water, bathed naked in a spring, praised Apollo, and inhaled hallucinogenic vapors. They also insisted that each client sacrifice a goat.

Skipping ahead a few years, the person generally credited with inventing the business of international consulting was one of my predecessors as secretary of state, John Watson Foster. This gentleman served in the Union Army during the Civil War, was later a journalist, and then led the department for six months under President Benjamin Harrison. After leaving office in 1893, he planned a return to his Indiana law practice; a decision he reconsidered after a fellow attorney at the firm described handling a time-consuming case about a hog. Thinking that he might find more stimulation in Washington, the ex-secretary hired himself out to U.S. companies that were exploring overseas markets, and to international powers (including China) that were keen on protecting their interests in the United States. Simultaneously, he continued to represent America, concluding eight trade agreements on the government's behalf and a ninth on seal hunting.

Foster was a born wheeler-dealer; I am not. When a child in England during World War II, I went with my parents to visit my uncle Honza, or Jan, who had also escaped from Czechoslovakia, bringing with him his wife and two children. My father and uncle had different personalities, and I often heard them quarreling late at night when I was supposed to be asleep. Honza, who was in the construction business, was always worried about his next project. My father was driven more by politics and public service. His passion was to help the Allies win the war so that we might return to our homeland and participate in restoring the kind of democratic republic that had flourished there prior to the Nazi invasion. I took after my father. I had a pragmatic side and no desire to starve, but international affairs are what stirred my soul. The bugle call I responded to was the public good, as best as I could discern it. Would leading a business mesh with my desire to be, and to be seen as, a person committed to shaping a better world? If asked that question prior to my years in the State Department, I might not have thought so. By 2001, I had changed my mind. Let me explain.

The end of the Cold War had given the democratic cause an enormous boost. For a brief period, many experts deemed the battle for political freedom to be all but won and thought people everywhere would benefit. Our dreams were realized, but only in some places. Men and women who had grown up under totalitarian regimes had been conditioned to rely on the government for jobs, shelter, basic social services, and political and moral instruction. Understandably, a substantial number had difficulty making the transition to greater self-reliance. Meanwhile, the new democratic leaders—eager to please—promised much that they could not swiftly deliver, causing expectations to rise more rapidly than living standards, which sometimes went down. People grew impatient. Promoters of free institutions, myself included, love to say that liberty is a universal yearning, but so is the wish to eat.

As secretary of state, I engaged in frequent discussions about how to remedy democracy's shortcomings and prepare the ground for liberty's growth. If democracy were a flower, we couldn't make it bloom just by tugging at it; that would tear it up by the roots. Instead, we needed a wide-ranging approach that would moisten the soil with fair elections, responsible political parties, competent police, unbiased courts, an independent press, and other attributes of a free society. As a metaphor, this sounded straightforward enough, but it sidestepped the issue of cost. How could governments muster enough resources to pay for all the nourishing elements that a democracy needs? Back in 1787, America's Constitutional Convention convened in response to precisely this challenge: financing the tools and safeguards required for a free government to operate. The more I thought about the issue, the more I was drawn to the role of the private sector.

In my travels as a diplomat, I had met regularly with local representatives of U.S. companies through the American Chambers of Commerce. These tended to be big meetings, however, so I sought out sessions with smaller groups. With them, I shared my view that U.S. firms had a diplomatic role to play and urged them to meet the highest standards of corporate responsibility. I also peppered attendees with questions. What are the obstacles to investment in emerging democracies? What must governments do to attract foreign capital and create jobs? What steps can the business community take to help blow the whistle on corruption? How can we aid local educators in equipping students with the skills necessary to compete in the global marketplace? How can we convince people who grew up in communist societies that free enterprise is a good thing?

Based on these questions and the conversations that followed, I was convinced of the need to get democratic leaders and forward-looking businesspeople into the same room. Each had much to gain from partnerships with the others. Yet if I were to go beyond issuing invitations and hoping for the best, I would have to learn more. I knew what it was like to be in government, participate in political campaigns, teach public policy, and advocate on behalf of democratic values, but I had never seen the private sector from the inside; that time had come.

THE ALBRIGHT GROUP, or, as we called it, TAG, set out with modest expectations. In choosing the company's name, we wanted to stress that the venture would be a collective enterprise. We hoped gradually to attract other creative partners, men as well as women, and to establish a niche as a company skilled at helping socially responsible companies prosper.

Among the principals, aside from me, were Wendy Sherman, Jim O'Brien, and Carol Browner. Carol had been the administrator of the Environmental Protection Agency (EPA) throughout the eight years of the Clinton presidency. Her love of nature came from hiking in the Everglades as a child, and her success in government from an ability to convince polluters that it was in their best interest to mend their ways. We became friends when I was UN ambassador and protocol dictated that officials line up at public functions in the order that their positions were created. Because EPA and the UN ambassador were last on the list, Carol and I spent many hours sitting next to each other, sharing indiscreet opinions about those of our colleagues who had better seats.

The Albright Group came together gradually, but by August 2001, the principals were all on board and ready to go. The experience was new to us, which made for both headaches and anticipation as we began building something out of nothing. Piece by piece, we assembled a business plan. Suzy found people to help set up a payroll, arrange health insurance, lease equipment, and rent space. Her husband, Nate Tibbits, provided shrewd input on our technology systems and marketing. We brought in an outside expert to advise on the shape of our logo and the color of our stationery. Eight hours and several overflowing trash baskets later, we had reached a consensus on both.

We also decided on the kind of firm we would be. Whatever the cost to our bottom line, we didn't want our children to think of us as creeps. We chose not to represent tobacco or gun companies and to look carefully before taking a dime from anyone. We would neither work for a foreign government, however sympathetic, nor lobby on behalf of a company seeking contracts with the United States. Most of us had spent a portion of our lives representing America, and we were not about to sit and negotiate from the other side of the table when U.S. officials were in the room. This was a big decision and one that cost us a boatload of money, but we had no doubt that, for us, it was the right course.

In October 2001, after several weeks of being open for business without any actual business to conduct, Wendy and Jim traveled to Kenilworth, New Jersey, and the corporate headquarters of Merck and Co., the American-based pharmaceuticals firm. There they made our pitch, essentially sharing with company representatives for free everything we hoped to charge them for, should they sign up. How else to demonstrate our value? The next day, a Merck official called to say, "We're prepared to sign a contract, but we don't want to be your only client. You do have others?" Wendy, who had taken the call, replied (almost) truthfully, "We have a number of companies in the pipeline." The contract showed up a few days later. We were on our way.

* * *

OUR ARRANGEMENT WITH Merck turned out to be a winner for precisely the reasons we had hoped. The drug company was a leading producer of antiretroviral treatments that could be used to keep alive patients with HIV/AIDS. In June 2001, it announced an agreement with Botswana and the Gates Foundation to help finance a comprehensive prevention and treatment program. Compared to many countries in its region, Botswana was relatively prosperous, but it had been hit brutally hard by the virus. A third of the adult population was stricken. The country's average life expectancy had dropped by 50 percent in the span of a decade. As secretary of state, I had visited a clinic there for women with AIDS. The doctors said half of those who learned that they were infected didn't tell their husbands or partners for fear of being shunned. The stigma meant that many refused to be tested, thus contributing to further infections. Botswana's president declared, "We face no less than extinction," and to dramatize his distress, he had himself tested for HIV on national television.

Merck's agreement with Botswana had been reached before TAG became involved. We soon discovered, however, that there were snags in making the arrangement work. Each of the three stakeholders had a different perspective and thought in its own terms. A business such as Merck is designed to be efficient and focused on doing one thing at a time, on time. A government has an array of priorities and must respond to each of the social and political forces pulling on it; this can lead to delays and mixed signals. The Gates Foundation was barely a year-old at that juncture and eager to find the combination of research and testing that would yield the best results. Our role—a modest one—was to help keep the lines of communication open and to break big issues down into smaller operational steps on which all could agree.

Fairly quickly, due largely to the determination of Botswanans to make the most of the help they had received, the country made large strides in counseling, testing, the availability of treatment, and reducing the transmission of HIV from mother to child. Between the mid-1990s and 2007, the level of mortality there declined by 50 percent.

Botswana was not the only country where gains were made. In Romania, thousands of young people had HIV because, as infants during the final years of communist rule, they had been given injections with dirty needles or received transfusions of tainted blood. Many who carried the virus were orphans or children whose families had abandoned them. Due to HIV/AIDS fears, they could not attend school, and without antiretroviral treatments, most would die.

In 2002, I stopped by an orphanage in Bucharest. My heart filled, while I nearly lost my tongue. What does one say to a girl or boy who seems to have neither a place in society at present nor any expectations for the future? There are no words. Quietly desperate, I went from there to a meeting with Romanian President Ion Iliescu. Joining us was Per Wold-Olsen, a senior executive at Merck. We talked about the lives that were at stake and the possibility that the company could offer large discounts on its medicines. Iliescu said wearily that, with Romania's minuscule health care budget, even rock-bottom prices would be too high. As my despair deepened, Wold-Olsen came to a decision. "Mr. President," he said. "We will provide the treatments for free." By the following spring, Romania was the first country in Eastern Europe, and among the few anywhere, to provide universal access to antiretroviral therapy.

Not only in Botswana and Romania, but in other countries as well, TAG supported Merck in its understanding that patients had to come first. The private sector is right to point out that the development of lifesaving medicines depends on financial incentives, yet companies will receive a fair hearing only if they show a commitment to people in need. Revenues lost in some places can be recovered by expanding markets elsewhere. In Poland, for example, we found that older women were the least likely to receive medical treatment of any kind. They spent their lives looking after husbands and children but neglected their own well-being. I was pleased to participate in an educational campaign that stressed the issue of women's health in every aspect. This benefited women who learned how they could prevent maladies such as osteoporosis (brittle bones), and it helped Merck, which had products for this purpose.

Most of our events with the company went smoothly; a couple did not. In Paris, I was told an hour before a scheduled speech that I was expected to deliver my remarks in French. This wouldn't have been a problem because I can speak that language, but we spent frantic minutes looking up the appropriate terms for gonorrhea (*blennorragie*) and sexually transmitted disease (*maladie sexuellement transmissible*). In Prague, I attended a presentation from doctors on genital warts. That wouldn't have been a worry, either, except the physicians had photographs—immense graphic images—that were projected on a screen directly behind where I was sitting. Ever alert, I shifted my seat before anyone could snap a picture of Madeleine Albright's face framed by an infected vagina.

The HIV/AIDS crisis was horrific. Like many people, I knew families that had lost loved ones to the disease. By 2001, more than twenty million men, women, and children had perished. Beyond that chilling statistic were devastating social impacts as communities in some regions were deprived of half a generation of teachers, public administrators, and health care workers. Whole nations were at risk of being hollowed out. There was a period early in the twenty-first century when I doubted that Africa would ever bring the epidemic under control and feared that it would continue its rampage through South Asia, China, Russia, and beyond. Ultimately, the tide turned not because of a cure-all vaccine, which was Merck's priority when we first engaged with the firm, but through the development of treatments that enable the afflicted to live productively despite having the virus.

The battle against HIV/AIDS is still far from won, but millions of people are still with us today because of a sustained global campaign that has included industry leaders, governments, public health warriors, UN agencies, and foundations. That is a blueprint for responding effectively to other potential catastrophes. The imperative is to act quickly and to cooperate across borders and sectors. A capable consultant can establish the connections to help bring this about—a proper calling for anyone.

FOR OUR FLEDGLING business, securing one client was cause for rejoicing, but we needed more. Accordingly, we cast bait in all directions and bragged about ourselves. We don't just open doors, we claimed, we also escort clients through them by developing and implementing strategies that will enable them to identify new areas for growth. Association with TAG, we promised, would help companies improve both their reputations and their bottom lines.

To impress prospective partners, we conducted research on everything from the global chocolate industry to ladies' clothing to furniture, plate glass, tractors, cars, airplanes, fiber-optic cable, electronic gizmos, security systems, and alternative energy. I also tried cold-calling women CEOs, such as Carly Fiorina of Hewlett-Packard, to let them know that we were around. After every significant meeting, I sat down like a dutiful schoolgirl and wrote notes expressing gratitude "for the chance to meet and learn more about your great company."

The hard work paid off. Client number two signed on, then three, then four. We began to hire researchers and communications people. I adjusted my schedule to include TAG meetings at home and abroad. I also had to learn how to think and talk like a businesswoman. Much has been made of the so-called imposter syndrome. This refers to the feeling that one is not qualified for the position one occupies and is, therefore, essentially a fraud whose inadequacies may be exposed at any moment. The syndrome was originally thought to be a characteristic of stressed-out females, but is now considered more a feeling than a condition and something that many people of both genders experience. I call it "being nervous." Whatever the label, I had always felt well cast as a professor and a diplomat; I had, however, never performed in the role of consultant. Thirty years after graduate school, I was back to being a student.

FOUR

"Do Not Be Angry"

JOHN SHERMAN (1823–1900) was President William McKinley's secretary of state. He had previously enjoyed a stellar career as a lawyer, member of Congress, and secretary of the treasury. His name is attached to a landmark antitrust law enacted in 1890, and his older brother was the renowned (in the South, notorious) General William Tecumseh Sherman, who brought the Civil War to a brutal end by devastating Georgia on his march from Atlanta to the sea. John Sherman was a celebrated figure in his lifetime, but he hoped also to secure his reputation beyond. In his final testament, he offered $10,000 to any respected scholar who would consent to write his biography. The money went unclaimed. The moral? If you want your story told, you'd better tell it yourself.

That was my plan.

I OFTEN ASSIGN to the classes I teach books that were authored by former presidents and diplomats so that we might analyze how those leaders arrived at critical decisions. My students are quick to point out, however, that the baskets in which people collect their memories often have holes; it is not unusual for officials to recall the same event in ways that conflict.

One of my predecessors, when preparing his memoir, drafted an account of an important meeting, then sent it to a friend for comment. His correspondent praised him for the excellence of the description. "You captured it all," he said, "except for one detail—you weren't at the meeting." To guard against comparable gaffes, I convened several sessions with former aides to discuss what we had done and why. Though we could all agree on the broad outlines of events, our recollections diverged on many of the specifics of motive and timing.

To ensure as much accuracy as possible, I needed to consult the written record. Unfortunately for me, but understandably from the government's point of view, I could not take many of my official files with me when I left office. They were the public's property, not mine. I had the right to consult them, however, and for this purpose was assigned a small, dank room in the State Department's large, dank basement. The arrangement, though cumbersome, enabled me to sort through stacks of documents and assemble a chronology of events. I also made use of the few journal entries I had found time to make and a few dozen handwritten notes—some of which had done double duty as shopping lists.

A book, of course, needs a publisher, and finding the right one requires good advice. For that I turned to the best advice-giver I know: Bob Barnett. I had first crossed paths with him in 1984, during the prodigiously unsuccessful Mondale-Ferraro campaign. Bob later helped Ferraro with her book, then did the same for scores of other authors, mainly, but not exclusively, from the arena of politics. He has become a legend in the business because he tells you things you need to know but didn't, understands the book industry inside and out, and responds to questions almost before you ask them.

When I sat down to talk with Barnett and his equally astute colleague Deneen Howell, Bob asked me to describe the kind of memoir I had in mind. Immediately, I mentioned *Present at the Creation*, Dean Acheson's meticulous account of his years at the State Department. Back in 1969, I had attended a party for the book, during which Acheson made brilliant though decidedly undiplomatic remarks, lamenting Franklin Roosevelt's "stupidity" and calling Dwight Eisenhower a "son of a bitch" for never inviting him to the White House. Acheson's book, the only one authored by a former secretary of state to win a Pulitzer Prize, is full of insights about how to conduct foreign policy. Barnett smiled at my comments, then shook his head. "Acheson's was a great memoir, just marvelous, but no one writes like that anymore—also, no one buys books like that anymore. The publishers are going to want something closer to the style of Katie Graham. If you're searching for a model, her memoir, *Personal History*, is the way to go."

Outwardly, I nodded because I knew Bob was right. Inwardly, I grimaced. I didn't want to be thought of in the same breath as Katharine Graham. For a professional woman in the nation's capital, the shadow of the *Washington Post*'s longtime owner was inescapable—precisely why I wanted to avoid it. I had met Graham at bridge parties in the early 1960s, before the death of her husband and at a time when we were both preoccupied with our domestic roles. We shared a fascination for journalism and had worked briefly, when young, as reporters. Our spouses had each served in the U.S. Army, and our marriages would be of the same length, twenty-three years. We also had a family connection of sorts: Graham's father, Eugene Meyer, had bought the *Washington Times-Herald* from Cissy Patterson, my ex-husband's great-aunt. Kay Graham was two decades older than I was and, as a friend of John and Robert Kennedy and the heroine of Watergate, moved in more exalted circles. For years, however, we lived within a couple of blocks of each other in Georgetown, where she hosted dinner parties and I invited friends over for the same, though with less famous guests, humbler wine, and plainer food. As much as I admired her, I wanted to be judged on my own merits, not in comparison to hers.

On the day I left office, Barnett began looking for a publisher. A leading contender quickly emerged. His name—respected then, infamous now—was Harvey Weinstein. In that era, Weinstein was best known for his film company, Miramax, which produced the Academy Award–winning best pictures *The English Patient* (1996) and *Shakespeare in Love* (1998). He called me in Mexico several times while I was on vacation and, despite cell phone reception issues, managed to get through. He had started a publishing company and urged me to join its stable of writers. Barnett arranged a meeting in New York with Weinstein and the rest of the Miramax team, headed by Tina Brown, the innovative magazine editor (*Talk, Vanity Fair*, the *New Yorker*), and Jonathan Burnham, a rising giant in the field.

While in government, I had developed at least a tissue-thin shield against flattery, because I knew that foreign diplomats in pursuit of favors would tell me whatever they thought I wanted to hear. Now that I was again a private citizen, my defenses were down, and Miramax quickly won me over. I had no inkling then that Weinstein would one day be accused by dozens of women of sexual harassment up to and including rape. The man of my acquaintance was a quick-to-laugh natural salesman with a big-city personality and an appetite for glamour. The sympathy I felt when the allegations surfaced, however, was not for him but for the women involved. Weinstein was big enough to know right from wrong, though apparently too small to act on that knowledge.

I HAD DONE a fair amount of writing in school at various levels, for think tanks, and for government. My father penned half a dozen books, and I had assisted with the research and editing of some. Though I had never written a memoir, I was confident that given enough time, I could do a serviceable job—not elegant, but blunt, informative, and funnier than most readers would expect. The way my new life was shaping up, however, time would be in short supply. I needed help. Miramax suggested that I hire a collaborator who had worked with other authors. I said no. I didn't see how an outsider could capture the way I thought or have the knowledge to explain the nuances of U.S. foreign policy. Instead, I asked my speechwriter from the State Department, Bill Woodward, to take on the project, and he agreed.

At the outset, Bill and I decided to split our assignment into two parts. I would draft the chapters that covered the first five and a half decades of my life, until I entered the State Department in 1993. Bill would try his hand at the years we had spent together in government.

Then we would begin the grueling labor of polishing and revising the whole. After considering and rejecting more exotic titles, we settled on *Madam Secretary*.

EAGER TO BEGIN, I started pecking away diligently at the keyboard only to have my enthusiasm dampened by doubts. My entire life I had wanted to fit in, but wasn't the point of writing a memoir to inform readers how the author stands out? I confronted the fact that I had never thought of my life as dramatic despite my family's early encounters with the followers of Hitler and Stalin and my coming to the United States as a refugee. In my generation, there was nothing unique about this: most Americans had been deeply affected by World War II. The photographs of loved ones lost were featured in albums and displayed on bedside tables in homes across the country. Post-war, from my arrival in New York at age eleven until my designation as UN ambassador forty-four years later, I had a few "in the spotlight" moments, but no claim to fame. How many readers, I wondered, would care to learn about my teenage humiliations, marital ups and downs, and long-delayed start to a professional career?

It was only after the words started to flow that I remembered something I never should have forgotten: a life doesn't have to be filled with earth-rocking escapades to be instructive or engaging. Much of literature, after all, centers on the everyday preoccupations that move with us from cradle to tomb: relationships across age and gender, the search for a personal identity, the interplay of desire and conscience, money worries, and reflections on our tiny place in a universe about which we know little. I decided that, as long as I was honest, readers wouldn't necessarily be bored by the mix of mundanities, quiet joys, and trials that were, to that time, the sum of my existence. That didn't, however, ease the challenge of reliving the worst of them.

The passages that proved most searing to write concerned the loss, half a dozen years into my marriage, of a child at birth. (This was another experience I shared with Katharine Graham.) I also had to describe my divorce and the circumstances surrounding it without straining relationships within my family. To that end, I confirmed what was true—that Joe continued to be an excellent father to our daughters. I found myself, as well, recalling my years as a budding homemaker. I had been reasonably happy, my memory told me, but then I came across an essay I had written in 1961:

> Two years after finishing with college, I am obsolete, like a filing clerk who was replaced by a data processing machine. When I stepped off the platform after accepting my BA degree, I was confident that I was stepping into one or a series of interesting jobs. Now, it seems incomprehensibly naïve for me to have thought that a woman could compete with men on an equal basis, particularly a woman who is married and the mother of twins, which I now am.

The dilemma, the essay continued, was that I had no good answers for a prospective employer who asked, as they all did, what would happen should my husband switch jobs again and we have to leave town, or if one of our babies became sick. This left me, like many women, following a script I had little part in writing. There was no need to invent my own character or even to think up original lines. The plot was all laid out. First, there was "Yes," then "I do," then "How was your day?" then "I'm expecting" then "Isn't he/she adorable?" then "How do I get the stain out of this shirt?" and so on. The story was not without high points—in fact, there were many wonderful moments—but there was also for me too strong a sense of boundaries. I felt hemmed in by barriers that men were allowed to climb over or walk around. In this, I shared a desire with many women of my era—and yes, later eras—for greater freedom.

I TREASURED BEING secretary of state, but that doesn't mean I went around whistling all the time. There were many days when I didn't get my way in a meeting and left with steam pouring out of my ears, vowing to get revenge when I wrote my memoir. *Just wait*, I thought, *I'll lay everything on the table, and the whole world will see that I was right and they were wrong and how unfairly I was treated.* When I began to reduce these incidents to paper, however, I found that I had either forgotten why I had been furious or was unable to explain what had happened in a way that proved my point.

For example, I had many disagreements over the years with National Security Advisor Sandy Berger and Secretary of Defense Bill Cohen. Our overall approach to foreign policy was similar, but I tended to be more action-oriented to the point of being called an interventionist. At one juncture, Sandy complained about people who talked about using military force "as if it were like having an orgasm." I stopped him and said I was tired of debates in which every time a person favored doing something, she was called bloodthirsty and in which every advocate of restraint was called a wimp. "Enough with the ad hominem attacks," I declared, "and besides, I have forgotten about orgasms."

For several seconds, we just stared at one another, then everyone laughed, and we resumed our squabbling. This story, which I initially included in the memoir, then timidly took out, was more R-rated than most, but not atypical of our discussions. Still, the differences between us were never personal, and our friendships remained strong. In any case, I found that I felt better when emphasizing the positive. I had also come to dislike the kiss-and-tell memoir of the sort first authored by James Monroe (about George Washington) and, more recently, by former staffers of Bill Clinton, who were made famous by him and then became even better known by slamming him in print. Finally, I recalled the words of Gabriel García Márquez, the masterful Colombian author, whom I had met years earlier at a state dinner in Mexico. I told him honestly that my favorite novel was *Love in the Time of Cholera*. Later, when we were together in Cartagena, we went for a walk during which he pointed out landmarks from the book. He also advised, "When you write your memoir, Madeleine, do not be angry."

*   *   *

AFTER WORKING ON the book for several months, we had written tens of thousands of words but were not yet close to a finished product.

We had rejected Miramax's suggestion for an outside collaborator but happily agreed to the ministrations of an editor. The woman chosen was someone with whom I got along well, and who encouraged me when writing to jump back and forth in time so that my memories when young would foreshadow the more public events of my maturity. The approach might have borne fruit in the hands of a more agile author, but what I produced tried too hard to make comparisons that didn't jibe. I kept waiting for the editor to apply first aid, but the draft chapters I sent were returned with question marks, not proposed improvements—and when I called her, she was usually busy doing something else. The partnership was not going to work. Enter editor number two.

Richard Cohen is a product of Birmingham, England. Tall and— per Richard's own edit—"well-chiseled," he looks like an athlete and is in fact a champion fencer who competed in the Olympics three times. His accent is a cultured sort of British, so, to my ears at least, he sounds smart. From the first day, he imposed discipline on our writing, mostly by weeding out excess verbiage and smoothing the narrative's flow from one event to the next. He told me that my stories and paragraphs should reinforce one another like "happy families."

Richard is a sublime but ruthless editor. Using tracked changes, he faced off against my finest prose, then impaled whole paragraphs on a thin red line as if running them through with his saber. When I complained about attending "endless" meetings, he pointed out that the meetings had in fact ended. He condemned the use of "very" as padding and "literally" as most often untrue. He assured me that my friends—if they were friends—would still like me even if their names and attributes (wise, good-looking, hardworking) were not cluttering up the text. With one eyebrow higher than the other, giving an ever-quizzical look to his face, he pushed me to stop dancing around my feelings. "What the reader wants to know," he said, "is not what you are comfortable telling them; it's what you really think. Stick to that, and your words cannot help but be of interest."

Because I was now so busy and because of all the wrangling over how best to tell my story, we needed an extra year to finish. Finally, with publication imminent, we sought to create some buzz, beginning at a booksellers' convention in Arizona. Upon arriving at the auditorium, I checked to see where I had been placed on the queue of speakers. There I was, right after the author of *Time to Pee!*, a manual on potty training. I was ready to be upset but, when listening, had to admit that my fellow writer knew his stuff. When my turn came, I eased the transition by exploring the similarities between what *Madam Secretary* had to say about managing world affairs and *Time to Pee!*'s advice on negotiating with a two-year-old.

As soon as my book was in the shops, so was I, flying from airport to airport, giving interviews and attending events both at bookstore chains and at such fine independents as Powell's (Portland, Oregon), Kepler's (San Francisco), Tattered Cover (Denver), Books and Books (Coral Gables), and Politics and Prose (Washington, DC). This was the endurance test known as a book tour.

I learned quickly that, amid the whirlwind of speaking and autographing, logistics matter. It takes stamina to sit for hours, smile constantly, and sign, sign, sign. To survive, one needs a smooth writing surface (with no tablecloth), a pen whose ink flows reliably, a wrist that is free of carpal tunnel, and a stack of sticky notes for people to spell out their names so I can inscribe the books correctly. Also required is the ability to exchange pleasantries without getting lured into debates that stall the line. However, we can't be in such a rush that the book is whipped away while I am still writing, and "Albright" shrinks to "Albri . . ." There are other trials. I found it impossible, for example, to keep a straight face when asked to dedicate my memoir, "To Chastity, have a fun life."

As a person of a certain age and reputation, I made clear to friends that I was not the sort to worry about how many people bought my book. My goals were high-minded: to educate, inspire, and add to the public record. At the same time, I decided there must be a reason that Tina Brown and Jonathan Burnham weren't calling every couple of hours with a sales update, so I helped by calling them. They were grateful, I'm sure, especially when I suggested that they might want to arrange for *Madam Secretary* to be displayed more prominently in Barnes & Noble and alerted them to the absence of copies in the Minneapolis airport bookstore.

Who am I kidding? It's a wonderful feeling to walk into a shop and see your life story on display, even when customers are striding past it in search of the latest Grisham. My mood lightened further when, just about this time, I was summoned to jury duty. Walking into the cavernous room at the DC courthouse where prospective jurors are made to cool their heels, I sat down next to a young woman. After a moment, she gave me a sidelong glance, as strangers in such a situation will do. I peered at the volume she was holding in her lap—*Madam Secretary.* The young woman did a double take, our eyes met, we bumped fists, and I yearned on the spot to adopt her.

EVERYONE WHO CAN should write a memoir, whether for publication or just to deposit in a drawer or beam to the cloud. There is drama in every life. Fame is irrelevant to one's worth and can sometimes be an obstacle to an appropriate appreciation of others. Further, the effort to reflect on our opportunities and choices is, for all of us, a challenge worth attempting.

I know that when I looked back on my life to that point, I found it easier to grasp the pieces than the whole. Cosmic meanings were beyond me. I wanted my final thoughts in the book to appear profound; instead, they were primarily about how grateful I felt—a genuine sentiment, but hardly original. I was, however, also struck by how much of my life seemed an accident, a narrative that could easily have turned out differently. If my parents had not been able to leave Prague so soon after the Nazis invaded, or had they gambled that it was safe to stay, the chances are near certain that none of us would have survived the war. My sister and brother, my children and grandchildren, would never have been born.

In 1948, when the Communists seized power in Czechoslovakia, we could probably have found a way to live in the country even though my father, a staunch democrat, would surely have been arrested. I will always wonder what direction my road might have taken had I come of age in a totalitarian state. Would I have simply kept my head down and my mouth shut? Would I have sought to curry favor by conforming to the dictates of power? Or would I have cast my lot with dissidents, braving hardships and risking jail?

What if, when leaving Czechoslovakia, my family had stayed on in Europe instead of coming to the United States? What if, instead of Joe Albright, I had married Elston Mayhew, my high school crush? What if I had never embarked on a professional career? The pondering led to no answers but underlined for me the unpredictability of all our lives. It is rare that we move from one step to the next in a logical progression. More often, like a small child crossing a wide stream, we launch ourselves from stone to stone, every leap bringing us closer to some destinations and farther away from others—but without a clear view of where our ultimate landing spot might be. Instead, we prepare for the next jump, then the one after, until after a lifetime of motion is past, we are startled, at least a little, by where we are and by what we have become.

FIVE

Quicksand

M Y DINNER PLANS were set. I was slated to share a meal with President George W. Bush's national security advisor, Condoleezza Rice. Concerned about being on time, I walked faster than normal along the narrow curving pathway that led to my garage. Just prior to reaching the door, I caught a heel in the crevice between two bricks, twisted an ankle, and came down hard with my shoulder and forehead bearing much of the impact. Stunned and unable for a moment to find my arm, I groped in the dirt for the keys that had slipped from my grasp. Rising unsteadily to my feet, I circumvented the ferns in urns and stumbled back inside where I called Condi's office to say that I would be late. Not until entering the bathroom to rinse off did I realize from the mirror that blood was pouring from a gash above my left eye. I looked like Sissy Spacek in *Carrie*, postprom.

My brother, John, appealed to by phone, rode to the rescue, driving me to Sibley Hospital, but I was so shaken I forgot my purse. That wouldn't have mattered had the lack of proper identification not brought the paperwork process in the emergency room to a screeching halt. To get things moving again, I said to the woman who had stopped filling out forms, "Perhaps you recognize me. I'm Madeleine Albright, and I used to be secretary of state." The woman gazed at me with a blank expression, taking in my ragged, bloodstained blouse with leaves sticking to it, ripped stockings, and mud-spattered shoes.

"No," she announced. "Colin Powell is secretary of state."

I replied, "Yes, you're right, Colin Powell. But I had the job before him."

A spark of comprehension flickered in the woman's eyes, "So," she said, "that means you're unemployed."

JUDITH MARTIN, ALSO known as "Miss Manners," was in my graduating class at Wellesley. For all her wise counsel, she never prescribed the proper etiquette for thinking about one's successors in a highly visible job. Publicly, you wish them well, but the ego being what it is, you don't want them to be placed on a pedestal at the expense of your own reputation. You also hope they don't flop so badly that everything you tried to accomplish is undone.

My successor, Powell, began work with the burden of high expectations. In 1993, as UN ambassador, I had served alongside him until his term as chair of the Joint Chiefs of Staff was up and he retired from the army. During those eight months, we engaged in a sometimes edgy debate about whether the United States should risk using force to stop ethnic cleansing in Bosnia. I argued the case for; he stressed how high the costs of intervening might be. I grew frustrated, as a mere mortal civilian female, trying to prevail in a dispute with the much-decorated hero of Operation Desert Storm.

Powell wrote later that my manner of talking about the U.S. armed forces nearly gave him an aneurysm and that he had felt compelled to explain to me patiently the military's proper role. In 1995, the United States and NATO did step in to good effect, thus ending the carnage in Bosnia and smoothing the way to peace. In time, the retired general and I became friends. When he sent me a copy of his book, he inscribed it "Patiently yours, Colin." Replying, I signed my note of thanks, "Forcefully yours, Madeleine."

President-elect Bush's choice of the former general as secretary of state was hailed by most as the ideal pick. Although I did not always agree with Colin, I was confident the department would be in skilled hands. Like him, Condoleezza Rice was a veteran of the George H. W. Bush administration.

As a Democrat, I was impressed and a bit mortified that a chief executive from the other party would be the first to appoint an African American secretary of state and the first to choose an African American woman as national security advisor. It was a good moment for the party of Lincoln. Having Powell and Rice represent the United States to the world sent a powerful message of inclusion. Condi especially made use of the fact to show that she (and by extension, the country she served) could empathize with populations that viewed themselves as disadvantaged. She noted that when America's founders talked about "We the People," they had not included her ancestors, and that her family had lived for many years in communities that were segregated. More than once she said that the United States "was born with a birth defect: it was slavery."

GEORGE W. BUSH ran for president the way challengers most often do: by drawing a contrast between his virtues and the more egregious flaws of the man he sought to replace. Throughout the 2000 campaign, Bush's signature pledge was to restore honor and dignity to the White House, an undisguised reminder of the Monica Lewinsky scandal. To this he added a pair of promises: to raise educational standards and cut taxes.

In that last year of the millennium, there were few other weak spots for a Republican campaign to exploit. Although the economy was beginning to slow, the Clinton era had become a synonym for prosperity. The federal budget, rescued from gargantuan deficits, had found a haven in surplus territory, while inflation, unemployment, and crime were down. Overseas, the United States was without a serious rival. When appealing for votes, Bush had little to say about foreign policy. His focus was narrow and shaped largely by his service as governor of Texas. His first international trip as president was to Mexico, just across the border from the Lone Star State. It wouldn't be long, however, before his mettle as commander in chief was tested.

Unavoidably, the Bush record in global affairs is defined primarily by the events that flowed from the September 11, 2001, terrorist hijacking of four commercial aircraft and their use as weapons to murder almost three thousand people. Between that day's serene dawn and its grief-ravaged dusk, America's view of the world and its dangers was transformed.

Later, I would find much to criticize in the Bush administration's foreign policy. Any fair judgment, however, must begin with a sense of what it must have been like to occupy a position of authority in the aftermath of 9/11. That very night, fear that another attack was imminent prompted the Secret Service to awaken the First Couple and hustle them into the White House's underground shelter. Within weeks, five people had died from exposure to anthrax contained in envelopes sent to media outlets. In October, the president's top aides were warned that they might have been exposed to a botulinum toxin that could kill them within hours.

I could imagine the pressures bearing down on senior officials. In August 1998, when I was secretary of state, terrorists bombed the U.S. embassies in Kenya and Tanzania, injuring thousands and killing 224 people, including 12 Americans and 40 local citizens who had worked for us. In the months that followed, we asked ourselves repeatedly if we could have done more to prevent those tragedies. The answer was that one can always do more. Every day, we put aside other business to track down threats to our military and diplomatic outposts, overseas travelers, and families at home. Yet, even while we followed the clues we had, we worried about what remained hidden.

In the wake of 9/11, Bush administration officials rose each morning uncertain whether further attacks were brewing. They had a formidable job: to reassure the nation, lock down the cooperation of allies, gauge the extent of terrorist networks, and sift the daily flood of intelligence data for nuggets that might foil a planned strike.

They also had to hit back. The perpetrator's identity was no secret. Osama bin Laden had boasted of his role. Al-Qaeda, the group he led, was based in Afghanistan and enjoyed the protection of the country's radical rulers, the Taliban. About a month after 9/11, Bush authorized a military intervention that drove the Taliban from power and forced al-Qaeda to scatter. I fully backed this operation and expected Bush to follow up by pursuing the remnants of bin Laden's organization, trying to stabilize Afghanistan, and rallying support across the globe to prevent the rise of other violent extremist groups. This was the logical strategy—and one I am sure that Al Gore, had he been elected, would have chosen—but it is not what Bush decided to do.

Over the course of 2002, the president let himself be convinced that the best way to defeat the enemy that had attacked the United States was to destroy an adversary that had not. Instead of sticking to the task of defeating al-Qaeda, Bush diverted vast amounts of military, intelligence, and diplomatic resources to the invasion of Iraq and the overthrow of its dictator, Saddam Hussein.

Why do this? The administration argued that, after 9/11, the United States could not live with the possibility that bin Laden would find a national leader (such as Hussein) who would willingly provide him with nuclear, chemical, or biological arms. To heighten the sense of urgency, a group of hawks in the Defense Department and on the staff of Vice President Richard Cheney claimed to have discovered a link between Iraq and al-Qaeda. Meanwhile, Iraqi exiles stirred the pot by declaring that Baghdad's weapons programs were more advanced than our experts had thought. The assertions were picked up by the *New York Times*, whose editorial writers urged the White House to show resolve.

To this day it remains unclear precisely when Bush made the decision to invade, but as the months passed, war fever took hold. In August, Cheney said there was "no doubt" that Hussein was amassing weapons of mass destruction "to use against our friends, against our allies, against us." In September, Rice warned that a failure to act might lead to a "mushroom cloud" over the Middle East.

Powell, alone among senior officials, raised questions about the wisdom of what was being planned. Interviewed later, he recalled telling Bush:

It isn't just a simple matter of going to Baghdad. I know how to do that. What happens after? You need to understand, if you take out a government, take out a regime, guess who becomes the government and regime responsible for the country? You are. So if you break it, you own it. You need to understand that 28 million Iraqis will be standing there looking at us, and I haven't heard enough of the planning for that eventuality.

Powell recommended referring the matter to the UN Security Council, and Bush did. In October 2002, that panel ordered a new round of inspections to determine whether Iraq did indeed possess forbidden arms.

Meanwhile, attitudes on Capitol Hill were influenced heavily by the events of a decade before. In 1990 and early 1991, most Democrats had opposed using force to roll back the Iraqi invasion of Kuwait, arguing that economic measures would eventually suffice while avoiding further bloodshed. We worried that a military campaign might turn much of the Arab world against us, embroil our country in a drawn-out war, and impose a high cost in American lives and treasure. Our fears proved groundless. The United States and its allies took just a little more than a month to drive Iraqi troops out of Kuwait, did so with overwhelming support from Arab governments, and suffered far fewer casualties than skeptics had predicted.

By the time of the Security Council vote in 2002, many Democrats were of two minds, wary of again being judged wrong yet not convinced that war was necessary. We hoped that the reintroduction of weapons inspectors would either resolve the crisis without violence or provide a clear basis for military action.

However, when the first review proved inconclusive, Bush decided not to wait for more data. He was sure he already knew the truth. To plead his case, he enlisted his most credible spokesperson: the secretary of state. Powell's address to the Security Council on February 5, 2003, was watched almost everywhere. I tuned in with a special interest because, years earlier, I had testified before Congress on the same subject—Iraq's weapons of mass destruction. To prepare, I had worked closely with CIA analysts who went over every word of my testimony. In several places, they inserted cautionary notes so that I did not make allegations that went beyond what the evidence told us. Basically, we were sure that the Iraqi military had produced chemical and biological arms before the First Gulf War; we didn't know if it still had them. We did, however, put Hussein's regime under constant scrutiny and felt that we could make him pay should he attempt an aggressive move.

In New York, Powell offered a narrative that began where mine had stopped, then took off in new directions. Iraq, he declared, had a stockpile of chemical weapons, was in the process of manufacturing more, and had "factories on wheels and on rails . . . [that] can produce enough dry biological agent in a single month to kill thousands." He accused Hussein of trying to reconstitute his nuclear program and charged that Iraq, in December 2000, had begun offering training to associates of al-Qaeda. The secretary then shared ominous intelligence interpretations (later proven wrong) about the images shown in certain satellite photos. The portrait he painted was of an Iraq bent on revenge, equipped with an arsenal of banned weapons, and in league with the 9/11 terrorists.

For many in America and abroad, the presentation was decisive. From my experience, I was sure that in such a setting, any claim made by the U.S. secretary of state could be verified. Indeed, Powell stressed that "every statement I make today is backed up by sources, solid sources. These are not assertions. What we're giving you are facts and conclusions based on solid intelligence."

Like me, Colin made the strongest case he could, based on the evidence he was shown. Unlike me, some of the "evidence" he had been given was bunkum. He was misled and so, too, was the world.

ON MARCH 19, 2003, U.S. armed forces invaded Iraq and occupied the country. The consequences, for better but mostly for worse, would be felt through the remainder of the decade and beyond.

In this period, I was often invited to appear on television and radio news shows. I told interviewers that although I could understand why the president had gone to war, I worried that he lacked a good plan for "what next?" I feared that our occupation of Baghdad, Islam's capital during that faith's golden age, would make it easier for terrorists to find recruits. I was bewildered by the administration's failure to anticipate sectarian violence and by its surprise at what should have been obvious from the outset: that the chief regional beneficiary of the invasion would be Iraq's longtime rival, Iran. I was also disturbed by the Bush team's impatience and "shock and awe" rhetoric, which wasn't going down well overseas.

Polls at the time indicated a sharp drop in backing for the United States coupled with growing cynicism about our intentions. One survey found that a majority of French, Germans, Russians, and Muslims believed the U.S. goal was to dominate the world by seizing control of Middle East oil. Further, in Afghanistan, the Taliban was enjoying a respite from pressure that allowed it to catch its breath, reorganize, and mount what would become a serious and decades-long challenge to the government in Kabul.

In September 2002, Bush told an assemblage of Republican governors, "I'm gonna make a prediction. Write this down. Afghanistan and Iraq will lead that part of the world to democracy." The president believed this because it was what his instincts, and some of his advisers, had told him. There is a price, however, for being wrong. The distance between Bush's desires and the realities of occupied Iraq caused his foreign policy team to come loose from its moorings. The Pentagon's plan for the early withdrawal of troops was abandoned. The State Department's ideas for reconstruction were ignored. A presidential appointee disbanded the entire Iraqi Army without prior notice to anyone. Cheney kept pushing hard-line policies through his daily talks with Bush and the network of loyalists he had established in key agencies. Then photos surfaced that showed U.S. military personnel inflicting sadistic treatment on captive Iraqis.

Although I was not privy to what was happening inside the White

House, I thought it plain that Powell was frustrated. His advice prior
to the war had been brushed aside. He was forced to defend decisions
in which he had played no part. As a career military man in a diplomat's role, he also had to be careful to stay in his own lane. Though he
had an acute understanding of the challenges faced by U.S. forces in
Iraq, he couldn't provide military analysis without trespassing on the
Pentagon's turf. To this, one must add the fury Powell later admitted
to feeling at being shoved on stage with inaccurate intelligence information for his speech in New York.

Powell's lack of clout within the administration was mystifying
if only because of his leverage. His judgment in matters of war and
peace was more widely respected than that of the president or anyone else in the White House. Surely, he would have received a fuller
hearing had he threatened to go public with his concerns. However,
the traits that make Powell so admired also made him less effective
as a bureaucratic infighter.

In one of his books, he writes:

> In the military, your superiors may have very different ideas than
> you do about what should be your most important mission . . .
> I never tried to fight my superiors' priorities. Instead, I worked
> hard to accomplish the tasks they set as quickly and decisively as
> I could. The sooner I could satisfy my superiors, the sooner they
> would stop bugging me about them, and the quicker I could
> move on to my own priorities. Always give the king his due.

Powell is, above all, an army man who believes in the chain of authority. He wasn't about to say anything that might undermine the
morale of U.S. armed forces or be interpreted as disloyal to the president. He was the ultimate team player, yet to Bush's inner circle, the
secretary's misgivings about the war made him an outsider. He had
originally intended to resign after a single term, then decided to stay,
then was pushed out in favor of Rice. He left office with his integrity intact, but not with the level of backing he would have preferred

after decades of service. In his memoir, George W. Bush writes, "I admired Colin, but it sometimes seemed like the State Department he led wasn't fully on board with my philosophy and policies." In hindsight, this seems like high praise.

By the end of 2004, Powell was not the only member of the administration who was unhappy; so was his boss. The president was disturbed that so much of what he had been led to believe about Iraq was untrue. The American military had been greeted as occupiers rather than liberators. There were no vans producing biological weapons, no stockpiles of chemical arms, and no sign of a resurgent nuclear program. Elections were bright spots but failed to curb the ethnic and religious rivalries that had turned much of the nation into a war zone. Around the Middle East, people viewed what was taking place in Iraq as a warning, not as a model for how they wanted their own countries to look.

In commenting to the public on all this, I was restrained by my hope that the U.S.-led coalition would ultimately succeed. With the lives of tens of thousands of American troops at risk every day, I was not about to predict failure. Instead, I emphasized the steps I thought the administration could take to salvage what had evolved into a tragic mess. Privately, however, I was appalled at the blundering.

SIX

Clubbing

I LOVE NATURE, TRULY, but there's only so much zip I can derive from an oak, a bug, or a bee. I draw energy from other people—not always positive energy, but energy. I'm happiest when bouncing thoughts off those who share my interest in trying to solve the world's many riddles. So, it is in the pursuit of happiness that I set out chairs, pour drinks, and organize groups.

My hunger for companionship can probably be traced to my childhood in Europe and to a family that moved at short intervals from one apartment, city, and country to the next. Never in one place for long, I wasn't able to acquire a settled circle of friends. I had my parents for company, my little sister and baby brother, and a few play dates here and there, but was often alone and didn't like it.

Beginning a new life in America, I was resolved to blend in. At church that first Thanksgiving, when singing "We Gather Together," I "aaahsked" the Lord's blessing with a pronunciation (picked up in England) that my Long Island peers chastened and hastened to laugh at. Because I didn't want to be different, I soon dropped the accent. Later, whenever I entered a new school, I started an international affairs club and named myself president. What better way to be sure of being included?

As a grown-up, I arranged car pools, volunteered for committees and joined in neighborhood projects. When appointed U.S. ambassador to the United Nations, I decided to convene regular meetings of all my female counterparts. *We'll need to reserve a conference room,*

I thought, but it turned out that women represented just 7 of the more than 180 member countries. My guests and I sat comfortably around my dining room table, handbags stacked on a spare chair. We called ourselves the G-7. After I became secretary of state, I formed a club of women foreign ministers that was twice the size. We assumed the name the "fearsome fourteen" and promised, at a minimum, to return one another's phone calls. When male foreign ministers from big countries complained that they couldn't get through to me as quickly as their female colleagues from Barbados and Liechtenstein, I said the solution was to have themselves replaced by a woman. There were no further complaints.

I also enjoyed the company of men. During my final days in office, the French foreign minister, Hubert Védrine, organized a going-away dinner for me near Paris with a group of fellow diplomats. I abhor national stereotypes, but in this gathering, certain traits were evident. There was no denying the Scottish flair for language in the red-haired British foreign secretary, Robin Cook; or the orderly thinking of Germany's Joschka Fischer; or the ebullience of Italy's Lamberto Dini; or the sober realism of Russia's Igor Ivanov; or the infectious zeal of Spain's Javier Solana, who sported the longest title: high representative for common foreign and security policy of the European Union.

Among ourselves, we quarreled often on topics that ranged from sectarian rivalry in the Balkans to the safety of consuming biogenetic products (dubbed "Frankenfood" by protectionist European farmers). Our national interests did not always mesh, and our temperaments varied, but we had no trouble setting aside professional differences in social settings. At the dinner in Paris, Ivanov presented me with a Russian tea set that had a little portrait of one of us on each cup and a matching plate inscribed: "Madeleine's Dream Team." Védrine gave me a beautifully bound two-volume edition of de Tocqueville's *Democracy in America*, implying that the French understand the United States better than Americans do. In the case of de Tocqueville, he was probably right.

* * *

AFTER LEAVING GOVERNMENT, I still traveled widely, including trips across the Atlantic for business meetings, to deliver speeches, and to participate in conferences. Between flights, I occasionally had a chance to connect with one or more of my former partners in diplomacy. Given the ominous turn that events were taking, especially in Afghanistan and Iraq, we always had more fears to voice than our fleeting encounters allowed. Robin Cook worried that a political chasm was opening up between much of Europe and the United States. Jozias van Aartsen, ex-foreign minister of the Netherlands, sounded the same alarm. Amid the clamor, my old instinct revived, and I invited friends, as in high school, to start an international affairs club, this one made up of former foreign ministers. I didn't nominate myself for president, but neither did I object to the informal name we adopted: "Madeleine and Her Exes."

The attendees from the dinner in Paris made up the new group's core, but others soon came knocking, and have steadily widened our circle. What we now call the Aspen Ministers Forum meets one or two times a year under the auspices, logically enough, of the Aspen Institute. I look forward to the sessions because, as one participant observed, "we treat each other with all the respect we believe we are owed." Because we no longer occupy official positions, we can exchange ideas without approved talking points or any sort of national agenda. We are free to be ourselves—in this company, a good thing.

It is, of course, more difficult for an ex-minister to have an impact on policy than someone still in office. A leader in government can always attract attention either by announcing a new program or by explaining an old one in novel terms. That same person, out of office, can turn cartwheels on the Avenue des Champs-Élysées without causing a stir. As a group, the "formers" have fewer responsibilities, but we do have a reservoir of experience in war and peace that still has value—or so we tell ourselves. In our hearts, we're not done. Over the years, we have undertaken joint projects, issued statements, written articles, and published a book of essays. We have invited younger people to our meetings in the expectation that they will profit from our perspective and we from theirs. Because of our diversity, we quibble over details but are united in thinking that when addressing global problems, effective diplomacy should be the first option, not a last resort.

MY MEETINGS WITH the former ministers helped assuage my appetite for discussions of foreign policy. However, they were not enough. Many months, sometimes a year, separated our sessions. In between them, my hunger returned; I needed another club.

The 34th Street Group—as it came to be known—was born in an office building on 15th Street, next to downtown Washington's McPherson Square. There, on the tenth floor, is where my consulting firm set up shop. We had a conference table that could seat twelve. Reluctant to exclude friends, I invited twice that number of veterans from the Clinton administration's national security team. Our mission: to talk about what we would be trying to accomplish were we still in power. Scrunched together, we devoured cold sandwiches and reviewed the troubled global scene, picking apart one another's arguments as we had done so frequently in the past. The difference was that when we finally arrived at a consensus, we had neither a decision memo to send out nor a bureaucracy to order into action.

Although we framed our deliberations around the needs of the nation and the public good, there was a partisan slant to much of what we said. At the table, in addition to me, were such close advisers to Bill Clinton as Sandy Berger and former White House chief of staff John Podesta; Al Gore's top aide, Leon Fuerth; and my counselor at the State Department, Wendy Sherman. For years, we had strategized the way Washingtonians do, with one eye on world problems and the other on American voters. We were sincere both in our desire to develop ideas that would serve our country well and our eagerness to help Democrats win back the power to put those ideas into practice.

After several cramped sessions in my business office, we decided we needed more space. My living room isn't huge, but it can, with a little rearranging, accommodate two dozen normal-size bodies in an equal number of below-average-size chairs. By 2003, that's where we were meeting, just about every month, at my address on 34th Street. Over time, we have expanded to include members of Congress and their key staff, retired military people, former ambassadors, and a sizable number of what Europeans call "apparatchiks" and Americans describe as "political junkies."

When our group began, I expected we would continue for a year or so, then move on. That hasn't happened. People still come, despite how hard it is to find a parking spot in Georgetown. Every month, I tell my staff, "Just you watch. Nobody is going to show up." But the doorbell keeps chiming. I take that as proof that in our era, the need for communal therapy has no bottom.

My job, aside from explaining the bathroom's location and where everyone's coats and backpacks should go, is to introduce the guest speaker (should there be one) and to kick off the discussion. Then I recognize people who raise their hands or, in some cases, just their eyebrows, keep the group on topic, and summarize what has been said. In the process of doing this a few hundred times, I have reached some conclusions about how different professional subspecies approach the same subject. Lawyers tend to begin with a thesis, and then list the main points in favor and against the proposition at hand. Sandy Berger excelled at this; he also liked to insist on a clear statement of goals. Professors—and I am one—emphasize lessons from history and the impacts of culture; we want to put as much data as possible into the pot. Those with a military background will likely highlight the practical; for them, *doable* is an adjective of merit and "if only" a phrase that wastes time. Media specialists focus on how to present ideas in a way that will attract the most attention—by choosing a catchy name for an initiative, for example, or by announcing it at just the right moment. Experts on Congress testify to what committee and party leaders are thinking and how politics influences everything.

Lucia, my longtime cook and household czar, assembles the meals. We always select entrees that can be cut with a fork: asking two dozen people to hack through steaks while balancing plates on their knees is to court disaster. It's also fortunate that women are skilled at multitasking, because I run the meetings while keeping a wary eye on the glasses of red wine that are stowed beneath chairs atop my vulnerable rug. For dessert, Lucia puts fruit and cookies on the coffee table in front of us. There the treats sit, undisturbed, until I rise to my feet and take one. Perhaps my guests are just trying to be polite or maybe they are afraid of being thought gluttons, but it's up to me to make the first move—the only duty I share with the queen of England.

As the 2004 election approached, politics intruded more deeply into our conversations. The 34th Street Group included many who would be active in the campaign. We talked about what we thought voters would care about most and how candidates could best frame the foreign policy discussion. The elders among us cautioned against making promises to get elected that would be impossible to implement should the Democrats win. The more ambitious pointed out that a candidate who loses can't implement anything. This tension between good policy and winning votes is what makes the political game so complex and, after one falls beneath its spell, hard to shake off.

MY OWN POLITICAL awakening came when I was just fifteen. Most of my classmates tuned their radios to hear the latest star singers (Eddie Fisher, Patti Page) and share in the new dance enthusiasms (La Bomba, the bunny hop). I did, too, but I also spent hours listening to speeches and commentary from the 1952 Democratic National Convention. How could any song or dance be more exciting than Adlai Stevenson? My parents were Democrats because Franklin Roosevelt had guided America through the war and because the party leadership had helped to build strong transatlantic institutions and the UN. Also, Democrats beyond the Jim Crow South were outspoken supporters of labor and civil rights. Still, when Stevenson lost to

Eisenhower once, then again, about the only states he carried were from below the Mason-Dixon line. By the time of that second defeat, I was attending college in Massachusetts, where I went around raising money for an outfit called Dollars for Democrats. Patrolling the streets of Boston with a sign in my hand, I was approached by an old guy who said with a wink, "Not one dollar for Democrats, but how about five bucks for you, baby?" Then being then, I laughed. In 1958, I got a job with the college newspaper and managed to land an interview with a U.S. senator who was up for reelection. I have no memory of the questions I put to John F. Kennedy, but I do recall asking for his autograph. Decades later, I am still shamed by my betrayal of journalistic standards and pleased to have the autograph.

During the tempestuous 1960s, I was busy getting married, rearing children, and pursuing a graduate degree at Columbia University. I also solicited money for the schools my daughters attended and on behalf of other worthy causes. In politics, a person with a proven record in fund-raising is like a lead tenor in the world of church choirs: always in demand. In 1972, I was asked to organize a dinner in support of Senator Edmund Muskie, who was angling for the Democratic nomination to oppose the incumbent president, Richard Nixon. Muskie's craggy face and homespun way of talking—he was from Maine—drew comparisons to Lincoln; as did his height: even his tie clasp looked down on me. I thought he would make a top-notch chief executive and hoped to impress him by ensuring that every detail of the dinner went just right. With help from friends, I designed invitations, approved the menu, nagged almost everyone I knew into buying tickets, and, to highlight Muskie's environmental leadership, decorated the hotel ballroom with potted fir trees.

The gala, with more than a thousand guests expected, was a sellout at the then-record-high price of $125 a seat. I was sure we were going to collect buckets of money and prayed that the night would proceed smoothly. Then, early in the day, a deliveryman showed up demanding cash for the fifty floral arrangements he had brought in his truck. "We didn't order any flowers," I said brusquely, "we have trees." I also heard about a phone call we had received from the embassy of Chad thanking us for its invitation but wondering when the limousine would be there to pick up the ambassador. We told him that, although we had no limousines, he would be welcome to come.

That evening, my nerves began to rattle when a second deliveryman, also expecting cash, arrived bearing a dozen cases of liquor. We turned him away, but not before he angrily pulled out his order sheet with our names written boldly at the bottom. Pizzas were next, two hundred of them, smelling the way only pizzas do, with special toppings. Just as I was dealing with the pepperoni crisis, I saw a man dressed in a batik robe enter the ballroom. I went up to him and said, "You must be the ambassador from Chad." "No," he said, "I am the ambassador from Kenya." *Uh oh*, I thought. Soon we had to find seats at dinner for more than a dozen emissaries from Africa and the Middle East, and their wives. Outside, there was an equal number of limousine drivers who claimed to have been hired for the event and wanted to be paid. This was madness.

Somehow, we were able to make space for all of our guests and I started to relax. Then in walked two more people I didn't recognize. I wondered, *Oh God, what next?* and raised my hand to halt them.

"We're magicians and have come to entertain the children."

"Leave," I said. "There are no children. Shoo, go away."

They told me that they really were magicians and that if I didn't allow them to stay, they would turn me into something terrible.

Oh, hell's bells, I exclaimed to myself. *What can it hurt?* "Come on in."

What had happened? We didn't find out until a couple of years later, when a pro-Nixon operative, Donald Segretti, confessed to orchestrating the whole shebang. He had thought about adding elephants but was unable to complete the arrangements. He and his co-conspirators did succeed, however, in releasing mice at a Muskie press conference, distributing racist letters on phony campaign stationery, and paying a young woman to run *au naturel* through the lobby of a hotel where the candidate was staying, yelling, "Senator,

I love you." The reason for the sabotage was that Nixon didn't want the Democrats to nominate Muskie, and as it happened, they didn't. Instead, we settled on George McGovern, a lovely man but for many voters too liberal. Nixon won in a landslide.

Muskie never became president, but he was a big reason for my eventually becoming secretary of state. In 1976 he asked me to be his legislative assistant, my first paying job since placing filler items in newspapers for the *Encyclopedia Britannica* about fifteen years previously. (Sample work product: "Ostriches are voiceless," says the *Encyclopedia Britannica*.) Joining Muskie moved me from one category of Washingtonian (volunteer parent) to another (professional policy wonk). The transformation took. Following my stint on Capitol Hill, I served on the National Security Council staff under Jimmy Carter and then advised two Democratic presidential candidates who lost. That experience and the contacts I met along the way led to my cabinet posts in the Clinton administration and to my status, by 2004, as a "former somebody."

A RULE OF thumb in presidential politics is that the economy and national security are the two issues that matter most. Other topics may loom large in contests for Congress and governor, but citizens look to the commander in chief to help them prosper and keep them safe. In his first term as president, George W. Bush had begun well, but with the war efforts in disarray, and unemployment higher than it had been under Clinton, his reelection was no sure thing.

The field of Democratic candidates was therefore a bulky one and included three prominent senators (John Kerry, John Edwards, Joe Lieberman), a longtime U.S. representative (Richard Gephardt), a retired four-star general (Wesley Clark), and a little-known governor from a small state (Vermont's Howard Dean). Of these, the one judged least likely to do well was Dean, who in 2003 proceeded to raise more money and achieve higher poll ratings than any other candidate. In an augury of campaigns to come, the governor began his crusade from the left, claimed to represent "the Democratic wing of the Democratic Party," and faulted the senators in the race for not opposing in advance the invasion of Iraq. For months he was the only contender who generated excitement. Ultimately, he fell short because of an inability to expand his base or to erase doubts about his ability to defeat Bush. His descent after the Iowa caucuses was mirrored by the rise of Kerry, a more traditional politician whose résumé included two decades in the Senate and meritorious service both in and against the Vietnam War.

As I moved around the country during this period, I frequently found time to participate in campaign events and to engage in heated debates with conservative commentators on radio or television. I enjoyed doing this for the same reason I loved meeting with the former foreign ministers and the 34th Street Group: the energy boost. I can be almost comatose from traveling and then feel the adrenaline flow when appearing before a group of voters or preparing for an interview. Formulating and defending opinions is like doing stretching exercises for the brain.

Throughout the summer of 2004, I felt close to the Kerry operation because its staff had taken over three floors in the building where the Albright Group was located. For months, every elevator ride put me in up-or-down contact with diverse members of the Democratic tribe: streetwise union organizers, veterans with flags sewn onto their vests, big-city mayors, and hordes of young people with cell phones attached to their heads like earmuffs.

The campaign's proximity also allowed me to play a minor role in a piece of political theater. Four years earlier, Kerry had been on the short list for selection as Al Gore's running mate, and the whole world knew when he was bypassed in favor of Lieberman. Now, the prospective nominee wanted to interview his own potential running mates in secret, thus sparing them a comparable ordeal. Because my office was so near, I hosted a meeting between Kerry and Senator Bob Graham of Florida. Despite our efforts to be discreet, Graham was seen entering our building, and word of the meeting leaked.

So, I called Kerry and said, "Why don't you use my house?" I didn't have to tell him where it was because he lived around the corner from me. He agreed, and a few days later, when I was out of town, my colleague Suzy George let him in the front door and John Edwards through a back entrance from the garage. Sitting together in my dining room, the two talked for hours while sipping soda and nibbling nuts. Evidently, the interview accomplished its purpose, for the meeting remained a secret and the Democrats nominated the Kerry-Edwards ticket at their convention in Boston. I had the honor of addressing that assemblage and later sat in the audience next to Hillary Clinton. Together we listened to the keynote speech given by a young U.S. Senate candidate from Illinois about whom we then knew little but would before long learn much.

SEVEN

Professor Maddy

D URING MY YEARS in the State Department, I strived to stay in shape physically, but the constant travel and frequency of official meals led me to tell friends that "my job is to go everywhere and eat for my country." In my new life, I was bent on making a fresh start. Three times a week, I set my alarm for 4:45 a.m. When the bell rings, I hit the button and turn over. Exactly nineteen minutes later, I launch myself up and take a bath. After having coffee and being depressed by the newspapers, I head for the Definitions Fitness Studio ("Train Harder. Burn Smarter.") on Jefferson Street, ten blocks away. There, under the eyes of trainer Margo Carper, I sweat. This has been going on since 2001. Within weeks, I began dropping pounds and feeling healthier.

In addition to the lifting and stretching, I have experimented with every diet conceivable, some more than once. What worked especially well was the Fat Flush Plan outlined in a best seller by Ann Louise Gittleman. I was pursuing that regimen when, in 2004, I went to Qatar to give a speech. The country's emir, noting my reduced figure, asked for the secret. I told him. He made me promise to send him a copy of the book, a pledge that went unfulfilled. I wasn't about to ship *The Fat Flush Plan* to a head of state who would not, I presumed, be opening his own mail. From what I saw on television later, the emir never did slim down. I console myself that he and other Arab leaders can hide an ample amount of waistline beneath those billowing white robes.

A few years into my exercise program, I made the mistake of boasting to a reporter that I could leg-press more than four hundred pounds—roughly twice the weight of a female giant panda. The claim caused a brief furor on social media. Some people accused me of fibbing, while gym enthusiasts said the feat wasn't particularly impressive and, anyway, it is never good manners to brag. Point taken. But just to be clear, as Margo is my witness, I could do ten reps.

Once I have settled on a routine, I tend not to change. For the past two decades, my schedule when in Washington has featured that early start, the thrice-weekly workouts, regular hair appointments, and the morning drive to my office downtown. The exception is on Mondays during the school year, when, following the example of my father, I teach.

MY HABIT OF rising before the sun had started when my daughters were little and I needed quiet time to pursue my graduate studies. In those days, I had thought about becoming a professor and in the fall of 1982—with a master's degree, a doctorate, and several years of government experience behind me—the chance presented itself. Georgetown University's Edmund A. Walsh School of Foreign Service hired me to teach international affairs and establish a program to train young women in a field that was then dominated by men even more than it is today. I would spend many hours urging the women in my classes to unlearn everything they had been taught about the virtues of humility and waiting one's turn. "Silence may be golden," I said, "but it won't win many arguments. If you have something to say, don't keep your ideas locked up; unclench your jaws and set those thoughts free. And don't be afraid to interrupt, because that may be the only way you are going to be heard."

When I was a teenager, my mother had worked nine to five as a secretary in the Denver Public Schools, while my father, when he didn't have classes, spent much time in the house. This peculiarity caught the attention of friends, who wanted to know why Dr. Korbel was so often at home in the afternoons. I said it was because he had little to do: a few hours of instruction, some student meetings, summers off. Being a professor was a breeze.

I soon realized how thickheaded an assumption that was. Well before my initial semester at Georgetown started, I was wearing myself out writing a syllabus, developing a reading list, preparing lectures, and trying to get enough sleep despite the weird dreams I was having about being a professor on the first day of school. When that day finally arrived, there weren't enough seats for all the students and, not surprisingly in Washington at the end of August, the temperature was so high in the classroom that it was hard to breathe, let alone think.

Start-up problems aside, I quickly saw the wisdom in one of my father's favorite expressions: "There is nothing better than to be a professor in a free country." Because of all the preparatory work, teaching is in many ways a solitary profession, but the rewards come through the constant back-and-forth with young people, the banter among mostly amiable colleagues, and the relaxed busyness of campus life. Further, I found that the discipline required to explain issues clearly in the classroom would carry over to other fields—first to television interviews and public speaking, then later to diplomacy and business. For nearly a decade, until I left for the State Department, teaching was also a form of personal training, and I enjoyed every minute.

IN 2001, AFTER leaving government, I returned to the Walsh School at the invitation of the dean. We agreed that I would teach a graduate class in the autumn and a larger undergraduate group in the spring. Georgetown, just a quarter mile west of my house, is known for its rigorous academic standards, a men's basketball team that once won the national championship (in 1984), and an athletic nickname, the Hoyas, that few understand. Let me satisfy your curiosity. The name first used by Georgetown's sports teams was "the Stonewalls." At some point in the late nineteenth century, this inspired a Greek scholar to come up with a matching exclamation: "*Hoya Saxa!*" which translates as "What rocks!" In time the Stonewalls became the Hoyas. Now you know.

In recent years, Georgetown has been coming to terms with its historic identity as an owner, exploiter, and seller of slaves. Responding to pressure from students, the administration has offered apologies, renamed buildings, and promised to finance projects that will benefit the descendants of those who were trafficked. The controversy remains ongoing. Ironically, the mother of the university's most revered president, Patrick Francis Healy (1874–1882), grew up a slave in antebellum Georgia. Though Healy identified with the heritage of his Irish father, he remains one of the few people of African American heritage to lead a predominately white university. During his tenure, the school built a two-hundred-foot-high flagship structure later named in his honor. Designed by the same architects who fashioned the Library of Congress, the building is part medieval, part Gothic, and possibly haunted. The tower is graced by a clock the hands of which students periodically detach and then send to famous people as an invitation to visit the campus. Among those to receive the hands was Pope John Paul II, who blessed and returned them but resisted the entreaty to come with.

The course I teach, America's National Security Tool Box, is designed to help students know the options available to a president when dealing with an international crisis or when trying to convince a foreign government to act in a certain way. The tools are surprisingly few but include incentives (aid, trade, arms sales), punitive measures (sanctions, military coercion), and diplomacy in all its forms.

Each semester, on the first day of class, I greet a roomful of well-scrubbed faces to whom even my oldest stories are new. After reviewing the rules (no laptops or cell phones permitted), we start. I urge students to leave behind any presumptions they might have and to begin with the basic puzzle of why countries do what they do. Here, I emphasize five factors that translate roughly into an equal number of questions: What are a country's strengths, and where is it vulnerable? Is its political system controlled from the top or driven by pressures from below? Are neighbors friendly or hostile? What is the nation's self-image? Are the people in charge decisive and vision-ary, or insecure and unable to see beyond the present?

The answers to these questions might tell us, for example, why in 2014 Vladimir Putin took the risk of stealing Crimea from Ukraine. He had sufficient power within Russia to make decisions unilater-ally. He thought the breakup of the Soviet Union had been a disaster and that Crimea—where he had spent his honeymoon—was a legit-imate part of Russia. A risk-taker, he wagered that annexing the re-gion would appeal strongly enough to nationalist feelings at home to outweigh the costs of global opposition. Finally, he sought to restore his country's dominance within the region, so that his neighbors would seek to please (and appease) him rather than the United States or Western Europe. All this was predictable, yet not anticipated by any Western intelligence agency.

For students, the highlight of the term is role-play weekend, when they are asked to assume the identities of ambassadors, cabinet ministers, and White House officials while I am privileged to im-personate the president. Since 2017, however, I have been in denial about the presidency and so, for the purpose of role-play, insist that the chief executive's name is "Pence." To provide the proper setting and adequate sustenance for our drama, the classrooms are divided into a combination UN Security Council, White House Situation Room, and food court.

Because of its size, the undergraduate class splits, with one cohort dealing with a crisis scenario on Saturday and the other navigating the same obstacle course on Sunday. The scripts, which I develop with the aid of my teaching assistants, and which my students claim I concoct while on drugs, might involve the discovery of a secret nu-clear site in Iran, Russia plotting to seize control of the Arctic, terror-ists detonating explosive devices all over the map, or a combination of the three. The pressure placed on students to make decisions not only challenges their reasoning powers but also reveals their con-ception of how the world works. Some students abandon diplomacy almost immediately and want to send in troops or start bombing, regardless of consequences. Others insist on avoiding bloodshed even when diplomatic measures are plainly doomed. For every role player who adapts quickly to a sudden twist, there are several who throw up their hands or become paralyzed. I don't judge too harshly because my scenarios tend to be outlandish from the start, but then, to enliven them further, I add the equivalent of a fire-breathing dragon at the last minute.

Imagine, for example, that you are a diplomat assigned to the UN the morning after a North Korean missile has veered off course during a test and slammed into a city in Japan, killing thousands. The tragedy appears to have been an accident, but North Korea has issued no statements and its leader, Kim Jong-un, has disappeared. What would you recommend to decision makers in your capital? And how would you respond when informed during the day that North Korean troops were massing along their country's southern border, an unidentified group had hijacked a plane traveling from East Asia to the United States, and a woman claiming to be Kim Jong-un's half-sister was plotting to oust him and seize power in Pyongyang?

Would you, in the manner of my Saturday group, seek authorization to launch military strikes against North Korea, or follow the lead of my students on Sunday and try to engineer a coup that would bring a new government to the North and end on a hopeful note? The scenarios were the same each day, but the outcomes were different because of the choices that my apprentice ministers made. The lesson was clear: leadership matters.

Role-playing gives students a chance to exhibit a range of skills, not least of which is the ability to adapt when, as my script ensures, the White House and Security Council are hit by a cyberattack that blacks out every electronic device. The cries of the suddenly deprived young are piercing, as are their shouts of joy when, an hour or so later, online access is restored. Not every student performs well, but some each year are thoroughly credible in their assumed roles. That is when I can close my eyes and feel as if I am listening to an actual squabble among the president's top advisers (albeit with fewer profanities) or a UN debate with less need for translation.

The role play is also a revealing laboratory for relations between the genders. During my first stint as a professor in the 1980s, I made a big deal out of having women take on parts that defied stereotypes—secretary of defense, for example, or a senior military officer. Over the years, the stereotypes have faded without disappearing. Young women are now more comfortable giving voice to their thoughts, while men are more apt than before to listen respectfully. Many exchanges are free-flowing. Even today, however, a woman is far likelier than a man to apologize for interrupting, worry that she is repeating arguments already made, or conclude her comments with the verbal equivalent of a question mark. The gender gap is narrowing, and I expect the trend will continue as more women are entrusted with powerful jobs in the national security arena, but it hasn't closed completely. Since I began teaching, the United States has had its first woman CIA director, its first two women national security advisors, and its first three female secretaries of state. I look forward to the day we run out of "firsts."

I HAVE HAD many discussions with my fellow elders who are dismayed by students' obsession with social media and their seeming disinterest in the study of history. I point out that every generation has had its detractors. One has only to listen to know that today's young have much that is valuable to say about intercultural relationships, economic justice, environmental ethics, and the whole notion of leadership. Many are gentle and caring and, at least in my classes, have already traveled widely. They are also extremely busy and must balance my list of recommended readings against a demanding array of outside activities, internships, and jobs. It is with genuine respect that I like to quote Robert Frost: "Now when I am old my teachers are the young."

Yet, even the most stimulating "teachers" can sometimes be irritating. For example, to gain admission to my course, students must enter and be chosen by a lottery. Why, then, do some think it's okay to skip classes? Why do a few attend session after session without opening their mouths? Why do some believe that, in grading, an A stands for "average" and for me to give them anything less is a war crime? And what was I to think of the young woman who said she thought "professor" was too formal a title and insisted on calling me "Maddy"?

My course emphasizes executive decision making, including its more humdrum and procedural aspects. I explain that when I served in the Carter White House, the president insisted that letters to Congress be drafted on paper that was a particular shade of light green. He read the drafts himself and returned them with spelling mistakes corrected, punctuation that pleased him, and often acerbic comments on the quality of grammar. When George Marshall was secretary of state, he demanded single-page memos that briefly cited the issue to be decided, presented the arguments from all sides, and included boxes he could check to indicate his wishes. Directives of this type (which stress form as well as substance) are typical of how governments operate.

That is why I ask my students to compose memos instead of lengthy papers and to adhere to a fixed format. Most comply. Some, however, rebel against any attempt on my part to dictate how they should present their ideas or how long it should take them to do it. I admire their feistiness, but not their job prospects. Due dates are also an issue. In real life, a decision memo that arrives too late is as useless as a screen window on a submarine. Knowing this, students who are tardy tend to be creative in their excuses: "My paper was stuck in my outbox for a week, and I didn't know it," claimed one. "My laptop was confiscated by the Transportation Security Administration," said another. "I was sick," complained a third. This last plea might have been accepted had not the physician's note neglected to cite any symptoms and been written on stationery with a San Francisco address and the heading "Doctors on Demand."

* * *

BEFORE SERVING IN the Clinton administration, I was a professor for eight years. After leaving office, I looked forward to returning for what I assumed would be a mere fraction of that time. Now, almost two decades later, I am afraid to take sabbaticals for fear the university's brass will decide that I have aged out. Thankfully, that hasn't happened. In 2019, I was pleased to join with John DiGioia, president of Georgetown, and Dean Joel Hellman in observing the one hundredth anniversary of the School of Foreign Service.

One advantage of my personal longevity is that the number of my former students who have become significant players in the State Department, Pentagon, foreign governments, or civil society keeps rising. Whether in Washington or traveling abroad, I bump into them all the time. In 2018, I even received a decoration, the Grand Cordon of the Order of the Rising Sun, from Japan's foreign minister and my former student, Tarō Kōno.

More than any other activity, teaching embodies my sense of who I am and what I aim to be. Here again my father's example serves as my North Star. In the words of one of his former students, "Professor Korbel was always hoping to challenge those who felt themselves infallible, and to encourage those who felt themselves inadequate." Korbel, wrote another, "was never anecdotal or trivial. His command of detail was awesome, but of greater moment was his genius for moral insight."

Beyond the family connection is my own experience. I had female professors at Wellesley who insisted that women could, and should, excel in the fields of international politics and law. In graduate school at Columbia, I was privileged to participate in a seminar taught by Zbigniew Brzezinski, a terrifyingly smart man who later, as Jimmy Carter's national security advisor, gave me my chance to work in the White House. More broadly, I have witnessed throughout my life and public career an intimate connection between human progress and the right kind of education.

As a professor, my ambition is simple: to bring to the surface the best qualities that already exist within my students. That process, repeated by instructors in classrooms everywhere many millions of times a day, is infinitely complex and never fully satisfying, but its importance cannot be overstated. British writer H. G. Wells observed a century ago that as the modern era advances, "History becomes more and more a race between education and catastrophe." That is a race we must win.

EIGHT

Bulls

"YOU CAN RENDER a valuable public service," said Senator Paul Sarbanes, a deep-voiced son of Greek immigrants who represented Maryland in the nation's capital for more than a quarter century. In the wake of scandals involving dot-com busts, accounting irregularities, revelations of insider trading, and calamitous bankruptcies, I had been invited in May 2003 to serve on the board of directors of the New York Stock Exchange (NYSE), the world's largest public platform for buying and selling stocks. I asked the senator, coauthor of the Sarbanes-Oxley financial reform legislation, if he thought I should accept the invitation. "Our system depends on trust," he told me. "Right now, we don't have it—not in banks, not in Wall Street, not in government. We need someone like you to transform the psychology."

The call that led to my two years on the NYSE board had come a few weeks earlier, when a friend asked my permission to contact the exchange's chairman and CEO, Richard Grasso, who was looking to recruit new members. Was I willing to be considered? Intrigued, I said, "Why not?" Grasso soon invited me to New York, where he told me politely that although he appreciated my interest, the Democratic seats were already filled. I thought this a curious way to talk about a nonpartisan position but thanked him anyway and prepared to forget the subject. Days later, however, an article appeared in the *Wall Street Journal* that raised questions about Grasso's compensation, hinting that his pay, which had not been publicly disclosed, might be excessive. Soon Grasso was back on the phone.

"Madeleine," he said, "I've changed my mind. If you'd like to be on the board, I can arrange it."

"Well," I replied, "I've been reading the newspapers and may have second thoughts, too. Let me think some more about it. I'll call you."

For a week, I deliberated. My staff supplied me with a short list of people, in addition to Sarbanes, whose guidance might be of value. Among them were former Office of Management and Budget director Leon Panetta, John Podesta, and a well-known New York financier, Bernie Madoff. I had time to call only the first two. I also consulted Bob Barnett, my counselor, who didn't see any upside to membership on the board and advised against. Other friends, especially the male ones, pointed out that I knew nothing about the technical aspects of running the world's number one stock exchange. My own cautious side, so often ignored, warned that I was already doing too much.

Then the dutiful part of me weighed in. Didn't I have a responsibility to help if I could? The NYSE was the embodiment of free enterprise and was—or should have been—a synonym for financial integrity even in turbulent days. Instead, homegrown critics were questioning its honesty, and al-Qaeda had chosen the World Trade Center, where many banking and investment firms were housed, as a September 11 target. As for my lack of expertise, my ego assured me that I could learn what I didn't already know. Curiosity and the desire to contribute won out. I called Grasso and said I would do it.

THE NEW YORK Stock Exchange traces its roots back more than two centuries, to the informal street trading of bonds during the American Revolutionary War. It had, over time, formalized a charter, beaten back and merged with competitors, adapted to such life-altering innovations as the telegraph and the telephone, and kept operating through harrowing investment cycles of climb, crash, and climb again. "Many a rapid fortune has been made in this street," observed Charles Dickens when, in 1842, he visited, "and many a rapid ruin." By the time of my involvement, the NYSE had developed

into an institution with several built-in tensions. Although known
to people everywhere, it resisted public scrutiny. Technically a self-
regulating organization, it was still accountable to the U.S. Securities and Exchange Commission (SEC). It claimed to have three
constituencies (brokers, companies, and investors), but only the brokers had a role in selecting leaders and approving rules. Owned by
its 1,366 seat holders, the exchange had no desire to share information about how it was run.

This reticence attracted little criticism when the economy was
humming, the case during much of the 1990s. However, the early
years of this century were not so carefree. The foundations supporting the long bull market proved rotten. In 2001, Enron collapsed
amid revelations of tax-evading shell companies and phony accounting. Next to fall was the telecommunications giant WorldCom,
which filed for bankruptcy in 2002 after it was caught cooking the
books. At about the same time, the manufacturer Tyco was brought
low by the avarice of senior managers, who looted the firm to support
their lavish lifestyles—symptoms of which surfaced in the form of a
six-thousand-dollar shower curtain and a two-million-dollar birthday party.

As investments turned to dust and once-respected companies fell
apart, the impression grew that insiders were manipulating stock
prices and siphoning off cash with no regard for the shareholding
public. Responding to the tawdriness, New York's camera-hungry
attorney general, Eliot Spitzer, won headlines by vowing to clean up
Wall Street. Meanwhile, the NYSE upgraded corporate accountability standards for the companies it listed, but neglected to apply the
same standards to itself.

This mattered because the clubby nature of the board invited sus-
picion. Some members were from sectors of the financial industry
that had enabled the bad behavior of Enron and other rogue corporations. In October 2002, Martha Stewart resigned from the panel
when under investigation for insider trading. The following spring,
Grasso tried to install the chairman of Citigroup as a "non-industry"

representative, a move akin to calling a fox a hen; adverse publicity stopped him. As the list of embarrassments grew, powerful state pension funds, other institutional investors, and federal regulators urged the exchange to take a look at its own practices.

Such a review was under way when, on June 5, 2003, I joined the board. A Special Committee on Governance, co-chaired by Panetta, had come up with a list of proposed changes that were approved at my first meeting. To prevent conflicts of interest, we decided that representatives of the financial industry should no longer be allowed to serve on the committee that recommended pay packages. To implement the new policy, we asked Carl McCall, former comptroller of New York State, to chair the panel.

From the outset, I knew that coordinating my schedule with that of the board was going to be tricky. I had to phone in to several meetings, as did others, especially those who lived outside New York. This separation made it impossible to fully capture the mood of a session. There was no body language to observe, no meaningful looks to interpret, no under-the-breath muttering to decipher. I nevertheless got a sense early on of what I would encounter.

One morning in July, as I sat with my ear to the phone in Washington, I heard someone—I still don't know who—enter the room where a hearing was about to begin and, unaware that I was listening, express his unhappiness that I had been asked to serve on the board. "The last thing we need is some former secretary of state coming in here and acting like Saint Francis of Assisi." This assertion was greeted by several seconds of silence. When it became clear that no one else would find a tongue, I exercised mine:

"Excuse me, I am Madeleine Albright and I am on the phone and can hear everything you say."

The guy didn't back off. Instead, he said, "Well, come on, Madam Secretary, you have to admit that you don't have much of a financial background."

I said, "That may be true, but I have solved a few hard problems."

We weren't done. At this point, another person, playing diplomat, interjected: "I am sure she can learn," causing the first man to grunt, "Yeah, right, and I can teach a monkey to play the piano."

Now my fuse was lit. I said, "This is the first time in my life that I have been compared in the same breath to Saint Francis of Assisi and a monkey; and if I had any doubts about whether I can contribute, you have just removed them."

As I replaced the receiver, I thought to myself, *So, this is how it's going to be*. Obviously, the NYSE was not my natural habitat. The creatures who flew highest there had built a nest for themselves that they were vigilant in protecting. I couldn't blame them; it was a comfortable nest, with a stunning view. Sadly, for them, the tree in which it nestled was on public land.

THERE HAD NEVER been a better leader of the exchange than Dick Grasso. Everyone said so. Wall Street is where his career began and where he worked for thirty-five years. Of Italian immigrant stock, Grasso grew up in Queens, the child of a father who deserted his family when the boy was a toddler and of a mother who hoped her son would join the police. Instead, after a two-year stint in the army, Grasso secured an entry-level position as a clerk at the NYSE, where he commenced to study, schmooze, and plot his way upward. Catering to the powerful, he attracted attention simply by knowing who everyone was, understanding the hurdles they faced, and mastering the rules of the game. Some found him immature and volatile, but all were impressed by his drive. In the early 1980s he was made the exchange's executive vice president; in 1988, its president; and seven years later, chairman and CEO.

Seizing the helm with intensity and flair, the short, balding man transformed the staid financial headquarters into one of the most compelling shows on earth. He brought live television coverage to the exchange floor at a moment when stock prices were jumping and cable news shows were garnering a huge audience. He made a spectacle out of the bell-ringing at each session's open and close, featuring in separate instances Muhammad Ali, Nelson Mandela, Snoop

Dogg, Liza Minnelli, Venezuelan President Hugo Chávez, Darth Vader, Mr. Potato Head, a lion, a cow, and me. Grasso hustled to outmaneuver the upstart NASDAQ, gain the allegiance of Silicon Valley CEOs, and attract new listings from corporate honchos across the globe. Then, just six days after 9/11 blew a hole in the heart of Lower Manhattan, he was somehow able to reopen the exchange. The first responders who were honored that morning cheered; so did much of the world.

As I learned when working alongside them, Grasso and those who seemed most closely aligned with him didn't fit the stereotype of a Wall Street controlled by families possessing inherited wealth. Many were people of modest backgrounds who had climbed to the top rungs of the economic ladder because they had made the best of every opportunity. They could be single minded in pursuing financial gain and determined not to let anyone get the better of them. They thought it only natural to trade favors in return for leverage and assumed that should they fail to grab an advantage, rivals would. They were, in important ways, honorable men—supremely capable, direct, loyal to their code, and generous in helping worthy causes. Were they humble? No. They were, in their own minds, human sky-scrapers, fragrant with testosterone; backslapping, hand-crunching, sports-talking deal makers who spoke a language alien to me and, while swearing imaginatively at one another, often giggled like kids. Observing them in action, I admired their intelligence and coveted their bonhomie, but felt less at home than when, as secretary of state, I had visited a Mongolian yurt.

SOMETIME IN JULY 2003, Carl McCall informed me by phone that his committee had approved an extension of the chairman and CEO's contract through the middle of 2007 and that, as part of the deal, Grasso would immediately receive the deferred compensation he had earned over the previous eight years.

"How much?" I asked.

"One hundred thirty-nine million point five," came the reply.

"*How* much?" I repeated.

Same answer.

I gulped. This was even more than the numbers that had been floating around in the media and far more than seemed reasonable or even possible. Grasso's salary, I discovered, was $1.4 million and had remained flat; his annual benefits package, however, traced an upward arc, ballooning from about $4 million in 1996 to more than $25 million in 2001. Funds not paid to him right away accumulated interest at a generous rate.

There was nothing illegal about this. According to contracts negotiated in 1995 and 1999, the money would belong to Grasso sooner or later. It didn't take a genius, however, to anticipate the uproar. The huge payday would look like yet another example of Wall Street greed.

I told McCall that I thought it would be a mistake for Grasso to take his money now. The funds were intended for retirement, so why rush? Carl said I should share my concerns with the chairman directly, and I did. Some other directors took the same step. On August 6, I was informed that Grasso had gotten the message. The question of extending his contract would be put off for another day, I was relieved.

The following morning, the board convened; I joined by phone, not expecting any controversy. Then McCall put Grasso's full compensation package on the table and asked that it be approved. I was stunned—and suspicious. Had I been lied to? Carl explained that his committee had decided, just an hour earlier, to reverse course and go ahead with the extension. Was Grasso behind the switch? Evidently so. After talking to other members, he had concluded that either the furor over his pay would be short-lived, in which case he might as well get paid at once, or the opposition would build, tempting a future board to prevent him from getting his money at all. Either way, he felt it best to force the issue.

Our discussion that morning was animated, confusing, painful, and long. McCall was unclear both about the terms of the contract and the procedures that had left us with no good options. Grasso's fan club insisted that he deserved every penny. I said again that I had nothing against Dick but thought it crazy, given all the negative press, for him not to wait. The debate grew so contentious that one board member, Jürgen Schrempp of Daimler-Benz, started speaking in German.

When McCall asked for a vote, I suggested that we decide on the contract extension and benefits package separately, voting first on one and then the other. Carl said we had to consider the two together. I abstained, then asked for a straw poll on whether to postpone paying in full. The result was close, but the majority aligned with Grasso.

The exchange waited three weeks (until August 27) to announce the new contract, hoping that press coverage would be minimal in the run-up to Labor Day. The ploy didn't work. The *New York Post* headlined its story "Grasso's Jackpot." Rank-and-file members of the exchange, until then kept in the dark about the issue, were outraged. The chairman of the SEC, whose annual salary was equal to about one-thousandth of the amount Grasso would receive, sent a letter to McCall demanding an explanation and stating, "In my view, the approval of Mr. Grasso's pay package raises serious questions regarding the effectiveness of the NYSE's current governance structure." That was only the beginning.

On September 2, Grasso received checks totaling $139.5 million. Later in the week, we learned that his contract extension included an additional $48 million in deferred compensation and benefits, bringing the total to nearly $190 million. Complicating the matter further, the press release announcing the deal had made no mention of the $48 million. When the media nevertheless found out, they demanded to know what had happened to the promised transparency. There was no good answer.

On September 9, the board met again via phone. We had to come up with a response to the SEC letter and somehow stop the public bleeding. For many, the focus was on the additional $48 million. What if Dick kept what he already had but rejected the extra money?

Right on cue, Grasso came on the line and said he was willing to do exactly that. To the board, otherwise sharply divided, this seemed a way out.

But it was too late. The unsparing judgment of public opinion had turned against the chairman and could not be reversed. The leaders of the three largest state pension funds called for his resignation. Hank Paulson, a board member who had different priorities from Grasso, began rounding up votes. I joined the anti-Grasso ranks alongside McCall and several of the chairman's former allies. For years, Grasso's daring eccentricity and brash salesmanship had made him the face of the exchange. Now his failure to comprehend quickly enough how others viewed him endangered the institution he had labored so hard to build.

For more than a week Grasso thrashed about, consulting widely, still hoping to save his job. If he was upset with me, the feeling was mutual. He had wanted me on the board to improve its image but made that impossible through his own demands. He hoped that I would be a box turtle, not a snapping one. But the problems he faced were of his own making. Finally, on September 17, he told us he would resign if asked. He dropped off the line, and we voted 13 to 7 to issue that request.

TO SALVAGE THE situation, we brought in another Wall Street veteran, John Reed, to replace Grasso on an interim basis. Working for a salary of one dollar, Reed moved quickly to overhaul the board and order an independent review of the Grasso compensation imbroglio, which found the chairman's pay to have been "grossly excessive." Years of litigation ensued, to no good purpose. Grasso was never found guilty of breaking any laws and the civil case against him was dismissed. He kept his money. Life went on.

Although I served on the NYSE board until resigning in 2005, I felt in hindsight that my decision to join had been a mistake. I hardly expected in the beginning that so much valuable time would be consumed trying to deodorize the head man's pay package. That was a disservice to the many stalwart professionals who work at the exchange and a distraction from other issues that warranted our attention. This was a period of technological transition, as the NYSE sought to keep pace with competitors and move away from its traditional modes of doing business in favor of electronic trading. The good news is that the reforms put in place in the aftermath of the ordeal have increased transparency, reduced obvious conflicts of interest, and made the institution more broadly representative and accountable. In 2006, the exchange became a publicly traded company, and in 2018, Stacey Cunningham was named its second woman president.

I emerged from this experience with enhanced respect for my long-suffering cautious side. Although I left the arena with a few new friends—future Secretary of the Treasury Hank Paulson among them—I could not claim to have become an expert on the ins and outs of Wall Street. Cast in a new role on an unfamiliar stage, I had less impact than I had hoped. What I did take with me was a reminder of how tone deaf even smart people can be, and how vital it is that checks on authority be built into every democratic institution. There is much to be admired in the personality and accomplishments of a figure such as Richard Grasso. But as a good Roman Catholic, even he might acknowledge that a little tip from the prophet Micah ("walk humbly") speaks to us all.

NINE

Democrats with a Small d

WHEN LEAVING OFFICE in 2001, I was offered the chair of the National Democratic Institute (NDI). A second later, I accepted. Of the hats I wear, this is the one that fits most comfortably. Nothing lifts my spirits more than the long voting queues and raucous shouts of "I disagree" that tell the tale of a healthy democracy. Nothing disturbs me more than the overflowing jails and cowed acquiescence of a society ruled by fear.

NDI is one of four organizations operating under the umbrella of the National Endowment for Democracy, which was created in the early 1980s. The thinking at the time was that while totalitarian governments crushed opponents before they could become a threat, democratic regimes were inherently fragile because they gave protest movements the freedom to organize. In a June 1982 address to the British Parliament, President Reagan sought to compensate for this vulnerability by announcing an initiative involving business, labor, and the two major American political parties, and that was aimed at assisting democratic development worldwide. Having just written a study on Poland's Solidarity movement, the struggle for liberty was much on my mind. When asked to become vice chair of the original NDI board, I leapt at the chance.

Setting out in its first full year, 1984, NDI had a mission but no road map. We weren't entering a field; we were inventing one. For inspiration, we headed to the Democratic National Convention in San Francisco, where we took note of the many foreign observers on hand. This gave us the idea to host a program every four years for visitors from overseas. So it came to be. At each convention, we reserve hotel space, sponsor seminars, bring in speakers, and give our guests a close-up view of American democracy in action. What they see is a frothy blend of educators, steelworkers, farmers, shopkeepers, retirees, and activists who have assembled from across the country to consider how the nation's many problems can be fixed. The spectacle of powerful politicians competing for the approval of such a disparate collection of delegates is heartening. Instructive, too, is the glimpse of a party—such as the Democrats in 1984—optimistically trying again after having been clobbered in the previous election. In many countries, a party that misses the goal with its first kick doesn't get another chance. Because their vantage point differs, foreigners may appreciate even more than Americans a process that, for all its faults, has legitimized the peaceful transfer of power since 1797, when our second president, John Adams, took the reins from George Washington.

Conventions, however, are unpredictable gatherings. One evening in 1948, the chairman was about to introduce the Democratic nominee and incumbent president, Harry Truman, when he was interrupted by a delegate from the host city of Philadelphia. Mrs. Emma Guffey Miller ascended to the dais carrying a towering bouquet of carnations that she intended to give to the candidate. Beneath the flowers was a container holding forty-eight "doves of peace," one for each state. When Mrs. Miller opened the cage, the birds, who had been confined for hours, swooped wildly about the hall. Sam Rayburn, minority leader of the U.S. House of Representatives, plucked a feathered friend from atop his bald head and flung it back into the crowd. The president's speechwriter's wife, startled to discover a bird, equally distressed, on her lap, quickly improvised a dove diaper out of a copy of the nominee's remarks. Due to all the flapping and dodging, Truman wasn't able to begin his acceptance speech until the witching hour had come and gone.

In Charlotte, at the Democratic convention of 2012, I had my own challenge to surmount. The doings were so jam-packed that NDI had not been able to obtain credentials for the foreign visitors we had invited. Without access to the convention floor, our guests would be left with little to occupy their time. I explored all the regular channels, to no avail. Finally, on the eve of the climactic day, I tracked down a senior party official who I thought could pull some strings. It was almost midnight, however, and he was standing, beverage in hand, amid a boisterous party.

Marching up, I yelled above the din, "I have to get my hands on two hundred sets of credentials for tomorrow—can you help?"

"Sure," he yelled back, "on one condition."

The next morning, NDI got its passes—and the following spring, I delivered the commencement address at the high school graduation of the man's son.

AN EARLY MILESTONE in the NDI story came in January 1990, when I led a multinational group of election advisers to Prague. Two months earlier, the Velvet Revolution had brought down Czechoslovakia's pro-Soviet dictatorship. The democrats who rose to power in its stead were a brave and talented bunch but ill-prepared to govern. In the lead was a dissident playwright, now the new president, Václav Havel. To my delight, he chose as his foreign minister Jiří Dienstbier, an ex-journalist whom I had met in the United States and who had provided valuable grist for my dissertation on the Czechoslovak press during the Prague Spring.

Jiří had been an outspoken radio commentator when, in 1968, Soviet tanks quashed the democratic revival in his country. His insistence on broadcasting the truth about the communist regime made him vulnerable to arrest, but sympathetic colleagues arranged for him to fly to America on assignment. They, and I, were stunned when he later decided to go back so that he might bear witness from within. He was jailed for a time, then barred from journalism and forced to find work as a furnace stoker. In that first January after the revolution, I rushed to embrace my friend in his office in the foreign ministry. My pleasure was doubled by the fact that I had been in that office before, decades earlier, when my father had served as the ministry's chief of staff in the months following World War II.

Jiří arranged for our delegation to meet Havel in Prague Castle, the Czechoslovak equivalent of the White House. I had looked forward to meeting the new leader, known for his provocative plays, humane rhetoric, and the deft touch he had displayed when persuading the communist government to relinquish power. Havel's central role in that pivotal postwar moment had made him almost overnight one of the world's most famous figures, yet our delegation was greeted by a man who appeared entirely without pretentions. Almost exactly my age (then fifty-two), he was wearing black jeans, a matching dark turtleneck, and a warm but shy smile. I had brought with me a copy of my father's last book, *Twentieth-Century Czechoslovakia*. Expecting a batch of international visitors, Havel hadn't focused on any local connections, so he seemed nonplussed by my gift.

"Oh, yes," he said. "Mrs. Fulbright."

"No, I am Mrs. Albright. Josef Korbel was my father."

Recognition dawned, and so began a friendship that would last for more than two decades.

Anxious to be of worth, our group offered to arrange for outside experts to help in drafting a revamped electoral law, a suggestion that Havel quickly endorsed and that we soon implemented. When I told the president's advisers that I had worked in the White House, they asked if I could recommend a staffing structure for his office. To that end, I sat for hours with my new Czech and Slovak pals in a restaurant near the castle, eating delicious bowls of greasy cabbage and drawing up bureaucratic flowcharts.

Five months later, in early June (this was still 1990), I returned to Prague with delegates from NDI and our sister organization, the International Republican Institute (IRI), whose most prominent representative was John McCain. This collaboration—between the Arizona senator and me—was to blossom into another long-term friendship. We were in Czechoslovakia to witness the fruits of the electoral law that NDI had helped to facilitate and to observe the country's first free parliamentary elections since 1946. I relished the chance to show my native city to McCain. He, like Havel, was a former prisoner but one who had been held under even harsher conditions, in his case by the North Vietnamese. Striding alongside him through Prague's winding streets, I could not imagine what it must have been like to be held captive and tortured for five and a half years in a Hanoi jail. Whenever he and I were in the same room, I stood a little straighter.

Between 2001 and McCain's final illness in 2018, we collaborated often as the chairs, respectively, of NDI and IRI. Although he is remembered now as the embodiment of political grace and civility, the senator shared his opinions with as much verbal hot sauce as anyone I have met in public life. He was a patriot to his core and, though hard to pin down ideologically (hence also a "maverick"), he had clear conceptions of right and wrong. His temper could melt diamonds, but when his mood was light, so could his laugh. I remember especially the night our organizations honored a courageous group of pro-democracy nuns from Ukraine. McCain began his remarks routinely enough, but then veered into a diatribe about the follies of domestic politics. He concluded with one of his pet jokes about the difference between a "caucus" and a "cactus." (With the cactus, the pricks are on the outside.) How the interpreter translated this, and what the Ukrainian sisters thought, I haven't a clue.

During those long-ago summer days in Prague, we immersed ourselves in the emotions of the moment. To celebrate democracy's resurrection, Havel arranged for Paul Simon to perform in Old Town Square, while McCain and I joined a more modest revel, singing "We Shall Overcome" with former dissidents at their headquarters across town. Through two days of voting that weekend, the turnout was 97 percent, and the parties associated with Havel earned a thumping victory. I thought to myself, *It doesn't get any better than this.* I was right. It doesn't—and it hasn't.

* * *

IN THE 1980S, when NDI started out, the Cold War had yet to thaw and its sudden end was unforeseen. The ideological competition between East and West still raged. NDI's commitment was to back democratic values in countries regardless of which camp they were in. One of its initial forays, in the Philippines in 1986, was to observe a snap election called by the nation's strongman, Ferdinand Marcos, a longtime ally of the United States. When the government tried to rig the vote, a fact confirmed by NDI, street protests forced Marcos to leave office. Two years later, the institute helped to secure an accurate ballot count in a plebiscite in Chile, thus prompting a second dictator, Augusto Pinochet, to depart the presidency at the end of his term. As the decade progressed, anticommunist despots came under severe strain, but so did communist regimes. It turned out that they weren't invulnerable to public pressure after all. In 1989, the Berlin Wall was torn down and by the end of 1991, the Soviet Union had broken up.

Thus began democracy's golden moment. In South Africa, apartheid ended, and the African National Congress (led by Nelson Mandela) assumed power. From Indonesia to Argentina, dozens of authoritarian leaders were voted out, shamed into retirement, or otherwise compelled to look for new employment. Nearly everywhere, the language of freedom was being spoken or learned. With head-swiveling speed, requests for assistance poured in. Hundreds of millions of people were exclaiming, "Hurrah, we have democracy! Now what do we do?" NDI, a magnet for this type of inquiry, answered the call.

In our offices at the time, there was no step-by-step manual for building a perfect democracy or even a reliably good one. That is still being written. Over the years, however, NDI and its sister organizations in the United States and abroad have developed and tested ideas about everything from forging an effective parliament to conducting a credible election observer mission. In keeping with our nonpartisan approach, we never favor one political party over another. Our programs are open to people from across the ideological spectrum, and we emphasize the importance of including women, minorities, and youth in all phases of public life. We stress that a free government requires more than a single election or protest, and that the creation of a democratic culture is as essential as the building of institutions. Our approach throughout has been to help where we can, then get out of the way. The prize we offer is not a clone of American democracy or dependence on the help we offer, but instead the capacity for self-definition and reliance; that is why most of those who work for us overseas are hired locally.

We also highlight the worth of international networks by encouraging democrats in one region to share what they have learned with counterparts from another—Latin Americans, for example, sitting down with Central Europeans; or South Africans talking about the complexities of post-conflict healing with the Catholics and Protestants of Northern Ireland.

By the early 1990s, we felt as if we were riding the crest of a grand movement. Training sessions drew overflow crowds. Even governments that were uncomfortable with us were afraid to say so for fear of being thought undemocratic. Instead, they tried when they could to make our vocabulary work for them. When one North African regime bragged about how free its elections were, NDI evaluated the claim. We found that voters were being given a choice of ballots color-coded according to party, then instructed to place the one they had chosen into a see-through plastic envelope that was dropped into a box in front of government officials. "Behold," said a spokesman, "our process is completely transparent." Years would pass before real democracy came to that country (Tunisia), and then only because the public had become fed up.

IN 2001, WHEN I returned to NDI after my time in government, much of the post–Cold War euphoria had dissipated. Democracies, instead of being compared to totalitarian states, were judged on whether they were meeting the expectations of their citizens—a much higher standard. Many cleared the bar, but others were falling short because of corruption, crime, a failure to meet economic benchmarks, and officials who viewed the responsibilities of democratic leadership in the same spirit with which Augustine originally embraced a vow of chastity: "Lord, make me pure, but not yet." Then came 9/11. Washington and much of the world shifted its attention to the fight against terrorism. Guaranteeing security became the paramount issue. American troops were deployed to Afghanistan and Iraq. Surveys showed broad support in some Muslim lands for Osama bin Laden. What did these developments portend for the future of popular government? The forty-third president thought he had the answer.

On January 20, 2005, George W. Bush kicked off his second White House term by declaring that "the policy of the United States [is] to seek and support the growth of democratic movements and institutions in every nation and culture, with the ultimate goal of ending tyranny." He continued: "America, in this young century, proclaims liberty throughout the world and to all the inhabitants thereof."

The president's rhetoric was infused with scriptural echoes and high moral purpose. Peggy Noonan, who had written for Bush's father, saw in the speech a case of "mission inebriation." The sentiments were noble, but what basis did they have in reality? Bush felt sure, for example, that his pledge of liberty would be welcomed by hard-pressed populations in the Middle East even though he had no viable way to deliver on the promise. There are Arabs, however, for whom freedom is related less to democratic voting procedures than to personal and national identity. With the memory of colonial rule still strong, they equate independence with emancipation from the West, not with allowing heavily armed foreign soldiers to pound on their doors and patrol their streets. So, when the president boasted about democratizing the Middle East while simultaneously occupying Iraq, some in the region interpreted his words as a threat.

As chair of NDI, I highlighted at every opportunity the merits of open political systems but also my view that democracy cannot be promoted effectively by military means. Democracy, by definition, is a choice that nations must be allowed to make for themselves. The principle is basic and yet it was being blurred by the administration's actions. With turmoil in Iraq dominating the news, I found it hard to tout democratic ideals without sounding—at least to many foreign ears—like Bush. Indeed, I had to spend an increasing amount of time defending NDI from baseless allegations: No, we were not engaged in a Judeo-Christian crusade against Islam; No, we were not conspiring to bring down any governments; No, we were not trying to help the United States seize the Middle East's black gold; and No, we were not invented by the CIA. The situation was frustrating because I wanted to spread the word about what NDI *was*; instead I had to prove continually what we were *not*.

One day early in 2006, I was invited to the White House along with other former secretaries of state and defense. The president welcomed us to the Roosevelt Room, a windowless space across a corridor from the Oval Office, then urged us to endorse his policy— which he equated with support for democracy. To set the stage, he asked the U.S. military commanders in Iraq to brief us, via video, on the most recent developments. I was alarmed to see that our technology was unimproved from my day: the audio went in and out, and the picture was not exactly high-definition. The glitches didn't stop the generals from painting a rosy-hued picture. We were told that the morale of our troops was excellent, Iraqis were grateful to us, and the momentum of events was on our side. When the commanders were done, the president thanked them, then went around the table soliciting our thoughts.

My colleagues asked good questions but seemed reluctant to criticize. I didn't see any alternative. I intended to tell Bush directly that his policy was dampening enthusiasm for democracy in many parts of the globe, strengthening the regional power of Iran, and complicating the fight against terrorism. When my turn came, I plunged in, but was just getting warmed up when the press was allowed to enter and take pictures. The meeting was over.

We old-timers exchanged glances, then rose to our feet. The president led us into the Oval Office to see how Laura had redecorated the furnishings. We thanked them both. In despair at an opportunity lost, I left.

COMPLICATIONS IN IRAQ were not the only hurdles to NDI's work or to democratic progress more generally. The post-9/11 focus on combating terrorism caused some to see a zero-sum choice between allowing people to exercise their rights and providing security. The rise of social media created demands for more responsive governments that even the best-intentioned leaders could not always fulfill. Long-standing internal divisions based on ethnicity, religion, or race plagued many countries. Numerous governments had trouble collecting the taxes needed to operate—and a few important states faced all these problems.

Nigeria is Africa's most populous country. It can boast of the world's tenth- or eleventh-largest reserves of petroleum, and its universities are among the finest in the region. Its sons and daughters include acclaimed writers, artists, entertainers, and filmmakers. Yet surveys showed that in the opening years of the twenty-first century, Nigerians' satisfaction with democracy sank from 84 to 25 percent.

As secretary of state in 1999, I had welcomed the inauguration of President Olusegun Obasanjo, a career military man and self-styled reformer who pledged to end corruption (as new leaders often do) and to bring his country's diverse population together. Helped by rising oil prices, he cut Nigeria's debt and took modest steps to improve services and invest in infrastructure. His standing sagged in 2006, when he was accused of trying (in vain) to strong-arm parliament into changing the constitution so that he might seek a third term. I wanted to think well of Obasanjo but couldn't help feeling, when I visited him in the lavish presidential villa in Abuja, with its gargantuan rooms and a menagerie of wild beasts patrolling the backyard, that he had more of a "Midas touch" than a common one.

In April 2007, I went with a sixty-member NDI observer team to witness the choice of Obasanjo's successor. We deployed to every part of the country. On the bright side, it was the first transition in Nigerian history from one elected president to another. Less positively, the voting was disorderly and unfair. Because ballots were slow to arrive, polling stations in many areas opened late, closed early, or never got started. Turnout was low due to threats of violence. Among the abuses our group noted were ballot stuffing, bribery, lack of secrecy, and underage voting. There were also technical difficulties. The village where I was observing had no electricity, so that when darkness came, officials had to halt proceedings and ask if anyone had a generator. Someone did. We all watched as he strung up a single bulb, casting just enough light for the clerks to resume tallying.

The scarcity of electric power was emblematic of Nigeria's divisions. The country was oil-rich, but the people energy-poor. In my hotel, I had to wear a jacket because the air-conditioning was set too high, yet the average Nigerian had to get by with batteries and matches. The initials for the state Power Holding Company were said by many citizens to stand for "Please Hold Candle." Adding to the unhappiness, the government commission that supervised the balloting was widely seen as a shill for Obasanjo's chosen successor, who duly won the election.

When asked by reporters how I rated the vote, I replied, "As many of you know, I am a professor. If the process I have just witnessed were the work of one of my students, I would give it a failing grade."

THE LANDLOCKED BALKANS region of Kosovo is near to my heart because of my role, when secretary of state, in trying to safeguard its ethnic Albanian population from violent repression by the government of Serbia. In 1999, after leaders in Belgrade rejected efforts to resolve tensions peacefully, NATO intervened, thus enabling Kosovars to govern themselves.

In many respects, their progress since has been remarkable. The Republic of Kosovo has a competitive multiparty system and a constitution that guarantees the freedoms of religion, speech, organization, and assembly. The country holds regular elections, provides for the representation of women and minorities in parliament, and boasts a flourishing civil society and a growing economy. NDI has worked closely with Kosovars every step of the way, most recently to encourage parliamentarians to hold town hall meetings with constituents and to promote public discussion of such chronic social problems as gender discrimination and domestic abuse. Kosovo is a place where people generally feel free to speak their minds, which is quite an accomplishment for a land that had never before known freedom, having been ruled successively by the Romans, Byzantines, Bulgarians, Serbs, Ottomans, and Yugoslavs.

There remains, however, much room for improvement. In the past two decades, I have visited Kosovo often. Each time, I stress the importance of reconciliation between the ethnic Albanian population and the Serb minority. Progress has been slow due to the persistence of bitter feelings on both sides. I have also emphasized the need to curb the corruption that has undermined public faith in government, infected the judiciary, and led to attacks on the investigative press. That problem, too, has lingered despite several high-profile initiatives to combat it.

In June 2019, I went to Kosovo to help mark the twentieth anniversary of the success of NATO's intervention. President Clinton was there also, the reception was wild, and the affection for America both palpable and refreshing. During a short parade, we marched past a statue of Clinton, a memorial to international peacekeepers, and a newly dedicated bust of me. We met with former refugees who are now lawyers, businesspeople, and civil society leaders. Thousands of people lined the streets or waved from balconies. The flags of the United States and Kosovo were everywhere. It was also hotter than Hell.

Developed under the guidance of its longtime president, Ken Wollack, and burnished by his successor, Derek Mitchell (former ambassador from the United States to Burma), NDI maintains a list of what it calls "lessons learned." These are on vivid display in the lives of many countries, Kosovo included. Among those lessons is the understanding that democracy everywhere is not an accomplishment but a pursuit—an unending effort to make governments more responsive, effective, and fair. In this quest, the development of a democratic culture is essential. But what is a democratic culture? It's a society where people honor each other's dignity and rights not only because they will get in trouble with the law if they don't, but because it feels natural and appropriate to do so. Kosovars continue to struggle with this, due especially to the different views of the past held by ethnic Albanians and ethnic Serbs. When I urge each side to treat the other as they would wish to be treated themselves, no one disagrees; they just nod their heads and wait for the other group to go first.

One of democracy's more delicate tasks is to prevent historic grievances from deterring people from joining in present-day projects. While a dictator can simply impose his will, a democracy must go through a process, often intensely emotional, of mutual education and debate. If the effort bears fruit, such a trial can provide an inspiring model for other countries. That's why democracies must help one another. In our era, little remains hidden. Men and women everywhere know when a system is delivering the right results and when it is falling short. NDI wants people in all regions to see democracy work. That's our mission, and we are as determined today to fulfill it as when the organization was founded.

TEN

A Foothold

AT THE END of each year, I evaluate how I spent the previous twelve months. As a visual aid, my staff draws up a paper showing a little bucket for each activity, consults the calendar, then does the math. In 2005, I delivered more than fifty speeches, devoted hundreds of hours to clients of the Albright Group, and allocated substantial swaths of time to NDI and to my spring and fall courses at Georgetown. I was busy as well with writing projects, and had it been an even-numbered year, would have flown from city to city trying to rustle up votes for favored candidates. The mix of what I did and where and with whom I kept company gave each day a design all its own, but the larger pattern was set. I was forever saying to aides, "Okay, that's done, what's next?"

Just one thought nagged at me: *Was I doing enough?*

The world, then as now, seemed to be spinning in the wrong direction. Before audiences, I lamented the latest grim news from central Asia and the Middle East, decried the ongoing violence against civilians in the Darfur region of Sudan, warned of the growing global divide between haves and have-nots, and voiced alarm about threats to democracy. When I paused, the question asked most often, especially by younger listeners, was "What can I do?" My usual response was something along the lines of "Uh . . . let me see. Volunteer? Vote? Study harder? Write a check?" I had trouble developing a satisfactory reply because I was putting the same question to myself. For all my many activities, I was without access to the levers of power. How and where could I have a more tangible impact?

* * *

THERE ARE POLITICIANS I know, including some I like, who will not use the word *poverty* in speeches because they think voters find the word depressing. Pollsters agree. Americans are uncomfortable with the term and even more so with the reality.

In wealthier societies, one can live day to day with mere glimpses of the poor. Our cities and towns are divided into upscale neighborhoods and those "on the wrong side of the tracks." Our transportation patterns sustain the separation, as do the schools our children go to, the supermarkets we patronize, the religious services we attend, and the entertainment options we select. Viewers who subscribe to HBO or who stream Netflix rarely make hits of shows that dwell on the lives of the chronically desperate. But travel widely enough and one cannot evade poverty and at least some sense of its harshness. Visit a crowded land such as Egypt or India, where tormented eyes and outstretched hands are seemingly everywhere; or the Central African Republic, where most people survive (barely) on a single meal a day; or Haiti, where tens of thousands of children are in orphanages not because they are without parents but because their families believe they will be safer and have more to eat in an institution than in a dilapidated village or slum.

As secretary of state, I was given malnourished children to hold while photographers did their jobs, and I whispered hopefully, "Everything will be all right" to a boy or girl in my arms. Then I handed the child back, headed home to the United States, and felt terrible. In Ethiopia, at an event to commemorate International HIV/AIDS Day, I sat next to a little boy who had been orphaned by the disease. I had a ballpoint pen in my pocket that I pulled out and handed to him; he returned it, saying in English, "No. Food, shoes." He was the same age as one of my grandsons but lived in a world of unsatisfied appetites and endless want. Poverty is an age-old problem; I knew that. I admired the work that our development professionals were doing to alleviate hardship, but I could not shake the feeling that our efforts were falling well short. Like hamsters on a treadmill, we were expending plenty of energy—but did we have a plan that would actually move us forward?

IN 2005, I met Dr. Hernando de Soto Polar. A businessman turned economist, de Soto has soft brown eyes, a near-perpetual stubble, and a frame that from head to heel is not much longer than mine. I first encountered him at an economic conference in Washington, where he talked about fighting poverty from an angle that few others were emphasizing, and none with his command of facts.

Twenty years earlier, de Soto had devised a plan in his native Peru to grant legal documents to three disenfranchised groups: farmers who had no deeds to the land they cultivated, businesspeople who lacked certificates of incorporation to the enterprises they had started, and families who had no title to the houses or apartments in which they lived. Backed by his government, de Soto's program gave legal standing to the poor even in sections of his country where they were being victimized by a brutal guerrilla group, the Shining Path. His strategy, dubbed "the Other Path," was so effective at undermining the guerrillas' call for revolution that they tried to kill him.

De Soto's core insight was that people who live outside the legal framework of a society cannot benefit from its protections, or, in his words, "monetize their assets." They are left without the rights that every citizen should have, vulnerable to exploitation by the more powerful, and unable to accumulate the savings required to escape poverty. He asked me to picture what my life would be like without credit, insurance, a medical plan, the deed to my house, or access to a bank. I said I'd probably be baking pies, if I could find an oven, and selling them on the street. "Well, that," he explained, "is how four billion of the globe's six billion people live."

De Soto's manner is that of an adventurous uncle who seems to have been everywhere and has stories to tell about each port of call. "In many countries," he declares, "more than eighty percent of all homes and businesses are unregistered; ancient Rome was more advanced!" Even in the United States, he goes on, huge amounts of money are channeled through the informal economy, allowing people to evade taxes but also making them easy targets for thieves, con artists, and loan sharks.

When he speaks, de Soto's hands move constantly, palms opening and closing, fingers pointing alternately at himself, his listeners, and the ceiling. Walk down a street in almost any city in the more depressed regions of the globe, he tells me, and the chances are good that the next person you see, whether it is a food vendor, rickshaw driver, maid, laundress, delivery man, or day laborer, will be anonymous to the government. Many proceed from their first breath to their last with no birth certificate or other proof of identity. Some can claim ownership to one thing only: a burial plot. How will they ever escape poverty? Without legal credentials, he concludes, these people are going to remain stuck in the same precarious conditions their grandparents endured. What is worse, their grandchildren will, too.

That winter of 2005, de Soto came to me with a proposition. He asked if I would join him as co-chair of the about-to-be-created international Commission on Legal Empowerment of the Poor (CLEP). This was the Peruvian's chance to display his ideas on a bigger stage. The United Nations and eleven countries, including Norway and the United States, had promised financial support. Would I sign on? Well, what could I say? Here was a multinational project that aimed to draw on the expertise of both the public and private sectors. It would attack from a fresh standpoint a failure that was holding democracies back, and it offered me a valuable chance to learn. If all went well, we could do some lasting good. He had me at "I need your help."

HISTORY AND POVERTY entered the world together and were followed, shortly thereafter, by promises of social justice. The lawgivers of ancient Babylonia pledged on their honor to protect the weak. The Hebrew Bible admonished citizens to refrain from exploiting the poor and to treat widows, orphans, and strangers with kindness. The ancient Greeks, under Solon, pioneered the idea of debt relief, and the Romans appeased the less fortunate with free rations of corn (bread) and civic entertainment (circuses).

More recent times have brought forth a wagonload of theories about how best to curb poverty, some focusing on individual improvement through universal education or, much less generously, workhouses and debtors' prisons. Others have called for the restructuring of society by means of class warfare, enhanced worker rights, welfare programs of different shapes and sizes, higher or lower taxes, and markets that are either tightly regulated or fully free. The topic remains a source of debate in virtually every country.

Mindful of such controversies, the commission attempted to avoid becoming entangled by them. We wanted our concept to be viewed as a useful addition to, not a replacement for, more conventional ideas. It was a nice try. Despite what we had hoped, our approach was greeted by many with skepticism, even anger. To the complacent, de Soto's desire to empower the poor was socially and politically threatening. To those wary of authority, his emphasis on legal record-keeping was viewed as a way to control, not help, the destitute. To radicals, his ideas were a distraction from what they saw as the real causes of poverty: the arrogance of the wealthy and corporate greed. Why, they asked, was de Soto trying to reform capitalism when he should have been striving to destroy it?

Having critics on all sides, however, didn't discourage me. I liked the fact that legal empowerment was politically ambidextrous, drawing from the left a desire for social justice and from the right an emphasis on personal initiative and responsibility. If de Soto had his way, I could see benefits flowing both to individuals who would be part of a legal economy for the first time and to governments that would gain by having more contributors to their tax base.

THE COMMISSION STARTED work in the fall of 2005 and met at regular intervals over the next three years. Our panel of some two dozen members featured Anthony Kennedy, a justice of the U.S. Supreme Court; Shirin Ebadi, a Nobel laureate from Iran; half a dozen former heads of government; and one future one (Ashraf Ghani of Afghanistan). To manage the workload, we split into five groups; and to ensure that we heard from as many people as possible, we tapped the brains of experts and made field trips. In November 2006, Hernando and I led a delegation to Nairobi's Toi Market, on the outskirts of Kibera, Africa's largest slum.

Imagine a vast square filled with five thousand tiny shops, each consisting of a stall, a table, or a blanket spread on the ground. Pyramids of onions, bananas, and mangos compete for space with stacks of sandals, and racks of T-shirts, bicycle parts, sunglasses, toys, and tea. Six days a week, chatter and fruity smells fill the air, while makeshift tents provide a partial barrier to the sun. The heat is stifling, but no one pays the thermometer any attention, for business is being transacted. Ten years previously, the shopkeepers had agreed to pay fifteen cents a day into a communal pool that makes small loans to finance civic improvements such as a public bath. Spending decisions are made democratically, with consent indicated at meetings by the wagging of fingers and the clapping of hands. To the minds of many, a slum is associated with idleness; in the Toi Market, people are as entrepreneurial as anyone from Silicon Valley or Mumbai. If Kenyans want to gain a foothold on the economic ladder, they have to hustle. Everywhere we looked, men, women, and children were doing just that.

Among the local leaders was Joseph Muturi, thirty-three, a trader in secondhand clothes. He was proud of the market and pleased with his own situation, but he was also aware that men with bulldozers could come at any time and flatten his stalls. "I know that in a matter of hours," he told us, "all this can disappear."

Another Kibera resident, a woman forty-nine-years-old, said that her income from selling cabbage was enough to send three of her children to school while her husband earned money doing odd jobs in the only middle-class neighborhood within walking distance. Nobody in her family had a birth certificate. Their shelter, too, was a bureaucratic blank space; the tiny tin dwelling had no address, did not show up in any legal record, and wasn't hooked up to a utility. The woman pronounced herself content; she worried, though, that if someone stronger should covet her living quarters or market kiosk, her family could be dispossessed and have to begin all over again.

In wealthier countries, we may think of courage as the pluck to play football despite a sore ankle, but in the Kibera slum, there were no streetlights, no electricity, no running water, and no government health clinics or hospitals. Workers shoveled sewage out of communal latrines and into the Nairobi River. Alcoholism was chronic due to the availability of cheap, high-potency liquor, which contributed to a pregnancy rate of about 50 percent for women between the ages of sixteen and twenty-five. In this environment, every day demanded bravery; the Toi Market was one of the few sources of hope.

A year after our trip, in December 2007, Kenya conducted a presidential election. The outcome, bitterly disputed, spawned an eruption of interethnic bloodshed that roiled neighborhoods throughout the poorer sections of Nairobi and demolished virtually every cubbyhole and stall in the Toi Market. A few weeks later, I received a letter from Mr. Muturi, who wrote, "We have gone back in time. It will take us many years to come back to the level where we were both socially and economically."

When Kenyans next elected a president, I made sure that the National Democratic Institute worked closely with all parties to ensure a fair campaign and prevent violence. Once again, the balloting was close, but on this occasion (in 2013) the losing party challenged the result in the courts, not the streets.

IN 2008, THE Commission on Legal Empowerment of the Poor released a nearly five-hundred-page report, *Making the Law Work for Everyone*. During its European unveiling at the discordantly elegant Peace Palace in The Hague, I argued that "legal identity is not a privilege; it is an entitlement too often denied those without wealth and power." The report underlined four essential rights: of individuals to justice under the law; of families to accumulate savings through legal safeguards for their property; of workers to be paid fairly and treated well; and of entrepreneurs to start and operate a business.

We also called attention to the psychological change in communities where citizens are exercising rights for the first time. There is a pivotal difference between people who believe their voice matters and those browbeaten into thinking it does not. Compare a woman who has full and equal legal standing to one who has no say in deciding whom she weds, no power within her marriage, no recourse if physically abused, no leverage in a divorce, and no right to inherit or own property. Contrast a town where farmers hold clear title to their fields to one where crops can be seized and land occupied by anybody with enough clout to do so. In a sense, the contrast is merely bureaucratic—a question of paperwork. The effect on the spirit, however, and on peoples' lives, is vast.

In preparing the CLEP report, I was grateful to panel members for being so deeply engaged. Justice Kennedy submitted a pungent analysis of the rule of law. Mary Robinson, former leader of Ireland and UN High Commissioner for Human Rights, stressed the indispensable role of women. Tanzania's ex-President Benjamin Mkapa underscored the need to convince citizens that when the government shows up, it is to help them solve their problems, not steal everything they own. Larry Summers, the head of Harvard, offered a revealing comment on the importance of ownership: "No one," he told us, "washes a rented car."

The final report has held up well, though one writer strangely faulted us for relying on "rational persuasion." Others pointed to the difficulty of putting some of our ideas into effect, a reality we acknowledged. It is easy, after all, to envision a world where everyone has the right papers and the promise of equal treatment before the courts. Getting there, however, will take time—especially, but not solely, in the poorest countries.

Today, the Global Legal Empowerment Initiative, founded in

2011, operates worldwide. Projects include the enforcement of environmental laws in India, land titling in Africa, and the creation of community law centers in Ukraine. Because of the CLEP report and Hernando de Soto's advocacy, legal reform is now an integral part of any serious discussion regarding the alleviation of poverty. That's worth celebrating and may have contributed, in recent years, to the number of people living in extreme poverty dipping below 8 percent (compared to 35 percent in 1990), the lowest rate on record.

ELEVEN

Things Unseen

IN A FOURTH-GRADE classroom one morning, an observant teacher pauses as she walks by the desk of a student, a nine-year-old girl with long auburn hair and, adorning her wrist, a silver charm bracelet. "What are you working on?" the teacher asks.

The girl glances up and answers with an earnest look on her face, "I'm drawing a picture of God."

"Very impressive," comes the reply, "but I'm sorry to say that people all over the world have been thinking about that subject for thousands of years, and nobody, not even the wisest and most holy, knows what God looks like."

"Well," says the girl, "They will in a minute."

Oh, for the confidence of that young lady! From the dawn of human consciousness, we have speculated about the nature of God, but with imaginations stunted by our less-than-divine desires and brains. Accounts in monotheistic Scripture leave us with an array of impressions. Is the supreme being remote and fearsome? Intimate and merciful? Jealous? Forgiving? Changeless? Moody? Lacking a definitive answer, we have sometimes amused ourselves by propounding our own ideas. In popular entertainments, God has twice been made to appear like Morgan Freeman but has also been depicted by, among others, Martin Sheen, George Burns, Alanis Morissette, and Whoopi Goldberg. Given the immensity of the universe, also beyond our power to conceive, I suppose it's possible that long ago, somewhere in the cosmos, there was a Hogwarts for apprentice deities. Instructed to produce a science fair project, one student created

Earth and the accompanying solar system, thereby earning from her professor an A for the oceans and mountains, a C for human beings, and extra credit for golden retrievers. Displeased by the mixed review, our scholar gave a mighty spin to her project—which she had named "Genesis"—tossed it high in the air, and moved on.

The unprovable essence of God has not stopped people of all ages and eras from investing faith in unprovable answers. Our diverse beliefs in things unseen, and the overlaps and clashes among them, have very visible consequences.

THE DAY AFTER the 2004 election, a map appeared on an internet message board showing North America in two parts: the first made up of Canada and the states that had voted for Kerry, the second, called "Jesusland," of those won by Bush. The meme, which went viral, implied that America was split between the sensible and secular on one hand and religious fanatics on the other. Quite a few Kerry voters, chastened by their narrow electoral loss, thought the image amusing; I did not. I did, however, think it revealing. According to surveys at the time, two out of every five Americans identified as evangelical Christians—40 percent. Why was it that even though I often attend church, I could count on the fingers of a single hand the professed evangelicals that I knew personally? Was I out of touch? Apparently so.

I am part of a generation that was taught to keep religion far from any discussion of public affairs and especially foreign policy. The reason is plain. To resolve a dispute, diplomats must persuade each side to settle for part of what it wants rather than prolong a squabble by demanding all. Finding the path to compromise is hard enough when the stakes involve land, money, or other tangible goods. It can be impossible when the issues are believed by one side or the other (or both) to involve God's will. Then, every acre of soil can be viewed as sacred, any sign of retreat as heresy, killing as holy, and dying (even by blowing oneself up) as martyrdom. Hence the traditional mediator's desire to frame questions in secular terms. I accepted this prudence as wisdom throughout my time in government.

In the early 1990s, when fighting broke out in the Balkans among Orthodox Christian Serbs, Roman Catholic Croats, and Bosnian Muslims, I asked all sides to focus on the rights of the individual, not the age-old grievances of their faith groups. In the Middle East, we urged leaders to formulate their positions based on legal rights and national aspirations, not religious inheritance. In seeking to cool other hot spots, I emphasized what contending groups had in common, downplaying religious differences. In each case, I stressed logic and prescribed compromise. It seemed the best strategy, but was it sidestepping issues that couldn't be ignored?

IN THE SPRING of 2004, Yale Divinity School invited me to come to New Haven and give a speech. The idea that I do so had originated with a friend, Clyde Tuggle, a senior executive at Coca-Cola who had in his twenties earned a master's degree from that institution. My hosts expected a critique of the Republican administration's foreign policy, but the prospect of sharing my views with divinity school students prompted me to re-examine some of my earlier assumptions. At the time, many of Bush's political opponents were mocking his penchant for inserting religious themes into his rhetoric. I agreed that the president could sound self-righteous, but so could many of his critics. I no longer accepted the view that questions of faith should be avoided when discussing foreign policy.

The 9/11 attacks sparked this modest epiphany but were merely the jumping-off point for my second thoughts. Worldwide, four out of every five of us are aligned with one spiritual tradition or another. This inevitably affects how the countries in which we live define their interests and values. If we are to anticipate and solve international problems, don't we need to take this factor into account? We know that religion has been linked at times to terrorism and war, but we also know that the sacred texts of every faith provide a firm foundation for helping others. Why shouldn't our leaders build on that?

My remarks at Yale were published in the divinity school journal, along with an essay by a professor of theology who accused me of being an inadequate Christian—to which I could only plead guilty. However, the criticism so misconstrued my purpose that I decided to expand my speech into a second book. To avoid any further misunderstanding, I made clear that I would be writing solely from the perspective of a foreign policy specialist and not as someone who saw herself as an authority on ethics or religious doctrine. I did claim one advantage, however. I had been raised a Roman Catholic, became an Episcopalian upon marriage, and later discovered that my family heritage is Jewish. "Interfaith dialogue comes naturally to me," I observed. "All I have to do is sit in a corner and talk to myself."

When I informed my European colleagues that I was planning to write about religion and foreign policy, they looked at me as if I had sprouted a second head. Many of them consider religion to be, at best, a balm for people unwilling to face reality and, at worst, a rationale for crackpots to destroy the lives of others via inquisition and holy wars. "Good people do good things and bad people do bad things," I was told, "but for good people to do bad things, that takes religion."

My purpose in writing the book was not to advocate for belief in the divine; others could make that case. My plan was to examine the immense impact that religious teachings and identities have on international affairs, then consider how diplomats could best deal with that reality. This struck me as a timely effort, given the "improvements" made over centuries in the means of killing. We have all read in our history texts about religious wars fought with swords, catapults, and battering rams. Our commanders now had weapons that could destroy all of human civilization—in fact, some believe Scripture foretells for us just such a fate.

A BAPTIST MINISTER, a rabbi, and an imam sat down at my dinner table in Georgetown. While we nibbled on rolls, salad, and chicken, I picked their brains. What can leaders do to ensure that religion brings people together instead of causing them to bash their neighbors' heads? Why do some people who proudly flaunt their religious identities know so little about the tenets of their chosen faiths? How can a person who prostrates himself before a God of love and mercy be blind to the rights and cares of others? Why can't we all get along?

However familiar the questions, I was delighted to have so much wisdom to draw on for my book. My three guests were of about the same age but their minds had been shaped by strikingly different backgrounds. Dr. Richard Land was president of the Ethics and Religious Liberty Commission of the Southern Baptist Convention, Rabbi David Saperstein was director of the Religious Action Center of Reform Judaism, and Imam Feisal Abdul Rauf was the head of a prominent mosque in the Tribeca district of Manhattan.

"Each of the major religions is a many-splintered thing," Land began. "It is dangerous, and unfair, to generalize about the beliefs of the whole based on the actions of a few. We can't judge Christians by the sins of the Ku Klux Klan, or Jews by the harsh rhetoric of the Jewish Defense League, or Muslims by the crimes of al-Qaeda."

Rauf offered a hearty amen to that. "The overwhelming majority of Muslims want the same things everyone else wants: life, liberty, and the pursuit of happiness," he asserted. "But if even a thousandth of a percent of two billion people are terrorists, we have a big problem."

Saperstein, who talks at roughly the rate that a hummingbird flaps its wings, argued, "Every religion has people within it who deny completely the validity of other faiths. When these factions have the upper hand, people everywhere can get hurt. But how do we prevent that? Outsiders can't do it. A Jew can't control what Muslims do; a Christian can't influence radical Jews; a Muslim isn't going to temper the extremism of some Christians. We each have to work from the inside and take responsibility for our own traditions."

I asked about religious literalism, the theory that despite its many contradictions, every word in Scripture must be true. This contrasts with the cynic's quip that the Bible is 100 percent accurate, but only when thrown at close range. "There is a difference," Land said, "between certitude of religious belief and certitude about how to apply those beliefs to current events." He added that when discussing the latter, he steps down from the pulpit to signify the contrast between what he knows and what he thinks.

Rauf was pressed to comment on the principle in Islam that those who convert to another faith should be put to death. He pointed out that early Muslims lived in a hostile environment and felt surrounded by enemies. In that context, a Muslim who abandoned the faith was switching sides in the middle of a war, the equivalent of treason, still a capital crime in many countries. He said that the modern enforcement of such measures tends to be lenient, varies widely, and depends on local culture and attitudes.

Then we had dessert.

THE PRESENCE OF Dr. Land, who had close ties to Republican leaders, added to my hope that the political right and left could work together on humanitarian issues. During my time in government, I had grown accustomed to hearing many Republicans denounce foreign aid to any country except Israel. Then, when testifying on Capitol Hill in the late 1990s, I detected a change. Suddenly, right-wing legislators were complaining that we were doing too *little* to help people abroad. Shouldn't we be investing more in the fight against HIV/AIDS? Why couldn't the United States take the lead in providing debt relief to the poorest nations? Early in my career, I had been accused of being a do-gooder in love with "foreign policy as social work." Now Kansas Senator Sam Brownback, deeply conservative, was arguing that the United States "must move humbly and wisely, not just for our own economic and strategic interests but for what is morally right."

To pick up on this theme, I approached Brownback in a corridor of the U.S. Capitol; this was early in 2005.

"I've been listening to you," I said, "and agree with many of the points you make."

Brownback's eyes nearly popped their sockets. "You have? You do?"
"Yes, and I have a proposition. Let's combine forces."

The outcome was a conference, Uncommon Leadership for Common Values, held that November at Georgetown in a hall packed with more than six hundred students and activists. Land and Saperstein spoke, as did U.S. Representative Frank Wolf and U.S. Senator Hillary Clinton. I said that we should not allow differences of party or ideology to prevent us from doing what we all knew was right. Brownback called attention to the needs of the poor in five especially hard-pressed areas: Darfur, North Korea, Burma, the Democratic Republic of the Congo, and Northern Uganda.

I had friends who faulted me for my partnership with the conservative Brownback. Too bad. The Kansan and I disagree on gay marriage, budget priorities, and all manner of other issues, but he favors the humane treatment of immigrants on biblical grounds and longs to help people who wake up each morning in the most wretched places on earth. How can I not see merit in that? Besides, he got plenty of grief from his friends for sharing a stage with me.

WHAT I REFERRED to casually as the "God book" appeared in March 2006. The formal title, a bit long-winded, was *The Mighty and the Almighty: Reflections on America, God, and World Affairs*. When the European editions were released, I crossed the Atlantic to give interviews and otherwise publicize the event. One afternoon, I had an appointment with a Dutch photographer, who strode into the room where I was waiting, carrying with him a stuffed bird. "This," he said, noting my arched eyebrows, "is a peace pigeon." I thought perhaps he meant a dove, but on closer inspection, I had to agree: it was definitely a pigeon. The photographer asked that I hold the bird in front of me as he circled the room in quest of the ideal angle. After several minutes of clutching a stuffed pigeon, I had trouble maintaining a dignified expression. This upset the cameraman, who said sternly, "Madam Secretary, you cannot smile. You must be serious; this is a serious pigeon."

* * *

WHILE WRITING *THE MIGHTY and the Almighty*, I began reading the
Bible every day and delved more deeply into my feelings about religion and its associated rites and teachings.

There are many passages in Scripture, especially the antiquated
legalisms and eye-for-an-eye aspects of the Old Testament (or Hebrew Bible), that make me want to beat my head against a wall. But
ever since I was a child, religion has been a part of my life. As my
family moved from place to place (five different countries before I
was twelve), praying came naturally because it was comforting for
me to think that somewhere up above, a kindly ear was listening. In
my bedroom, I set up a mini-altar and pretended to be a priest—an
early sign of ambition from a child who was both Roman Catholic
and female.

This is how I grew up—with a temperament inclined to faith. I
was one of those rare students who looked forward to catechism class.
I had a prayer book with Latin on one side and English on the other.
The graceful rhythms of the language entranced me: *Ave Maria, gra-
tia plena . . . In nomine Patris et Filii et Spiritus Sancti.* I was taken,
too, with the simplicity of what worshippers asked: to be forgiven
for sins, shielded from evil, and to receive our daily bread. Church
music, though dirge like at times, can also lift spirits. I defy anyone
not to smile when singing "Joyful, Joyful, We Adore Thee." As with
the best literature, Scripture provides much to challenge, comfort,
and confuse: amid the lessons it imparts to human hearts are sagas of
exile and redemption, grand prophecies, instructive parables, and the
promise of a light entering the world that darkness cannot overcome.
There is a lot to think about in all of this.

The religious influences I derived from my family were mixed. My
mother attended services regularly, but my father just at Easter and
Christmas. He objected to the Church's practice of putting family
identification numbers on the weekly offering envelopes, a tracking
system that to him seemed despotic.

Later, as a young mother on Long Island, I wrote in my journal:

*January 9, 1966: In the morning we took the twins to Sunday
School. They really enjoy it. Both are singing hymns and reciting
prayers. Last Christmas Eve, when we went with them to
church in Vermont, they were excited, but it was terribly hard
to keep them quiet, so we didn't stay long. I did notice that they
both sang "Away in a Manger" to every song. When asked why,
Anne replied, "It's the only one we know."*

I AM ACQUAINTED with people whose religious devotion stems from
a rock solid sense of personal revelation, a conviction that their communication with God is literally a two-way affair. I envy them, but
lack the same certainty. I have had no startling visions of the Virgin
Mary; nor have I felt touched by an angel or dreamt that Jesus sat
down beside me for a talk. I am also acquainted with scholars who
can lecture on the parallels between Sumer-Akkadian and Hebrew
flood myths and put a name to twenty different Christian heresies;
I envy them as well. The only course on religion that I took while in
school was at Wellesley, a required one on the Bible (Old Testament
in the fall, New in the spring), taught by a professor of literature.

Having written the God book, I am sometimes asked to appear
on panels where I am grilled on the philosophies of Augustine, Aqui-
nas, Buber, and Niebuhr. Rather than admit ignorance, I dodge the
questions and tell jokes. In England for a conference one summer,
I was assigned to a guesthouse at the University of Cambridge. Inside, I met a man who was wearing a clerical collar but whose name
I didn't catch. Figuring that religion would be a topic of mutual interest, I ran through my repertoire of stories on the subject, ending
with an account of my audience with Pope John Paul II, my email
relationship with The Most Rev. Desmond Tutu, and my many conversations with the Dalai Lama. Basically, I dropped every name I
could before glancing at my watch and concluding, "Now, if you will
excuse me; I have to get ready for dinner. I am to be the guest of the
former archbishop of Canterbury." Two hours later, when I walked
into the university's lovely old dining hall, I was greeted warmly by

the same fellow. This time, I did catch his name: Rowan Williams, former archbishop of Canterbury.

My lack of religious expertise is hardly unusual. Church educators admit that faith communities are often united less by a cohesive set of theological convictions than by a blend of inherited habits, an urge to belong, the hypnotic lure of ritual, and anxiety about what, if anything, comes after death. This can be the case regardless of the creed involved. During coffee hour at church, I have often heard parishioners inquire of the priest, "What do we believe?" on this topic or that. Hardly a belief, though, is it, if one must ask? I have also taught many students who identified with a faith the core teachings of which they had but a passing familiarity. Such is the way of the world. In my experience, people tend to speak more than they think and to hold strong opinions without always asking themselves why.

There is, nonetheless, a huge market for religious education beginning at a tender age and continuing until "meeting one's maker" no longer seems just a figure of speech. Religion attracts truth-seekers because it corresponds to the human desire to feel part of something larger and more universal than oneself. Religion is not the only way, but it is a means of coping with questions about life's origins and purpose, and about our place in the seemingly boundless realms of time and space. Coping with questions, however, is not the same as finding answers of which we can feel sure.

I am a believer who harbors doubt—admittedly a wishy-washy state of mind. Much remains opaque to me, despite years of trying to arrive at a clear view. Given the multitude of injustices small and large that we witness on this planet, the theory that an all-powerful, all-merciful, always-attentive supreme being is in charge seems preposterous. However, it feels about right to believe that we, the inheritors of free will, are engaged in a constant struggle between good and evil, with discerning the difference a pivotal element in the ordeal. If God is always with us, so much the better, even if the visible outcome depends on what we do, not on thunderbolts from above.

In me, this is where faith plants its hook.

I cannot willingly accept a world utterly devoid of divine spark, where all is explained by physical and biological interaction and there is no larger meaning to anything. If this is indeed the case, so be it, but leave me out. I'm reminded of a story about a group of scientists who challenge God's unique status as Creator, claiming that given enough time, natural processes would bring all manner of life forms into existence out of a single handful of soil.

God responds, "I'll take that bet and give you all the time you want, but on one condition."

"What's that?" a scientist asks.

Says God: "You have to supply your own dirt."

What do I (and so many others) mean by a divine spark? I can't explain it even to my own satisfaction, but every day, I see generosity of spirit in people around me, people who regularly exhibit kindness with no thought of credit or material gain.

When I was secretary of state, I met a boy in Uganda, five years old, and asked the usual question: how are you? He said, "Fine, and you?" I soon learned that, a few weeks earlier, his mother had been killed in a massacre and that he had crawled out from beneath her body and walked miles to a refugee camp, carrying his little sister, Charity, on his back. The orphans were being cared for by volunteers from World Vision International who, for years, had been trying to protect people from the Lord's Resistance Army, a gang of thugs that kidnapped children and butchered families in the name of the Ten Commandments. The camp was the kind of place that might be called godforsaken, except that it had not been abandoned by the people of faith who ran it. I asked them how they dealt with the sweltering heat, constant hardships, and danger. They replied that they were grateful for the chance.

Gratitude is one reason I see value in prayer. To an atheist this will seem silly, but I pray daily to a God whose existence I cannot verify and whose form I cannot grasp. My prayers are for people I know (and many I don't) who are ill in body or mind, or who are threatened by war or some other source of hardship. My devotional routine makes me consider with sympathy, for a minute or two each day, those whom I might otherwise forget. Such thoughts sometimes lead to a visit, a call, a note, a favor, an appeal, perhaps a charitable contribution, or a bit of community service. Multiply my tiny experience by that of the billions of others who pray and suddenly this possibly imaginary God is as powerful an influence for good—real, tangible good—as any force on earth. Does that prove God exists? If it did, we could be certain of Santa Claus because of all the letters we write. But if prayer has benefits, and it does, why not give a little credibility to the source of devotion?

I SHOW UP at religious services as often as my schedule permits. In Georgetown, I go to St. John's Episcopal Church and, when staying at my farm, to another Episcopal parish, also named for Saint John, in Harpers Ferry. The latter is located a short distance from where the Shenandoah flows into the Potomac and where West Virginia, Maryland, and Virginia touch. Built in 1899, the church in Harpers Ferry is small, with nine pews to a side, a modest altar, a piano, an organ, and a crimson carpet set off by a stained-glass window and brown walls. The attendance in peak season is about twelve, just enough for a party of apostles.

Because the congregation is so tiny, finding a preacher has been a strain. For a long time, we had a high-spirited woman who led discussions on everything from how to interpret the Bible to the principles that separate just from unjust war. Eventually, she moved to the West Coast and was replaced by John Unger, who, in addition to our services, presided over those of the local Lutherans and Methodists. This made him very busy on weekends, and he was also a leading member of the West Virginia State Senate. The minister liked to relate an anecdote about the time, years ago, when he told his grandmother that he had been awarded a Rhodes Scholarship. She was delighted. "You'll have a job forever," she told him, thinking that in West Virginia there is no more reliable an employer than the state's

Department of Roads. To a Washingtonian, Harpers Ferry can seem remote from the tribulations of the world, but Unger had experience as a missionary in India and working with refugees fleeing violence in Vietnam and Iraq.

One Memorial Day, friends in the parish invited me to a jazz festival held nearby. I went and took away with me a tale shared by a musician who resembled Lou Rawls (and if you don't know who that is, be grateful for your youth). The story is about a murder victim who applies for admission to Heaven. The angel Gabriel greets him and explains that to get in, he must spell one word correctly. That word, he says, is *love*. The man passes the test and proves so well thought of in the celestial community that he is appointed Gabriel's assistant.

Months later, when Gabriel is on leave, the murderer, having also died, shows up at the Pearly Gates and asks to be admitted. The virtuous man recognizes his assailant right away. His first impulse is to banish his foe to an eternity of brimstone and fire, but in Heaven, the redemption of sinners tops the list of what angels are expected to seek. So, he restrains his temper and says to the murderer, "To be absolutely fair, I will give you the same test I was given; spell one word correctly and you will be allowed to enter." The evil man grins with relief and says, "Oh thank you, thank you, dear angel. What is the word?" The guardian of the gate smiles back: "Czechoslovakia."

TWELVE

Advise and Dissent

"WAR CRIMINAL OR Role Model?" One or the other. The newspaper headline offered no third alternative.

I am a person who wants very much to be liked. For more than two decades, I have also been accused by some of starving babies and feeling good about it. The allegation has been kept alive online and by social media, but it had its origin on the granddaddy of television news shows, *60 Minutes*. On May 12, 1996, the program broadcast footage of a shabby, ill-equipped hospital in Baghdad, featuring close-ups of sick and starving children. The accompanying report might as well have been narrated by the Iraqi government, which had arranged access to its medical facilities for a CBS camera crew. The heart-tugging segment was capped by a conversation between the network's top journalist, Leslie Stahl, and the U.S. ambassador to the United Nations—me. "We have heard that half a million children have died [as a result] of UN sanctions on Iraq," said Stahl. "I mean, that is more children than died in Hiroshima. And, you know, is the price worth it?"

I can't recall exactly what thoughts flitted through my head at that moment, but judging by the result, none that was useful. I should have challenged the interviewer's premise or rephrased the question myself, but lacked the quickness of mind to do so. I had already laid out the reasons for our opposition to Iraq's dictator Saddam Hussein, a policy that had robust international support and the backing of both parties in Congress. Still, there is no valid excuse for how I replied to Stahl's question: "I think that is a very hard choice, but the price, we think, the price is worth it." Better I had cut out my tongue. I can't blame people who saw that program or read the transcript for regarding me as insufferably callous, and I have since apologized a thousand times for answering as I did. For some, the chronicle of the cold-blooded granny has continued to define me no matter what else I do or say.

Because the network's report had the aura of a truth-telling exposé, it was rewarded with an Emmy. In fact, the producers of *60 Minutes* were duped. Subsequent research has shown that Iraqi propagandists deceived international observers, convincing them that, due to sanctions, children were dying by the hundreds of thousands. Per a 2017 article in the *British Medical Journal of Global Health*, the data "were rigged to show a huge and sustained—and largely non-existent—rise in child mortality . . . The objective of Saddam Hussein's government was to heighten international concern and so get the international sanctions ended." The article, which draws on three separate studies, concludes, "There was no major rise in child mortality in Iraq after 1990 and during the period of the sanctions. Conversely, there was no major improvement in child mortality after the downfall of Saddam Hussein."

This is not to deny that UN sanctions contributed to hardships in Iraq or to say that my answer to Stahl's question wasn't a mistake. They did, and it was. The impression I made in the interview is wholly at odds with the way I feel about the harm done to innocents as a byproduct of conflict, whether military or political. I despise the euphemism "collateral damage," and think commanders should be applauded, not accused of being weak, when trying to avoid civilian casualties stemming from military action. Economic sanctions, though sometimes necessary, should be designed to apply pressure on leaders, not to make life more painful for average citizens. This is what I believe, but I failed to make those convictions clear in the interview, and critics were right to fault me for the oversight.

Where they were wrong was to confuse cause and effect. Iraq's agony was directly traceable to the criminality of its government.

Hussein's decision to invade his neighbors—Iran in the 1980s, Kuwait in 1990—ravaged Iraq's economy, its medical infrastructure, and its standard of living. After the First Gulf War, his military's near-genocidal attacks against Shiites in the Southern region of the country and Kurds in the North generated further harm.

The *60 Minutes* report convinced a large slice of the world's population that the principal villain in the story was not Hussein but America. Many compassionate people were misled, while others saw an opening: "More than 600,000 Iraqi children have died due to lack of food and medicine... You, the USA, together with the Saudi regime, are responsible for the shedding of the blood of these innocent children." So, in 1996, opined Osama bin Laden, who later cited this cleverly manufactured lie as a principal justification for the 9/11 attacks.

U.S. policy throughout the 1990s was to prevent Iraq from reconstituting its most dangerous weapons programs. Short of another war, UN sanctions were the best means for doing so. Had the dictator complied fully with the requests of international weapons inspectors, the penalties would have eased. Had he spent Iraq's money on basic civilian needs, his people would have benefited. Instead, he lavished funds on his family and cronies and built palaces that included a multitiered complex about five times the size of the White House. The truth is that Hussein had every chance to put an end to Iraq's misery. Instead, he chose to prolong its pain at great cost to his people and, ultimately, himself. Further, the sanctions worked. While they were in place, UN inspectors destroyed more of Iraq's weapons of mass destruction capacity than had been eliminated during the entire Gulf War. That is why, when the United States invaded Iraq under President Bush, there were no such weapons to be found.

IN 2002, WASHINGTON Governor Gary Locke invited me to deliver the commencement address at his state's university. Despite the cross-country trek, I accepted because I was honored to be asked and because I love graduation ceremonies. Such an event is where academia most closely resembles church, with all the fine robes, music, and hallowed rites. Over the years I have watched with pride as each of my daughters has risen from her seat, crossed the stage, and been handed her degree. The first wave of grandchildren has begun now to follow in their footsteps. Each time, I marvel at how brief the interval is between diapers and diplomas.

Prior to a ceremony, I enjoy watching the extended families gather in groups, one generation with canes, another with strollers, all exchanging hugs with the giddy (and sometimes hungover) graduates-to-be. Then the program begins, and I savor each segment: the often-awkward welcoming remarks, the distribution of diplomas, and the entertainment furnished by string quartets, rappers, and rock bands. I also look forward to the student speakers, most of whom manage to be brilliant, hilarious, curiously moving, and transparently unrehearsed—an impression that cannot be achieved without hours of practice.

In Seattle, on the morning of June 15, 2002, the crowd nearly filled Husky Stadium, among the nation's largest. The governor was there, and so, too, the faculty, in full regalia of purple and gold. Sunlight was bouncing off the Cascade Mountains, and I felt great. Then the student speaker, instead of addressing her peers, cast a baleful eye on me. Referring to the CBS broadcast, she accused me of being a horrible person who had helped to murder Iraqi children. To dramatize the point, she urged her classmates to stand and turn their backs when I began to speak. So much for hilarious and curiously moving.

When I took my turn at the lectern, a number of students, though far from the majority, did rise and turn their backs. Repressing the impulse to flee, I said, "I want you to know that I respect you and your views, whichever direction you stand. This is your day; I didn't come three thousand miles to spoil it. So, please, make yourselves comfortable." To my relief, most of those who had joined the protest sat down.

Since leaving office, I have delivered an average of three commencement speeches a year. In 2019, I gave four in one exhausting week, two on each coast. Though some academic institutions offer a substantial fee, I will not accept anything beyond expenses. Occasionally there will still be hostile signs or a student orator who cites the *60 Minutes* interview, even though few of the graduates now are old enough to remember the 1990 war or why sanctions were imposed against Iraq. Often, to clear the air, I have arranged to meet privately with protest organizers either before or after a speech. Results vary. Some students accept my explanation; others do not; many in both categories request a souvenir picture. I can't say that I will ever enjoy being called a modern-day Cruella de Vil, but I do remember being young myself and think that the capacity for moral indignation, whether or not properly directed, has value.

IN THE UNITED STATES, the commencement tradition extends back to Harvard's first graduation ceremony, in 1642. Among those present were the colonial governor, a clutch of local dignitaries, and nine graduates (referred to as "commencers") and their families. To show how much more academically accomplished (or not) we have become since those primitive days, consider that students back then delivered orations in Greek, Latin, and Hebrew, before proceeding to a debate on philosophy, also in an ancient language. In subsequent years the festive weekend acquired a reputation for partying or, as one puritanical college president complained, "disorder and profaneness." In 1797 an elephant participated, along with people dressed as mermaids and mummies, and the local Indians (as they were called) whupped the graduating scholars in an archery contest. Forty-one years later, Ralph Waldo Emerson entertained those receiving degrees from the university's divinity school by denouncing the "evils of the church." His address was greeted with outrage, usually a good sign, and though his prescriptions for moral living are more hazy than precise, the text still reads well.

Over the decades, I have given speeches of many types, but commencement addresses (along with remarks at funerals) are the hardest to prepare. At my own graduation, the principal speaker was the secretary of defense, who advised the young ladies of Wellesley to find suitable husbands and raise smart children.

Today, National Public Radio maintains a list of what it calls the greatest commencement speeches; there are about 350, including Emerson's and, I was gratified to discover, two of mine. As encouraging as that is, I never attempt such a speech without fearing I will disappoint. A friend compared the challenge to that of kissing. In a romantic mood, one wants to surpass expectations, but there are perils associated with trying too hard, and there are only so many ways to go about the procedure. To stay on topic while avoiding triteness requires a rare combination of imagination, felicitous timing, and dexterity. That's a lot to ask of a commencement address. Daunted, most orators play it safe by centering their ideas on a handful of Hallmark-like themes: You can be anything you want to be. Don't be afraid to fail. Get ready for the real world. Follow your passion. And above all, devote your life to what really counts.

While trying to breathe energy into such material, a graduation day speaker must maneuver across minefields. Borrow even a self-deprecatory joke and you may find yourself accused of plagiarism. (For example, "A commencement speaker is like a corpse at an Irish wake. Your presence is required, but you're not expected to say very much.") Also, never assume that the ceremony is about you. The day belongs to the graduates. Talk too long, and the audience will fidget and reach for their phones. Once, when I was secretary of state, a member of my staff had the idea of using the ceremonies as a backdrop for policy speeches. He thought it would attract publicity. It didn't, and students were rightly unhappy about being used as props.

Tone, too, is crucial. It is better to be funny than pompous, but not many students yearn to be sent off into the world by a stand-up comedian. The young of every era pretend to have life all figured out, but most are as bewildered as their elders. Today's college graduates grew up in an environment marred by terrorism, war, economic disparities, climate fears, opioid addiction, evolving attitudes toward gender, and a crisis of faith in democracy. They deserve at least a few minutes of straight talk lifted by hopes that are as real as one can make them without becoming mawkish. If a speech is to have a compelling moment, this is where it will be, not in the funny or ironic lines. At the same time, students' memories are relatively short. They're not about to recall where they were when John Kennedy was assassinated, or the Vietnam War ended, or the *Challenger* space shuttle blew up. To them, Bill Clinton might just as well have been Napoleon. If words are to have an impact, they must be placed within a setting that young audiences will understand.

Finally, a speaker should expect to be interrupted—if not by protests, then by things unforeseen. At the University of Arizona, graduates had a tradition of throwing tortillas at one another, like Frisbees; this is not a custom about which I had been warned. At Smith College, a person dressed as a six-foot-tall bird strolled down the center aisle during my speech and just stood there, quietly chirping. Did that happen every year? No.

After years of trying, I have never departed a commencement confident that graduates would recall what I had said even the next day. The whole premise behind these ceremonies is that the old have something important to teach the young. This, to the coming generation, is hardly a self-evident proposition. However, in the years right after 9/11, I was able to grab the attention of some audiences with the following:

> One of the moving stories to come out of that nightmarish day involved a former high school football hero named Tom Burnett. On September 11, he called his wife from the hijacked United Flight 93, realizing already that two other hijacked planes had crashed into the World Trade Center.
>
> "I know we're going to die," he said. "But some of us are going to do something about it." And because Burnett and his fellow passengers fought the hijackers and brought down their

plane, many other lives were saved, and the football hero became a hero for all time.

When you think about it, "I know we're going to die" is a wholly unremarkable statement. Each of us here this morning could say the same. It is Burnett's next words that were both matter of fact and electrifying. "Some of us are going to do something about it."

Those words, it seems to me, convey the fundamental question put to us by life. We are all mortal. What divides us is the use we make of the time and opportunities we have.

Another way of thinking about the same question is to consider all the publicity lately about the similarities between the genetic code of a human being and that of a mouse. We are ninety-five percent the same.

Perhaps each night we should ask ourselves what we have done to prove there *is* a difference. After all, mice eat, drink, groom themselves, chase each other's tails, and try to avoid danger. How does our definition of "have a nice day" depart from that?

The problem, of course, is that we are all so busy using time-saving devices that we don't have time for anything else. We may understand what it means to answer the call of conscience, but instead of acting on that understanding, we tend to wait—until we are out of school, until we can afford a down payment on a house, until we can pay for our children's education, until we can free up time in retirement, until we can take that vacation we have always dreamed about.

We keep waiting until we run out of "untils." Then it is too late. Our planes have crashed, and we haven't done anything about it.

ON MAY 14, 2016, I delivered the commencement address at the all-women Scripps College, in Claremont, California. My invitation, issued by a committee of students, caused grumbling within a small circle of professors and led to the *Los Angeles Times* headline cited in this chapter's opening paragraph. In the accompanying article, the students who selected me are quoted as saying that they were delighted by their choice, given that Ellen DeGeneres couldn't make it. Less pleased was a young lady who wrote, "I'm deeply disgusted that on the happiest day of my life (up to this point) I have to sit quietly and smile at the cameras of my parents and grandparents while this woman tells me to go out in the world and be amazing."

Sure enough, at the ceremony, the student speaker upbraided me for all the usual reasons. I replied that "there is a special place in Heaven for anyone who speaks truth to power." This bromide soothed the audience and enabled me to go on with my speech, which did indeed urge the graduates to go out in the world and be amazing.

War criminal? I plead "not guilty." Role model? That's not my call. Optimist? Now you're talking.

Were I to stand in front of a graduating class and speak in resigned terms about the impossibility of human progress, I would see shoulders sag, eyes go flat, and attentions wander. Predictions of doom are not what the young want to hear, and certainly not what I would ever broadcast. People of all ages respond with the greatest energy when summoned to innovate, heal, build, and—yes, when necessary—protest. We each desire to be useful and to have a task in front of us that matters as we wipe the sleep from our eyes and begin the new day. So long as that is true, and I believe it to be an intrinsic part of how most of us are constructed, I will trust in our collective ability to learn from the past. Despite more evidence to the contrary than I would like, I have not lost hope that, in time, "all shall be well, and all manner of thing shall be well" or—if not quite that—at least a little better from year to year.

THIRTEEN

Companions

PEOPLE WHO ASK me how I feel about getting older are advised to duck, as are those who profess their astonishment that a person of my age still has the mental capacity to utter a coherent sentence. The subject is a sensitive one. There are many in my parents' generation of Central European immigrants who believed that speaking openly about one's age risked attracting notice from the angel of death. They would readily admit how old they were when they came to America and in what year they arrived, but beyond that, let others do the arithmetic. In their culture, they did not plan for "when Aunt Janika dies," but rather, for what to do "should something happen." I am (a little) less superstitious but still see no cause to tempt fate. My thinking is that because I have no interest in death, death should have no interest in me. This is the kind of quid pro quo that Emily Dickinson wrote poems about.

I do not often become ill. I am, however, a hypochondriac. When I feel an ache or a twinge, I fear the worst and begin asking friends if they ever experienced something similar and survived. Then the twinges go away, and life moves on until the following day, when I forget my keys and think my memory is slipping. Still, I am reluctant to visit doctors because too many of them insist on talking politics when all I want to know is whether my inner organs can still do their jobs.

I observe sensible precautions, such as carrying an EpiPen due to allergies (anaphylaxis) that I learned about the hard way. When I was a young mother, a bee stung me for no good reason; my throat swelled up so much that I could barely breathe. Then, in 1976, at a Democratic Platform Committee meeting in Denver, I ate some bouillabaisse for lunch and later developed itchy palms. My thought at the time was that with itchy palms and all that handshaking, I had no future in politics. What I actually have is a hyper-sensitivity to the iodine in shrimp.

I also suffer from idiopathic scoliosis, a mild curvature of the spine that is incurable, nonfatal, usually not progressive, and causes back pain. King Richard III had it, too, prompting Shakespeare to label him—unfairly, in my opinion—a "poisonous bunch-backed toad." I was diagnosed in 2007 and find the infirmity annoying because it makes me look a little bent when I walk, thus even shorter than I am.

Thankfully, youthfulness of spirit is contagious. I am grateful for the chance to interact regularly with the twenty- or thirty-somethings in my classroom, as a businessperson, and when speaking at public events. On trips, I enjoy conversing with aides who are a fraction of my age, especially in those moments when my activities have worn them down and they are too exhausted to escape. I don't pretend to be younger than I am, but it is energizing to be involved with people of any vintage whose minds are filled more with plans than regrets. I am convinced that for seniors, nostalgia is a trap: once the longing to look back starts to consume you, it is hard to shake free.

When Benjamin Franklin reached his seventieth birthday, he decided that was quite enough and began counting in reverse. Fourteen years later, at age fifty-six, he succumbed to pleurisy. On May 15, 2007, when I turned seventy, we marked the date with a dinner party for women only on the rooftop patio of the building where I worked. Hillary Clinton was there, along with Geraldine Ferraro, and the senior senator from Maryland, Barbara Mikulski. We talked of current projects, future plans, absent friends, and old adventures—such as the time Gerry and I were in Moscow and I went foraging for food at night, after the supermarkets had closed. I managed to scavenge a can of caviar, a bottle of vodka, and a bag of Fritos. Recalling our repast, Ferraro said she had never been so sick. Mikulski, who is ten months older than I am, summarized her career (and that of many women) by saying that "it took me only twenty-five years to be an overnight success."

THERE IS A stage in the life of most young children when they knock over or try to eat everything they touch. In the next phase they become miniature Rembrandts, and among the subjects of their art is Mom. Typically, her arms and legs are made to resemble sticks, her body an oval, and her head a perfect circle topped with a scribbly halo of hair. On her face is a toothy grin, and her flesh may or may not seep creepily over the lines. The portraits require just a few minutes to draw, but then spend years attached to refrigerators and office walls. For most of us, assuming we do nothing to merit the attention of a police sketch artist, this will be the last occasion anyone sees fit to capture our likeness. Given that the average smartphone today contains about four billion selfies, why bother? The omission would have been fine with me, but at the State Department, a secretary's final duty has traditionally come after leaving office: to pose for a portrait, get framed, then hung.

On April 14, 2008, my portrait was unveiled during a ceremony hosted by my successor plus one, Condoleezza Rice. I had steeled myself to show approval of the painting regardless of what I really thought, but in the event, had no cause to mask my opinion. The artist, Steven Polson, did a stellar job. I am shown in my favorite blue suit and my best attempt at a Mona Lisa half smile. I had expected that the sittings would be a bore; instead, they were a lark. Polson's studio loft in Brooklyn has enormous windows to let in the light, he put me at ease with his gift for lively talk, and there was an Italian bakery just a few doors down. We worked hard and ate well.

The completion of a portrait is no big deal; our nation's capital has them by the score. However, the unveiling ceremony on April 14 included a modest dash of something long overdue. I try not to obsess over the topic of gender, but the State Department has more than forty officially designated "diplomatic reception rooms." Of these, just two are named for women (Martha Washington and Dolley Madison), and both are bathrooms. For eight years, I had marched down corridors in the department that were lined with paintings of men. I had often fantasized that the walls shook a little when I passed, and that the fraternity of bewhiskered old dudes would eventually find a way to call security and have me kicked out of their club. But perspectives change. After the names of Rice and Clinton joined mine on the roll call, my granddaughter Ellie (six years old at the time) remarked: "I don't know what the big deal was about Grandma Maddy being secretary of state. Only girls are secretary of state."

THE DEDICATION OF my portrait doubled as a family reunion. The quality of the company there caused me to reflect, and not for the first time, that I must have been a perfect mother, or possibly Joe Albright was the perfect father—or maybe our three daughters became perfect on their own. Whatever the case, they certainly started out well. The twins' first report cards, from what we cheerfully referred to as Miss Stoddard's School for Very Little People, testified to the excellence of their small motor movements, admirable demeanor on the playground, and above-average skills at cut-and-paste. They tried hard to behave even when, at four and a half, they both spent a week confined to home with chicken pox, exercising their dolls—all apparently named Sweetie or Madeleine. They also looked out for me, letting me know when my hair was a mess or my clothes were wrong, and exhorting me when I went off to my own classes at Columbia to be "good in art."

Much later, when I was busy in government, these early signs of a parental instinct paid dividends. My daughters balanced my checkbook, urged me to be more economical when shopping, prevailed on me to get more sleep, and worried that I was becoming reckless.

Once, when CNN reported that a mob had hurled rocks and clods of mud at my car in the Balkans, I received a stern phone call from Anne. "What were you thinking?" she demanded. "Why don't you show more sense? You could have been killed. From now on, you have to tell us before you go anyplace dangerous." I suspect, had she the ability to enforce such an edict, I would have been sent to my room.

Since leaving government, I have been able to take better care of myself and have had more time to watch the trio of younger Albright women mature, raise their own families, and earn respect within their communities. My bias may be showing, but they're fabulous, and I can prove it.

Anne Korbel Albright is an associate judge on the Circuit Court in Montgomery County, Maryland. Years ago, shortly after graduating from law school, she worked in the county public defender's office and called to tell me that she had to break a dinner date. I asked where she was. She said, "At the jail." I heard "*in* jail," and almost had a heart attack. Before her appointment to the bench, she spent fifteen years as a partner in a two-lawyer meat-and-potatoes firm that specialized in helping families sort out legal problems. As a judge, she avoids all potential conflicts of interest and plays no favorites. If I were ever to jaywalk, I would not do it in Montgomery County. Anne is married to Geoff Watson, and they have two children, a son John (called Jack) and the brilliantly named Maddie, or Madeleine.

In 2013, Alice Patterson Albright, Anne's twin, became CEO of the Global Partnership for Education, which, as the name implies, is dedicated to enabling children wherever they live to have access to quality schooling. More than sixty-five developing countries are active members, along with a host of donors and other supportive organizations. Earlier, she was executive vice president and chief operating officer of the Ex-Im Bank, and before that, chief financial officer of the Global Alliance for Vaccines and Immunizations. In decades of travel, I have racked up millions of miles on my personal odometer, but Alice has had a more up-close and personal look at how most people live. She is fearless, dedicated, and, to choose an ordinary adjective that truly fits only extraordinary people: good.

Alice and her husband, Greg Bowes, are the parents of David and Daniel. When David was fifteen, I went with him on an excursion to the Arctic sponsored by the National Geographic Society and the Aspen Institute. The theme was climate change; the scenery included ice becoming water and stressed polar bears. I wish every consumer and voter could go on a similar trip. I can understand why global warming might not seem real to a family huddled indoors during a midwinter snowstorm, but to be personally confronted with how quickly the polar ice caps are shrinking is a lesson neither David nor I will forget.

Then there is Katie: after teaching in a nursery school that she helped to found in Nairobi, Katharine Medill Albright became a lawyer because of her desire to advocate effectively for the young. Her first client was a twenty-six-year-old grandmother; her second, a teenage rape victim. From these and other cases, she learned both the power of law and the importance of a supportive community. Having focused nearly full time on pro bono work in private practice, she later served in San Francisco as a deputy city attorney and led campaigns for universal preschools and high-quality teaching. Since 2007, Katie has been CEO of Safe & Sound, an organization dedicated to the well-being of children and their families. On visits to the Bay Area, I have seen my youngest daughter in action. She is a forceful and eloquent communicator who takes full advantage of the fact that (in contrast to her mother), English is her native language. She and her husband, Jake Schatz, have two other major accomplishments: Benjamin (Ben) and Eleanor (Ellie).

When I reached the age of eligibility for AARP, I found that milestone difficult to accept; now my children have qualified as well. The tiny and needy have long since grown up. Those of you who are parents can appreciate how that feels, including the inevitable sense of loss. Time, like one's shadow, cannot be outrun. I am gratified, however, that my headstrong daughters, with their Jo March–like independence and diverse talents, have pursued careers that powerfully reinforce my own. For all our differences, I have a welcome feeling that in our jobs and volunteer activities we are pulling in similar directions. I couldn't ask for more.

When the grandchildren were younger, I knitted mittens for them and little ski hats that looked like tomatoes. Now all six are taller than I am, and I have moved on to the production of large socks. Anne and Alice live in the Washington area, so we get together often, for which I am thankful. I try to drop in on Katie whenever I am in California, and she visits as often as she can. As a foursome, my daughters and I have a decades-old tradition of arranging "girls' weekends," featuring restaurants, mani-pedis, and shop-till-we-drop excursions.

My sister, Kathy, and brother, John, and his wife, Pam, also live in Washington, which makes it easy to remain in touch. In 2016, I was delighted to host at my farm in Virginia the wedding of my nephew, Joe Korbel, and his wife, Magda. The daughter of a Bosnian Muslim father and a Serb mother, Magda came to the United States as a refugee from the Balkans War. John and Pam were the proudest of parents, and Joe's brother Peter a charming best man, as we partied all afternoon with lively music and a variety of libations. In fact, we had so much fun that the police saw fit to stop by, I presume to make sure we were all right.

I frequently attend movies or the theater with Kathy, with whom I am as close now as ever before. At the end of each year, most of the clan assembles in Colorado to ski, drink hot chocolate, and sing Hanukkah songs and traditional Czechoslovak carols before a Christmas tree and menorah. We also reminisce. I fear that I have told my tales so many times that the family can recite them word for word, but if so, they are too polite to let me know. If I do lose my mind, they will keep me safe.

WINI SHORE WAS in my sixth-grade class in Great Neck, on Long Island, where my family lived for a year after arriving in the United States. My first week at Wellesley, I walked into political science class and there she was again. We reconnected right away, and our rapport has never flagged through the many stages our lives have since taken. We started out comparing outfits and boys, then watched as our children played together, then our grandchildren. Our bond was sustained by the many interests we share and by our loyalty to the same causes. For as long as I can remember, Wini has been a champion of women's issues, a trait that served her well in her career as a consultant on work and family policy. I don't suppose any friendship fully reaches the ecclesiastical standard of "all desires known and from whom no secrets are hid," but, for me, Wini comes close.

Down the hall from the room where I lived at Wellesley were two other girls who became longtime buddies. Susan Dubinsky from St. Louis was the kind of student who inspired envy in English class because she understood *The Sound and the Fury* and didn't have to read a Shakespeare line five times to figure out what it meant. She also wrote poems alive with haunting images, seductive rhythms, and words that rhymed when she wanted them to. Now Susan Dubinsky Terris, she is one of America's best poets and has twice as many grandchildren as I have.

Emily Cohen was a child of New York who was attracted to politics and became an outspoken feminist. She invited me to spend the occasional weekend at home with her family, where she introduced me to the Bronx outlet of the legendary Loehmann's, a shrine for bargain hunters. While I had wanted to become a journalist, Emily made good on that ambition, specializing on Asia and reporting for British television and, for more than twenty years, *The Economist*. Along the way, she wrote firsthand accounts of the Chinese Cultural Revolution, the Bangladeshi War of Independence, and the rivalry between India and Pakistan.

When we are young, our universe is confined by the boundaries of crib, playpen, and home. As we grow, it widens by virtue of travel, exploits, and the acquisition of friends. As we age, it begins again to diminish. For as long as possible, I prefer a big world. One obstacle to that desire is the fact that companions don't last forever.

Emily was taken by a brain tumor not long after I left the State Department. In 2011, Gerry Ferraro, the gutsy and combative political trailblazer, succumbed to myeloma. Four years later, leukemia claimed the polling guru Andrew Kohut, founding director of the Pew Research Center. Andy and I had often shared ideas about what questions to include in Pew's wide-ranging surveys. He was the world's foremost authority on what people everywhere were thinking, yet he was always curious to learn more.

Evelyn Lieberman also died in 2015. She had served as my undersecretary of state for public diplomacy but made her mark as a confidante for a mini-galaxy of leaders in my generation and as a counselor to scores of younger people, as well. The dignitaries who spoke at her memorial service included Bill and Hillary Clinton, Joe Biden, Marian Wright Edelman, David Skorton (the secretary of the Smithsonian Institution), and me. She was a woman of many qualities, honesty above all, and known for adding salt to her words but never mincing them.

Two years later, at eighty-nine, Zbigniew Brzezinski, my professor and mentor, passed away. I had many recollections of him, including my terror at the possibility of turning in a paper for class with his name misspelled. (I made sure I never did). Hard to forget as well was the long ago party he hosted during which the men donned horse costumes and I, like a lady at Ascot, sported a replica of Audrey Hepburn's gown from *My Fair Lady*. Our whole group could be silly then and had no thought of becoming old.

Loved ones who depart leave holes that cannot be patched up. Their absence does not stop us, when something dramatic happens, from wanting to get in touch with them to compare impressions. When a new idea pops into our heads, we would like to share it and see what they think. For a time, the urge to contact lingers, like a reflex awaiting the stimulus to respond. But then the phone rings and we realize whose voice won't be on the other end of the line. At holiday celebrations, theirs is the laughter no one hears. That is why so many songs are written about memory.

I mentioned earlier that I spent my first week as ex-secretary of state at a spa in Mexico with two friends. These were Wini and Susan. After we returned from that trip, Susan wrote a prose poem about the three of us relaxing amid "newspapers, books, shoes, half-empty wine glasses, sweat socks and mugs of Red Zinger tea—an adult version of our college rooms where we've (again!) strewn our clothes everywhere, walked around in various states of undress complaining about our figures, discussing laundry but not doing it." The essay includes her account of our plot to escape the spa's lean cuisine by slipping through the gates in pursuit of a fat-laden Mexican feast, complete with mariachi band. An uplifting picture? Maybe not. But I remember it well.

FOURTEEN

Digging Out

NEAR THE BEGINNING of President Bush's second term, I attended a dinner of former secretaries of state in honor of the new one, Condoleezza Rice. Like the other guests, I was presented with a small crystal piano as a party favor. The gesture put me in mind of the symbols we use to hint at our identities. Condi had been a music major and was still a superb pianist. I had a personal connection to her through my father, who had taught her as an undergrad at the University of Denver and served as a mentor on her PhD dissertation. At my father's funeral (in 1977), I noticed among the floral gifts an unusual piano-shaped planter. My mother explained that it had been sent by my father's favorite student. In 1987, I tried to recruit Rice for the presidential campaign of Michael Dukakis only to discover that she was a member of the other party. Now she was secretary of state and would be called on to bring to the global stage all the skill and discipline that enabled her to excel at the keyboard.

GEORGE W. BUSH had campaigned for reelection in 2004 on a platform that included deeper tax cuts, a scheme to partially privatize Social Security, and immigration reform. The president's political advisers hoped to create a permanent Republican majority by according citizens more control over their retirement savings and by convincing the country's burgeoning Latino population that the GOP had its back. Whatever the merits of these proposals, Bush's blueprint for an "opportunity society" went straight from the White House into the shredder. Seniors rebelled against any proposed tinkering with their retirement insurance; conservatives had no interest in helping illegal immigrants become citizens; and the already gargantuan budget deficit made further tax cuts a nonstarter. Worse still, the administration botched its response to Hurricane Katrina, a storm that in August 2005 laid waste to much of the Gulf Coast and nearly drowned New Orleans.

Internationally, the tidings were equally gloomy. In Afghanistan, the Taliban, in disarray just a couple of years earlier, had recovered and gone on the offensive. Between 2004 and 2006, the number of bombs detonated by the insurgents doubled, armed assaults on government and allied troops tripled, and suicide bombings quadrupled. Despite billions of dollars spent to recruit and train the Afghan military, the government was forced to cede control of much of the southeastern quadrant of the country. What had begun as a simple "quick in, quick out" mission to uproot terrorists would soon become America's longest war.

This didn't have to happen. In the words of Pulitzer Prize–winning journalist Steve Coll: "Military history is rife with examples of generals and presidents who squander strategic advantage by failing to press a battlefield triumph to its conclusion. Here was the same story again, involving not only complacency but also inexplicable strategic judgment, fractured decision making, and confusion." Bush and his team should have made sure of their first war, in Afghanistan, before assuming the burdens of a second, in Iraq.

As for that second war, the bombing of a venerable Shiite mosque in February 2006 signaled the start of a furious round of hostilities between Shia and Sunni militias. The chaos enabled al-Qaeda to attract new recruits and shake up the entire country. Each morning on the streets and in the alleyways of Baghdad, wary residents came across the modern-day victims of a medieval religious schism contested now by means of explosives, automatic weapons, and, in the grisliest of cases, power drills.

Bush stoutly defended his decision to oust Hussein but later admitted that the "summer of 2006 was the worst period" of his presidency.

He acknowledged that many people had grown tired of his administration and wrote that he felt as if he had an anvil on his shoulders when meeting with military families, visiting the wounded, and writing condolence letters to the loved ones of those who had died.

To its credit, the administration did not deceive itself that all was well. In her memoir, Rice wrote that when Bush asked her to take charge of Foggy Bottom, she told him "we had repair work to do with our allies and that we'd need to reaffirm the primacy of diplomacy in our foreign policy. That would also mean reaffirming the role of the secretary of state as the principal agent of the development and execution of that policy."

This was a change in tune. After four years of undermining and disregarding the State Department, White House officials concluded that the time had come for a more traditional approach. Even then, the president was reluctant to make major changes in personnel.

If Bush had truly desired a clean break, he might have persuaded his vice president, Dick Cheney, to refrain from joining him in the run for a second term. To some, the veep was an appealing figure: he dressed informally whenever he could, looked like the westerner he was, possessed a courteous manner, and didn't squander words. In contrast to others in the administration, he was less a crusading neoconservative than an old-school hawk. He didn't see much point in trying to democratize foreign governments but had no qualms about running over anyone he thought stood in America's way. In his view, if others feared us, they were more likely to bend to our wishes. This thesis wasn't working out as well as he hoped, however, and Cheney was blamed by many for pushing the United States into a disastrous war, endorsing the utility of torture, and poisoning relations with longtime allies. The vice president was conscious enough of his image, and sufficiently familiar with *Star Wars*, to dress his dog one Halloween as a Dark Lord of the Sith.

As for Rice, Bush was comfortable in her presence, appreciated her discretion, and didn't hold her responsible for the bonfire of male vanities that had singed his first term. The chief executive and his new secretary of state shared a devotion to physical fitness and a firm faith in the merits of political freedom. Both were sincere in believing that their intentions, to them so obviously benign, would be recognized as such by others.

With Cheney and Rice remaining on board, and the irascible Donald Rumsfeld still in charge at the Pentagon, the new Bush team had much in common with the old. Not until November 2006, following a Democratic victory in the midterm elections, did Bush accept Rumsfeld's resignation, appointing in his place the quietly capable and far less ideological Robert Gates.

By then, Rice had launched what she referred to as "transformational diplomacy"—an attempt to reclaim the high ground after years of headlines about Guantanamo, waterboarding, and degrading prison photos. With much fanfare, the administration sought to mend the rupture that had opened between the United States and Europe, and to pick up where Bill Clinton had left off six years before in bargaining with North Korea and leaders in the Middle East. The initiatives showed that the United States had not abandoned the search for multilateral solutions, but scored no breakthroughs because the specific ideas put forward by the Bush team lacked creativity and came too late.

More positively, toward the end of 2006, the president began to rethink his Iraq strategy. In the process, he did much of what he had failed to do prior to invading Baghdad. He consulted extensively with Iraqi leaders and with U.S. military and civilian experts. He asked probing questions of the intelligence community and took care to develop a plan that had political and economic as well as military dimensions. Instead of rushing to judgment, he delayed a decision several times while studying alternatives. The plan he announced sent roughly 21,000 additional U.S. troops to Iraq with a mandate to help Sunni Muslim factions who opposed terrorists and who were open to reconciliation with the government, including its Shiite leadership. This "surge," as it was called, proved effective at reducing sectarian violence and led to a commitment negotiated by

Bush for the withdrawal of U.S. troops from Iraq no later than the end of 2011.

With his job approval rating down to about 30 percent during his final two years in office, the president and his advisers began to compare their administration to that of Harry Truman. Truman had also been plagued by sub-basement poll numbers, in his case because of a sluggish economy, a seemingly endless war in Korea, and the nation's hunger for change after almost twenty years of Democrats in the White House. Historians, however, have a generally positive view of Truman. They give him credit for laying the institutional groundwork for the postwar world, standing up to the Soviets during the Berlin crisis, and reinforcing civilian control of the military.

To me, the comparison between Truman and Bush seemed a stretch. Among the hats I was now wearing was that of president of the Harry S. Truman Scholarship Foundation, created by Congress in 1975, following Truman's death. I had always had a warm spot for the thirty-third president because he was the chief executive when, in 1948, I arrived in America and because of his skill in handling multiple international crises simultaneously. He showed how the United States could lead while also sharing responsibility with others through alliances and global institutions. When I was secretary of state, I worked with Congress to name the State Department's building in his honor.

Bush's team argued that scholars would eventually see in their president the same perseverance and sound judgment that characterized Truman. Rice told an audience in London: "I know we've made tactical errors—thousands of them, I'm sure. But when you look back in history, what will be judged is, did you make the right strategic decisions? And if you spend all your time trying to judge this tactical issue or that tactical issue, I think you miss the larger sweep."

She was surely correct that the Bush administration's place in history will be determined by "the larger sweep." I doubt, however, that strategic acuity will be viewed as among the president's outstanding attributes. The Iraq decision alone would seem to disqualify him.

Bush's strengths could be found in his personal qualities—his charm, sunny disposition, and desire to do what he thought was right. With bipartisan support from Congress, he made a hefty investment in fighting HIV/AIDS in Africa and, if not sidetracked by Cheney, might have shown at least some leadership on climate change. He also had progressive ideas on immigration, worked hard, and never shirked his responsibilities.

Presidents, however, are not graded on effort alone. In the end, Bush was betrayed by his own instincts and by advisers who underestimated the limits on American power and misread the motivations of leaders in the Middle East. As president, Bush was resolved to separate himself from his father's legacy and be his own man. Sadly, foreign policy was not for him the best arena in which to display independence.

Since leaving the White House, Bush has joined Bill Clinton in a series of constructive diplomatic and humanitarian ventures and has spoken eloquently in support of a return to civility in public discourse. He also put together a moving volume of portraits that he painted of American military veterans. In 2017, during a conference at his presidential library, he gave me a copy. The images are haunting and, especially given the artist's lack of prior experience, skillfully done.

MY FIRST TWO books, *Madam Secretary* and *The Mighty and the Almighty*, had performed well enough in stores to lure me into considering a third. While the Bush administration was laboring through the final lap of its time in office and the campaign to succeed it was taking shape, I considered what I might say if given the chance to advise the victorious candidate, whether Republican or Democrat. The result was *Memo to the President Elect: How We Can Restore America's Reputation and Leadership*.

The book begins, in parallel with my course at Georgetown, by describing the national security tools available to any chief executive. I then offer suggestions to the incoming president on choosing a staff and on dealing with Congress and the press. Included are chapters on how to make the most effective use of force, intelligence, sanctions, and diplomacy. Along the way, I point out that some presidents (or future presidents) were more adept at bargaining than others. When Ulysses Grant was eight, or so the story goes, he received permission from his father to buy a horse. The youngster walked a mile to the nearest farm, approached its owner, and said, "Papa says I may offer you twenty dollars for a colt, but if you don't take that, I am to offer twenty-two and a half, and if you won't take that, to give you twenty-five." Transaction complete, the apprentice diplomat rode home happily, though with empty pockets.

The book also examines the many questions that the winner of the 2008 presidential election would have to confront in regions of disharmony and tension. Why, for example, do so many Arabs and Israelis declare their desire for peace and then do all they can to make a resolution of their differences impossible? How did Iran become our enemy and Saudi Arabia our friend? How can the United States peacefully accommodate the rise of China while protecting its own interests and those of its allies in Asia? And most urgently: what must be done to prevent terrorist ideologies from spreading not only from one country to the next but also from the current generations onward?

My hope in exploring these and other puzzles was to give readers a deeper understanding of world events. Like individuals, countries often act for reasons they are reluctant to acknowledge and proclaim principles they ignore in their own actions. I wanted to help Americans understand why some objectives are harder to achieve than they might think and why U.S. intentions are not always taken at face value. I also describe the mechanics of how important policy decisions are reached and why they can be so difficult to carry out. To that end, I cite several presidents who made promises that backfired or gave orders that weren't followed. Among them was John Kennedy who, during the thirteen taut days of the Cuban Missile Crisis, issued half a dozen instructions to his military commanders that were either misinterpreted or ignored—this despite the possibility that even a small mistake might trigger a nuclear war.

Looking back, I am chagrined to see that in the book's prologue, I drew a dismissive contrast between the significance of the subjects covered in the memo I was writing and the kind of routine communication most frequently found in Washington. To illustrate what I meant by a trivial memo, I cited those "outlining, for example, a federal agency's new policy on . . . the retention of e-mails."

If only my crystal piano had been a crystal ball.

FIFTEEN

Making of the President 2008

"COULD YOU PLEASE call her?"

"Okay, sure, we can talk about foreign policy."

"No, she doesn't care about that. She loves to knit."

The time was December 2007; the place, Iowa. I was volunteering as a surrogate for Hillary Clinton in the days preceding the first formal balloting of the 2008 presidential race. My job was to tout Clinton's experience in government and to vouch for her credentials as a future commander in chief. Because the Iowa caucuses are at the head of the line, campaigns strive to identify and track every potential vote. Hence, my phone call.

"So, I hear you enjoy knitting," I began.

From there, the woman and I had the most cordial of conversations about purling, joining, ribbing, slip stitches, figure eight casts, and warm woolen mittens, interspersed with asides on my part about how much Hillary was counting on her support and what a fine president the senator would make. After about forty minutes, I bid farewell to my new friend and sent word to the campaign that I expected the lady who loved to knit would caucus for Hillary. Just as swiftly, the woman called a reporter to say that she remained undecided.

EARLY IN 2007, Barack Obama informed me that he planned to run for president and asked that, should I not endorse him, at least to refrain from publicly backing another. I told him that I was sorry and would be supporting Clinton, a decision he had no doubt anticipated and accepted without any hint of rancor. I had a high regard both for Obama and several of the other Democratic contenders, but my bonds with Hillary were tight. We had met about twenty years earlier when she spoke at a fund-raiser for the Children's Defense Fund, after which I introduced myself to her as a fellow graduate of Wellesley. In 1995, when she was First Lady, we collaborated in planning America's role in the Fourth World Conference on Women. The event was held in Beijing, where Hillary managed to rebuke the host government for its poor record on human rights while still avoiding a major diplomatic breach. The following year, when on separate official trips, we met in Prague where we were entertained by the recently widowed Václav Havel. With the president as our escort, we strolled through Wenceslas Square and visited the Old Jewish Cemetery. Hillary and I also took a Fourth of July boat ride during which we conversed amiably above the sound of fireworks and the chatter of gulls while gliding atop the delicate little waves of the Vltava River.

Our friendship established, the First Lady and I got together socially on numerous occasions in New York and Washington and had long talks. One evening, the American-born Queen Noor of Jordan joined us in the White House dining room. I had a link to the queen through her parents, whom I knew, and because she had attended the same middle school in Washington as my daughters. A few months previously, I had watched Noor's husband, then gravely ill, prevail upon Arab and Israeli negotiators to settle their differences and thereby "fulfill the responsibility you have to your peoples and especially to your children." Cancer soon claimed the king's life, but time has only magnified the poignancy of his words.

The night of our dinner, Clinton, Noor, and I shared thoughts on world affairs, writing books, relationships with men, and the strains— more for them than for me—of always being in the public eye. The queen had long been among the world's most famous women, known for her thoughtful commitment to charitable works, her beauty, and her fairy-tale romance with King Hussein. No one, however, had experienced a more intense level of scrutiny from the media than Hillary Clinton. Every project she undertook, every opinion she expressed, every interview she gave, and even every change in her hairstyle was chewed over by columnists, TV pundits, and radio talk show hosts. Wherever she went, she was the center of attention. The miracle is that she hadn't become either a self-absorbed diva or a lunatic. As we dug into our final course (chocolate, fruit pie, *and* ice cream), I wondered how she had remained so normal to those who saw her up close. The reason, I supposed, lay in her past.

HILLARY RODHAM WAS born in Chicago, the capital of Middle America, around the middle of the twentieth century. She had middle-class parents, received a middle-class upbringing, and was a Brownie, a prodigious earner of Girl Scout merit badges, and a nickel-by-nickel fund-raiser for charitable events. She played softball for a team sponsored by a candy brand (Good & Plenty), went skating on the frozen Des Plaines River, and possessed the shiny optimism typical of well-cared-for children in that time and place. She was, however, neither pampered nor sheltered. In her memoir *Living History*, Hillary writes that after moving into a neighborhood at age four, she was reluctant to leave her house for fear of being bullied by Suzy, a girl who lived nearby. Finally, her mother ordered her to go outside and play, with permission to hit back if Suzy struck first. Not long after, Hillary returned in triumph, "I can play with the boys now," she announced, "and Suzy will be my friend."

Young Rodham's below-average eyesight was more than offset by her intelligence and nerve. Beginning in elementary school, she was an insatiable learner, spurred on by her interest in the community and guided by the "do all the good you can" doctrine espoused by the leader of her United Methodist youth group. Of staunch Republican stock, she helped her party try to prove that John Kennedy had won the 1960 election only because of voter fraud in Chicago. Registration lists in hand, Hillary wandered alone around the city's rough South Side, knocking on doors, asking questions, checking names against addresses, and even venturing into a bar. She was thirteen.

In 1959, the year I graduated from Wellesley, the big news was the

Greeting my successor, Colin Powell, at the State Department in January 2001.

Lifelong companions: my brother, John Korbel, and my sister, Kathy Silva.

Denver University's Josef Korbel School of International Studies, named for our father. Here his image (with pipe) looms above my left shoulder. Next to me (seated) are Kathy and John.

Josef Korbel in the classroom (c. 1960).

Our mother, Anna "Mandula" Korbel (1945). Father called her "the most talkative girl in Bohemia." We remember her with love as a worrier and protector.

Růžena Spieglová, our maternal grandmother.

A quartet of Albright women: with my daughters, Anne, Katie, and Alice.

The next wave: my grandchildren in 2008. *From left:* Maddie, Daniel, Ellie, David, Ben, Jack.

State Department portrait: art imitates reality (or is it the other way 'round?).

My partner in democracy, John McCain—owner of a warm smile and an unyielding conscience. I miss both.

To Madeleine Albright
With best wishes,
Laura Bush   *George Bush*

Honored to be at the White House with my mentor, Zbigniew Brzezinski, and our hosts, President George W. Bush and First Lady Laura Bush.

"Madeleine and Her Exes" in Morocco (2018). We may lack power, but we will be heard.

The ex-mins at play. That's Portugal's Jaime Gama raising my left hand.

Commencement address at Scripps College (2016). Graduation speeches are the hardest to get right.

Ready for college, my senior year (1958).

Best friends: on my right, Wini Shore Freund; on my left, Susan Dubinsky Terris.

Signing books. A greeting, a signature, then another, and another. Great fun, but the light at the end of the tunnel is carpal.

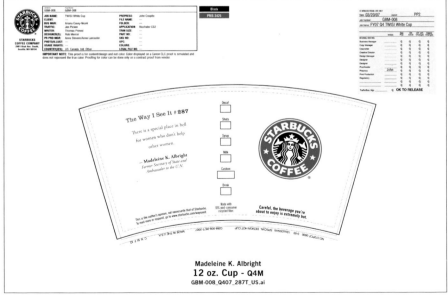

The Way I See It # 287

There is a special place in hell for women who don't help other women.

— Madeleine K. Albright
Former Secretary of State and Ambassador to the U.N.

Madeleine K. Albright
12 oz. Cup - Q4M
GBM-008_Q407_287T_US.ai

Brimstone with your coffee?

opening of the Saint Lawrence Seaway, the entry into the union of Alaska and Hawaii, and the introduction of the Barbie doll. Hillary received her diploma at the tail end of a far stormier decade, a period in which America nearly came apart. The country watched in ago-nized disbelief as JFK was murdered in 1963 and, five years later, the Rev. Dr. Martin Luther King Jr. and Robert Kennedy were struck down within the space of two months. Meanwhile, demonstrations on behalf of racial justice and against the war in Vietnam reflected tensions in many cities and on campuses, leading to incidents of vio-lence and causing some universities to cancel classes and shut down.

In this atmosphere, students at Wellesley demanded and were given the right for the first time to have one of their own speak at commencement—Hillary being the obvious choice. In her remarks, she warned that the weight of fear that had descended over the country would lift only when the generations began again to trust one another. She argued that people in power should not feel threat-ened by those who, like her, questioned traditional attitudes and in-stitutions. She defended the legitimacy of social protest and said that the rising cohort would not be satisfied with politics as the art of the possible; instead, it would strive for what conventional wisdom sug-gested couldn't be done. Her speech caught the attention of several major newspapers and was cited in two of the nation's leading mag-azines: *Time* and *Life*. Hillary spent the summer after graduation in Alaska, where she earned a paycheck by slicing open freshly caught salmon then removing their guts.

Over the years, I have heard people insist that Hillary would never have become well known had she not bumped into a student in the Yale Law Library whom she thought resembled a Viking. But Bill Clinton had nothing to do with Hillary's election as president of the student government at Wellesley or with her acclaimed graduation speech. He didn't help her to gain admittance to Yale Law School or to land a job as staff lawyer for the Nixon impeachment investigation on Capitol Hill. He didn't contribute to her work for the Children's Defense Fund or the scholarly articles she wrote in support of its reform-minded agenda. Ms. Rodham's career was sailing along well before her Viking appeared. Bill Clinton didn't invent Hillary (nor did he ever claim to have done that); in fact, he may have slowed her down.

Later, as First Lady, this diligent woman was not able to please everyone or, at times it seemed, anyone. When she answered questions about floral arrangements and holiday decorations, activists accused her of reinforcing gender stereotypes. When the president put her in charge of his mammoth health care initiative, the hidebound raged at her presumption. During the administration's first years, Hillary's time as a partner at the Rose Law Firm in Little Rock crept back to haunt her when one former associate, Vince Foster, committed suicide, and a second, Webb Hubbell, pled guilty to wire fraud and went to jail.

These incidents, and others, gave birth to stereotypes about Hillary that would prove impossible to shed. Sexism undeniably played a role. William Safire, a widely read polemicist for the *New York Times*, and a man famed for choosing his words with care, called Hillary "a congenital liar," not because he had evidence but because he thought the phrase clever. Clinton's dilemma was that she could not be all things to a nation deeply split about what it wanted her to be. Traditionalists didn't think a First Lady should be involved in politics. Those who yearned for a feminist icon couldn't understand why she had agreed to change her last name or, worse, stayed loyal to Bill despite the straying. Those who thought a woman should be deferential found that she was not, and those urging her to lead a revolution found that she would not.

Hillary's decision, in 2000, to run for the Senate from New York State was her declaration of independence. By taking that step, she showed the mettle of someone unafraid to fail, the confidence to have a career of her own, and the toughness required to do well in the political arena. More important, once elected, she performed. Her celebrity would have made it easy for her to hog the spotlight in the Senate had she chosen to do so, but instead she defied expectations and fit in. The lingering trauma of the 9/11 attacks reinforced her hawkish side, and as a member of the Armed Services Committee, she supported military families as she had also done while First Lady. She forged partnerships with Republican senators on significant but less-than-flashy issues and participated diligently in hearings that many of her colleagues didn't bother to attend. In the stable of hackneyed political analogies, she was a workhorse not a show horse. In 2006, when running for reelection, she carried all but four of New York's sixty-two counties.

I HAD LOOKED forward to the 2008 presidential campaign because I sincerely believed that my party could do a much better job than the Republicans who had been in power for almost eight years. I also knew that I would be welcome to participate in Hillary's effort, which I was sure would bring down barriers.

By then, Barack Obama's capacity to excite was no secret. I had been in the room during his electrifying keynote address at the 2004 Democratic Convention and had testified before committees on which he served; everyone could see that he brought his own spotlight. After I wrote my book on religion and foreign policy, I received letters (with many exclamation points) from correspondents who thought Obama so "too good to be true" that he must therefore be the Antichrist. According to the Book of Revelation, I was informed, the Antichrist was prophesied to be a man, roughly forty years old, of Muslim descent. By dint of his craftiness and charm, this devilish creature aims to hoodwink billions by spreading false hopes for world peace. Once in power, he will show his true colors and DESTROY EVERYTHING!!! I replied to this nonsense by saying that I had met Obama and was impressed by him. They said, "Of course you were. That proves our point."

Although Hillary sprang from the campaign's starting gate as a legitimate betting favorite, Obama was never the long shot many at the time portrayed him to be. His racial heritage drew attention, but what made him a formidable contender was his cool demeanor and his ability to make being smart charismatic. More significantly, he had voiced opposition to the Iraq War five months before the conflict began. This was a lever he could use against Hillary, who along with many other leading Democrats had voted to authorize the president to take military action should diplomatic alternatives fail. Her vote, though defensible at the time—I, for one, defended it—looked much worse in light of the Bush administration's rush to war, its discovery that Iraq did not possess prohibited weapons, and its subsequent mismanagement of affairs in Baghdad. The emotions Iraq aroused among Democratic voters gave Obama the broom he needed to sweep aside concerns about his lack of experience in public office. Seasoning was a virtue only if it led to good decisions, and on the paramount issue of war, his judgment had been validated.

In January 2008, I attended an Iowa caucus on Clinton's behalf. The outcome for her was not what I had hoped, but observing the process was intriguing, nonetheless. The caucuses are held in school gymnasiums or community halls. As the long winter night descends, neighbors come in from the cold to greet one another, listen to short speeches, and split into groups according to their choice of candidates. If a group is too small, its members must disperse, but can still pledge their allegiance elsewhere. This shifting around is often where the contest is decided. In the caucus I witnessed, the Obama representatives used calculators to figure out exactly where and when to pounce on orphaned voters. The Clinton loyalists distributed home-made cookies. In the showdown between cookies and calculators, technology won.

Later that night, when speaking at a hotel in Des Moines, Hillary accepted the loss. I was among those standing nearby, trying to keep my upper lip stiff. The next morning, commentators drew a contrast between the multiracial gaggle of Millennials surrounding Obama in his moment of triumph and the not-so-young types (exhibit one: M. Albright) onstage with his opponent. Obama represented the future, we were told, while Hillary and her gang were yesterday's news. The comparison was unfair—Clinton had backers of all colors and ages—and I didn't feel I owed an apology to anyone for being born so early. During the remainder of the primary election season, however, I avoided the cameras when she was onstage. To campaign arbiters, old was out, and the senator from New York, after Iowa, was surely headed in the same direction.

Yet she refused to quit. Throughout the campaign, she held her own in debates with Obama, whose mantra of hope and change was undeniably inspirational but whose policies, when picked apart by someone as knowledgeable as Hillary, were less than groundbreaking. Further, Clinton helped herself by doing precisely what a candidate, especially a woman, is not supposed to do. During a meeting with voters in Portsmouth on the day before the New Hampshire primary, she was asked how she managed to remain upbeat despite setbacks. She replied that "It's not easy, and I couldn't do it if I didn't passionately believe it was the right thing to do." With her voice cracking and her eyes appearing to well up, she added softly, "You know, this is very personal for me. It's not just political. It's not just public. I see what's happening, and we have to reverse it." She continued: "Some people think elections are a game, lots of who's up or who's down. It's about our country. It's about our kids' futures. And it's really about all of us together."

The consensus reaction was that she had, by almost weeping, blown her last chance. Like many others in my generation, I thought back to the 1972 campaign, also in New Hampshire, when tears (or melting snow) trickled down the cheek of the Democratic frontrunner, Ed Muskie. I was a Muskie partisan and almost shed tears myself when his candidacy was derailed by the display. Hillary, however, received a boost. Despite her gender, no one doubted the steel in her spine. Her problem was the opposite of what most women face. Voters had wanted to know if she had emotions that were real and that she would be willing to express in public. Her words in Portsmouth evinced an unscripted sincerity that hadn't come through previously.

Hillary scored a stunning win in New Hampshire, setting the

stage for an intraparty duel that would continue for months. I did my best to clear my schedule.

PEOPLE WHO SPEND most of their time in Washington and fancy themselves experts on politics should escape the capital whenever they can. The results of a phone survey tell one far less about American attitudes than sharing a bucket of fried chicken with voters who may or may not get by on a fixed income, ride a bus to their jobs, rely on their local library for access to a computer, wash their clothes at a Laundromat, have relatives sleeping on the couch, play the lottery, shop almost exclusively at discount stores, lag behind on their credit card payments, have at least one child in the military or police, love to hunt or fish, and, at a ball game, actually sing "The Star-Spangled Banner." The majority of Americans check at least some of these boxes; many pundits don't. Speaking personally, if I went to a ball game, I would sing.

In Michelle Obama's memoir, there is a lovely description of her first ventures into rural living rooms to speak on behalf of her husband's campaign. There she is, five feet eleven inches tall, African American, a lawyer, a product of the Ivy League, and a city dweller all her life, speaking to people who had never before set eyes on someone like her. Yet, simply by sharing her life story, she found much in common—a father with a blue-collar job, a stay-at-home mom who was active in the PTA, a beloved piano teacher, and friends with big dreams. This process of finding connections across differences is how democracies must work if they are to thrive.

In the end, I didn't enjoy the 2008 campaign as much as I had hoped, especially the primaries. Friends were lined up on both sides of the divide, including veterans of the Clinton administration who wrote articles disparaging Hillary in terms they must have known were untrue. Shame on them, I sniffed, but then there I was on national television accusing Obama of being naïve for advocating direct talks with the leaders of Iran. I had negotiated with North Korea, for Pete's sake. My only excuse is that the talking points developed during almost any political campaign can sully one's soul.

Even more disturbing was the feeling I had when knocking on doors and giving short talks in central Pennsylvania, remote from the large urban areas of Philadelphia and Pittsburgh. I was encouraged that voters were receptive, and indeed, Clinton would win these areas handily. What unsettled me was my fear that a significant number of these citizens were supporting her largely because Obama is black. No one came right out and said it, but my antennae go on alert when people are adamant about their intentions without being articulate about their reasons.

The Illinois senator did, however, have offsetting advantages. First, much of the press was all aquiver about him because of his personality and because they liked the narrative of an upstart taking on the presumed establishment candidate, albeit with half or more of the party hierarchy behind him. To my dismay, Ted and Caroline Kennedy endorsed Obama, as did John Kerry, Al Gore, and, more important, Oprah Winfrey. Second, Obama had assembled a talent-rich staff that began early and remained on message throughout. Many insurgent campaigns fall apart because of internal rivalries, a lack of discipline, and an inability to cope with pressure. His did not. He also had an edge in that those who signed up to work for him did so out of conviction, not because they were confident from the outset that he would prevail. Hillary's campaign was bolstered by many true believers, but her early front-runner status also attracted opportunists hoping for an easy ride to the White House. Obama's campaign was sleek and disciplined; Hillary's was skilled and bloated.

On June 7, after months of wins slightly outweighed by losses, Clinton conceded, arguing that her opponent had proven by his strength and grit that the United States was ready for an African American president. As for women, she told supporters, "Although we weren't able to shatter that hardest, highest glass ceiling this time, thanks to you, it's got about eighteen million cracks in it. And the light is shining through like never before, filling us all with the hope and the sure knowledge that the path will be a little easier the next time."

She was right that there would be a next time, wrong that it would be easier.

OBAMA'S NARROW VICTORY in the primaries left him with a relatively open road to the Oval Office. His strategy for getting there was twofold: tie John McCain, the Republican nominee, to the unpopular Bush and avoid mistakes that might call into question his own qualifications. With Clinton out of the race, I did all I could to help him.

Senator McCain had been a more attractive candidate in 2000, when he first ran, than he was by 2008. Especially compared to Obama, he looked cranky and battered. Beyond appearances, he found himself in the same trap Al Gore had been in eight years earlier and that Hillary would try in vain to escape eight years later. His party had held the White House for two terms, and now a majority of the electorate felt eager for change.

McCain was also a poor salesperson. Like Hillary, he found bragging about himself awkward and didn't get much joy out of campaigning. He honestly didn't see what others saw in Obama. The Arizona senator was determined, however, to run in an honorable manner, and he did. There were a hundred ways to whip up hatred against a black liberal Democrat with the middle name of Hussein, and he didn't indulge in any of them. He even lectured one supporter for calling Obama disloyal.

In late August, McCain took a high dive into Lake Unpredictable by inviting Alaska Governor Sarah Palin to be his running mate. Commentators scratched their heads, but Palin's speech at the Republican Convention in Saint Paul, Minnesota, knocked the roof off the Xcel Energy Center and awakened the hibernating Republican base. For a time, Democrats were unnerved. What would happen to the party's advantage among women? How could we respond to a folksy, wisecracking former beauty queen with a new baby and a husband who looked like a lumberjack? Even I was almost sucked in by Palin's colorful manner of speaking ("Youbetchya") and self-description ("just your average hockey mom"). Predictably, the honeymoon didn't last. Palin showed in interviews that she had paid little attention to events outside Alaska. She was bright and learned quickly, but she was also thrust into a spotlight for which she was unprepared. Instead of being an asset, her presence on the ticket raised damaging doubts about McCain's ability to make good decisions.

The final blow to the Republican campaign was the economic mayhem that rattled the nation and much of the world that fall. The stock market slid, housing prices took a dive, and many a financial empire went belly-up. Obama didn't pretend to have all the answers, but he could credibly assign blame to the other party, which was, after all, supposed to be in charge. McCain, meanwhile, urged people not to worry and called for an emergency meeting at the White House during which he had nothing to say.

I had expected the 2008 election to be historic, and it was. According to my pollster friend Andy Kohut, however, this was not because it represented a break in how Americans thought about the role of government or because of any specific change of perspective regarding events across the globe. "There's no indication that ideology drove this election," said Kohut. "It was driven by discontent with the status quo." The campaign was a triumph for Democrats, but starting in January, it would be their crew, with Barack Obama in the pilot's seat, who would represent the status quo.

SIXTEEN

First Light

A S THE SUN crept above the horizon on January 20, 2009, a million George W. Bush countdown clocks were tossed in Dumpsters, their work done. Hordes of excited men, women, and children assembled in Washington to welcome our forty-fourth president. Bundled against the cold, many carried signs that reflected the jolly mood, but words seemed inadequate to the occasion. Yes, the inauguration was a democratic rite marking the beginning of a new chapter in the nation's history, but this year it was also something more: a day that many had thought they would never live long enough to see. For African Americans especially, Barack Obama's raised hand embodied a moment when "free at last" seemed closer than ever to a description, not merely a hope.

The new president, unsurprisingly, nailed his speech. There were echoes of FDR in his denunciation of greed and a conjuring of JFK in his summons to unity and collective action. Each of his priorities (the economy, health care, the environment, and protection from terror) earned a mention. His choice of a signature phrase, "New Era of Responsibility," was forgettable, but his vision for the nation was infused with grace:

> We know that our patchwork heritage is a strength, not a weakness. We are a nation of Christians and Muslims, Jews and Hindus, and nonbelievers. We are shaped by every language and culture, drawn from every end of this Earth; and because we have tasted the bitter swill of civil war and segregation, and

emerged from that dark chapter stronger and more united, we cannot help but believe that the old hatreds shall someday pass; that the lines of tribe shall soon dissolve; that as the world grows smaller, our common humanity shall reveal itself; and that America must play its role in ushering in a new era of peace.

Aside from the president's remarks, I suspect that everyone had one or two parts of the ceremony they liked best; mine were Aretha Franklin's soaring rendition of "My Country 'tis of Thee" and the eighty-seven-year-old Rev. Joseph Lowery's rainbow-hued benediction: "Help us work for that day when black will not be asked to get back; when brown can stick around; when yellow will be mellow; when the red man can get ahead, man; and when white will embrace what is right." Amen. With a seat near the edge of the platform, I froze along with the rest of the happy crowd and felt wonderful despite losing track of one of my daughters. Cell phones were inoperative in the security zone, so I might have panicked had she not been forty-seven years old.

THE NEXT MORNING, I drove up Wisconsin Avenue to the National Cathedral for the postinaugural prayer service, a faith tradition dating back to 1789 that brings public servants and private citizens together to praise God beneath high ceilings and stained-glass saints. The Cathedral Church of St. Peter and St. Paul is the world's sixth-largest structure of its kind and is guarded by 112 gargoyles (rain diversion devices with a spout) and more than 1,000 grotesques (without a spout), including one in the image of Darth Vader—all meant to repel evil spirits. When my daughters were attending schools affiliated with the church, I served for a while on its governing board. At every meeting, members hailed one another cheerfully, then prayed, then started to bicker—sometimes about the cost of maintaining the gargoyles.

That Wednesday morning, I had a seat to the right facing the altar; on the left were religious dignitaries clad in Roman Catholic and Protestant vestments, tallits and kippahs (yarmulkes), Muslim tunics and abayas, sherwanis and saris. Particularly striking were the representatives of the Orthodox Church, with their ebony beards and loose-fitting cassocks; encircling the neck of each priest was a thick gold chain attached to a cross. The assemblage looked very sixteenth century, and thus right at home in the surroundings. I smiled when President Obama and the First Lady entered, causing the whole diverse group to jump to its collective feet and begin snapping cell phone pictures with the exuberance of high-schoolers on a class trip.

The president, wearing a black suit with a powder blue tie, appeared affable and surprisingly well rested as he and Michelle assumed their seats in the center, next to the Bidens, with the Clintons completing the front row. When all were in place, the cathedral's dean raised his arms in welcome and pointed out that in 1968, Martin Luther King Jr. had delivered his final sermon from the same pulpit. The service that followed was a reminder that, as Dr. King's career had borne witness, God and flag have often been linked in American history despite the technical separation between church and state. From the War for Independence onward, the divine has been appealed to regularly to bless the United States, stand beside her, guide her, and mend her every flaw.

In the sanctuary that morning, this overlap between piety and patriotism was on full display: a soloist squeezed every drop of joyous redemption out of "Amazing Grace"; the preacher observed that at least since King David's time, power has carried with it a moral duty; and the choir sang, "He's got the whole wide world in his hands," referring explicitly to the Almighty and, by inference, to Mr. Obama.

The First Couple, seemingly relieved to attend an event where neither was called on to speak, participated quietly. Bill Clinton, peering at his hymnal through glasses balanced on the end of his nose, sang every hymn with the gusto of the choirboy he had been.

Exiting the cathedral and searching for my car, I reflected on the degree to which Americans have come both to demand too much of our presidents and to exhibit too little respect for the office. There used to be boundaries beyond which partisanship was inherently self-defeating. A politician who was overly strident would be shunned. That is no longer the case, and the blame falls on both parties.

Might Obama be able to remedy this? I thought so at the time. His intelligence was undeniable and his temperament reassuring. For all his self-esteem, he appeared a patient listener, with the capacity to grow while in office. Also, notwithstanding the plethora of words generated by his campaign, he entered office with room for maneuver. As he frankly admitted, his candidacy had been a kind of Rorschach test. Many voters embraced him as an agent of change without inquiring too deeply into the nature of the reforms intended. This vagueness could be helpful to Obama because he had made few specific pledges that he could be faulted for not keeping; the corresponding danger was that many of his followers were imagining a far more profound transformation in American society—and in their own lives—than they were likely to see.

WEEKS EARLIER, I had been driving in Georgetown when my car's phone sounded. I pulled over. On the other end of the line was Hillary Clinton, who said that she had surprising news. Obama had asked her to be secretary of state. She had turned him down, but when he inquired again, she had promised to sleep on the idea. What did I think? I recalled how much we had enjoyed our international travels together and said that she was a natural diplomat who was already on a first-name basis with many global leaders. I warned that heading the State Department required an all-consuming commitment but said that I also couldn't imagine a more rewarding use of her energy.

"You should definitely do it," I told her. "It's even better than being president, because you can spend all your time trying to solve problems across the globe without having to worry about domestic issues like health care."

Hillary replied, "I like worrying about health care."

Hanging up, I was pretty sure she would accept Obama's offer because she was not someone who would back away from a test. This meant that the president would begin his term with a secretary of state who appreciated the value of diplomacy, was admired by many in Congress, and knew the issues. His decision to tap Clinton was further evidence of Obama's confidence. Three years earlier, Doris Kearns Goodwin had written *Team of Rivals*, a classic history about a president who enlisted the help of politicians who were also eager to burnish their reputations. That president, Lincoln, had no fear of being outshone. Neither did Obama.

After our conversation, I lent Hillary a conference room in the Albright Group's office to help her prepare for her Senate confirmation hearing. There was zero chance that she would fail, but neither would she glide through in the manner of World War II hero George Marshall, who in 1947 had been approved as secretary of state roughly three hours after he was officially nominated. With Marshall, the Senate didn't trouble itself even to hold a hearing or have a recorded vote. Clinton, though, could expect tough questioning on everything from the wars in Afghanistan and Iraq to North Korea's nuclear weapons program and the impact of the global financial crisis.

Foreign policy is an inexhaustible subject, and Hillary shares with me the desire to earn good grades. She showed up at our office with a mountain of briefing books to work her way through and did so meticulously. She knew that every ambassador in Washington would be waiting to hear what she had to say about the countries and regions that were of interest to them. She was also aware that the press would scour her words for signals of what the new administration had planned. As for the senators, many would be far less attentive to her thinking than to their own efforts to seize the spotlight. Opportunistic legislators understand that the surest way to attract cameras is to pose hostile questions, turn the "hearing" into a "yelling," and provoke the witness into losing her cool. A wise nominee will respond to each such attempt by smiling, praising the questioner, and agreeing that America is, indeed, a great country. This approach lulls the camera operators to sleep and, with luck, consumes the senator's entire allotment of time. Hillary did her homework well, for she was confirmed by a vote of 94 to 2.

* * *

A PRESIDENTIAL TRANSITION, especially from one party to another, is a unique period in Washington. For Sale signs pop up throughout the metropolitan area as one batch of political appointees leaves town and another starts to trickle in. Many people involved in the winning campaign, even those on the margins, wish to obtain prestigious government jobs. The process for doing so, however, can be opaque. Letters are sent, résumés are compiled, phone calls are made, and then the waiting begins, while rumors fly regarding who is in, when decisions will be made, and how best to influence outcomes.

I have friends who, back in 1977, relieved the tension by preparing a fake employment application for the incoming administration of Jimmy Carter. In deference to the new president's southern roots and devout nature, the document includes space to record the lyrics to "Dixie," describe the difference between cornpone and fatback, and show the dates when the applicant was born for the first time and also the second (born again). Other lines are marked "Position applied for" and "Position you might actually hope to get."

My own period of high anxiety came in 1992, after Bill Clinton won. I was asked to head the transition team for the National Security Council and thought I might be offered a slot either there or at the State Department. I had not been part of the campaign's inner circle, however, so wasn't sure of anything. Waiting for a phone call that refused to come, I shuttled between my home and office, buffing shoes that didn't need polishing and reorganizing files that were already in perfect order. Finally, the call came through, and I went to Little Rock to be unveiled as ambassador-designate to the UN.

In 2009, I was over seventy years old and no longer in the market for a position. That may explain why President-elect Obama chose me to represent him in meetings that winter with the G20 heads of state. I wasn't a threat to anyone. I did, however, hear from people who thought I might be able to assist in brightening their own chances. Dozens of friends, acquaintances, and some total strangers called seeking permission to use my name as a reference or to ask that

I contact the Obama team on their behalf. For those genuinely qualified, I did, and with some success. Even for the many I couldn't help,
I felt sympathy because I have a high regard for public service and
had walked in their shoes. One caller, however, I found aggravating
to the point of being funny. This was her pitch:

> Madeleine, dear, how are you? I'm just calling to say that Her-
> man and I have done well these past few years and so, despite
> the economic catastrophe now under way, don't worry about
> us; we're comfortable. But it just doesn't feel right for me to sit
> on the sidelines when I have so much to contribute and there is
> historic work to be done. It's like a summons to duty that I just
> can't turn down. You of all people should know exactly what I
> mean. So I've decided to allow you to put my name forward for
> an embassy. What do you think? Madrid or Rome would be
> best perhaps, but Asia would be okay if it's Tokyo; we can't do
> Beijing because of Herman's allergies. I could also be undersec-
> retary of state. Just let Hillary know; I'm sure she'll be enthu-
> siastic. I tried to reach her directly and couldn't get through.
> This is a big sacrifice for us, but I owe it to the president, don't
> you agree? When can you let me know?

A WEEK AFTER the inauguration, I was invited to dinner, as was usually the case at some point in January, by Fred and Marlene Malek.
I had known the couple for decades, but they always danced on the
Republican side of the political ballroom. Marlene, less conservative
than Fred, was a champion of cancer research and of women in the
arts. Basically, she rocks. Fred, the son of a Chicago truck driver, was
a former president of Marriott Hotels and Northwest Airlines. He
was a year older than I am, and of Czech and Croat descent. I liked
him in part because he seemed to like me, which counted for a lot,
and because I enjoyed working with him on projects for a group that
Fred organized: the American Friends of the Czech Republic.

The guest list at the Malek residence that Friday night was enough to make a liberal dive under the couch. The first person to show up after me was Jeb Bush, the ex-governor of Florida, about whom there were already rumors (ten days into the Obama presidency) that he would run in 2012 for his father's and brother's old job. Bush was followed through the door by Dick Cheney, Senate Minority Leader Mitch McConnell, former Federal Reserve Board Chair Alan Greenspan, McCain, and Palin. I had never met the Alaska governor and was naturally curious. Everyone wanted to know if she was smart, but there could be no doubt about her charm and the twang that enlivened her every sentence. I shared with her my own impressions of life as a hockey mom, memoirist, and grandmother; from there we veered into some lighthearted banter about Russia, which—contrary to a *Saturday Night Live* vignette featuring Tina Fey—she had never claimed to be able to see from her front yard. After the embarrassments of the last campaign, it was difficult to picture Palin as a future candidate for national office, but I felt she had the personal magnetism to be a force in the media for some time.

While friends were curious about Palin's IQ, the question with Cheney was whether he had horns. He doesn't, but he does have a bad back. I suggested that we sit and so ended up alongside him on a sofa. With both of us searching for a safe topic, we talked about Wyoming, which he calls home and where I spent a memorable holiday, at the Cheyenne Frontier Days rodeo, when in college. Switching gears, I brought up the transition process and how tough it can be to leave a position of power and then watch your successor occupy the office you once filled. Cheney said he had been bothered more in 1977, when Carter defeated Ford, for whom he had served as White House chief of staff. "It hurt worse then," he said, "because we had expected to win."

The issue of the day was the global economic crisis. Between helpings of salad, beef, and fish, the Republicans dismissed President Obama's just-proposed stimulus package as too big, too small, too slow, and, above all, not their idea. If there was hope for a new spirit of bipartisanship in Washington, I did not feel it that night. I had to keep from rolling my eyes when my dinner companions began moaning about the size of the federal deficit, which grows like kudzu when they're in office and for which they never take a shred of responsibility. Mr. Greenspan was sitting next to me, and I naturally tried to mine his fertile brain, but he was as cryptic at the dinner table as he had always been at congressional hearings. His words flowed smoothly enough, but the meaning was hard to pin down. His conclusion, however, was sobering: the economic mess was of a type that happens only once a century, so there was nobody alive who knew how to deal with it. I asked for more wine.

THE 9/11 ATTACKS and subsequent terrorist incidents spawned numerous efforts by civil society to help Muslims and the West clear away misunderstandings. I participated in several such programs, including, three weeks after Obama's inauguration, the U.S.-Islamic World Forum in Qatar. Although ordinarily skeptical about how much a conference of that type can achieve, I arrived in a positive frame of mind. The war in Iraq was winding down, and speculation had begun about a new peace initiative in the Middle East. More important, the United States had a commander in chief who didn't look like any of his predecessors and who would feel no need to defend past errors.

I urged listeners at the forum to consider what Obama's election showed about Americans' ability to overcome historic divisions and suggested that if my country could achieve such a breakthrough, so could other nations. I pointed to the president's willingness to talk frankly to any leader and praised his intention to deliver a major speech to Muslims worldwide. An incoming chief executive has but a short time to establish the tone of his administration. In Qatar, and everywhere else I went in those expectant days, I found audiences eager to hear what Obama would have to say.

SEVENTEEN

Thought and Purpose

As imperialists, the British of a century or two ago had their faults, but as originators of slang, they were unparalleled. To those Englanders of yore, a "think tank" was a synonym for the human brain—logical enough, when you picture it. A new meaning developed during World War II, when the term referred to the hideaway in military headquarters reserved for officers to share secret information and plot their next moves. Postwar, the modern conception came into vogue: a research organization dedicated to public policy.

Not everyone is fond of such bodies, though I can't understand why. To me, the sight of smart people wrestling with life-altering questions is more fun than a puppy.

In the late 1980s and early 1990s, I was president of the Center for National Policy (CNP), a think tank sprightlier than its name. The group's public mandate was to advance the economic and security interests of the United States. Its unspoken purpose was to help Democrats restore their party's credibility after getting thrashed at the polls by Ronald Reagan. My tenure coincided with the fall of the Berlin Wall, a moment when history sped up and dozens of previously undemocratic nations tore off their old uniforms and tried on new ones. I warned my students that although the world had suddenly become freer, it might not, because of the churning, be any less dangerous. Indeed, a rash of conflicts soon broke out as nations and subnational factions sought to assert themselves. CNP had a transformed global landscape to explain, but I had barely begun to reorganize my mind when President George H. W. Bush let the economy trip him up and lost the 1992 election to Bill Clinton, who hired me.

From research organization to government was a well-worn path and one that has traffic moving both ways. After eight years at the State Department, I made the return trip. One of my first stops was a natural, given my affinity for Colorado. The Aspen Institute was founded in 1949 and had since evolved into a house of many intellectual and artistic mansions, featuring projects on music, design, film, photography, books, medicine, global security, and much else. The institute sponsors research, but it is also a convener and, collectively, a doer. While teaching at the University of Denver, my father had been a resource, often giving talks on history and participating on panels.

In 2002, I joined its board of directors and looked forward to my first meeting, which did not go well. I felt as if I had walked into the wrong movie at the Cineplex—in this case, a poorly edited documentary with many topics brought up and none successfully thrashed out. The following year, a new leader took charge, and the Aspen experience evolved from a snooze into an adventure.

I had met Walter Isaacson when I was in government and he was a correspondent for *Time*. A man with rare gifts, he has the ability to command a room, write groundbreaking biographies (Franklin, Einstein, Jobs, da Vinci), and bring people together across every conceivable geographic, social, and intellectual boundary. Under his direction, Aspen established a global presence and inaugurated an Ideas Festival, held each July, where timely issues are scrutinized and prominent personalities are asked to share their thoughts and, occasionally, carry a tune. Details are confidential, but we have seminars that can produce moments one might never expect to see. Only at Aspen could a former secretary of state be observed singing "Hello, Dalai!" to commemorate a visit by the spiritual leader of Tibetan Buddhism.

My involvement with Aspen has remained close under Isaacson's superb successor, Daniel Porterfield, a former president of Franklin &

Marshall College who possesses strong skills as a leader and coordinator of diverse personalities and groups. The connection also dovetails nicely with the course I teach at Georgetown about the process by which national security decisions are made. Research organizations often play a pivotal role in such judgments by giving public officials the information and guidance they need to make smart choices. The value of sound advice, of course, has been a constant through history.

In ancient Egypt, Joseph taught a bewildered pharaoh the right way to interpret his dream about seven fat cows and seven lean. In sixteenth century Britain, William Cecil counseled Queen Elizabeth on how to rule while sidestepping the traps of gender and religious politics. In the nineteenth century, Otto von Bismarck's vision of a united Germany gave shape to the ambitions of Kaiser Wilhelm. Secretary of State John Hay helped William McKinley make America a world power; and then there was Rasputin, who had a salutary effect on Tsarevich Alexei, but otherwise served as a cautionary tale against employing an aide with a dire hairstyle and the nickname "Debauched One."

Gradually, as societies modernized and became more crowded, the demand for expertise outstripped the capacity of any one individual to provide it. Even the brightest counselors had to rely on advisers of their own to help their bosses manage large bureaucracies, adapt to new technologies, interact with distant cultures, maintain favorable public relations, and prepare continually for the surprises that lurked seemingly around every corner. From this litany of needs the think tank emerged—and with it, theories about how to transform the art of civic administration into a science.

To that end, philanthropists invested large sums to develop rules that, if observed, would lead to more capable governments and higher standards of international behavior. The intentions were noble and contributed to advances in rule making and arbitration procedures on which we continue to build today. Not every wish was fulfilled, however. In 1910, a Scottish American steel baron founded the Carnegie Endowment for International Peace in an effort to put an end to armed conflict. Through no fault of the endowment, four years later, in Sarajevo, the Great War began.

A second tycoon, Robert Brookings, made his fortune selling rolling pins, paper bags, and other household necessities to pioneers who had ventured into the wilderness west of the Mississippi River. As a businessman, Brookings was as tough on competitors and as well organized as modern-day Amazon. He anticipated the wants of his customers and then supplied the desired goods with neither a nickel nor a minute wasted. Wishing to share what he had learned, in 1916 he founded the Institute for Government Research, which was dedicated to the efficient management of the national economy. This haven for people wearing green eyeshades soon hooked up with another of the founder's projects, a graduate school, and became the Brookings Institution.

A third think tank had its origin in the collapse of empires and the realignment of nations that followed World War I. Faced by unrest on every front, President Wilson launched "The Inquiry," a band of scholars tasked with designing a postwar order. The all-male enterprise produced Wilson's famous Fourteen Points, while triggering a debate within the United States about the country's proper international role. Weary of war and wary of new commitments, many Americans were eager to turn their backs on global engagement, an attitude that alarmed business and professional leaders as well as the academics who had participated in the Inquiry. Meeting regularly over brandy and cigars, they looked for a means to counter the isolationist trend. Their solution: the Council on Foreign Relations (CFR). To raise funds for the project, former secretary of state Elihu Root went where the money was, writing letters to the thousand richest Americans.

Because of its Wall Street origins, and subsequent financial backing from the Ford, Rockefeller, and Carnegie Foundations, CFR was and still is considered a center of the U.S. foreign policy establishment. As such, it has been the subject of conspiracy theories from left and right, many of which portray it as powerful, highly disciplined, and traitorously eager to make America bow to the dictates of a world government. The allegations are hilarious to anyone who has witnessed a CFR meeting and heard members disagree on just about everything while grumbling that no one listens to them. Despite the complaints, admission to the council has always been prized. Among those I personally nominated for lifetime membership, years ago, was the then-governor of Arkansas, Bill Clinton.

THE FIRST GENERATION of U.S. think tanks produced studies intended for use by leaders regardless of political party. That began to change when, in 1971, the American Enterprise Institute (AEI) prepared a well-argued treatise on federal funding for the proposed supersonic transport aircraft and then didn't release its report until *after* Congress had voted on the project. Why the delay? The AEI president said he had not wanted to influence the vote. Such an attitude, which prized purity over relevance, could not last.

In more recent decades, bipartisan bodies have continued to form, the Center for a New American Security (founded in 2007), being a prime example. During this same period, however, the club of research organizations expanded to make room for a whole new category. Rather than resist partisan warfare, many groups now thrive on it. Conservative stalwarts include the Heritage Foundation and the Family Research Council. Liberals can point to the Institute for Policy Studies and People for the American Way. Libertarians boast of the Cato Institute and a flock of Ayn Rand fan clubs. There are many more.

The ascendance of overtly political think tanks is a mixed blessing, which I admit even though I have been complicit on the Democratic side. Most of the more prominent groups contribute information of value to public discussion. Most are sincere in their beliefs and in their desire to serve the public good. Once partisanship takes hold, however, there is no obvious stopping point. Every faction wants to win the battle of ideas and so looks for arguments that will excite its base and create distance from the opposition. This is the way to attract attention, establish an identity, and raise funds. Unfortunately, the resulting competition can often generate fog where clarity is needed.

In 2013, one liberal group estimated that an immigration reform bill pending before Congress would boost the nation's gross national product by more than a trillion dollars over ten years; a conservative rival concluded that the same bill would cause a net loss of six trillion dollars over fifty years. Each side had its talking points, neither budged, the deadlock persisted, and nothing constructive was done.

Further, as the media stage fills with partisans, quieter actors are drowned out. Like paper enfolding rock in the ancient Chinese hand game, noise defeats reason. When interviewed, I often begin answers by saying, "it's complicated." Why? Because most important issues *are* complicated. However, many people don't want to hear that. Instead, they crave the sound of certainty echoing from either end of the political spectrum. Experts who insist on being cautious, temperate, and precise may also be ignored.

It is true that none of us are objective in all things at all times. I have often told my students that the only completely open mind is an empty one. But just because no organization is pure does not mean that each is the same. There is a critical difference between a think tank that tries to be balanced, checks its facts, and recruits scholars who have a range of perspectives and one whose overriding purpose is to make the case for a pre-existing point of view.

This distinction, which should be obvious, is becoming increasingly blurred as partisans define and peddle their own versions of reality and, in the fervor of competition, try to undercut the whole notion of disinterested research. There is grave danger in the fiction that a professionally conducted study is no more reliable than one that cherry-picks its data to justify slanted conclusions—the political equivalent of a tobacco industry analysis of the health risks of smoking. Public debate, if it is to be rational and informed, depends on facts which, though often subject to more than one interpretation, can usually be pinned down with the right will and sufficient effort.

"Words are grown so false," complains Feste in *Twelfth Night*, "I am loath to prove reason with them." Research organizations should be a remedy to such problems, not a contributor.

* * *

EARLY IN 2009, I flew to Houston to deliver a speech in support of the city's Holocaust Museum. I was interested to learn from the exhibits that the author of *How the Grinch Stole Christmas* had drawn political cartoons during World War II. The rhymes and lines of Dr. Seuss—full name Theodor Seuss Geisel—had enlivened many a story hour with my young daughters. Given all the glorious silliness involving cats in hats and fox in socks, I hadn't known that the writer and illustrator had a more somber side. At the museum, I saw characters drawn in the man's distinctive style warning against Hitler, pointing to the dangers of isolationism, and speaking on behalf of the allied cause. One might fairly debate whether the pen is truly mightier than the sword, or whether one picture is in fact worth a thousand words, but in the hands of Seuss, the blend of image reinforced by language carried undeniable power.

The grim warning reinforced by the drawings and by the Holocaust Museum as a whole had not been far from my mind. The previous year, I had co-chaired with Bill Cohen, the former secretary of defense, a task force on the prevention of genocide. In our report, we made recommendations for how our government, working with others, could best organize itself to stop mass killing. We timed the study's release to coincide with the transition between Bush and Obama, hoping the new administration would incorporate our ideas.

The word *expert* is derived from the Latin *experiri*, or experience. By that standard, our globe has fostered far too many experts on genocide. Even within recent memory, when Yugoslavia broke apart, extreme nationalists moved to seize territory and settle old scores through campaigns of ethnic cleansing and terror. In 1994, Hutu extremists slaughtered their countrymen in Rwanda. Later in the decade, horrific civil wars broke out in Liberia, Sierra Leone, and East Timor. In the early 2000s, the government of Sudan brutally repressed opposition groups in Darfur.

The recurrence of such tragedies caused many to ask if human-caused horrors were an inevitable part of existence or whether we might, through wiser policies and more resolute action, consign them permanently to the past. For Americans, the query touches directly on the nature and extent of our leadership. Given our position in the world, do we have a special responsibility to act on behalf of endangered populations? If so, why, how, and under what circumstances can we fulfill that duty? For me, the task force offered a chance to dig deeply into issues that I had worked on when in government, later taught about, and that continued to gnaw at me. I could not conceive of a more fundamental shared human responsibility than to prevent genocide.

In the think tank world, Bill Cohen and I were a well-matched pair (a Republican man, a Democratic woman) with a proven ability to collaborate. I had known Bill since the 1970s, when he was a U.S. representative from Maine, and I worked for a senator from the same state. Because of our shared coastal constituency, we learned more than we ever thought we would about fish. When I was secretary of state, Bill was in charge of the Pentagon. We had our disagreements but generally got along well, and upon leaving office, organized our afterlives in parallel. He, too, started a consulting outfit and named it after himself. We both gave speeches and worked on books, though he alone dared to try his hand at fiction, penning such thrillers as *Dragon Fire* and *Murder in the Senate*.

Our challenge in putting together a report on genocide was not just to say how appalled we were; based on our knowledge of how governments work, we were determined to identify practical steps. We reviewed case studies from the recent past and concluded that no one in the executive branch in Washington had the job of preventing and responding effectively to humanitarian disasters. We proposed to fix that by designating a White House office to monitor the globe for warning signs and to set off alarms whenever the people of any country appeared at risk. Our goal was the national security equivalent of an AMBER Alert system.

Ordinarily, when a think tank releases a report, the event may be noted briefly in a news report, commented on during a couple of cable shows, and mentioned by a columnist or two. Then, like a passing sunbeam, the study regretably fades to black. Not this time. In August 2011, President Obama identified the prevention of genocide as a national security priority and established an Atrocities Prevention Board (APB) within the executive branch. He directed all federal agencies, including the intelligence community, to cooperate with the board and to respond urgently to early indicators of trouble. Further, he made clear that these steps were based on our task force's recommendations.

Under Obama, the APB was credited with sharpening the American response to potential outbreaks of violence in Burundi, to the civil war in the Central African Republic, and in 2014, to the rescue of endangered Yazidis from terrorists in Northern Iraq. The board also played a role in developing U.S. strategy against the barbarous Boko Haram in Nigeria and in trying to contain and end atrocities directed against Rohingya Muslims in Myanmar (albeit with scant success). The interagency group was not called into action on the Syrian Civil War because that conflict already had the attention, if not effectively so, of top policymakers. More recently, despite the change in administration, a renamed version of the APB remains in place and active.

ABOUT SIX MONTHS after we released our report, Bill Cohen visited the U.S. Holocaust Memorial Museum in Washington, DC. The facility was scheduled to present the premiere of a play written by Bill's wife, Janet Langhart Cohen, envisioning a conversation between Anne Frank and Emmett Till. While Bill waited near the entrance for Janet to arrive, an eighty-eight-year-old man walked into the museum, pulled a rifle from a bag, and fatally shot Stephen Tyrone Johns, the security guard who had just opened the door to greet him. The assailant, who was quickly apprehended, carried with him a notebook in which he had written "The Holocaust is a lie. Obama was created by Jews. Obama does what his Jew owners tell him to do. Jews captured America's money. Jews control the mass media."

The shooter was a navy veteran, reputed to be of well-above-average intelligence, and an admirer of Adolf Hitler.

Where does genocide find its roots? The sobering answer, wherever one lives, is close to home.

EIGHTEEN

The Serpent's Tale

"YOUR NEXT BOOK should be about your pins."

I took a sip of water.

"I'm not kidding. Listen to me. A coffee table kind of book, with lots of pictures and the story of how you used pins as a diplomatic tool. Readers will love it."

I put down my water glass. Stared.

"Be honest. Wherever you go, people come up to you and ask why you're wearing such-and-such a pin. That shows interest. No one has put together a book like that before and definitely no former secretary of state. It'll be educational and show how much fun you can be. What do you think?"

"I think," I said, "that you've lost it. You want the first woman secretary of state to publish a book about her jewelry? I won't do it, not in a million years."

And that, I felt sure, was that.

But Elaine Shocas can be stubborn. When I first met her, in 1986, she had fang marks on her wrist, courtesy of a snake she had encountered while on an election observer mission in the Philippines. She survived; the snake died. In the State Department, Elaine had been my chief of staff, looking out for my interests and often advising me to think thrice before speaking. A former federal prosecutor and aide to Senator Edward Kennedy, she continued to assist in my post-government afterlife. One day in 2004, she came into my office, sat down, and made her case. I said no, but she kept bringing the subject up and I kept telling her she was crazy.

There wasn't any way I would choose to write a book about my pins at a time when America was fighting two wars and I was fully engaged on projects involving poverty, genocide, and the future of democracy. All my life I had wanted to be listened to with respect. Now that my voice was being heard, why would I jeopardize that? I was pretty sure that Henry Kissinger wasn't composing an ode to his ties, and that James Baker wouldn't soon be writing a book about his most flattering suits. Going overboard about pins would be like standing in the middle of Chauvinist Boulevard with a sign reading, "Tread on Me." I wasn't going to do it.

Years passed, and I didn't change my mind. Then more time passed.

IN 2010, EARLY summer:

Secretary Clough, thank you very much for your kind words of welcome. The Smithsonian is our national museum, with a proud history and collections that include everything from the Hope Diamond to dinosaur bones. So you can imagine how grateful I was when the institution chose to put my pins on display—instead of me.

Yes, I had surrendered. Not only had we published a book rich with photographs, *Read My Pins*, but we had also collaborated in a touring exhibition. Starting the previous fall, more than two hundred of my pins had been transported from New York to Little Rock to the Smithsonian Institution in Washington, DC. From there, they would journey to museums in every part of the country, and to most of the libraries dedicated to former presidents, Democrat and Republican, going back to FDR.

What had happened? In part, Elaine wore me down by conspiring with mutual friends to badger me. Partly I began to appreciate how many women, and some men, asked about my pins when I traveled. Mostly, I just decided that the world might profit from a little lightening up. Per medieval superstition, every time we sigh, we lose a little blood: why not try to compensate by kindling a few smiles? I had already found that talking about my pins was a way to make foreign policy seem more human and less foreign. Still, I had mixed feelings. I heard from some professional colleagues who agreed with my initial reaction, arguing that if women were to be taken seriously, we should intentionally downplay feminine interests and attributes. That is how my generation had been conditioned to think. To have a chance at equal treatment, we should imitate men.

The impulse remains. Female politicians still become indignant when reporters insist on writing about their appearance and fashion choices. Was my situation any different? Perhaps. After many years in government and all the subsequent speaking and writing, I was assured that I need not worry about being thought frivolous. Besides, hadn't the time come for the world to accept that women can wear earrings and other jewelry without losing their wits? A punctured earlobe doesn't mean a leaky brain.

THE STORY OF my pins began in the early 1990s. Like most tales, it required both a good guy and one who was not so good. In this case, in the eyes of the Iraqi government, I wore the black hat. As America's UN ambassador, I had criticized that regime for ignoring Security Council resolutions, a bit of truth telling that apparently hurt the feelings of Saddam Hussein and his minions. There appeared in the Baghdad press a poem entitled "To Madeleine Albright, Without Greetings." The translation begins, "Albright, Albright, all right, all right, you are the worst in this night," and goes on to warn that no one "can block the road to Jerusalem with a frigate, a ghost, or an elephant." The poem concludes by referring to me as an "unmatched clamor-maker" and an "unparalleled serpent."

Not long after this felicitous verse saw the light of day, I met in New York with Iraqi diplomats and wore a pin in the shape of a serpent. The press picked up on the connection, and the game began.

From that time forward, I challenged both the media and foreign diplomats to decipher the meaning of my pins—and they eagerly took the bait. Whenever I walked into a meeting, the peering started, and so did the questions: "What's with the ladybug? "Why the spider?" "Does the angel mean you're in a good mood?" "That wasp—does it sting?"

People ask me now how I accumulated so much bling, and the short answer is: coals to Newcastle. Everyone knew I liked pins, so they always shopped for me in the same aisle. In the diplomatic world, costly gifts are the exception because, due to concerns about bribery, one is not allowed to keep such items. That's why I have had to bid farewell to a Bahraini Rolex, a Kuwaiti necklace, a Mongolian horse, and, from Mali, an endearing if opinionated goat. But a brooch doesn't have to be expensive to be lovely, and I was the happy recipient of, among many other pin designs, a lion from the British, a maple leaf from Canada, a flower from the leader of NATO, lacquer snow scenes from Russia, and a sparkly carbuncle from France. One of my challenges while in government was to remember, if a foreign minister had recently given me a pin, to wear it when we met again.

The irony is that until 1982, the year my marriage dissolved, I rarely shopped for jewelry of any kind. A woman usually didn't. One either inherited pieces or received them as gifts from men. But left on my own, I had extra time to duck into stores and so began to buy a pin here and there. I enjoyed the looking, the comparing, the pondering, the yielding to temptation, and, upon arriving home, the unwrapping.

One such expedition took place shortly before Bill Clinton nominated me for secretary of state. I came across a French antique pin with rose-cut diamonds and a gold eagle with widespread wings. I loved the piece but not the price and decided I would buy it only on the off chance that the president chose me. When he did, I went back to scoop up the brooch, which I thought would be perfect for the swearing-in ceremony. What I failed to notice was that securing the old-timey clasp was a multistep process. At the big moment, I had one hand on the Bible and the other in the air to take the oath when I looked down: my pin had come undone. The following morning, news photos showed me standing next to the president with my beautiful eagle flying sideways.

The shape of a different bird, a dove, is that of a pin given to me by Leah Rabin, the widow of Israeli prime minister Yitzhak Rabin. During my first year in office, I had been reluctant to venture into the quagmire of Middle East peace negotiations, but in the summer of 1997 a series of terrorist incidents left me with no other choice. If leaders couldn't persuade cooler heads to work together, extremists on every side would be emboldened and the possibility of Arab-Israeli reconciliation, for which the prime minister had given his life two years before, would be lost.

That August, at the National Press Club, I outlined Clinton administration ideas on the region and announced plans to go there. The speech drew a full house that, when combined with the television lights, warmed the room. I felt flushed and would probably have fainted had I not been petrified of what the media might say about a woman being unable to stand the heat. Somehow, I finished my remarks without embarrassing myself. Meanwhile, from her vantage point in Israel, Mrs. Rabin saw that I was wearing her pin.

A few weeks later, in Jerusalem, Leah came to my hotel room. She brought with her a companion necklace, composed of a flock of doves, and handed me a note that read, "There is a saying: 'One swallow doesn't announce the spring'—so maybe one dove needs reinforcements to create a reality of peace in the Middle East. We need hope which is so much lost—I do wish you will restore it. With all my sincerest wishes, Leah."

In the three years that followed, I devoted more time to the Middle East than to any other region. Although I often wore the dove, I found cause, when impatient, to substitute a turtle, a snail, or a crab. Regrettably, none of the pins proved equal to their assigned task. Today, long after Mrs. Rabin's well-meant gesture, the dove remains in need of reinforcements.

As the symbolism of Leah's gift suggests, what we wear on our shirts and jackets can convey a concise message about our identities and beliefs. Over time, pins have been employed to denounce war, the slave trade, HIV/AIDS, breast cancer, indiscriminate logging, vivisection, homophobia, the exploitation of workers, and a long list of other ills. The year 2020 marks the one hundredth anniversary of the adoption of the Nineteenth Amendment to the U.S. Constitution, guaranteeing to women the right to vote. One of my more expressive pins shows the glass ceiling in its ideal condition: shattered.

In the past, the more people commented on my pins, the more self-conscious I became. Even now, when my days as a professional diplomat are behind me, I use the jewelry to send what I hope will be an appropriate signal—but like almost everything else in my life, that requires preparation. Before any trip, I set aside a few minutes to think about which items to bring along. Though I have been tempted, showing up at a public event *sans broche* is hardly an option. First, most of my jackets are pockmarked with holes; I need to wear pins to conceal the damage done by wearing pins. Second, should I arrive at a speech without something on my lapel, the host will want to know why. The few times I have forgotten, women have plucked off their own pins and pressed them into my hand, putting me in a position where neither accepting nor rejecting feels comfortable.

ELAINE AND I had known the book we were planning would be tricky to produce, and we were right. In theory, all we had to do was select some brooches, photograph them, write some explanatory text, and the task would be complete. But which ones to choose? Who would take the pictures? Explain what? We began by emptying drawers and bags at my house, covering the bedspread in the guest room, and sorting the jewelry by species—patriotic emblems over here, fauna over there, flowers in that corner, and family heirlooms (among them a clay heart made by Katie in kindergarten) in the middle.

In previous books, we had used a photographer who specialized in portraits. Who specialized in pins? The answer is: very few, but

John Bigelow Taylor and his partner, Dianne Dubler, had produced books on antiques, sculpture, and interior design, plus one on Elizabeth Taylor's jewels. With John behind the camera and Dianne in charge of the layouts, we were in business. It really wasn't until I saw their photographs that my doubts about the book began to dissolve. In their skilled hands, the pins seemed truly alive, the flag poised to flutter, the bumblebee ready for flight, the beetle starting to crawl, the kangaroo about to hop, and the aliens dangling from their gold-plated spaceship doing some weird dance—the moonwalk, perhaps?

Pretty soon we had our images of everything from campaign buttons and costume jewelry to designer pieces and museum reproductions. This, however, was but the beginning. To use the photos, we had to obtain the permission of the people who had designed the pins. That could have been a roadblock. I had not been in the habit, when receiving a pin as a gift, of saying, "Why, this is very nice. Where did you buy it?" Of my own purchases, I could remember the source of some, not all. Many of the inexpensive pieces, the majority, had been mass-produced and lacked any telltale markings. Some were antiques, crafted by artisans long since dead, or sold by shops that had gone out of business. Although we were unable to track everything down, we did our best and ultimately listed all the information we had gathered in the book's "Pindex."

We also had to meet expenses. No one thought *Read My Pins* would be a best seller (though it turned out to be), and there was a limit to how much anyone would pay to produce it. I put in money, so did Elaine, but it would not have been published without help from the California-based clothing company St. John Knits. Even more, we couldn't have managed the costs of the museum exhibit if not for the generosity of Bren Simon. I knew Bren, a successful businesswoman, from her involvement with the National Democratic Institute and her steadfast support for cancer research, child health, and abuse prevention programs. How did I convince her to help with the pins exhibit? I didn't; she just stepped up and did it.

The museum tour had been Elaine's brainchild as well; I never thought enough people would be interested. She began by approaching officials at a couple of the fancier galleries in Washington; they said the idea was ridiculous. *Aha*, I thought, *my suspicions are confirmed*. Then she tried her luck in New York, and those same doubts were confounded. The curators of the Museum of Arts and Design, David McFadden and Dorothy Globus, agreed to eyeball the merchandise, displayed this time on tabletops that made my house look like a pin addict's pawn shop. David and Dorothy came, checked everything out, and said they thought the pieces would work as an exhibit in their showplace. From that point, word of mouth has carried us along from city to city.

I can't claim that the *Read My Pins* tour was met with the frenzy accorded King Tut's mummified liver, but it has now been visited by millions of people, from toddlers to totterers, in twenty-two museums and libraries. In the displays, my pins are accompanied by panels that explain where and why I wore the pieces and that serve, or so we intend, as teaching tools. With the exception of one woman who misunderstood and was drawn to the show out of her love for pens, most visitors have gone away satisfied. Even though a decade has elapsed, we could probably continue indefinitely. I'd rather stop too early than too late, however, but that doesn't mean I'll be getting my pins back. Instead, they will be donated to the State Department and the newly opened National Museum of American Diplomacy, another project in which I have been deeply involved.

THE IDEA FOR a museum that would tell the story of American diplomacy was suggested to me while I was still secretary. My successors, and several of my predecessors, have also subscribed to the effort, and in 2014, a shovel brigade (consisting of Secretaries Kissinger, Baker, Powell, Clinton, Kerry, and me) broke ground for the new facility. Not yet complete, the museum will eventually include interactive displays, space for educational programs, and four exhibition halls. Among the highlights is a chunk of the Berlin Wall signed by more than two dozen international leaders who helped to end the Cold

War. By coincidence, one of my pins also contains fragments of the Berlin Wall; it should feel right at home there.

Looking back, I can see that I worried for nothing. When I am discussing the book, even at museum openings, audiences switch readily from the topic of pins to questions about the more consequential aspects of foreign policy. At most locations, and especially the presidential libraries, we have had events featuring a back-and-forth between students and me. The core message, about the varieties of diplomatic communication, has been widely grasped. In the opinion of Robin Givhan, the Pulitzer Prize–winning fashion critic for the *Washington Post*, "Albright has done what no glass-ceiling busting, power-brokering, globe-trotting diplomat has attempted: written a book that speaks directly to her personal style and emerged with her brainy reputation unscathed."

A brainy reputation? If not for the pins, I would never have known.

NINETEEN

Muscles in Brussels

IN JANUARY 2009, nine days into the Obama era, I accepted the National Collegiate Athletic Association's Theodore Roosevelt Award. This was not an honor I expected; when the organization called, I said they must have the wrong person. The list of prior winners is dominated by Olympic champions, sports executives, and figures otherwise associated with physical prowess. In college, I swam, rowed, and played field hockey with maniacal fierceness but was never a star. When I told my daughter Anne about receiving an award from the NCAA, she said, "Mom, I am a lawyer, and you are a fraud."

During that month and the next, I invested my energy in fundraising events for numerous organizations, including Denver University's Josef Korbel School of International Studies, named for my father. I attended Secretary of State Clinton's swearing-in ceremony and gave speeches in Florida to a library association and an insurance convention. I also submitted to my publisher the final draft of *Read My Pins* and helped attract attention to the task force reports I had worked on. I met with Walter Isaacson to discuss what the Aspen Institute's agenda might look like under the Obama administration and to thank him for supporting the Aspen Ministers Forum, aka "Madeleine and Her Exes." The 34th Street Group continued to convene regularly, and Andy Kohut of the Pew Research Center came by to see if I had thoughts on a poll he was preparing to gauge global reaction to the first flowerings of the Obama presidency. I then flew seven thousand miles to Qatar, where Georgetown's School of Foreign Service had established a presence and, while there, attended

business meetings. In free moments, I engaged in talks with unoffi-
cial representatives from Israel and the Palestinian Authority aimed
at improving the climate for Middle East peace.

One day that hectic spring, Hillary Clinton called me. She said
that the North Atlantic Treaty Organization (NATO) was assembling a group of experts to recommend revisions to its strategic concept, a document last amended in 1999. She cautioned that the job
would demand a lot of time and travel, but asked, "Would you be
willing to represent the United States?" I didn't hesitate.

"Count me in," I said, "and thanks for thinking of me." I rang off,
took a long look at my schedule, and exclaimed to myself, "Madeleine, you must be mad."

NATO WAS CONCEIVED in dismay. Western leaders had hoped their
wartime partnership with Stalin would endure beyond the Axis surrender and that the newly organized United Nations would become
an effective guarantor of global security. "I had assumed," said one
American diplomat, "that the inevitable differences of opinion could
be resolved without serious difficulty."

It was not to be. Postwar talks among the major powers called
for free elections in Eastern and Central Europe, but in some countries, these never took place, and in others the outcomes were pre-
determined by Moscow. Czechoslovakia became the last state in
the region to be subjugated when, in 1948, the Communist Party
stormed to power and began locking up democrats. Alarmed by the
debacle, Western officials feared that the Soviets wouldn't be satisfied until they held sway also in Southern Europe, the Korean Peninsula, the Middle East, and, eventually, Latin America. The West
vowed to stand its ground, setting up a clash that the UN Security
Council was helpless to prevent because each side had the power to
veto initiatives by the other.

President Truman and his counterparts in Western Europe concluded that just as they had needed an alliance to prevail in World
War II, so they had better build one to contain Communism. NATO,

with a dozen original members, was born on the fourth day of April, 1949. Among its midwives was newly appointed Secretary of State Dean Acheson. At the signing ceremony in Washington, he used language befitting a minister's son to promise "refuge and strength" to the seekers of peace and "woe" to those "who set their feet upon the path of aggression." The secretary praised the coming together of countries that, in centuries past, had often been at odds, but later remarked on the peculiarity of the military band selections chosen to accompany the birth of history's greatest alliance: "It Ain't Necessarily So" and "I've Got Plenty o' Nuttin'."

DIPLOMATICALLY, WE LIVE today in an era of mild enthusiasms, 50 percent faiths, and modest dreams. NATO, by contrast, had the highest aspirations. Countries that were just beginning to emerge from a devastating war vowed to show strength and thus deter future aggression. Under their new pact, NATO members pledged to consult one another in the event of security threats and to consider "an armed attack against one or more of them . . . an attack against them all." This covenant gained yet more urgency when, in August 1949, the Soviet Union became, after the United States, the world's second nuclear power.

NATO hurried to set up a command structure and establish a headquarters in Brussels. The alliance's primary military mission was to safeguard territory within its boundaries; its related political function was aimed at the whole world: to showcase governments that provided a vibrant and democratic alternative to the harsh conformity dictated by communist rule. Both missions were accomplished. By preventing the Soviet Bloc from exploiting its sizable advantage in conventional military might, the alliance carved out, over four decades, a reputation as freedom's most potent protector. Although the Cold War had plenty of hot spots, the Berlin Wall was ultimately dismantled (in 1989) without NATO having to fire so much as a pistol.

In 1993, Bill Clinton became president, and I joined the government. Immediately, we began asking: is the work of our alliance done? We were no longer concerned that Russian tanks would crash through the front lines, because there were no front lines; the barbed wire strung across Europe's midsection had been replaced by signs of greeting: *Willkommen, Vítejte, Witamy,* and *Üdvözöljük.* So, was NATO still necessary? We decided that it was. Even though the Soviet Union had shattered, other threats were on the horizon. For example, when ethnic cleansing caused bloodshed in the Balkans, the alliance was the only institution we could rely on to end the atrocities. We valued it as well for what it espoused: liberty, the rule of law, and a commitment to peace. These were permanent, not temporary, ideals.

A new era, however, demanded adjustments. Going back centuries, the area separating Germany from Russia had been a battleground whose borders were fought over by smaller nations and ignored by the big. We worried that with the Iron Curtain lifted, the scramble for advantage would resume. NATO could prevent that. The alliance offered nations in the region an incentive, in the form of prospective membership, to strengthen their democratic institutions and avoid destructive quarrels. The strategy paid off. At a ceremony in 1999, I had the pleasure of welcoming the Czech Republic, Hungary, and Poland into the alliance. Other countries soon followed.

There are those who will tell you that building a bigger NATO was a mistake because Moscow didn't like it. The theory, apparently, is that Russia's reward for losing the Cold War should have been a veto over alliance decisions. That doesn't make sense. The argument also presumes that Russia would pose a lesser threat to a smaller, weaker body than it does to a larger, stronger one. That, too, is twaddle. We cannot know for certain what Europe would look like had the alliance decided either to disband completely or to tell aspiring members that they would have to search elsewhere for security guarantees. However, the probability is that without NATO to generate mutual confidence and purpose, the continent would be more prone to strife than it is. Historically, Europe was frequently split into rival empires or blocs. For all the disagreements today, that kind of stark division ceased in the 1990s. Make no mistake, expansion was the right call.

In 2001, shortly after the 9/11 terrorist attacks, the collective defense provisions of the North Atlantic Treaty were invoked for the first time. The allies labelled the strikes an assault on all of them, not just the United States, and their aircraft were soon flying patrols over the Eastern Seaboard. The Bush administration could have reinforced this sense of shared mission by asking NATO's help in destroying al-Qaeda; instead, America invaded Afghanistan virtually on its own. European leaders were dismayed by this approach, which showed a lack of faith in an organization whose value the United States had always stressed. Eventually, NATO was given a training mandate and, after U.S. armed forces became bogged down in Iraq, a more ambitious role that included taking on the Taliban insurgency. Every NATO member has participated in that campaign, which prevented a victory by the extremists but could not fully stabilize the country.

As long as Bush was president, European governments were eager to avoid a renewed squabble over Iraq, and thus reluctant to engage in a frank discussion concerning NATO's future. When Obama was elected, the time seemed right for the alliance, like any sixty-year-old, to take a long look at the shape it was in and consider how best to gird itself for future tests.

INITIALLY, THE NATO experts group was to number twenty-eight, one for each member of the expanded alliance. However, the organization's new secretary-general, Anders Fogh Rasmussen, thought that too many. He cut the group to a dozen and asked me to serve as chair. I agreed, and when friends from the countries that had been left out complained, I told them it wasn't my decision and they should go yell at Rasmussen.

Among the more vital of our tasks was simply to remind people that NATO remains in business and is still helping to keep our countries from harm. There is neither any substitute for it nor any lessening of the dangers we confront. To get that message across, the advisory panel solicited the views of civilian and military leaders, courted the media, and held seminars in Luxembourg, Slovenia, Norway, and Washington. In the process, we listened to experts from every corner of the alliance, weighed their concerns, answered their questions, and evaluated the changes they proposed. We also saw value in explaining even to potential adversaries what NATO's intentions were, and why no law-abiding nation (with emphasis on the adjective) need fear its actions. To that end, we boarded a plane and headed for Russia.

WHENEVER I VISIT Moscow, I bring baggage from the past. My old boss Zbigniew Brzezinski was of Polish heritage and had antagonized a succession of Soviet governments simply by describing honestly their policies and actions. To officials in Moscow, he was an unrepentant cold warrior, and, by association, so was I. Given my family's history, I had my own issues with the Kremlin, and although I got along well enough personally with most Russian diplomats, I have never been among the Americans judged friendly to Putin or to the power brokers around him.

In December 2006, the myth of anti-Moscow Madeleine took a bizarre turn when reports surfaced that I had a "pathological hatred of Slavs." The information had been gleaned not from anything I had said, but from the report of a Russian security official who had undergone hypnosis in an effort, which he claimed was successful, to commune with my subconscious. This was a novel form of espionage, aimed at my thoughts rather than my words or deeds. Who would take seriously such a nutty brand of spying? Well, based on exactly that, a retired KGB general told reporters that I was someone who "resented the fact that Russia had the world's largest mineral reserves" and that I believed the country's petroleum and other resources "should be shared by all of humanity under the supervision . . . of the United States."

Given my Czechoslovak ancestry, the notion that I dislike Slavs, whether consciously or subconsciously, is absurd, and I have neither the desire nor the power to deprive Russia of its oil. The fable wouldn't be worth mentioning had it not since been referred to repeatedly in such prominent publications as *Pravda* and *Kommersant*, and by officials high up the chain of command, including Putin. Why all the attention? Kremlin leaders want their citizens to think that the West hates them and is trying to destroy their country. The more Russians believe this lie, the easier it will be for their government to justify the quashing of political liberties and to blame outsiders when official policies don't work.

In February 2010, I arrived in Moscow intent on defending NATO's interests without handing further ammunition to critics. While there, I renewed my acquaintance with Sergey Lavrov, who had been Russia's ambassador to the UN when I was in New York and had since been promoted to foreign minister. Lavrov, a dapper but also dour fellow, inquired about my pin, which was in the shape of a braided gold rope tied in the middle. I said the knot represented the tight bond between Moscow and the West. Lavrov nodded and smiled, but his body language suggested Siberia in January.

The two of us, and our delegations, then argued for hours about why NATO had expanded, whether Russia had the right to boss around its neighbors, the meaning of democracy, and whether Moscow's resentment toward the West is justified. Finally, we paused and Lavrov gave me one of his stubborn looks. After a gulp of lukewarm tea, I gave him one of mine. Then I made a last plea to move beyond our stale disagreements and focus instead on the prospects for future cooperation. "There is no reason," I argued "why the new NATO and the new Russia can't get along. The alliance, at least, is looking for partners, not enemies." Lavrov wasn't buying. He said in his deep rumbling voice that the person at the table who was arousing unpleasant memories was me. I was the one, he insisted, whose mind was stuck in the Cold War. "The bond your pin represents," he declared, "is James Bond." *And you, Sergey,* I thought, *will always be Doctor No.*

I TELL MY students that when diplomats sit at a table, history lingers alongside and has much to say about how countries think. So it was with the NATO group of experts: present attitudes were shaped by the memory of past events. To our Polish and Latvian members, the preeminent reason for NATO's existence in 2010 was the same as it had been in 1950: to keep Russia from grabbing what it didn't rightfully possess. Their nations had spent decades on the wrong side of the Berlin Wall, forced to comply with Moscow's every wish, and didn't want to repeat the experience. That's why NATO membership was so important to them; it provided a guarantee that such a fate would never again befall their homelands.

Our experts from Western Europe understood that fear but considered it overdone. To them, Putin was an irritant but not (then, at least) an international pariah. Much of the continent depended on Russia for oil and gas, and its leaders looked to Moscow for help in dealing with the threats posed by terrorists and Iran. Half a dozen allied governments thought the Kremlin had been right to condemn the U.S. invasion of Iraq, and few outside Poland and the Baltics worried that Russian armed forces would dare attack a NATO member. Finally, to European governments with imperial histories, Putin's desire to maintain a sphere of influence around his country's borders was natural. Russia had, after all, been invaded before.

The differences in perspective between NATO's East and West surfaced every time the experts evaluated future dangers. This, in turn, affected each aspect of our plans. A mother who is about to take her children outside will prepare them differently for a hot, dry day than for one that is chilly and wet. In the same way, NATO tailors its activities to the nature of the international climate it perceives; but what did the geopolitical forecast tell us? Was Russia still NATO's number one threat? Or should the allies pay equal or even greater heed to more distant, so-called out-of-area, risks?

To the majority in our group, the answer seemed plain. By 2010, the alliance had swelled to more than twice its original size, giving it a much larger territorial base to defend. It was also training forces in Iraq, helping to maintain order in the Balkans, protecting maritime traffic off the coast of Africa, and debating how to respond in the Arctic, where global warming (and melting glaciers) had enabled the establishment of new shipping routes and military bases. Then there was the mission in Afghanistan, more than 1,800 miles from the alliance border.

In addition, cyber warfare had emerged as an economic and security peril, thus raising the question of whether, under the North Atlantic Treaty, an attack on electronic infrastructure should be treated in the same manner as an invasion by ground or air. Looking further ahead, we knew that advances in weapons technology powered by robotics and artificial intelligence had the potential to transform the battlefield more dramatically than at any time since the dawn of the nuclear age. To complete the metaphor, it seemed as if Mother NATO might have to prepare her children for all kinds of weather, equipping them with the military equivalents of an overcoat, an umbrella, a tube of sunscreen, a GPS, and a Swiss Army knife.

THE EXPERT GROUP'S report, *NATO 2020*, was published in May 2010. To reassure Central Europe and the Baltics, we emphasized our ongoing commitment to collective defense: "No one should doubt NATO's resolve if the security of any of its member states were to be threatened." To highlight the value of versatility, we noted that "as the alliance matures, it must prepare itself to confront an array of fresh perils."

In presenting the report, I stressed that membership in the treaty organization was a privilege, not a right, and that every nation, no matter how small, had obligations to meet. Under NATO policy, each member is expected to devote at least 2 percent of its gross domestic product to defense. These are not payments to NATO, itself, which is funded under a separate formula. The 2 percent standard refers to the expenses that governments incur when operating and equipping their own armed forces. At the time of our report, only six of twenty-eight members were meeting the prescribed threshold.

The experts' recommendations provided the foundation for NATO's revised strategic concept, approved later that year. In the time since, however, those worried that Russia cannot be trusted have had their fears validated. Alarmed by the Kremlin's opportunistic policies in Ukraine and Syria, its complicity in cyberattacks, and its failure to comply fully with the Intermediate-Range Nuclear Forces Treaty, the alliance has deployed troops to Poland, conducted military maneuvers in the Baltics, and stockpiled equipment in both.

The renewed growling of the Russian bear has put a lot of people's teeth on edge (and, more important, destroyed thousands of human lives) but has thus far provided few tangible benefits for Russia. After two decades in power, Putin leads a country that is economically stagnant and militarily still weak. Rather than view the West as a partner whose friendship could yield enormous returns, he insists on treating it as a rival. He acts as if he were still a member of the KGB. His clear intent is to divide Europe internally and to loosen the ties that bind the transatlantic community. His hope, ultimately, is that NATO will lose its sense of common purpose. To accelerate the process, he aims through propaganda and the sabotage of elections in other countries to blunt the moral edge that democratic nations claimed when the Berlin Wall crumbled. Though Putin's hand is not strong, he generally plays it well. This is due both to his cleverness in public relations and to a lack of effective teamwork on the part of U.S. and European leaders.

MY INVOLVEMENT WITH the experts group reinforced my long-held belief in the need for solidarity among free nations, while also heightening my concerns about Western complacency. If NATO is taken for granted, or if its members drift further apart, the alliance will surely go in precisely the direction that Putin hopes.

I was reminded of this risk when, in the fall of 2019, I delivered the Green Foundation Lecture at Westminster College in Fulton, Missouri. Seventy-three years earlier, the lecture had been given by Winston Churchill who warned about the descent of an "iron curtain" across the continent of Europe. In the face of grave danger, he called for "a new unity . . . from which no nation should be permanently outcast." Churchill's core message was that democratic societies must stand together to shield themselves from two "gaunt marauders": tyranny and war.

The NATO of my dreams has canny leaders, a clear chain of command, the muscle to deter potential conflicts, and missions that are well understood and supported on both sides of the Atlantic. At its best, the alliance forged in Washington in 1949 has met this high standard. Its overall record is a strong one.

But let us be honest. NATO's performance in Afghanistan was less effective than it should have been. The contingents of some countries fought valiantly, but others were prevented by their governments from going into harm's way. NATO has been hurt as well by the perception that it is merely an extension of American power. During much of the Cold War, that view was not worrisome because the United States was held in high regard. Recently, however, support for many aspects of U.S. foreign policy has diminished, while doubts about the steadiness and commitment of American leadership have increased.

These and other disturbing trends were in evidence when, in London in 2019, the alliance held a rather joyless celebration of its seventieth birthday. The goal of organizers was to avoid outward signs of disarray and to paper over differences in how to respond to Russia and China. Also avoided was any serious discussion of an even more worrisome topic: the alliance's waning identification with democratic ideals. During the Cold War and the decades immediately after, this was NATO's decisive advantage. Yet the government of Hungarian Prime Minister Viktor Orbán has openly embraced nondemocratic policies, and Poland's leadership has tiptoed up to the line. Turkey, under Recep Tayyip Erdoğan, is increasingly both aggressive and repressive and, in a sharp departure from alliance practice, an unrepentant buyer of Russian arms. Meanwhile, the U.S. commander in chief, Donald Trump, has shown more interest in berating allies over money than in coordinating with them to protect shared interests. The spectacle is alarming. Put bluntly, a NATO whose embrace of democracy is in doubt would have a much lesser claim to public approval than it has enjoyed in the past—and the alliance needs all the backing it can attract.

This explains why my message today on both sides of the Atlantic resembles closely that of Churchill nearly three quarters of a century ago. We need to wake up. Every ally has agreed to dedicate 2 percent of its wealth to national and collective defense, and all should meet that standard. But more important, each should devote 100 percent of its energy to the values of democratic constancy that brought NATO together in the first place. It's not too late, but neither is it too soon; the true measure of any alliance is not what it has done, but what it is prepared to do.

TWENTY

A Bigger Sea

Late in 1997, I traveled to a refugee camp in Pakistan about twenty-five miles from the Afghan border, not far from the Khyber Pass. The mountainous landscape was barren, with no trees or even shrubs to provide shade. My destination was a tiny school where a couple of dozen women and girls were waiting, among them a doctor and several teachers.

The women explained to me through interpreters how the Taliban in their native Afghanistan had prevented them from holding jobs, attending class, or even leaving their homes unless accompanied by an adult male. A girl described the death of her sister, who had leapt from a sixth-floor window to avoid being raped by men who had broken into her family's apartment.

As we talked, I sensed the refugees' nervousness. Many still had relatives across the border and feared that their willingness to meet with me could, if revealed, have severe consequences.

Later, I went outside to address a larger gathering of Afghans of both genders and varied ages sitting on rugs in a makeshift courtyard. The sun was getting low, and I could see along the camp's perimeter the shadows of the marksmen who were protecting us. I told my listeners that the job of America's secretary of state was to care about issues of war and peace and about whether people in need receive the food and shelter they must have to survive.

I said that I, too, had once been a refugee. Although I could not compare my experience to what they had endured, I did know that war is cruel and that life can be very hard when you aren't able to live in the place you call home. I added that no country can become prosperous unless women and girls are allowed to go to school and are shielded from exploitation and abuse.

When I was done, I walked forward to say hello. The youngest were seated in front, cross-legged. I extended a hand, but the children were so small we couldn't connect. I was afraid that if I bent over any farther, I would tip over. So, I got down on my knees and greeted them that way. Their fingers were thin and wiry; their eyes dark and haunting. I have not forgotten their smiles.

DURING MY FINAL year in office, the United Nations established the Millennium Development Goals, a set of ambitious benchmarks for the world to achieve by 2015. Among them was a commitment to eliminate gender disparity in access to education. Contrary to the expectations of many, that objective has since been reached due in large measure to progress in South Asia, where more girls than boys now attend primary school. In still-fragile Afghanistan, substantial gains were made when the Taliban were forced out after 9/11; however, much work remains to be done there and elsewhere. In many places, needed change has been slowed by security fears, the continued incidence of child marriage, a shortage of qualified female teachers, a lack of resources, and bias. Across the globe, an estimated 130 million girls who should be in class each day are not.

Rooster Cogburn, the rugged one-eyed cowboy featured in the western novel *True Grit*, tells his fourteen-year-old female employer: "If you don't have no schooling, you are up against it in this country, sis. No sir, that man has no chance any more. No matter if he has sand in his craw, others will push him aside, little thin fellows that have won spelling bees back home." Rooster spoke the truth—and what applied in his mind to "little thin fellows" is pertinent now regardless of gender. For any nation seeking to foster economic and social gains, educating girls is an essential step. The more schooling women have, the better the choices they will make and the more likely it is that those choices will be heeded in their homes and communities.

Knowledge breeds confidence, which begets power. That's precisely why patriarchal systems strive to keep women ignorant, and why preparing women to be effective leaders and advocates is so beneficial. History has shown that, when women's voices are heard, the cycle of poverty becomes easier to break, children are healthier, environmental standards improve, and socially constructive values are passed on with greater frequency to the young.

I HAVE OFTEN spoken of my affection for Wellesley College and of my gratitude for the friends I made there and for the knowledge I acquired during my years there both about myself and about the world. As the decades passed, I kept in touch with my alma mater by attending reunions, participating in alumni activities, and later, following my stint in government, speaking on panels and at commencement ceremonies. Not long after I left office, a group of my classmates, led by Wini Shore Freund and Mary Jane Durnford Lewis, proposed a more enduring and tangible connection: an institute in my name to train young women for global leadership. Wellesley's twelfth and thirteenth presidents, Diana Chapman Walsh and Kim Bottomly, embraced the idea and, over several years, helped put the pieces together. In January 2010, I traveled to Massachusetts for the inaugural session.

The Albright Institute was founded on the belief that a student doesn't have to major in international relations to have a global mind-set. By giving young women the chance to work in partnership with peers from a variety of disciplines and countries, we encourage them to see differences of perspective as a strength and even as a tool to help solve complex problems. To that end, we provide an intense course of study over a three-week period between the fall and spring semesters, complemented by summer internships. Of the hundreds of Wellesley juniors and seniors who apply annually, forty are selected. In the first two weeks of each session, we offer classes run by professors, former government officials, nonprofit leaders, and businesspeople. During the final seven days, the fellows work in teams to analyze and make recommendations regarding a thorny international problem. At the end, they present their findings, which we pick apart and discuss.

A key element of our approach is to give women with different academic interests a chance to work together. On any team of fellows, one might find, for instance, a budding scientist, an economics major, and an aspiring poet. Our program challenges them to pool their talents and develop innovative plans for addressing the subjects we assign. The results are often surprising: that science major might have insights into the climate-related causes of poverty; the economist might identify a novel link between corporate responsibility and the workforce of the future; the poet may have thoughts on the way language can be used to encourage reconciliation between contending factions.

A principal aim of the institute is to instill enough confidence in the value of collaborative problem solving that participants are eager to nourish that same attribute in others. Students learn from what they hear and see, and we want our graduates (who already number more than four hundred and come from dozens of countries) to have an impact far beyond the classroom. In our vision, they will become teachers themselves, whether directly or indirectly by the examples they set, thus inspiring others and spreading knowledge outward for generations to come.

We have made a good start. In January 2020, under the leadership of Wellesley's current president, Paula Johnson, we observed the tenth anniversary of the institute, during which we centered our discussion on the legacy of the 1995 World Conference on Women. I had led the U.S. delegation to that event and was pleased to share my thoughts about the gains that had been made in its wake—and the hard work still to come.

AMONG WELLESLEY'S TRADITIONS is the annual hoop-rolling contest for graduating seniors. The competition requires participants to hike up their ceremonial gowns, tie down their mortarboard caps, and employ a stick to steer a circular piece of wood along a path. When I was a student, the prize for the winner was the expectation that she would be the first in her class to land a husband. In my year, the victor chose instead to go to law school and eventually became a judge. I didn't come close to winning the contest yet still made it to the altar less than one week after graduation. Later, living in Washington and New York in the 1960s, my husband and I were part of a group of young couples with buoyant hopes and egos to match. At parties, we speculated about which of us might one day end up on the cover of *Time* magazine—which of the men, that is. Earlier, I had sought employment as a journalist but was told by an editor that it was against newspaper guild policy for me to work for the same publication as my spouse; and to write for a competing paper, he said, would be out of the question.

As for a career in foreign policy, that was beyond my imagining. In those days, the sole way a woman could have an international impact was to host a diplomatic reception and pour tea on an unfriendly ambassador's lap. Only single women were allowed to join the Foreign Service, and those who did, should they then get married, were promptly fired. Of course, male diplomats faced trials, as well: they were judged on how socially presentable their wives were. The evaluation forms used to assess their performance included space for supervisors to make comments.

In this same period, one of the few female CEOs, the *Washington Post*'s Katharine Graham, admitted to a heavy burden of personal insecurity, telling an interviewer, "In the world today, men are more able than women at executive work . . . I think a man would be better at this job I'm in than a woman." Consider, if she felt that way, what the workplace climate was like for the generation of women just starting out.

I cite this history because, though most often praised, the Albright Institute has also been chided for being "unabashedly careerist" and for encouraging women to make a difference in the future instead of concentrating on the joys of learning for its own sake. I don't see how one option excludes the other, but the criticism does touch on a question with which Wellesley graduates and women more generally continue to wrestle. How do we describe what constitutes a fulfilling life? Cloudiness about the answer has even affected the old tradition of hoop rolling. In the 1980s, the winner of the graduation event was presumed no longer to be the first bride but, rather, the first CEO. A little later that distinction was also deemed too narrow, and now the victor is acknowledged to be the first who will obtain success—as she defines it.

Women who are young (and not so young) often seek advice about how to achieve what they call a work-life balance or what I have always referred to, perhaps anachronistically, as juggling. For many who approach me, the request is casual. They aren't desperate; they're just looking for tips. While they refuse to accept that they can't have it *all*, most no longer expect to have it *all at once*. More than a few, however, are in anguish because the harder they try to excel on the job and also as a parent, wife, daughter, friend, and community member, the more they worry that they will fall short in each area. They attempt too much and feel life getting away from them without knowing how to rein it back in. Pressure from colleagues and trepidation at losing ground professionally make them loath to reduce their commitment to work; but the pull of home and family seems to leave them with no other choice.

It's an old story and one that I have been grappling with to some extent all my adult life, whether personally or through my daughters or in sympathy with comrades. I wish I had better answers, or at least words of guidance that didn't sound like they were culled from a magazine article. I have often said that every woman's middle name is "Guilt," but that we should not be blamed for what we feel.

When I was just starting out, women who worked and found themselves "with child" tried to disguise the condition by wearing tents while on the job. The doings of adorable offspring weren't discussed for fear that such talk would imply a lack of focus on the office, and the mothers of preschoolers who applied for positions were given a pat on the head and then turned down flat. Attitudes have changed since, but a lot of employers in both the public and the private sectors still miss the main point. When they help women to cope with the competing demands of work and family, they are not doing the women a favor; they are helping themselves. It's smart for them to be flexible. After all, the wider the talent pool, the more first-rate employees will be found. Further, studies indicate that people who return to jobs after a period caring for their young at home have more emotional maturity and an enhanced ability to confront problems without becoming flustered. It's true that most women can't go full speed in all directions without tearing themselves apart, but it's equally the case that they shouldn't have to.

WELLESLEY AND ITS sister schools weren't conceived to make life simpler for women to navigate, but to give us a bigger sea. The founders of the college (Henry and Pauline Durant, in 1870), sought to enable their students to do well in the workplace and to play an equitable role in society. Despite a long history of impressive female accomplishments, the idea that women have the intellect, character, and stamina to thrive in the most demanding professions still strikes many as revolutionary and requires daring and innovation to implement. That is the challenge that the Albright Institute has taken up with a vigor that is reflected in the burgeoning network of former fellows who regularly get together to share their experiences as budding leaders, not just in the United States, but in many countries.

Education, at bottom, is an act of faith, and what I see when the institute convenes each year reinforces my optimism about the future. That's why I look forward to my annual winter journey north where I will find a fresh contingent of students eager to deploy their talents across cultural and academic boundaries, and to show the way on issues of universal concern.

The institute is but one program, of modest size, at a single college. It isn't going to transform civilization or save it. However, by preparing young women for central roles in unraveling the mysteries of tomorrow, it is a contributor of value. That is all we can claim, and it is enough.

TWENTY-ONE

Puzzles

I N ENGLAND DURING the war, when I was very young, I learned to skip rope. Beyond the basic jump, I did not advance far—no crisscross, double under, Awesome Annie, or donkey kick (which involves a handstand). I was, however, pretty fast. Had my life not been disrupted so often and had I a mentor to guide me, I might have become an all-star, or so I like to believe. Training rarely makes perfect, but it does help us do more with the gifts we have.

In the world of business, I needed practice to find my way. Though I had no formal instructor, I gained by observing and by asking questions of the executives I had come to know through my consulting company, the Albright Group (TAG). The relationships gave me a chance to study a cornucopia of corporations up close. I didn't learn much in the way of fancy maneuvers, just enough to move along briskly without entangling my feet in rope.

My best moments in business are those that most clearly inform and complement other aspects of my life. That is when the projects we work on have tangible social benefits—fortifying the economy of a struggling democracy perhaps, or helping people in remote regions to gain access to modern medical treatments. Ideally our enterprise would always do well by doing good, but I have yet to find anyone who thinks that as a business plan, altruism is enough. A commercial operation is just that, not a charity. Payrolls depend on bottom lines, which is why most of our advice is aimed at helping clients to achieve or maintain a competitive edge. However, when I was in the State Department, I established an annual award for companies that met the highest standards of social responsibility. I insisted then, and believe now, that integrating ethical and civic-minded behavior into a corporation's culture is both possible and smart. This isn't just a matter of public relations. Employees work more diligently and stay longer with firms that are good local citizens and whose priorities they respect. We want to be proud of what we do.

By contrast, companies go astray when they tolerate unsafe working conditions, trash the environment, dip their fingers into corruption's fetid pool, or cook up pay scales that over-feed the few at the top while serving only crumbs and scraps to the rank and file. "Greed is good," said the fictional Gordon Gekko, but taken to excess, avarice is stupid. A bad corporation may fly high for a while, but the truth has wings, too; ultimately, a company will either have to shape up or shut down. The problem, in the meantime, is that the worst firms taint by association the better ones, thereby undermining the credibility of free enterprise itself. There are those who say the market lacks a conscience. If so, we—and here I mean especially the business community—must supply one.

THE EARLY YEARS of the Albright Group coincided with 9/11, the bursting of the dot-com bubble, the entry of China into the World Trade Organization, mayhem in the Middle East, and increased anxieties about climate change. Each of these events had an impact on clients. A major labor union, for example, sought to ensure that in the rush to find new security guards to protect facilities from terrorism, governments would not hire people who were unqualified. A leading soft drink company was concerned that its identity as an American icon was hurting its business in regions where, due to the Iraq War, the standing of the United States had declined. TAG partner Carol Browner's credentials as the former administrator of EPA attracted notice from companies affected by environmental issues. One such firm specialized in the safe disposal of mercury used by dentists; another wanted help in combating rumors that their chocolate bars contained unacceptable levels of cadmium and lead. (They didn't.)

Global advice-giving can be rewarding, but contracts mirror performance; the pressure to add value is unrelenting. To contribute all I can, I prepare for meetings as meticulously as when I was secretary of state. Here, my curiosity is an asset. I never have to feign interest in what clients have to say about their aspirations and worries. Whenever I am presented with a dilemma to be addressed, my mind fills with questions, the names of men and women to contact, and possible routes to a solution. In the same way that some people look forward to their morning crossword puzzle, I am energized by clients looking for answers. I also draw on the benefits of experience.

Years ago, when I was the legislative assistant to Maine Senator Ed Muskie, a big part of my job was to help constituents, whether individuals or companies, in their dealings with the federal government. My assignment was to ensure that the citizens of the Pine Tree State were treated fairly and to convince even the skeptical that Muskie was looking out for their interests. In the process, I studied the effect of laws and regulations on disabled veterans, apple growers, lobster harvesters, paper companies, people on fixed incomes, homeowners who couldn't pay their heating bills, and the opponents and proponents of building a hydroelectric dam in New England's northernmost woods. To enhance my usefulness, I developed a network of contacts within federal agencies and among other Senate offices and committees. I learned about conflicts of interest and the difference between legitimate and inappropriate requests. I wrote letters, made phone calls, arranged meetings, and drafted bills.

Decades later, I discovered that consulting is an advanced form of congressional casework: you are presented with a problem or a set of goals and must find the optimal strategy for moving ahead. Each new client presents a story with its own plot and cast of characters. Your role is to think about how the next chapter should unfold and, ultimately, help write an ending that satisfies.

Being in business also provides an additional reason for travel, which has its own rewards. Returning from one trip on the fancier-than-average Emirates airline, I had to transit a bar to get to the bathroom. I excused myself while trying to maneuver around two men who were having drinks. They wouldn't let me pass. Instead, one exclaimed, "Oh Mother, it is so wonderful that you're here. May I give you a hug?" His companion bowed from the waist and requested that I bless him. On my way back, I asked a flight attendant if she could find out who the tipsy two thought I was. She soon had the answer: "Mother Teresa." This was a first. I have been mistaken many times for Margaret Thatcher, but Mother Teresa is even shorter than I am, far better qualified to dispense blessings, and since 1997, deceased. I was left to wonder how many drinks it takes for someone to imagine a halo above my head.

WITHIN A YEAR of its founding, the Albright Group was paying its way and within three years, it had begun to prosper. To make room for a larger staff, we moved a few blocks to a building with glass walls overlooking a vast undeveloped lot that was sometimes rented out by a professional tennis team (Serena Williams!) and, on other occasions, by a trapeze school. It wasn't long before we branched out. In 2005, I joined the other TAG principals, plus Gregory Bowes and John Yonemoto, in founding an adjunct investment firm, Albright Capital Management. The firm (which is still going strong) is adept at navigating emerging markets and delivering commercial returns while focusing on projects that have a positive social impact. TAG itself still had four partners aside from me: Wendy Sherman, Carol Browner, Jim O'Brien, and Suzy George. We had surpassed expectations, but we also knew that change was coming.

Our company's principals had come from government, and to government several hoped to return. In 2004, that prospect was postponed by Bush's reelection. Four years later, when Democrats reclaimed the White House, Obama immediately tapped Carol Browner to head the administration's new Office of Energy and Climate Change Policy. Wendy Sherman, too, was in demand and would soon be offered the number three position at the State Department. Suzy and Jim were also being recruited. Putting some or all of them back to work on behalf of the public would be good for them and for the country, but what would it mean for the Albright Group? We had deliberately limited our growth by taking on only those assignments that were of interest to at least one of us. Clearly, we had a chance to expand, but that would require new people and a different approach.

When I was secretary of state, I was in contact nearly every day with Clinton's national security advisor, Sandy Berger. I had known him for decades. He was a trade lawyer who shared with me a love of foreign policy and an affinity for politics; we had worked together in both the Carter administration and the Dukakis campaign. There were moments when in advising the president during Clinton's second term, we tried to occupy the same space at the same time, causing our egos to bump, but never hard enough to wound our friendship. Upon leaving office, we each formed a global advisory firm. Sandy's was called Stonebridge International, a partnership that also included Tony Harrington, Michael Warren, and a former Republican senator from New Hampshire, Warren Rudman. Sandy was a bright and creative thinker, with an aversion to false flattery, whether given or received. He was no Clint Eastwood, all squints and grunts; like me, Sandy loved to talk. I have met few men with whom I made a better team.

Given our past collaboration and the opportunities we saw in front of us, the idea of a merger between TAG and Stonebridge started to put down roots. I often had dinner with Sandy and his wife, Susan. We compared notes on what we were each doing and thought it might be exciting to combine forces again. There seemed little doubt that it would make good business sense. The two companies had complementary geographic strengths, their own fields of expertise, and structures that were distinctive enough that we could learn from one another. Over time, I had more conversations with Sandy; Suzy and Jim went back and forth with their contacts; we mulled, hesitated, and finally dived in.

* * *

IN 2009, TAG went to consultants' heaven, and the Albright Stonebridge Group (ASG) was born. The merger required a host of adjustments, which we expected. Most of the leading personalities meshed, but making decisions became more complicated because additional voices had to be considered. A sense of separateness lingered until, in 2015, we were able to find an office suite big enough for all, on the tenth floor of a century-old building about four blocks from the White House. Like TAG, ASG does not lobby the U.S. government.

Albright Stonebridge has grown rapidly, and I am excited by the challenge of managing a firm that has offices on six continents and has been active in some 110 countries. Sadly, Warren Rudman died in 2012, and Sandy in 2015. Suzy George left to work in the Obama White House. Jim O'Brien, however, has evolved into an indispensable figure within the company, and we have an all-star cast reporting for work each day, including my co-chair, former Secretary of Commerce (under George W. Bush) Carlos Gutierrez, other partners, former cabinet ministers, ex-ambassadors, and bright young people of many nationalities.

The assemblage of talent reminds me of my time in government, and so does our organization. Our staff has regional teams and groups whose members possess special expertise in discrete areas, such as health, high technology, and sustainability (both environmental and social). The quality of their analyses and forecasts compares favorably to that of the intelligence assessments I relied on when in public office. Our outposts abroad are similar to embassies in their blend of American and locally hired staff and in the breadth of their responsibilities to research, report, and represent. Back in Washington we strive for the right kind of corporate culture by requiring annual ethics training, taking a zero-tolerance approach to sexual harassment, participating in community service projects, and deploying a battalion of tech experts to foil the many attempts made to hack us. It used to be that security meant locked doors and a safe. Now it demands that we be smarter than the Russians, the Chinese, the North Koreans, and the whole predatory universe.

ASG describes itself as the world's leading commercial diplomacy and geopolitical risk firm. Our clients are an eclectic mix, including foundations, manufacturers, financial enterprises, service providers, and nonprofit groups. Our mission is to help them steer a sure course through the labyrinth (unique to each country) of government, public opinion, economic conditions, and local customs. We aid them in identifying the people they can rely on and in discerning the difference between a solid verbal or contractual commitment and one likely to collapse under stress. More and more, we are demonstrating the ability to anticipate challenges before they fully emerge, so that clients will have answers to questions that their competitors may not even have considered. Our goal is to enable companies to operate more wisely and to expand into foreign markets at the ideal time and in the right way, so they do not later regret the attempt.

To illustrate, consider a firm that is on the leading edge of genomics, the branch of molecular biology focused on the study and mapping of genomes. Recent advances in the field have the potential to revolutionize preventive health care, but they involve techniques that didn't exist until this century and remain unfamiliar to many. We know from history, and more recently from experience with HIV/AIDS treatments and polio vaccines, that innovative health care practices must be explained carefully and repeatedly if they are to overcome public skepticism. A company can't simply march into a foreign country and set up shop without first addressing the anxieties of the host government, local physicians, and opinion leaders. In this era, when damaging allegations can go viral in minutes, a passive approach is not enough. Genome sequencing technology can be extraordinarily beneficial, but how, why, and at what cost? A strategy is required to lay out the facts and foretell problems in each market a company seeks to enter—and tailoring strategies is what ASG does.

Our firm has also done a lot of work involving the clash between social media and governments. I have been intrigued by this because the stakes involved bear directly on the future of democracy and the balance between the rights of the individual and those of the community. They reflect, as well, the need to respond to break-throughs in technology. Here, young people have the edge in know-how, but their elders, having seen many bright ideas come and go, have the advantage of seasoning.

In London during World War II, my father was the director of broadcasting for the Czechoslovak government in exile. At the time, radio seemed at the outer reaches of what was possible. Imagine be-ing able to speak directly from a cramped BBC studio in England to listeners huddled around illegal receivers made from coat hangers and toilet tissue rolls in the attics of Prague. Incredible. In the 1960s, my young family watched with wonder as the U.S. and Russian space programs turned the fantasies of science fiction into reality; by de-cade's end, the Man *in* the Moon had become the man *on* the moon. In the late 1970s, I was employed by the Carter White House when Ayatollah Khomeini sparked an insurrectionary movement in Iran via the medium of the cassette tape—the same idea as Twitter, just slower and with longer messages. Technological revolutions are not new, and their consequences are frequently overestimated. Novel gadgets affect lifestyles far more than they do human character. Yet it is already clear that the impact of the internet and the rise of social media is of a magnitude all its own.

Almost every client of ASG is touched by the transformation in how data are communicated, how information is stored, the veloc-ity with which facts (and lies) are spread, and the need to play both offense and defense in protecting a company's credibility and honor. Social media platforms in particular are being tested, as the original concept of a fully free and unregulated online space gives way to a demand for discipline. What obligation does such a platform have to ensure that the content it transmits is not inflammatory, bigoted, or marred by outrageous falsehoods? Who is the judge of what crosses the line? Who enforces that judgment? How do we prevent personal information from being exploited in ways that violate trust? How do we properly weigh the private desire for confidentiality against the imperative of protecting the public against terrorist conspiracies and other forms of subversion? These are difficult, novel questions, to which there remain no consensus answers. They are among the many controversies on which, each day, ASG seeks to shed light.

I HAVE A soft spot for all ASG clients, but occasionally one comes along who is unique. Christo Vladimirov Javacheff, better known as just Christo, is an environmental artist with a flair for scale. Born in Bulgaria, he is my elder by two years. He and his wife, Jeanne-Claude, began the public phase of their joint career in the streets of Paris when, in 1962, they built a partition to symbolize (and satirize) the Berlin Wall. In subsequent decades, the couple created tempo-rary but spectacular works of art in many venues, including the si-multaneous display of thousands of oversize umbrellas in Japan and California, the installation of saffron-colored fabric panels to form a kind of golden river in Manhattan's Central Park, and a system of floating yellow piers that enabled participants to walk on water, or seem to, over Lake Iseo, in Italy.

We had already been working with Christo for several years when, in 2015, he asked ASG for help in coordinating with the government of the United Arab Emirates. His plan was to use thousands of oil barrels to fashion a structure in the shape of a mastaba, an ancient Egyptian tomb that resembles a flat-topped pyramid. I went with him to the proposed site in the arid Al Gharbia region of Abu Dhabi.

Christo is an exuberant man with curly gray hair who wears black-rimmed glasses and consumes raw garlic with yogurt each morning for his health. En route to our destination, we were passed repeatedly by cars going extremely fast. Arriving at the hotel, I found that we had stumbled into a convention sponsored by Ferrari. Company rep-resentatives learned I was there (because I introduced myself) and offered me a ride. I said, "Sure, but I get to drive." Off I went with a Ferrari pilot—Ferraris don't have drivers; they have "pilots"—who took me down the road a piece. Then we switched seats, and I hit the gas on the way back, arriving without damage either to myself or to the cherry-red car.

The next day, I accompanied Christo many miles into the desert to see where he intended to site his work. For transport, we relied on a rugged four-wheel-drive truck known as a dune buster. There is, I soon learned, a difference between a pile of sand in, let us say, the Cape Cod National Seashore and one in the middle of the desert in Abu Dhabi. The dunes of the Arabian Peninsula can climb hundreds of feet high, and some are so steep that people zoom down them on snowboards. Dashing through the glistening mountains at the speed of a leopard in full stride makes one grateful for a light breakfast. Going up, my head was pushed back into the seat like an astronaut's at liftoff; descending, I leaned forward with my stomach whimpering softly. I was having such a good time that I asked the guides if they would let me take the wheel; wanting to live, they said no.

What made the day even more memorable was the late-afternoon blend of whiter-than-alabaster sand, azure sky, pure air, shifting angles of sunlight, and Christo explaining with infectious verve the mechanics of what he was planning. As dusk fell, my bare toes played in the dune, and I thought of how the figure beside me never stopped imagining what might come next.

At ASG, I work with Millennials every day, but sometimes it takes an older client to rekindle inspiration and hope.

TWENTY-TWO

Inferno

SHORTLY AFTER I turned fifty, I became a talking head. The television show, *Great Decisions*, was on PBS and adhered to a format well known to any high school debater: one issue, a moderator, and commentators from opposing sides. For the Republicans, former Reagan National Security Advisor Richard Allen; for the Democrats, me. Each week, between 1989 and 1991, the two of us matched sound bites on a broad sweep of foreign policy issues.

Though raw at the outset, I soon grasped the basic rules: speak crisply, stick to the point, eschew hand or arm gestures, strive to have the last word, and be sure of your makeup. When someone else is talking, don't react, just sit like a mannequin and listen. Though the television lights may be hot, you should not be: harsh words are magnified by the medium, and in that era, civility was still deemed a virtue. My GOP debating partner checked every box. He was soft-spoken, polite, and didn't make claims he couldn't defend. Years later, I learned that Allen had recommended *Great Decisions* to President George H. W. Bush who, on Camp David stationery, typed his reply:

> I will try to catch a show or two. Actually it comes at a good time for me when at CD 'cause I am catching up on paper work—and I know that a jolt or two from Madeleine Albright might be better than bran flakes (crossed out)— make that coffee.

The skills I developed on PBS proved valuable upon my entering government. While in office, I was interviewed regularly on the Sunday network news programs and on cable broadcasts hosted by, among others, Larry King and Christiane Amanpour. In the years since, when foreign policy has been in the headlines, I have continued to share my thoughts. During the presidency of George W. Bush, I was most often a critic of administration policy, though I tried to be a fair one. When Obama took office, I faced a subtler challenge: how to be objective about a chief executive whose election I had endorsed and whose secretary of state was a longtime friend.

The answer is that I wasn't—or not entirely. There were occasions when I bit my tongue. In the beginning, though, I saw no need for reticence. After the first sixty days, I told an audience at Georgetown that "although every new American president inherits headaches, Mr. Obama inherited the entire emergency room." To illustrate, I pointed to the economic crisis, two wars, violent extremism, rising nuclear threats, a potential flu pandemic, global warming, and that scourge unique to the twenty-first century: Barbary pirates with cell phones.

My conclusion? Amid a sea of troubles, Obama was managing the early stages of his voyage well. Wherever I traveled, I found America's friends relieved and its critics mute. The president had star quality and a predecessor against whom he compared favorably in the eyes of most. There was no guarantee, though, that either advantage would last.

Obama had campaigned on a pledge to orient U.S. foreign policy toward the East. He saw Asia as a continent rising in economic clout, downloading energy from the tech-empowered young, and increasingly central to U.S. interests. To lead in the Pacific, however, required that America disentangle itself from the Middle East and especially the war in Iraq. Withdrawal from that conflict would also ease the strain in relations between the United States and the worldwide Muslim community, thereby undermining the appeal of al-Qaeda and its terrorist brethren.

On June 4, 2009, when addressing a largely Muslim audience in Cairo, the president promised to close the prison at Guantanamo within a year, to remove U.S. combat troops from Iraq by 2012, and to revive the Middle East peace process. In addition, he voiced support for democracy while separating himself from Bush by emphasizing that "No system of government can or should be imposed on one nation by any other."

IN THE WAKE of the Cairo speech, the State Department asked me to lead Partners for a New Beginning (PNB), a program to expand America's educational and economic ties to Muslims. I agreed. As busy as I was, there were few priorities more urgent. While in office, I had added Islamic holidays to the official State Department calendar and hosted annual Iftar dinners in recognition of Muslim Americans. In the time since, the need for more substantive arrangements had grown. We could either build on shared interests or lurch backward to a time when Jews, Christians, and Muslims routinely slaughtered one another. Building seemed the better idea.

Like the administration it served, PNB sprang swiftly from the starting blocks. My vice-chairs were both on my list of friends: the Aspen Institute's Walter Isaacson and Muhtar Kent, CEO of Coca-Cola. Because we wanted to avoid the stigma attached to foreign aid, and because we didn't have any money to give away, we explained that ours was not a traditional assistance program. The initiative would thrive or dive depending on our ability to persuade corporations to invest in economically and socially constructive ventures. For a brief period, we seemed to be pushing on an open door. In Indonesia, ExxonMobil developed a rural education project. Microsoft and Intel began mentoring students in Tunisia, where with the joint sponsorship of Secretary of Commerce Penny Pritzker, we held a regionwide conference on entrepreneurship. Coca-Cola established a new bottling plant in the West Bank. In Turkey, Cisco Systems had a strategy to help women get started in business. In the academic arena, we planned to connect schools in America with their counterparts in the Middle East and to increase student exchanges. Within three years, we had inaugurated chapters of PNB in eleven countries and laid the groundwork for more. After the promising start, however, that open door swung shut.

Looking back, I concluded regretfully that the program had been the right idea at the wrong time. The public-private approach could have made a tangible difference in Muslim societies by sparking economic diversity and improving relations between them and the United States. It could have done so, however, only with substantial operational support from the State Department, which it didn't get, and if other elements of the Obama game plan had come together, which they didn't.

Special Middle East Envoy George Mitchell spent two years shuttling from capital to capital in search of leaders who would take risks for peace; not finding many, he resigned. Shuttering Guantanamo proved harder than the president had expected—impossible, in fact, due to congressional resistance and controversy about where to send detainees. U.S. troops left Iraq on schedule but had to return when terrorists went on a rampage. Meanwhile, civil unrest spread through large parts of the region, causing foreign investors to close their wallets and look elsewhere. With these events piling up, the administration's long-term agenda was subsumed by near-term needs, and the new beginning dissolved into the same old story.

I don't like to fail, but after half a dozen years of trying in every way we could, I decided that PNB was like a Lego set whose pieces didn't fit; we had no choice but to move on.

IN TUNIS ON December 17, 2010, Tarek al-Tayeb Mohamed Bouazizi, a street vendor made desperate by the hostility and corruption of local authorities, set himself on fire. Eighteen days later, he died from his burns. He wasn't the first young Tunisian to immolate himself, but social media decide on their own when to erupt, and Bouazizi's act of rebellion touched a nerve in an aggrieved population. Tunisians by the thousands took to the streets demanding change and soon were joined by thousands more.

On January 14, the nation's leader, Ben Ali, yielded to the pressures gathering from below and abdicated after twenty-three years in power. The decision was both a shocking conclusion to his reign and a preface to further disruptions. Suddenly, the discontented in North Africa and the Middle East had cause to believe that revolution might also be possible in their countries. Exhilarated by the prospect, they summoned the courage to initiate protests of their own. As political frictions increased, long-frozen power structures began to thaw, and the Arab Spring began.

Of the countries affected, Egypt was the most prominent.

When I first met Hosni Mubarak, I was a rookie secretary of state, just getting a feel for the job. Mubarak had already been president of his country for a decade and a half. Elegant and stocky, he appeared the very model of a moderate Middle Eastern leader: secular, pragmatic, risk-averse, and tough without seeming cruel. He owed his longevity to the support he enjoyed from Egypt's enormous bureaucracy and its deeply entrenched military-business establishment. The partnership worked well for the insiders who banded together to reward friends and to ensure that rivals were held down. It is no wonder that, in my conversations with him, Mubarak played the role of senior statesman, confident in his position and secure in the knowledge that America thought him irreplaceable.

Since Reagan, every U.S. president had courted the Egyptian leader not so much because of his virtues, but because of what he was not. He wasn't a hard-line nationalist in the mold of a predecessor, Gamal Abdel Nasser. He didn't invade his neighbors like Iraq's Saddam Hussein. He wasn't an eccentric egotist in the manner of Libya's Muammar Gaddafi. Westerners could easily imagine a head of government in Cairo who would be far worse. That explains why the name "Mubarak" turned up so often in diplomatic discussions with the phrase "pillar of stability" attached.

But in the Middle East of early 2011, sturdy pillars had suddenly begun to resemble thin reeds.

Mimicking the uprising in Tunisia, protestors swarmed the Egyptian capital's Tahrir Square. The dissidents did not have a charismatic leader or a coherent agenda. They did have legitimate grievances, including the government's inefficiency, its lack of political openness, and the cronyism that had always marred Mubarak's brand of leadership. The president sought to cool the crisis by pledging to reform the constitution and not run for reelection. The dissenters rightly viewed the gestures as symptoms of weakness and pushed even harder. For all their differences, they were united in demanding that Mubarak either leave or be jailed. Egyptian police, caught off guard by the opposition's militance, were unable to disperse the angry crowds and denounced for trying.

Back in Washington, Obama administration officials argued amongst themselves about whether to cut the beleaguered Mubarak loose immediately or to seek gradual change. Publicly the signals they sent were mixed, calling for democracy yet warning of chaos. One reason for the uncertainty is that, out of deference to a longtime friend, U.S. intelligence agencies barely operated in the country; the United States couldn't make good predictions based on information it didn't have.

Asked to appear on CNN, I called the State Department for guidance and was informed that the administration favored "a smooth transition." So, it seemed that Obama wanted the Egyptian leader to go. During my interview, however, the network ran videos of Secretary Clinton and another American diplomat (Frank Wisner) warning about the disruption that might ensue if he did. Pressed for my own recommendation, and not wanting to upstage the White House, I deployed some of my favorite waffle words—*complicated, delicate, difficult.* I added that the decisive force in the nation might well be found among moderates who supported neither the government nor its best-organized opponent: the Muslim Brotherhood. Egypt, I said optimistically, had many citizens who were educated and civic-minded and who could, given a chance, build a modern democratic society.

On February 11, a few days after my interview on CNN, Mubarak, with encouragement from Obama, stepped down. This was the high point of the Arab Spring—and the beginning of its descent.

The removal of the Egyptian president was a shattering event, but hardly the revolution it might appear. Power was simply transferred to a military council, more a cosmetic change than a real one. Eager to move beyond that first step, demonstrators pressed the council to hold early elections. Though understandable, the rush spelled disaster for the moderate democratic parties, who were small, poorly financed, and unready to compete. In November 2011, when voters began going to the polls, they chose a parliament dominated by the Muslim Brotherhood and other Islamist groups.

The presidential election was next, and as chair of the National Democratic Institute, I hoped that our expertise might be of value. We were not given a chance to find out. On December 29, Egyptian security forces raided NDI offices in Cairo and two other cities. Without a warrant, they confiscated equipment, documents, and money and shuttered the programs. They proceeded to arrest and press criminal charges against dozens of people who worked for NDI, the International Republican Institute, and other pro-democracy organizations. The irony was grating. Under the autocratic Mubarak, NDI and groups with a similar mission were at least allowed to operate. In the new and supposedly more democratic era, we were not.

For years, I had elicited laughter from audiences by referring to the "grumpy old men" who control power in the Middle East. In the case of Egypt and NDI, my unhappiness was with an ill-tempered woman who might well have held a personal grudge against me. When I was America's ambassador to the UN, Fayza Abul Naga was an aide to the organization's secretary-general, Boutros Boutros-Ghali, a man with whom I had frequent disagreements and whose effort to win election to a second term the United States had, on my watch, vetoed. In 2012, Abul Naga was the Egyptian official who took the hardest line against NDI, making it impossible for us to do our work. Her title was minister of planning and international cooperation, but noncooperation was more her style. Perhaps our second run-in was mere coincidence; to me, it had the odor of revenge.

WHILE THE THEATRICS in Egypt held one stage, another drama began in neighboring Libya. The opening act was familiar—demonstrators clashed with defenders of the status quo—but in this case the violence quickly escalated into full-scale civil war. Lightly armed rebels advanced before being beaten back by better-equipped government troops. The country's flamboyant figurehead, Gaddafi, who had held power since 1969, compared the opposition to "cockroaches" and warned Libyans about foreign agents who "are making your children drunk and sending them to hell." He vowed to annihilate any who rose against him. On March 17, 2011, the UN Security Council authorized the establishment of a no-fly zone and "all necessary measures" to protect civilians and prevent Gaddafi from turning his domain into a slaughterhouse. In the next days, European and American ships and aircraft destroyed the regime's ability to attack rebels from the air. The balance of forces tipped in favor of the opposition, but the fighting dragged on, city by city, for months. In late August, the dictator's military disintegrated, and on October 20, he was injured by shrapnel while trying to flee, captured, stabbed, and shot dead.

BY THEN SYRIA, too, was in flames. Earlier that year, on March 15, two hundred mostly young protestors marched in Damascus. In April, the confrontation spread to ten cities, then twenty, fueled by calls for the country's dictator, Bashar al-Assad, to resign. Syrian security forces sought to intimidate the nonviolent crowds with artillery and sniper fire, killing scores and arresting many.

As tensions swelled, so did the Syrian opposition. Within its ranks were defectors from the military, Kurdish separatists, liberal intellectuals, Islamist fighters, and ordinary citizens eager for something different. With help from Turkey and Gulf Arabs, they won several early victories. However, when they tried to take Aleppo,

Syria's largest city, the two sides fought to a blood-drenched stalemate, destroying whole neighborhoods, claiming thousands of lives, and setting in motion a vast exodus of civilians. Government artillery and bombs did most of the damage. Having already seen two Arab dictators fall, and with a third (Gaddafi) on the verge of doing so, Obama tried to get ahead of events by calling on the Syrian dictator to step down. This was, however, more of a wish than a policy because, although the administration wanted Assad to leave, it had no plan in place to force him out.

As the fighting intensified, some in the West did urge an armed intervention comparable to that mounted by NATO in Libya. But Syria was bigger, and the regime had some powerful, albeit unsavory, friends. Iran and Hezbollah sent fighters to help Assad, and Russia later did the same. Moscow could also be counted on to shield Syria from any attempt by the UN Security Council to take effective action to protect civilians. There would be no internationally blessed military operations against Assad. By the end of Obama's first term, an estimated sixty thousand Syrians had died due to the conflict.

AGAINST THIS STARK backdrop, I was asked to chair another task force, this one on an evolving tenet of international law known as the "responsibility to protect." The request from the U.S. Holocaust Memorial Museum stemmed from growing feelings of frustration. In 2005, world leaders had agreed that preventing mass atrocities should be among their core goals. In that spirit, they acknowledged a "responsibility to protect," or R2P, based on three reinforcing propositions. The first is that every government has an obligation to safeguard its people from genocide and crimes against humanity. Second, nations should help one another to fulfill that mandate. Third, countries should be prepared to take collective action under the UN Charter if a state, such as Syria, fails in its duty.

In 2008, Bill Cohen and I had tried to add teeth to these principles by calling for the creation of an Atrocities Prevention Board in the United States, a recommendation implemented by Obama three

years later. Now, in 2012, we were again facing a humanitarian catastrophe that everyone could see and no one could stop.

My working group sought to remind world leaders of the vows
they had so recently made. Our report, issued in 2013, centered on
the question of whether, under international law, there is a limit to
the crimes a government can commit against its own people. Dictators typically say there is not. We asserted that, in extreme cases,
there definitely is. In fact, that is where the responsibility to protect
arises. We pointed to the Holocaust as the prime example, but also
to Cambodia under the Khmer Rouge, Rwanda during its genocide,
and Serbia during Milosevic's assault on Kosovo. Just as parents are
not free to murder or enslave their children, so governments should
not be allowed to perpetrate atrocities against their citizens.

When releasing our report, I stressed the importance of taking
early action to prevent catastrophic situations from evolving. No
president or prime minister wants to face a choice between sending
the country's armed forces into the middle of a foreign firefight or
standing aside and allowing a monstrous genocide (there is no other
kind) to occur. The wise course, therefore, is to invest in diplomatic
tools, including economic aid, the nonviolent mediation of disputes,
and support for political pluralism and human rights. World leaders
should engage in constant efforts to identify and ameliorate problems before they grow worse. That will not guarantee success in every
instance, but it may well save thousands, even millions of lives.

THE ARAB SPRING, brief though it was, touched on nearly every
element of my professional activities. I was asked with increasing
frequency to appear on news shows. At NDI, we worked hard to preserve the integrity of our programs in the affected countries. I spent
many hours with clients, analyzing the impact of both the democratic opening and the resistance to it. In my class at Georgetown,
I asked students to put themselves in the shoes of the president and
secretary of state and to think about how they would respond to the
tumultuous developments.

I also thought back to the commission I had co-chaired with Hernando de Soto on legal empowerment of the poor. The Tunisian fruit peddler Mohamed Bouazizi killed himself because the police confiscated two crates of pears, a basket of bananas, three boxes of apples, and an electronic scale. These were virtually his only possessions. Bouazizi had no legal way to recover his losses because his business was not officially registered. In Tunisia at the time, the cost of establishing a formal business was more than three thousand dollars. The young man had wanted to take out a loan and buy a truck but couldn't use the family house for collateral because he couldn't afford to register a deed. In the months after he set himself afire, more than one hundred other North African Arabs, many of whom were also street entrepreneurs, did the same. It wasn't just flames that doomed them; it was a system that made hard work irrelevant and left them with no way up and, in their eyes, no other way out.

TWENTY-THREE

R-E-S-P-E-C-T

I N 1963, BY executive order, John F. Kennedy established the Presidential Medal of Freedom, the nation's highest civilian award. The criteria are imprecise. To qualify, one must make "an especially meritorious contribution" to whatever purpose the president sees fit to recognize. Kennedy's choices favored the arts and included singer Marian Anderson, author Thornton Wilder, cellist Pablo Casals, and painter Andrew Wyeth. Tragically, before the awards ceremony could be held, Kennedy was assassinated. His successor, Lyndon Johnson, presided in his stead, distributing medals and adding posthumous honors to JFK and Pope John XXIII.

The selections made by later presidents provide a window into their personalities and interests. Carter was partial to southern writers, Reagan to businessmen (not business*women*), and Clinton to lawyers and jurists. Barack Obama roamed across every field. In 2012, his thirteen choices were broad enough to encompass a labor organizer (Dolores Huerta), a women's basketball coach (Pat Summitt), an astronaut turned U.S. senator, (John Glenn), one of America's foremost novelists (Toni Morrison), a future Nobel laureate (Bob Dylan), and me.

The awards ceremony was held in the East Room of the White House. I had been there many times when Clinton was president, so it felt odd to return to a familiar setting in a new role, but I couldn't have been happier. Once the audience was seated, the honorees filed in. Thanks to the alphabet, I was first in line. The last, wearing dark glasses because of the television lights or just because he wanted to, was Dylan. I wondered why he didn't come earlier in the list until I remembered that his birth name is "Zimmerman" and thought maybe that was the reason.

For a full minute, we stood at attention while the friends and guests sitting in front of us recorded the scene on cell phones. Then, accompanied by a flourish of trumpets, the president strode in. He had on a striped shirt and, in the lapel of his suit, an American flag pin. I, too, wore a U.S. flag pin, about twelve times the size of Obama's. Receiving the Medal of Freedom was not an occasion for subtlety. My eyes were on the chief executive, but I also stole glances at the many members of my family who were there. I was enjoying this.

Standing behind a small lectern and in front of a gold brocade curtain, the president told stories about each of the recipients, again starting with me. He referred kindly to my efforts in government, humorously to my pins, and seriously to my experience as a refugee. After completing his remarks, he dangled a medal on a blue ribbon around each of our necks and fastened it in the back. This was followed by more pictures.

Glancing down at the decoration, I could say at last that I had something, if only this, in common with such earlier awardees as John Wayne, Lucille Ball, and Joe DiMaggio. The memento's design includes thirteen small gold stars within a blue circle against the background of a larger white star, and around the edges are five gold eagles with outstretched wings. After the ceremony, when I casually let slip to Colin Powell the fact that I had received the Medal of Freedom, he congratulated me heartily. I asked if he had one; he said no. He has two.

IN FEBRUARY OF that same year, I attended a concert at the Kennedy Center featuring Chris Botti. I had met the ultra-cool jazz trumpeter and bandleader a month earlier at a state dinner for China. He had performed; later we chatted. Visiting backstage before the Kennedy Center event, I wished him good luck. He thanked me and added that he sometimes invited members of the audience to come up and try their hands at the drums. Having never played a percussion instrument, I might logically have kept my mouth shut. Instead, I inquired, "Really?"

The show was well under way when Botti approached the microphone, said that I was in the audience, and asked me to come forward. This caused a few in the crowd to clap and many to laugh. I had on a dark jacket, a heart-shaped pin—this was Valentine's Day—and a skirt made of clingy black leather, which being of sound mind, I rarely wore.

My first challenge was to maneuver in heels across the enormous Kennedy Center stage without tripping over what seemed a snakes' convention of electric cords. Safely ensconced behind the drums, I listened for a few minutes to a duet played by Botti and violinist Caroline Campbell. The piece, "Nessun dorma" ("No one sleeps"), is from Puccini's opera *Turandot*. The music the two of them made was lovely beyond words, sweet, haunting—but in keeping with the ominous script, also threatening. Years earlier, when I was a child, my parents had taken me to a performance in Belgrade of *Madama Butterfly*. I decided then that if I couldn't realize my ambition to be a Catholic priest, I would become an opera star.

Now I was onstage with Chris Botti, making like Ringo. I thought, *Don't screw this up.* Also: *There are a lot more drums here than I expected.* My adrenal glands pumped, my hands twitched, my cue finally arrived. Raising the sticks I had been clutching, I began rapping them in time to the beat shown to me by the regular drummer, Billy Kilson, who was nearby pounding one hand into the other. When he mimed a buoyant stick-swinging gesture, I did the same, a split second late but with no lack of ham. I even hit the cymbals a time or two. When we were done, the audience screamed its approval and I was well and truly amped. Kissing everyone once and Botti twice, I exited stage left, sticks held high.

The roots of this epic musical interlude extended back to my years in government and to an underrated foreign policy tool: cultural diplomacy. Presidents and cabinet secretaries may like to think that they shape America's international image, but the truth is they have plenty of company. Filmmakers, television shows, athletes, corporate brands, universities, tourists, and others contribute as much or more to perceptions overseas—and no art form is more gloriously American than jazz. Some of our country's finest ambassadors have been named Armstrong, Davis, Ellington, Fitzgerald, Goodman, and Holiday. That explains why, when in office, I thought it appropriate to host a reception each year for a global competition run by the Herbie Hancock Institute of Jazz. The venue provides a showcase for talented young performers on every continent, and it gave me a chance to advertise the intimate connection between political liberty and artistic freedom. It also allowed me to forge a friendship with Hancock, another illustrious ambassador of music, who presides over the event.

In September—this was still 2012—Hancock was joined as co-host of the competition by none other than Chris Botti. The two decided to recognize my work on behalf of cultural diplomacy and invited a member of royalty to join in the festivities.

Earlier that year I had participated in a project for the UN High Commissioner for Refugees, during which I had lip-synched my way through an abbreviated version of "Respect." Now, onstage, was the universally acknowledged Queen of Soul rocking the house with renditions of the R-song and "My Funny Valentine." Then, Aretha Franklin congratulated *me*. I have to say that, onstage with Hancock, Botti, and Franklin, I truly felt like a natural woman. Next, at a nod from Botti, I reprised my performance on the drums—a little louder this time, more assured. I had found my niche.

AT THE RISK of too jarring a transition, let's shift the topic of our discussion from the world of trumpets and drums to that of cloaks and daggers—from jazz to the CIA. Established by the National Security Act of 1947, the CIA has a well-known mandate to supply top U.S. officials with the information they need to make good decisions and, when directed by the president, to carry out specific missions, usually secret, on America's behalf. I never served in the agency, but between 2009 and 2017, I was a member of its External Advisory Board. That panel's assignment was to offer thoughts on how the spy outfit could better manage its operations and explain itself to the world. The need for improvements in both policy and public relations was obvious given the CIA's role in the lead-up to the Iraq War and subsequent revelations about its involvement with clandestine prison sites and torture. The advisory board met several times a year, received briefings, and shared its ideas with the director, Leon Panetta, and his top aides. There were fourteen of us, including one of my new partners at ASG, Warren Rudman. It was a collegial group, experienced and not afraid to probe or find fault.

In this age of WikiLeaks, any attempt to maintain secrecy in foreign affairs is likely to be ridiculed as impossible or attacked as an effort to engage in some sort of devilish conspiracy. I concede that national security officials restrict access to more documents than they should, but that is usually evidence of too much caution, not malign intent. Confidentiality does have its place. Fans of Julian Assange may think of themselves as agents of truth, but one reason some secrets must be kept is to protect real truth tellers in repressive societies from being exposed.

Back in 1987, I visited Czechoslovakia as part of a program run by the U.S. Information Agency. The Cold War was still in full chill and a communist government was in firm control of the country. Nevertheless, a public affairs officer from the U.S. embassy agreed to help me get in touch with a dissident—a brave member of Prague's political underground. The diplomat told me to wait for a man in a trench coat at an exact time, in front of a certain building, near a church on a well-known square. I followed instructions, and tried not to betray my nervousness, but couldn't help scanning the street for a rainproof coat on this partly sunny afternoon. Suddenly, I heard a whisper: "Follow me. We're taking the Metro to a stop several minutes away. Don't ask me which."

On the train, more whispering: "Keep close to me. We'll pretend that we're lovers, and no one will notice." I then received a convincing smooch from a man I didn't know on the way to a destination at which I could only guess. After exiting the Metro, we walked a few blocks to a nondescript building, then headed down to a basement apartment—literally the underground—where we were able to talk. As I might have deduced from the stacks of *Rolling Stone* magazine that filled his shelves, the whisperer was also a musician. He had joined the Jazz Section, a group that came together in 1971 but soon discovered that, under an authoritarian regime, artistic expression could not always remain separate from politics. This was the lesson that, years later, I would emphasize when speaking at the competition with Herbie Hancock and friends.

The Jazz Section, along with the plays of Václav Havel and a Frank Zappa–inspired rock band, the Plastic People of the Universe, was at the center of Czechoslovakia's cultural and political opposition to Communism. That day in Prague, my new friend and I discussed the strategies that the dissidents used and the obstacles they faced. Before leaving, I gave him some cash and offered to send another two hundred dollars, and then more if the funds actually got through. He told me where to address a money order, which I dispatched as soon as I returned to Washington. When I told my mother what I had done, she was furious, sure the payment would be traced. I told her not to worry. My beneficiary wrote and thanked me for the "two hundred kisses," but when he was later arrested (for reasons unrelated to the money), my mother insisted she had been right.

Moviemakers and mystery writers love to romanticize intelligence work, and to propagate myths about how much the CIA knows and what it can do. From my vantage point as a policymaker, I came to respect the agency's wide-ranging capabilities, but also to temper what I expected. The CIA operates in a bazaar peopled by power seekers, con artists, tall tale tellers, zealots with a cause, mercenaries, and a surprising number of men and women who stun cynics by being honest. The agency's budget is finite, and its actions constrained—or should be—by the tethers of policy and law. During my years on the advisory board, our attention was drawn to four vital aspects of its mission: stopping terrorists, halting the spread of nuclear and other weapons of mass destruction, defending our electronic infrastructure from cyberattacks, and predicting what would happen next in the war zones of Afghanistan, Iraq, and Syria. These were impossible tasks to fulfill perfectly, but when the CIA is properly led, and top executive branch officials allow it to function as it should, I do not think anyone can do them better.

In 2012, I was asked by Panetta's successor, David Petraeus, to coordinate a study on the CIA and women in leadership. He was concerned that relatively few women were being promoted to the Senior Intelligence Service and suspected that flawed management practices might be responsible. Working with a group of CIA officers, we found that women in the agency face even greater obstacles than their counterparts in the private sector. In the intelligence field, jobs that are all-consuming, and therefore hard on families, are common. Even now, a high-intensity workload is more likely to disrupt the career decisions of a woman than a man. Because the cadre of senior women is small, there are relatively few role models for younger counterparts, thus perpetuating the imbalance. Meanwhile, the traditional macho culture, though expressed less overtly than in the past, remains. The solution is to ensure that gender equity is considered whenever decisions are made on recruitment, work schedules, promotions, and pay. That is an easy prescription to write out, but it's up to the patient to follow through.

After submitting our report, I went to Langley to talk about its recommendations and to join in marking Women's History Month. While there, I explained to a gathering of employees that when I became America's ambassador to the United Nations, I had to overcome sixty years of social training. Until that time, my habit in a meeting had been to listen first, then speak only after I had a feel for the conversation and what other people were saying. In the Security Council, I couldn't be so reticent. In front of me was a nameplate reading, "United States." It was my responsibility, more often than not, to set the agenda and establish the framework for debate. I couldn't sit around and play it safe; I had to jump in. After a while, I got used to interrupting when I needed to, and insisted that others respond to me. The point of my story was that in any group, someone has to lead, and it might as well be a woman—provided she has done the work necessary to prepare.

EARLY IN 2017, I received a phone call from Mike Pompeo, the newly named CIA director. He thanked me for my service as a member of the agency's External Advisory Board. Then he fired me.

I will always have my drums.

TWENTY-FOUR

"You Are Just Like Your Grandmother"

THROUGHOUT OBAMA'S FIRST term, as I constantly switched hats, I also thought about moving ahead with another book. Since leaving government, I had produced *Madam Secretary*, *The Mighty and the Almighty*, *Memo to the President Elect*, and *Read My Pins*. Why stop? There was one project I had long contemplated. Toward the end of the First World War, a legion of Czechoslovak soldiers found themselves stranded in Russia amid the Bolshevik Revolution. Unable to exit the country through an embattled Europe, the band was forced to fight its way to the Pacific along five thousand miles of the Trans-Siberian Railway. My father had wanted to write of the odyssey and was doing research when, in 1977, he became ill and died. The soldiers' tale was a daring one, full of diplomatic double-dealing, hairbreadth escapes, engineering miracles, and the ransoming of boxcars filled with Romanov gold. My father recorded his notes on Dictaphone tapes that were stored in my garage. I was tempted to have a go at finishing what he had started, then reconsidered. As stirring as the saga of the legion was, the plot was light on roles for women, and my own connection to it was thin. The more I went through the papers in my garage, the more I was pulled in by another drama, closer to home.

PRAGUE WINTER WAS published in the spring of 2012. The book describes the opening eleven years of my life set against the backdrop of a country and a continent ripped asunder by Hitler, then Stalin. The text is a blend of first-person narrative and history informed by the writings of my parents and their contemporaries. Chapters cover my family's life in the democratic Czechoslovakia of the 1930s, followed by the 1939 German invasion and our subsequent escape to England. There my parents and I lived during the war, joined in 1942 by my newborn sister Kathy. After the German surrender, we returned only to witness, in 1948, what amounted to a communist coup. This forced my family (now also including little brother John) into exile for a second time.

I told my publisher that I wanted to write the book because it was in those war-ravaged years that I learned how to be who I am. Repeatedly uprooted, I felt like a migratory species fleeing each unwelcome change in the climate. I couldn't help but develop a measure of self-reliance. At the mercy of large events, I also became a watcher constantly on-edge at a time when foreign policy decisions shaped my life and those of everyone around me. My mother, Mandula, was the worrier. This was among the ways she expressed her love. Even now, when I or one of my daughters becomes anxious, we say that she is having "a Mandula moment." My father saw the world the way I try to: as a place, though infinitely complex, that can be made freer, more just, and more humane by people unafraid to pursue those goals.

For almost all of my first sixty years, this was my universe, shaped by my family's experience as I understood it. I knew where I had come from, what I believed, and why. Then, with shattering abruptness, I discovered that I had known far less than I thought.

About the time I became secretary of state, I learned that my heritage was Jewish and that more than two dozen members of my family, including three grandparents, had died in the Holocaust. The discovery was public, laid out by a reporter in the pages of the *Washington Post*. When I said that I had been unaware of these facts, many commentators accused me of lying and suggested that for reasons of personal ambition, I had taken pains to conceal my Jewish ancestry. This was a mortifying accusation that left me feeling helpless and yet made no sense, given that I hadn't even held a professional job until I was thirty-nine. Why keep secrets? In hindsight, I had to acknowledge that the clues to my family's roots were there, but I had not looked because I had felt no reason to dig beneath the surface of the world I already knew. I had never doubted what I was: an ethnic Slav, a proud (and grateful) American immigrant, and an Episcopalian convert who had been baptized Roman Catholic.

To write now about the period between 1937 and 1948, I would have to replace the lens through which I had always viewed the past. I would have to find out all I could about the lives and fates of family members that my sister, brother, and I had come of age not knowing we had. I would have to confront emotions I was unsure I could handle: to think deeply for the first time about people my parents had never stopped loving but who were long since dead. I would have to cope with a sense of guilt because I had not asked questions that would later seem obvious. I would also have to write about the Holocaust, a tragedy I didn't feel I had the standing to describe. I am no Elie Wiesel, who was imprisoned at Auschwitz and Buchenwald. I am a survivor in a sense, but not of the Shoah. My wartime experiences, though occasionally harrowing, do not compare.

Starting in 1997, my siblings and I began to learn more about our family's past. In February, Kathy and John went to the Czech Republic to visit the town (known now as Letohrad), where our father had grown up, and also to nearby Kostelec nad Orlicí, home village of our mother. Given the demands of my new job, I could not travel with them at the time, but instead flew to Prague in July, where I saw the names of our family members inscribed on the interior walls of the Pinkas Synagogue, along with those of more than 77,000 other Czechoslovak Jews who had perished during the war. With help from local Jewish officials, we were able to form in our minds a general outline of what our ancestors had gone through during the Nazi occupation—but an outline was not enough.

Two dozen relatives. Three banal words. What were the life and death stories behind them? Wiesel had written, "Not to transmit an experience is to betray it." My sister, brother, and I couldn't revisit the past without sadness, but we couldn't fail to do so without leaving unpaid our debt to the dead and incomplete our own understanding of who we are.

I HAD AN older cousin named Dáša, or Dagmar. She had known me as an infant in prewar Czechoslovakia and had stayed with us for a time when I was with my parents in London. Our paths diverged after the war, when the Iron Curtain descended, and she chose to remain in Prague to marry her sweetheart instead of leaving with us for the West. Her mother, Markéta (Greta) Deimlová, was my father's sister. After deciding to write *Prague Winter*, I contacted my cousin to probe her memories. I also asked for her help in translating letters that until 1997 I had not known she had—letters that my paternal grandmother, Olga, had sent to Greta during the early years of the war. Those messages gave us insight into the period when Nazi cruelty was bearing down on Czechoslovak Jews, depriving them of jobs, pushing them into ghettos, restricting their movements, starving them, and requiring them to wear the infamous yellow star, with "Jude" inscribed on it in black.

In July 1942, Olga wrote that she and her husband (my grandfather) were to be transported by train to Terezín, a town in the northwestern part of the country that had been set aside to house Jews. The Germans described the town as a spa; the inhabitants knew it to be a prison. "I have to get used to the thought that we are actually leaving," wrote Olga. "I hope that once I get [to Terezín], I will calm down. I am not calm right now. In fact, I haven't been calm for a long time . . . I would like to ask you, my dear Gretichka, not to waste your strength worrying about us. You will need it for yourself. I promise that I have a very strong will to survive. Somewhere, in some foreign land, we will meet again."

ON JULY 30, 1942, beneath a soggy sky, Arnošt and Olga Körbel departed Prague along with 936 others. To my grandfather's relief, a neighbor had agreed to care for Drolik, his beloved fifteen-year-old fox terrier. But in Terezín, amid the grossly overcrowded conditions he encountered, Arnošt's fragile health soon failed him. On September 18, he succumbed to bronchial pneumonia. Two months later, my aunt Greta arrived in the ghetto accompanied by her husband, Rudolf Deiml, and Milena, their eleven-year-old daughter. Greta was put to work in the prison hospital, where in February of the following year she was among those whose lives were claimed by an epidemic of typhoid fever.

While Rudolf, a doctor, did carpentry work, Milena took her place as one of the young artists of Terezín, in a setting where education and culture were revered despite the wretched surroundings. After the war, some twenty of her drawings were among those found crammed into suitcases in an attic of the girls' dorm. My little cousin drew pictures of trains, animals, and of families standing outside their houses beneath a sun that sometimes smiled.

Terezín had no gas chambers. It was not a death camp—though thousands died there—but rather, a jail and transit point. For almost three years, Jews were sent east at irregular intervals from Terezín, most often to Auschwitz, where they were separated into groups judged either fit to do work or unfit and therefore to be killed. Rudolf boarded a train on September 28, 1944. He was followed, on October 23, by my grandmother Olga and little Milena. Theirs was the third-to-last transport. My grandfather's brother Karel and his wife were on the final one. At the time, their young son Gert was in a labor camp near Auschwitz. Early in 1945, when the site was evacuated, Gert was sent on a forced march back to Czechoslovakia. Enfeebled by malnutrition and typhoid, he died in a barn just a few days before liberation.

SINCE LEARNING WHAT I did in 1997, I wondered how my mother and father could have shielded me so completely from the fears they must have felt during the war. After the first months in London, they would have had no direct way to communicate with their parents. As the fighting intensified, they would likely have had only general knowledge about Terezín and nothing verifiable regarding the jammed transports that were taking Jews from there to Auschwitz. When poring over old transcripts, I discovered that my father's broadcast team in London explicitly warned the Nazis against killing Czech Jews, and that in one case, the publicity succeeded in delaying a mass execution, but only for a month.

After the war, my mother and father rarely talked about this part of their past and never about what had happened to my grandparents. I was told that they were old and had died, which I accepted as the fate of people who grow old. I neither saw tears nor shed them.

Then, when searching through a box of my father's papers in pursuit of material for *Prague Winter*, I came across some pages he had typed up years before; it was the draft of a short novel about a young Czechoslovak diplomat who returns home after the war. Eagerly, the man anticipates a reunion with his mother, only to be overwhelmed by grief when he finds that she and every relative to whom he had once been close had been taken away; they were no more. He doesn't ask why, nor does he speculate. He knows why. In despair, he returns to his hotel and collapses, sobbing, on the bed. Later, he makes his way to the countryside, to the house in which he had lived as a boy. He knocks on the door. A stranger answers. The young supplicant tries to explain himself, but after several awkward attempts to communicate, realizes that the man standing before him cannot hear him nor can he formulate words of his own. The narrator finally gives up and takes his leave. As he exits, he thinks to himself that the encounter must have been a sign: "The past was to be deaf and dumb," wrote my father. "It was to be neither heard, nor spoken."

WHEN *PRAGUE WINTER* was published, many people whose lives were touched by the events described in it reached out. First, a woman wrote that she had been among the few babies born in Terezín during the war who had survived. Then an eighty-six-year-old called from Toronto; I recognized her name from the research I had done. As a teenager, Vera Schiff had been imprisoned at Terezín and forced, while working in the prison hospital, to confront an unspeakably difficult moral choice.

At a Jewish Community Center in New Jersey, I met Hana Stránská, who had once been a trusted assistant of my father in London and Prague. Ms. Stránská could no longer talk very clearly, but she smiled and her eyes sparkled when I held her arm. I had included an anecdote from her own writings in *Prague Winter*; it described how impossible it was for her to forgive Germans after the war, even though she had grown up speaking their language.

I was also in contact with a woman living in Austria who had been on the same train to Auschwitz as my grandmother and little cousin Milena. The woman, then a teenager, had been accompanied by her twin sister. While on the train, the two were counseled to say to the Germans that they had been born a year apart, because waiting to interrogate them on the station platform would be the Nazi doctor Josef Mengele, who had an abhorrent fascination for twins.

What struck me about such accounts is that the women who related them had, seventy years earlier, faced imminent death. If the Nazis had prevailed in their plans, each of these individuals would have long since been exterminated. Instead, they were still alive in the twenty-first century, proof in the flesh of the failure of the Third Reich, which Hitler had boasted would last a thousand years. The reversal of fates is one reason I find it impossible to be cynical.

HAVING COMPLETED *PRAGUE WINTER*, I thought I knew as much of my family's story as I would ever learn. Most moving to me were the letters that my paternal grandmother, Olga, had written in the months before she and Arnošt departed for Terezín. Her vivid accounts helped me imagine the character and feelings of this unique person who had once cradled me in her arms, but whom I had been too young to remember and not had a chance to know.

Though grateful for what I had discovered about Olga, I knew little concerning my mother's mother, Růžena Spieglová. I was aware only that she must have suffered greatly during this period. Her husband, Alfred, died in 1936, and her daughter Máňa lost a battle with kidney disease in February 1941. My brother figured out that Růžena had lived in the town of Poděbrady, and we learned from government records that she was sent to Terezín in June 1942.

Years earlier our grandmother had been a shopkeeper in Kostelec nad Orlicí assuring customers that her family's coffee was the finest in all Bohemia. At the time of my birth, she helped my mother to care for me and called me "Madla" or "Madlenka," after a character in a popular stage drama. (My birth name was Marie Jana.) In the first days after Hitler's invasion, she again took me in while my parents were in Prague devising a plan for our escape and sleeping in a different place each night to avoid arrest. When I was young and indulging my love for swimming in cold water, my mother used to exclaim, "You are just like your grandmother." This was all I knew of Růžena.

After *Prague Winter* was released, I continued in spare moments to sort through the notebooks, writings, and letters that had belonged to my father. I had moved some of this material to a public storage facility when I was in government and the Diplomatic Security Service took over my garage. Most of the papers were related to my father's writing projects or to his years teaching at the University of Denver. I was amused to find, given that my Georgetown course is called America's National Security Toolbox, that he had long ago written an article entitled "The Tools of Foreign Policy." I also uncovered a collection of his sweet-smelling pipes. What was clear was that most of the cartons in the storage facility had not been opened in a long time. The documents in them were yellowed, curled at the corners, and bound by rubber bands so brittle they snapped at first touch. The containers stacked in the corners and on shelves higher up were the last to come down. One day in 2014, I grabbed hold of a cardboard box and brushed away the dust. Inside, I found some folders and loose sheets—nothing unusual there— but also an object with a different appearance, more formal, almost elegant. It was a worn leather-bound book, maroon, six inches by nine. The binding at the bottom had broken off; the leaves were gilt-edged.

On one page, there was a drawing of a bird on a tree branch. Clearly it was a journal, and as with my repeated efforts to keep a diary over the years, it began on January 1. The year in this case, though, was 1942. The handwriting, in Czech, was unfamiliar. Then my eyes were drawn to the opening salutation, "Dear Andulko."

What was this? Andulko was an affectionate variant of my mother's name, Anna. I could feel blood drain from my face. All these years, out of sight, sitting in a box. I looked again at the date and knew in a flash what I was holding. I was well over seventy years old and would only now, for the first time since infancy, be given the chance to hear, albeit in writing, the voice of my maternal grandmother. How had the journal come to be there? We will never be sure. Once again, I regretted not knowing earlier the full story of our family. Eagerly I started to read, then stopped. January 1, 1942—on that date, my parents and I had been in London for almost three years. It was around that time that the Germans had decided as a matter of official policy to put to death every Jew in Europe. I would read what my grandmother had to say, but not all at once.

WHENEVER I HAD started a journal, I had done so with the intent of recording my thoughts each day. Růžena evidently had the same goal. For the first three weeks there are regular entries. On New Year's Day she recalls life earlier in Poděbrady with her daughter Máňa, who was my mother's sister and my aunt. Among the subjects they talked about, my grandmother wrote, was Madlenka "and all the cute things she used to say." But now, Máňa is dead and Růžena is alone, "I don't have my dear daughter here anymore. So I don't really worry about too much." She continues:

> *We here are waiting as we hear everywhere that we will be moved to a camp—about ten transports left from Prague already . . . People here are sad and everyone is taking the war with difficulty. This includes Aryans and non-Aryans, to use this rather peculiar naming into which God's creation are now*

divided. We wear stars as you know, some proudly, some hide
them even though you are not allowed to . . . Today, I celebrated
the New Year and went for a walk to some field not too far
away, since Jews cannot leave town and cannot go into any
village. And if I had to write all the things that can't be done, it
would take too long so again, some other time. Now I am sitting
in that small room under the eaves. I am warm, and I am
waiting for some ladies who visit me sometimes.

As the days pass in that bleak January, Růžena comments on the
steady flow of military trains; the scarcity of vegetables, fruit, eggs,
milk, and cheese; the inventorying of Jewish possessions; German
boys yelling, "Jew, Jew"; the fact that "in this very difficult time, a
person stops being normal," and the prohibition on listening to foreign radio broadcasts (where, had she a receiver, she would surely
have heard my father's voice). In mid-month, despite frigid temperatures and heavy frost, Jews are ordered to give up fur coats, hosiery,
and wool underwear, so the items may be sent to the Eastern Front to
warm the bodies of Axis soldiers. Houses are being inspected, which
prompts Růžena to worry about where to hide her journal. On the
sixteenth, she writes, "I want to systematically remember what has
already happened to the Jews." A few days later she mentions that
new German leaders have taken charge in Prague and that the repression has become even worse. She notes, as well, a report that foreign
parachutists had landed in Czech territory and that authorities had
found the parachutes, not the men.

After January 21 there are but two entries. On February 8, Růžena
marks the first anniversary of her daughter's death and describes with
a gentle sadness the courage Máňa had shown in her final days. On
April 22, she writes that she had been called to the Jewish Center to
prepare for departure. She undergoes a physical exam and is judged
able to work. Her expectation is that Jews will be moved out of
Poděbrady. It "is possible," she writes, "that the troubles, which await
us, I will survive. Perhaps, we will see each other, dear ones, who are

abroad. May God give you health. When I come back (I hope I will today, a person never knows), I will write down what it was like."

Růžena's decision to keep a journal is made more poignant by the message-in-the-bottle aspect; she had no way of knowing whether or by whom her words would be read. She was alone, and this was her attempt to reach out from one generation to the next, not sure whether a connection would ever be made. It was an act of faith in a context where there were no grounds to have faith—and also an act of rebellion.

Five weeks after my grandmother's last notation, a British-trained Czech expatriate who had dropped into the country by parachute hurled an antitank grenade at the Mercedes carrying the German overseer in Prague, Reinhard Heydrich. After lingering for a week, Heydrich died of wounds suffered when the explosive sent shards of metal, glass, and seat stuffing into his guts and chest. The man known as "the Butcher of Prague" had been a protégé of Heinrich Himmler and had helped plan the Holocaust. He was the only high-level Nazi assassinated during the war. Hitler spoke at his funeral and, with the assailants still at large, vowed revenge.

On June 9, 1942, the day Heydrich was buried, a train departed Kolín, just south of Poděbrady, en route to Terezín. Instead of being imprisoned there, the Jewish passengers were sent farther east. Precisely what happened at the end of their journey is not known, except that there were no survivors. Almost certainly the train stopped in German-occupied Poland. Terezín records suggest the location as Trawniki, the site of a forced-labor camp established the previous year. Among other purposes, the facility was used by the Nazis to teach Russian and Ukrainian prisoners how to become concentration camp guards. As part of their education, the students were required to shoot prisoners. Růžena Spieglová was on that train.

As a child, I had understood that my grandparents had died because they were old, an explanation, I noted earlier, that from my youthful perspective made sense to me. But perspectives change. I

To Madeline — Thanks for your extraordinary service to our country!
Michelle Obama

An exemplary president, an incomparable First Lady; we owe them both.

Receiving the Medal of Freedom from President Obama (2012). Behind me: space hero and senator John Glenn.

Photograph by Charlie Archambault

Flanked by former secretary of defense Bill Cohen and Janet Langhart Cohen.

AP Photo/Carolyn Kaster

Ceremonial groundbreaking, National Museum of American Diplomacy (2014). Digging in with me are (*from left*), former secretaries of state Clinton, Kissinger, Kerry, Baker, and Powell.

A shattered glass ceiling, a dove, a serpent, and a book cover that says it all.
Pin photographs by John Bigelow Taylor and Dianne Dubler. From left to right:
Breaking the Glass Ceiling *by Vivian Shimoyama;* Peace Dove *by Cécile et Jeanne;*
Serpent, *designer unknown*

Book cover photograph by Diana Walker; Liberty *pin by Gijs Bakker*

Campaigning in New Hampshire for Hillary Clinton (2016). A good candidate, she would have made a great president.

Celebrating my eightieth birthday with two very special surprise guests.

That's Chris Botti on the trumpet and you-know-who with the sticks.

Tribute to jazz with Herbie Hancock, Jennifer Hudson, Colin Powell, Dianne Reeves, and the Queen of Soul, Aretha Franklin (2011).

Presenting a laptop (his first) to the new president of Czechoslovakia, Václav Havel (1990).

Havel's memorial service: a truth teller at rest (2011).

Sharing a laugh with Madam Secretary ('Téa Leoni).

Dueling over waffles with Leslie Knope (Amy Poehler) of *Parks and Recreation*.

Wishing a happy birthday to Rory (Alexis Bledel) on *Gilmore Girls*.

Paul Morigi/AP Images for National Portrait Gallery

National Portrait Gallery (2018). Robert Redford! Still waiting to exhale.

Alexis Krieg

Madeleine of Arabia. Barefoot in the desert with Christo (2015).

was seventy-four years old when I wrote *Prague Winter*; my grandmother was only fifty-four when she was murdered.

WE PUT DOWN in writing what our senses tell us because humans, alone among species (as far as we know), believe it important to remember. Rickety though it may be, memory is the one railing we can hold on to in our unequal duel with time. Loved ones die, but their faces, words, favorite expressions, teachings, characteristic movements, and the distinctive shape of their mouths when smiling remain with us, crisp for a while, then less so. Months pass, then years, and the images fade, only to recover suddenly their sharpness when a sight or sound jogs our brains. Is it pleasure that we feel then, or pain? I see a man with a pipe and think of my father. A woman telling fortunes or drinking tea may conjure up my mother. No one now alive has a personal memory of Růžena Spieglová. My family has two photographs; now we have her words.

TWENTY-FIVE

Leaving

"MR. PRESIDENT, MR. Prime Minister, distinguished guests from around the world, family and friends of Václav Havel, I am honored to participate with you in this celebration of an incomparable man."

I have delivered eulogies before, but not with a heavier heart or in a setting so imposing. Prague's Metropolitan Cathedral of Saints Vitus, Wenceslas and Adalbert, with its three-hundred-foot-high tower, Gothic arches, and vaulted tombs, embodies the paradoxical blend of humility and grand design that characterized medieval worship. Within its walls are the Czech crown jewels and the remains of Holy Roman emperors and Bohemian kings. The cathedral is where the history of the Czech people is witnessed and recorded. Yet, on the afternoon of December 23, 2011, Václav Havel would surely have preferred to be someplace else.

I AM OFTEN asked, "Who is your hero?" The older I become, the more uneasy I am with the term. We may judge specific actions to be heroic, whether of soldiers or civilians, but no one can live up to that billing all the time. In our era, even comic book superstars have flaws. As he was quick to admit, so did Václav Havel. He lacked discipline in his personal life, his political reflections could be maddeningly abstract, and his reputation was magnified by his presence in the spotlight when history was ripe to be made. At a different place or time, or with worse luck, he might never have gained recognition beyond the theater. Nevertheless, I would have followed him anywhere.

Why? Because he insisted on injecting kindness into debates on how human beings should be governed. He saw forgiveness as an essential component of social and political relations. He rarely met a person with whom he could not laugh. Above all, he was honest; from his first breath to his final days, he pursued truth without hesitation.

On one of my last visits with him, Havel told me about a teacher he had in grade school during the German occupation of Czechoslovakia. The instructor was so strict that his students, including young Václav, feared him; yet this teacher had a virtue. He, alone among his peers, refused to go along with even the most convenient of lies. The Germans claimed that they had invaded the Czech lands out of self-defense and that the regime they had established in Prague did what was best for all people. They demanded further that schoolteachers in the land they had conquered funnel this nonsense into the ears of the young. Risking death, Havel's instructor would not. He told his pupils frankly that Germany's attack had been unprovoked and that the government it had set up to rule over them was a cruel fraud.

When, as an adult, Havel looked back on that time, he saw the teacher as representing an ideal. He knew that the leader of a political movement, no matter how just, could be motivated by hunger for acclaim, because he perceived that appetite in himself. But the teacher had neither any expectation of praise nor any realistic hope that his stance would make a difference. He was loyal to the facts because of an inability to be anything else.

HAVEL'S COLD WAR manifesto, *The Power of the Powerless*, was written in 1978. The essay showed how living and acting in truth could expose the communist system as one so hollow that even party members had ceased to believe in it. The author's boldness inspired dissidents throughout Central Europe and popularized themes that democrats everywhere still stress. Havel was arrested and imprisoned the following year, but his commentaries and plays, wherein political content is often masked by clever allegories, continued to pass from hand to hand. The Charter 77 movement, which Havel helped organize, collected signatures in support of free expression. When the Soviet bloc began to crumble, he negotiated behind the scenes, using street demonstrations to provide leverage. Crowds rattled their keys to emulate bells tolling the end of communist rule, while chanting, "Havel na Hrad" (Havel to the Castle).

On December 29, 1989, the wordsmith with the imp's grin was sworn in as president. Three days later, he addressed an anxious nation:

> For forty years you heard from my predecessors on this [New Year's] day different variations on the same theme: how our country was flourishing, how many million tons of steel we produced, how happy we all were, how we trusted our government, and what bright perspectives were unfolding in front of us.
>
> I assume you did not propose me for this office so that I, too, would lie to you. Our country is not flourishing.

By then my father had been dead a dozen years, my mother just a few weeks. If alive, they would, I am sure, have applauded the ideas and words of the new Czech leader. I am less certain of what Josef Korbel, who wore a dress shirt and tie when fishing, would have thought of Havel's informal style. The playwright president ditched his predecessor's limousine for a small car and rode down castle corridors on a scooter. Instead of suits, he often wore blue jeans, or what the Czechs call "Texas pants." He claimed credit, while on trips, for reintroducing cigarettes to both the Kremlin and the White House. And during his first year in office, his aides found a hotel for him to work out of while on a trip to Bratislava. Havel was delighted with the place and went to the bar, where he held court until his staff noticed that the other guests were uniformly attractive, female, and wearing not much. Though the president would have been pleased to conduct the public's business from a brothel, his advisers dragged him away.

Havel was a marvelous writer but an indifferent orator. When he spoke, even to television interviewers, he avoided eye contact. He told me it was a habit he had picked up in prison. During interrogation, he found it easier to stonewall a questioner by not looking at the man directly. I told him that "to succeed as a politician, you have to engage people with your eyes." Absorbing the advice, he replied, "I understand and will try to do better," while staring at the floor.

Despite his elusive gaze, Havel was a delight to talk to. He referred to himself as "a Czech bumpkin" and approached even heavy topics with a touch of grace. He resisted making definitive statements and instead found a silver lining in every cloud and a shadow cast by every sun. He could not place his full trust in language because, as his own verbal dexterity suggested, words could be twisted and deprived of meaning. He subscribed to no rigid doctrines because life was too fluid and circumstances too varied to conform to a fixed set of principles. He could not invest complete confidence in individuals because he did not think highly even of himself. In Havel's plays, the characters that most resemble the author are often betrayed by their own impulses. They mean well but exhibit weakness when tempted or tested.

Hypocrisy, whether his or that of others, nagged at Havel, but his commitment to public activism was real. At the age of ten, he envisioned a factory that would produce not goods but *good*, repairing a broken world. As an adult, he disliked having to shave every day, but that did not, he insisted, mean he was a nihilist. He understood from his own experience, and that of his nation, that official policies and programs were important. "You can't spend your whole life criticizing something," he wrote, "and then, when you have a chance to do it better, refuse."

Havel served more than two years as president of Czechoslovakia and, after the Slovak secession, a pair of five-year terms as president of the Czech Republic. In the latter's parliamentary system, the prime minister is the head of government, and the president has little formal power. Havel had moral authority, however, and expended much of it to reinforce the values he had emphasized all his life: reconciliation, inclusiveness, honesty, and respect for the well-being of the community. As time passed, he clashed often with another Václav, Prime Minister Klaus, whose rigidly pro-market economic policies struck the president as inhumane and likely to lead to corruption, or what he called "Mafia capitalism."

From the time he became politically aware, Havel felt that those who witnessed injustice should try to stop it. That's why, before the revolution, he stayed in Czechoslovakia and served years in prison when he could easily have made a living as a writer in Hollywood or New York. It is also why, late in his career, he refused to gratify the lesser politicians who longed for him to retreat to the sidelines and shut up. Havel would not have been who he was had he run from a fight. "Even a poet has teeth," he said.

THE GUEST OF honor in the cathedral that December afternoon might have preferred a jazz band to the sweet-voiced choir, but the ever-polite Havel would have appreciated the effort that went into his funeral. From the chancel, his portrait, draped in black, had a clear view of the Czech officials, foreign dignitaries, and Velvet Revolutionists who were there to pay him a final tribute. His coffin was cloaked in the national colors: white, red, and blue. The air shimmered with the light of a hundred flame-topped candles; the aroma of incense felt thick enough to eat.

As I sat motionless in my chair, awaiting the ceremony, I thought back to the spring of 2005 and Havel's two-month stay in Washington as a guest of the Library of Congress. He rented a house around the corner from mine and stayed there with Daša, his second wife, and their two boxers, Sugar and Madlenka. This was the only chance Havel had to study America up close, or at any rate one rarefied part of it. His verdict:

Washington is populated mainly by gentlemen who wear a tie all day, who work politically in the morning, then have a political lunch, then work again politically in the afternoon, only to go from work to some kind of political dinner. And throughout all this they remain good-natured, calm, handsome and charming. This is also true of their wives and of the political women.

Havel's principal complaint was the absence of salt at a catered lunch, after which he carried his own packets in a pocket. He was mystified by the tendency of Americans to drink water at meals instead of beer or wine, to him a barbarian practice that conjured memories of prison. He also objected to gum chewing, oversize cars with their "herds of useless horses under their hoods," and sandwiches so fat that when he tried to eat them, their insides escaped and stained his shirt. He graciously made himself available for dinners at which he was expected to supply wisdom on demand, as if he were Yoda with a Czech accent. The flattery embarrassed him, and the effort to converse at length in English wore him down, but he was entertained by the interplay of ideas and enjoyed studying his hosts. Americans, he concluded, are fond of stories with happy endings, a trait he found "endearing."

Sitting in the cathedral, I thought, too, of Havel's final play, *Leaving,* which I had seen in Philadelphia a couple of years earlier. The tragedy, or comedy, centers on a politician who, after years in office, stands by befuddled as his successor takes his place in the public spotlight, hires key members of his staff, blackmails him into vacating his villa, and coerces him into taking a job as an adviser to the former secretary of his former secretary. Amid borrowings from Chekhov and Shakespeare, the play finds more pathos than nobility in the pretentions of artists, journalists, and politicians. Reviews were mixed but beside the point. Continuing to write was Havel's way of keeping his mind aglow and of remaining relevant. That drive, to remain relevant, acquires urgency with age and is a yearning the two of us shared. The distinction, it seems to me, is that Havel did not want people to think he took himself too seriously. I worry that if I don't take myself seriously, others won't either.

There were more than a thousand people in the cathedral. Outside its gates, ten times that number stood watch despite the bitter weather and the "rude wind's wild lament." All week, the citizens of Prague and beyond had been depositing flowers and candles along the castle's perimeter fence. They had gathered in groups, rattling their keys one last time. Later, many would assemble in Great Lucerna Hall, which Havel's grandfather had built, and listen to music from, among others, the surviving members of the underground band Plastic People of the Universe, still with long hair but now well into their seventies.

Michael Žantovský, one of the late president's closest advisers, wrote that Havel, despite his intellectual credentials, had little trouble connecting with average citizens. He wasn't ostentatiously folksy, in the manner of many American politicians, but instead found qualities to admire in almost everyone, and they returned the favor. One afternoon while the Communists were still in charge, Havel stopped his car to help pull the secret police vehicle that had been tailing him out of a ditch. Another time, he asked the agents surrounding his house to please buy some beer so that he and his compatriots might have a party. The agents complied.

Until his final hours, Havel lived for the moment, moving to a rhythm both elegant and all his own, and with a zest-filled spirit that no prison could contain. In the cathedral, when the time came for me to speak, I rose and climbed a few steps toward the altar, bowed in the direction of the casket, and positioned myself behind the standing microphone. There was no podium or lectern, so I held my notes tightly, saying of my friend:

> He cast light into places of deepest darkness and reminded us constantly of our obligations to one another. Those who thought him naïve could not have been more mistaken. Václav Havel was fully conscious of human weakness, but he saw the conscience as a living organ, to be nourished through regular exercise. He prized liberty not as an end but as the means through which we might finally ensure that truth shall prevail.

* * *

IN NORTHEASTERN BOHEMIA, there is a verdant swath of countryside known as the Eagle Mountains. According to legend, the area is watched over by a lovely woman of generous temperament. Her name is Kačenka, or in English, Katie. Good-hearted travelers who make their way through the scenic hills can count on her help, though the lazy or dishonest may find themselves in trouble. It is to be expected that a maiden so fair would attract suitors of royal blood. No one should be surprised, then, by the visits of Krakonoš, the bachelor king, who arrives each year to court Katie and beg her to come away with him. She turns him down every time, for she would never willingly abandon her realm or the many creatures who live there. Krakonoš, who has a high opinion of himself, takes the news badly no matter how gently his advances are rebuffed. Enraged, he hurls thunderbolts and whips up hurricanes, venting wrath until creeks are flooded and woodlands drowned. Eventually, he returns in sorrow to his kingdom, only to renew his romantic endeavors the following twelvemonth, again in vain.

On September 20, 1909, my father was born in a small farming community nestled between those same Eagle Mountains and the Bohemian-Moravian Highlands about ninety miles east of Prague. The following spring, in a village nearby, my mother also entered the world. Though the region is now modern in many respects, the continued hovering of magical maidens and frustrated kings does not seem far-fetched. Hikers will attest that the hills are of emerald green, the brooks burble, and sky-borne predators shriek and dive as if with tales of their own to tell.

To my grandchildren, city kids all, their visit to Letohrad and Kostelec nad Orlicí was something new. Until then—this was 2015—their idea of the countryside was my farm, which is next to a busy road, not far from a mall, and has a pool. In much of the United States, even the areas set aside for wilderness feel domesticated. Here, in the more rural parts of the Czech Republic, nature still runs free. The time of our family homecoming was midsummer, so the fruit trees were in bloom and the sugar beet fields were starting to display their wares. It wasn't hard to suppose, as we gazed at the crimson and golden wild-flowers, that these were the direct descendants of the plants that, a century earlier, had delighted the eyes of Josef Körbel and Anna (Mandula) Spieglová.

Wandering through the local churches, museums, shops, and streets, we reflected on what life must have been like when my father was young enough to play tricks on the village policeman (so fat that his "trousers hung like an accordion,") and my mother went to the forest on fine days to pick wild berries and mushrooms. It was in this setting that my father, hoping for better luck than Krakonoš, first approached my mother.

"Hello," he said. "I am Josef Körbel, and you are the most talk-ative girl in Bohemia"—whereupon she slapped him.

The Spiegel family sold flour, barley, spices, jellies, and a locally renowned brand of coffee to other shops in villages far around. I was intrigued to discover, when researching *Prague Winter*, that Mandu-la's grandmother Klara (mother of Růžena) was primarily responsi-ble for running the business. She survived her husband by two and a half decades and refused to retire, working well into her seventies. I found curious as well an anecdote I came across narrated by a niece of Klara's. It seems that the old woman was visiting friends when, on the recently invented contraption known as the radio, she heard the voice of a singer she knew personally. Immediately, she grasped her hands as if to pray, then lifted her arms in front of her and cried out a greeting to the singer, anticipating an answer as if the sound were being transmitted both ways. For years after, relatives mimicked Klara's excited reaction when they wanted to show amazement. By coincidence, one of my earliest memories is of London during World War II, when I was four years old. Upon hearing my father's voice coming from the large green radio in our apartment, I responded with rapture, sure that he was hiding inside.

* * *

OUR FAMILY TRIP to the Czech Republic in 2015 also marked my grandchildren's first visit to Prague. Luckily for them, they had in me the perfect guide. Over the years, I had shown many companions the sights of that enchanted capital. Now I had a new set of eyes and ears to impress and, as I have learned in government and other arenas, preparation is everything. To be sure to captivate my grandchildren, I had brushed up on some of Prague's many legends.

After an early breakfast at our hotel, we headed out. Walking along, I told the children about the sprites who make their homes on the rocks, embankments, and beneath the bridges that span the whirling and swirling waters of the River Vltava. Their job is to place the souls of the drowned into jars for safekeeping. In the olden times, when business was slow and not enough people were drowning, it is said that the sprites would sometimes help the process along— parents had to watch very carefully to prevent children from venturing into the river above their knees.

Our main destination that morning was an area near the center of ancient Prague, adjacent to Old Town Square. Here, there is an oasis of smallish houses, built centuries ago, that would have been demolished had it not been—well, it's a long story.

In the distant past there existed in Bohemia, as elsewhere in Europe, an order of Templar Knights, most of whom were executed during a period of political repression. The leader was among those who had his head chopped off, after which he and his horse still managed—under the rules that govern legends—to find quarters in an apartment on Temple Street. Each night they patrolled the neighborhood with the ghostly knight carrying his helmet (with his head inside) in his left hand. Eventually, after a century or so, the horseman grew parched and acquired the habit of stopping by a pub at a corner near Tyn church. At first, his drinking caused a fuss because the ale he poured into his mouth passed immediately through his hewn-off neck and onto the floor. Then a sharp-witted barmaid suggested that he place his head back atop his shoulders before imbibing and all was well, except for a little dribbling and the fact that the knight sometimes had a few too many.

More years passed and with them a host of changes altered the face of Prague. The headless templar was dismayed to find that developers were destroying the old city of which he had been so fond, tearing down the vintage houses, building modern apartments, widening and straightening the narrow crooked pathways. As familiar sights disappeared, the poor knight had fewer and fewer streets to patrol. What was he to do? The construction activity took place during the day when no ghost could wander outside. Then something a bit out of the ordinary happened. The templar, riding by the house of the lord mayor late one evening, plucked his own head out of the helmet and found a way to substitute it for that of the municipal official. In the morning, the mayor with his new noggin gazed upon the city with a wide-eyed appreciation he had not previously felt for its ancient gables, balconies, and chimneys. Immediately, he ordered a halt to the demolition in the old neighborhood. The beautiful houses were preserved and still stand to this day. Later the mayor and the horseman exchanged heads once again and everyone lived happily ever after.

As I told this story, my sister, Kathy, and I herded the grandchildren along and eagerly pointed out the landmarks. "That's Tyn church," I said. "That's the street where the templar lived," we exclaimed. "Those are some of the houses that were saved," I shouted with a wave of my arm. A brief silence ensued as we walked, and my sister and I looked this way and that. I thought to myself how thrilling it was that everyone was having such a fabulous time. Finally, at the corner of James Street, I saw it. "That's the pub where the knight used to get drunk," I yelled deliriously. It was then that I overheard one of my grandchildren say to another, "She's crazy."

THE NEXT MORNING, after a full day of enjoying the peculiarities and calories of Prague, we drove north to Terezín, a place about which there are many stories but no fairy tales. In a much more sol-

emn mood, we toured the grounds, including the prison where political dissidents had been kept under brutal conditions, a cemetery,
a crematorium, and the museum that had served as a dorm for boys
in the Jewish ghetto during the war. The guides told us that fifteen
thousand children were sent to Terezín, of whom perhaps one in ten
survived. I had been to the museum before, but I was nonetheless
unready to see my grandchildren studying the photographic images
of boys and girls their own age who had been imprisoned. Of my
six grandchildren, only Ben and Ellie are being raised in the Jewish faith. No matter; the blood is the same. Hitler, if he could have,
would have killed them all.

At the museum, there is a space set aside for people to commemorate loved ones who had been confined to the ghetto. After *Prague
Winter* came out, our family decided to commission a plaque. My
brother, John, did most of the work to make this happen. We put the
plaque up during our visit to Terezín. On it are twenty-six names.

THE MUSEUM AT Terezín is one of many around the globe dedicated
to Holocaust education and remembrance. The attribute separating the Czech prison from most others is the range of cultural activities that inmates were able to engage in there. Despite the many
hardships and long hours of forced labor, the residents produced an
astonishing amount of literature, art, and music.

Among the poems written in Terezín is one by thirteen-year-old
Hanuš Hachenburg, called "May." The verse reminds me of Václav
Havel's ability to see in something its opposite—the potential for future sorrow, for example, amid current gladness. The young author
offers images of a flowery spring and then undercuts them so that
the "blushing" dawn is accompanied by the sound of a hurricane,
the "dew that falls on the field" is seen by the "mocking light" of the
moon, and when life awakens from its winter slumber, it does so with
"arms bloodied and torn with death." Elsewhere, the poet imagines
his heart to be in flames and cries, "I haven't the strength to put out
fire." He describes a summer's day, but encompasses the radiance in

"shackles, bloody shackles." Eager for beauty but surrounded by ugliness, he writes in frustration, "I learn to dream."

Havel was surely right when he wrote that "even the most ordinary and inconspicuous life is an unbelievable miracle . . . a fairy tale at times beautiful, at times suspenseful, and at times terrifying."

TWENTY-SIX

Cradle of Civilization

IN ONE OF their many films, Laurel and Hardy find themselves tasked with moving a piano. The sole path open to them is a decrepit wooden bridge strung across a ravine between a pair of mountain peaks. The bridge is narrow, barely the width of the piano turned sideways. Obviously, teamwork is essential. With determined faces and sweaty brows, Laurel drags the piano from in front while his friend shoves from behind. They are inching their way forward when Hardy's foot suddenly breaks through a slat. The thickset man topples and falls until, caught by an ankle, he is left dangling headfirst over the abyss. Disaster looms. Though initially bewildered, Laurel maneuvers delicately on tiptoes around to the other side of the piano and gives his partner a lifesaving hand up. Exhaling with relief, the duo return to their project with renewed vigor and begin at last to make headway. Then, within sight of their destination, they are confronted, between the piano and the far side of the bridge, by a gorilla. Welcome to diplomacy in the Middle East.

SECRETARY OF STATE Clinton called Syria a "wicked problem." John Kerry, her successor, struggled beyond the point of exhaustion to piece together a solution. Diplomats from Washington, the United Nations, Europe, and the Arab states held scores of meetings and, against a backdrop of sickening bloodshed, announced cease-fires that didn't last, humanitarian convoys that didn't go through, and turning points that became dead ends.

When in August 2013 the Syrian Army launched rockets packed

with sarin gas into a suburb of Damascus, killing 1,400 civilians, the Obama administration seemed poised to respond. A year earlier, the president had referred to the use of chemical weapons as a red line that, if crossed, would "change my calculations significantly."

I hoped the administration would see the attack as a chance to hasten the departure of Syrian dictator Bashar al-Assad. Had I been secretary of state, I would have recommended to the president that he authorize strikes against a significant range of military targets in Syria, especially those being used by the regime to assault civilians. I would have suggested that he notify our allies and leaders in Congress of his intent, but not wait for their approval. Obama did order the Pentagon to prepare strikes but decided not to go forward with them unless Congress agreed, which appeared unlikely. The issue became moot when a diplomatic avenue opened that led to the destruction at sea of Syria's declared arsenal of chemical arms. On one hand, the Obama administration gained the removal (although incomplete) of the deadly weapons, and the UN organization that monitored their disposal was awarded the Nobel Peace Prize. On the other, the killing continued as if nothing had happened.

GIVEN THE COMPLEXITIES of his job and the shortcomings of the chief executives who served fore and aft, Obama's performance in the White House was of a high order. He set intelligent priorities and stuck to them. He appointed able advisers, soaked up information from many sources, asked insightful questions, was attentive to morality, and took pains to explain his thinking to audiences, national and global. *Merriam-Webster* defines "presidential" as behavior befitting a president. Obama exactly.

By his own admission, however, the forty-fourth commander in chief's conception of America's global role was more modest than audacious. He told an interviewer early in 2015, "You take the victories where you can. You make things a little bit better rather than a little bit worse." He thought the United States was most likely to err when it overestimated its ability to influence others. In addressing international issues, he emphasized shared responsibility, a contrast to George W. Bush, who defined America's mission as largely a solo enterprise aimed at nothing less than "ending tyranny in our world."

Obama's steady engagement and reasoned approach enabled him to repair much of the damage that the previous administration had inflicted on America's alliances. He directed a relentless campaign to eliminate the remnants of al-Qaeda, including Osama bin Laden. Following Russia's annexation of Crimea, he united Europe behind a formidable catalogue of sanctions. He took the politically risky but long overdue step of normalizing diplomatic relations with Cuba. He put American prestige and resources behind a plan to end Colombia's decades-long civil war.

Further, with help from Kerry, Obama enlisted China's aid in support of the first comprehensive global agreement to combat climate change. The sight of Kerry signing that pact while bouncing his granddaughter on his knee melted many hearts, exactly what climate change is doing to the polar ice caps. Most issues profit from the clash of opinions; global warming—with its record temperatures, rising sea levels, loss of arable land, forced wildlife migrations, disastrous algal blooms, out-of-control forest fires, and now-frequent "once in a century" storms—is a scientific fact. The politicians who have denied its reality should cringe every time their children gaze at them. Their sins (of omission and commission) have placed on future generations what may be an insurmountable burden. What is worse, most of them know it and simply lack the spine to tell voters the truth.

Obama was on the right side of the climate debate. The same is true of the Iran nuclear deal.

At the UN General Assembly in 2013, Israeli Prime Minister Bibi Netanyahu denounced Tehran's "vast and feverish" effort to build a nuclear weapon. He claimed that Iran's actions posed a mortal danger to his country and demanded that the world compel a halt. That same day, Obama rang up Iranian President Hassan Rouhani, thereby spurring a multilateral round of diplomacy that culminated two years later in the Joint Comprehensive Plan of Action (JCPOA). That pact required Iran to ship 98 percent of its enriched uranium out of the country, shut down two-thirds of the centrifuges it was using to enrich uranium, fill the core of its plutonium reactor with concrete, and abide by an invasive verification regime that extends to all phases of the nuclear supply chain. The JCPOA turned the clock back on the dangerous aspects of Iran's nuclear activities, thereby lengthening the so-called breakout time should Tehran renege on its word. It was the kind of deal that were we ever to achieve something similar with North Korea, would be hailed as a triumph by all.

Netanyahu might have thanked his counterpart in Washington for dealing creatively with the peril his country faced. Instead he condemned him. The prime minister never warmed to the U.S. leader even though the Obama administration showered Israel with aid. The reason is that the president had a broader and, in my view, a more realistic sense of how to safeguard Israel's longtime security. Combativeness, untethered to diplomacy, can daunt foes for a while, but is unlikely to produce lasting stability or the kind of trust that allows people on any side to sleep well at night.

When I was secretary of state, Netanyahu had just become prime minister for the first time. In a note to myself, I termed him "a manipulative liar who gets away with a lot." My impression was that Americans thought more highly of him than they would had he not mimicked the manner of a Western politician and expressed himself in English without an accent. Netanyahu doesn't hide his convictions, however. He told me frankly that he believed that war between Israel and her enemies in the region was almost inevitable. His goal was to ensure that should hostilities begin, the Jewish state would be strong and her adversaries weak. He had little interest and no faith in negotiations. Given demographic trends within the current borders of his country, I wonder how wise that attitude is. In 2013, the year of Netanyahu's address to the UN, the single most popular name for male infants born in Israel was Muhammad.

* * *

WITHIN MONTHS OF his inauguration, Obama referred to himself as "America's first Pacific president," and spoke about his desire to rebalance U.S. foreign policy, with East Asia enjoying pride of place. Yet, from the beginning of street demonstrations in Damascus in 2011 until the day he left office early in 2017, the president wrestled with demons unleashed by the war in Syria. The brutality of that conflict can be traced primarily to Bashar al-Assad, the country's despotic leader and a man whom I met twice during my final year as secretary of state.

Our first encounter was brief, an offering of condolences on my part on June 13, 2000, three days following the heart attack that claimed the life of Assad's father. I spent most of my time on that occasion with my escort from the Syrian ministry of health, a talkative fellow who served as a character witness for the incoming president. He said that the thirty-four-year-old Assad had abandoned his original plan to become a surgeon upon discovering that he was squeamish and couldn't bear to cut open a human body with a knife. However, he did enjoy looking into people's eyes and so became an ophthalmologist. The sensitive young man had trained in London, I was told, where he also acquired a liking for the new information technologies. Once in office, his primary goal would be to modernize Syria and prepare its people to take their rightful place in the world economy.

Four months later, in Saudi Arabia, Assad and I had a more substantive meeting. My agenda was no secret. I wanted to know whether this relative newcomer would choose to model himself after the autocratic father he had barely known, or instead—as the health ministry official had indicated—fling windows open and welcome fresh air into the Middle East. Our conversation gave me hope. Unlike the austere patriarch he had succeeded, the younger Assad radiated enthusiasm. He spoke with fervor about his wish to transform his country and sounded as if he would have been at ease in a brainstorming session at a dot-com start-up. As I flew home, I dared think that the new president's arrival might be the beginning of something positive for Syria, with favorable implications for the entire region.

It was not to be. The decade that followed proved a harsh disappointment. Reactionary advisers surrounded Assad, allowing him to engineer minor economic changes, but no significant political liberalization. As the years passed, the evidence grew that the eye doctor lacked vision and, worse, that he wasn't squeamish after all.

In 2011, when the demonstrations against him began to spread, Assad offered concessions that seemed a desperate attempt to delay the inevitable. In the exuberance of the moment, the opposition was confident it could prevail. One reason is that the dictator's political base was surprisingly narrow for someone whose family had held power for forty years. Assad is an Alawite, a member of a religious sect that is an offshoot of the Shiite branch of Islam. Historically, the Alawites had been looked down on by the country's Sunni majority, and so both he and his father had depended on force to remain in power; they knew no other way. Because of this, the Syrian Civil War quickly became a question of survival. Assad could either leave or fight; he chose the latter and ordered his military and police to crush those trying to defy him.

As the clashes intensified, some Obama advisers thought it might be possible to organize, train, and equip a moderate Syrian opposition, then employ U.S. air power to shield the insurgents from enemy helicopters and planes. The Pentagon, and ultimately the president, however, worried that such a move would embroil the United States in yet another lengthy conflict whose outcome we could not control. They were skeptical as well of our ability to mold an effective fighting force out of the rebel groups, who were split into factions so numerous and incompatible that no one was ever able to develop a definitive list. Government lawyers also pointed to the lack of any legal authority for U.S. military operations in Syria. We could hardly claim self-defense, and only the Security Council, where Russia had a veto, could authorize the use of force under the UN's "responsibility to protect" doctrine.

These were high hurdles, but they had to be measured against a widening humanitarian catastrophe. The world had spent centuries developing legal standards for waging war; Assad ignored them. His military intentionally destroyed hospitals and clinics to prevent members of the opposition from receiving care. One hospital was hit four separate times in a single morning, after which the town's other medical center was struck as its personnel ministered to victims of the earlier attacks. The Syrian police tortured tens of thousands of suspected dissidents and took gruesome photos (later circulated by whistleblowers) to document their own crimes. The armed forces lobbed artillery shells and dropped barrel bombs on civilian neighborhoods.

With houses and apartments destroyed, families lived much as they had in the Iron Age, cooking over open fires and washing their clothes in pots. In large portions of the country, there was no electricity even in winter. While the world watched, half the Syrian population was displaced, schools were shut down, children went for months without the taste of fruit, infants had no formula, and average life expectancy dropped by twenty years.

Neighboring countries shared in the misery. In 2013, I convened the annual National Democratic Institute board meeting in Amman, Jordan. While there, we visited a camp where families that had fled the fighting in Syria were crowded together in trailers parked end to end as far as the eye could see. Almost overnight, the haven had become one of the most populous cities in the region. King Abdullah told me that the impact on his country of the refugees living in and outside camps was the same as if, in the space of two years, the United States had welcomed sixty million new residents. Sixty million.

THEN THE SITUATION became worse. In 2014, the terrorists of ISIS captured large chunks of land and such major settlements as Mosul in Iraq and Raqqa in Syria. The insurgents met little resistance from Sunni Muslim communities that, in each country, felt disenfranchised by their governments. ISIS declared that it had effectively redrawn the international legal boundary and created its own mini-empire, a caliphate. This claim was swallowed, inexcusably, by the *New York Times* and many others in the media, who obligingly referred to ISIS as "the Islamic state," despite the fact that it was neither a recognized state nor reflective of the core tenets of Islam.

Still, unlike al-Qaeda, ISIS did control territory to which it could summon loyalists to serve under its black flag. For those receptive to its quasi-religious bilge, the group offered a sense of holy mission. ISIS also had enough revenue from plunder, smuggling, and extortion to offer paychecks to many who, in their home countries, sat around on stoops all day and had no jobs. Via social media, terrorist recruiters painted a picture in two dozen languages of an idyllic existence for ISIS recruits, complete with happy families, pets, and amusement parks. To entice young men who had spent their lives in socially repressed societies, ISIS auctioned off female sex slaves, who came with notarized sales slips. Just as sickening, the group looked unstoppable. In 2015 alone, it organized or inspired strikes in Iraq, Syria, Afghanistan, the United States, Denmark, France, Turkey, Egypt, Saudi Arabia, Kuwait, Lebanon, Tunisia, Yemen, Libya, and Bangladesh. With Syria in chaos and Iraq split, ISIS seemed a fair bet to overrun Baghdad and eventually Damascus as well, thus plunging into savagery the lands that many historians refer to as a "cradle of civilization."

When the extent of the danger posed by ISIS became apparent, the United States, to its credit, did just about everything right. Obama assembled a coalition that included most Arab states. The Pentagon worked with partners to destroy ISIS assets and prevent the terrorists from moving except in small groups. Diplomats prevailed on governments in the region to control their borders and thus curb the flow of enemy reinforcements. The strategy took time to implement, but the design was smart, and the impact reassuring. Within four years the vaunted caliphate had virtually disappeared, its original leaders were dead, and its fighters were mostly killed, scattered, or in hiding. The bloodthirsty movement is far from extinct and could revive quickly (under its own name or some other), if given a chance. However, its plan to exercise sovereignty over a large block of territory has, at a minimum, been put on hold.

Tragically, the campaign against ISIS had an unintended beneficiary: Assad.

In the fall of 2015, Russia sent troops and planes to bolster the Syrian government, using the fight against terrorism as the rationale. With the boost from Moscow, the dictator's position became stronger and his leave-taking, which had once appeared imminent, could no longer be assumed. For reasons both humanitarian and strategic, Kerry made it his mission to end the war but found himself without the leverage to do so. Having called on Assad to step down, the United States demanded that he be excluded from any future government. Should U.S. negotiators abandon that position, they would lose the support of the rebel groups. If they didn't, the regime, having regained the advantage, would continue to fight. With no chips on the table in front of him and cards in his hand that didn't match, Kerry could neither win a showdown against the other players nor call their bluff.

THE TURMOIL THAT accompanied the Arab Spring and the Syrian Civil War created a demand in foreign policy circles for transformative thinking about America's approach to the entire region. Fred Kempe, director of the Atlantic Council, asked me to co-chair a project that would take a look at all the major issues and formulate recommendations that might be of use to the victor in the 2016 U.S. presidential election. When I pointed out that the Middle East was nowhere near the Atlantic, Kempe just harrumphed. My Republican co-chair was Stephen Hadley, who had been national security advisor in the second term of George W. Bush.

In setting to work, we agreed not to dwell on the policy errors either of Hadley's old boss or of Obama. Instead, we focused on our mandate, which was to figure out why the Middle East remained such an incubator of violence. Consulting far and wide, we found that while governments tend to blame their problems on either the legacy of imperialism or the danger of terrorism, the public is more likely to complain about the backward thinking of their own leaders. With power in the region tightly controlled and freedom of expression limited, there exist few legal ways to register dissent. This pushes the advocates of change into exile or hiding, drives many to see armed resistance as the sole means of achieving their ends, and fosters contempt for the law and those who enforce it. Economies are rigidly controlled, which is why most countries produce little (aside from petroleum) that the world needs. Budgets, too, are strained because few taxpayers willingly send money to governments that steal or squander every dinar or riyal they receive.

When testifying before Congress on the recommendations in our report, Hadley and I ran into a wall of skepticism about the possibility that any of this would soon change. The doubts are unsurprising. Leaders in the Middle East will always protect their own interests, as they perceive them, and their citizens, as a rule, don't place much faith in the advice of Westerners. The ancestors of the Syrians attacked by Assad in this century were shelled in the 1920s and '30s by the French. Iraqi civilians, in the same period, were bombed—what Churchill called "aerial policing"—by the British. After invading Baghdad, Americans are in a poor position to lecture others about the value of solving problems through diplomacy. Beyond that, governments that seek above all to preserve their own privileges generally do not welcome exhortations to allow their people a larger voice.

Hadley and I did, however, detect currents of energy in many parts of the region that may have been helped along by the otherwise disappointing Arab Spring. For example, a revolution in schooling is under way in some countries, especially Qatar and the United Arab Emirates. The elected government of Tunisia is encouraging an open press and has allowed civil society to bloom. Governments in Jordan, Morocco, and Egypt have sought to diversify their economies and have made visible, if not wholly convincing, efforts to combat corruption. In Algeria in 2019, after our report was issued, the aging, ailing, and out-of-touch President Abdelaziz Bouteflika stepped down rather than seek a fifth presidential term. A few months later, Sudan's long-serving dictator Omar al-Bashir was also forced from office.

The common view of the Middle East today is of a region still archaic in much of its thinking, irretrievably divided along religious and ethnic lines, and handicapped by strife both within and among nations. I have lost count of the number of meetings, conferences, and panel discussions in which I have participated regarding its problems, none of which are likely to be resolved by mere talk. The fundamental need, in my view, is for people in the region to view their differences in a new light. The separation that matters most is between those of every nationality and creed who want to build their communities and to live in peace with their neighbors and others who are intent on destroying opponents and imposing their will. In this view, a forward-looking Palestinian schoolteacher will have much in common with an apolitical Syrian craftsman, an idealistic Iranian nurse, a mind-his-own business Kurdish farmer, a Saudi Arabian businesswoman, and a well-intentioned soldier undergoing basic training in the Israeli army. Notwithstanding what their leaders might be telling them, these people should be allies not enemies.

My hope is with the young, of whom I have encountered many in my travels. The entrepreneurial force is with them, as is the desire to judge, and to be judged, on their own terms, free from the prejudices and cramped expectations of the past. They have all the energy they need but have received little help from their elders (whether in or outside the region) in recognizing their shared interests, combining forces, and moving their societies in a positive direction. That mission, it appears, is one they will have to undertake themselves.

Although it is up to the people of the Middle East to decide what kind of future they will have, the responsibility of the United States is nevertheless clear: to lend what help we can to the builders and to the searchers for peace while exhorting the entire global community to do the same.

TWENTY-SEVEN

Breathless

THE FIRST WEEK of May 2015, I was on the way to a company retreat when my stomach dispatched an urgent 911 message to my brain. Arrowheads seemed to be assaulting my rib cage and nausea my whole body. What was going on? To the hospital I went, scared but less panicky than I might have been. My heart seemed unaffected, and I knew that as long as I was in agony, I was still in the land of the living. After being installed in a room, I was scrutinized by a doctor who poked me in an unhurried manner, a positive sign. Eventually, he laid down his instruments, stepped back, and said, "I think it's your gall bladder."

The gall bladder: I wasn't even sure what the organ—if it was an organ—did. Was it divided into three parts? I learned the truth soon enough: pear-shaped, the gall bladder sits beneath the liver and diligently stores up bile to secrete when called on to aid in the digestion of fats. Torment arrives when the bile builds up and hardens, creating blockages. The good news is that it is not among the body's essential workforce. If it were a federal employee and the government shut down, it would be free to stay at home and watch cooking shows. Similarly, when the blockages are severe enough, the treatment prescribed isn't to help the organ heal, but to yank the thing out.

Thus, within twenty-four hours of entering the hospital, I had what I could neither spell nor pronounce: a laparoscopic cholecystectomy. My gall bladder had been deposited in the dustbin of history, and I wouldn't miss it. The bad news is that I would be unable to deliver a speech I had been invited to give, honoring the seventieth anniversary of V-E Day. The ceremony, on May 8, was to be held at the World War II Memorial on the National Mall. Thousands of veterans would be on hand. I yearned to drag myself out of bed and join them, but the doctors were firm.

I asked my sister if she would pick up the baton. Kathy is not timid, but she had never done something quite like this before. It helped that because of our shared experiences, her feelings about V-E Day and all it represents are similar to mine, so she was comfortable with the text we had prepared. Everyone I knew who was there said she rose to the moment and came through like a star. The operation made my stomach feel better—Kathy's speech did, too—and a week later I received from my staff a birthday present in the form of a gall bladder–shaped plush toy. This was proof that just about anything we want, and much that we don't, can be purchased online.

ONE OF MY more common travel destinations is Silicon Valley. This is the headquarters of several ASG clients; it's close to San Francisco, where my daughter Katie and her family live; and it's a place where people keep busy testing and marketing new technologies yet still find time to read books and attend speeches. Whenever I am there, I brag that "I was not just the first woman secretary of state; but also the first to have her own website." It's true that I am old enough to remember a time before credit cards and when Tupperware and frozen vegetables were the next big things, but that doesn't mean I live in the past. From Velcro and DVDs to laser surgery and Spanx, I have always been a fan of new ideas. At the State Department, I practically invented the international conference call, which I employed to stay in touch with NATO foreign ministers despite time and language differences—and bursts of shouting when someone's home team scored a goal in the World Cup. It took a while, however, for me to adjust to the online world.

Although email made its way to Foggy Bottom in the 1990s, I didn't use it or have an account of my own until after I left office—a deficiency that, in hindsight, might have been for the best. Back then,

cables from embassies abroad were still printed on paper and distributed to each office daily in three-inch-high stacks. At night, the documents were retrieved, placed in burn bags, loaded into shopping carts,
and thrown in the basement furnace. That's one way we heated the
building. For most of the decade, the few State Department computers
with access to the World Wide Web were confined to the library. We
did use the internet to trace my travels as secretary, however, and I had
many interactive events with students, but didn't personally do any
electronic mailing or surfing. Even now, I prefer to call close friends
on their birthdays, rather than text, and I rely on snail mail to send
messages of gratitude or condolence. In recent years, I have become
paranoid about the possibility that every email I dispatch will eventually get abducted and become fodder for a supermarket tabloid or Fox
News. So, when I am tempted to vent or overshare online, I don't.

I also resisted the idea of establishing a presence on Facebook or
Twitter. The reason was not philosophical, but pragmatic: I already
felt inundated with information. In 2013, however, I finally yielded
to the prodding of assistants who were adamant that if I weren't on
social media, I might as well not exist. To start out, I tweeted in reference to Condi Rice and Hillary Clinton: "First of 3 female secstates;
last to join Twitter; better late than never." We accompanied it with a
picture of a pin I had found at a Denver airport shop showing a little
bird chirping.

In October 2014, my aide Alexis Keslinke came into my office
and, with some trepidation, showed me a tweet from the television
personality Conan O'Brien: "I picked out my Halloween costume,"
he announced. "I'm going as 'Slutty Madeleine Albright.'"

Taken aback, I was silent for a moment before asking, "Why does
Conan O'Brien think I'm a slut?"

Alexis replied, "No, it doesn't mean that. It's supposed to be
ironic—like a slutty nun."

"Well, why does Conan O'Brien think I'm a nun?"

"He doesn't. He's just trying to be funny."

I pondered this for a moment, ruminating about the whole relationship between male humor and adjectives describing women, then pulled out my Twitter finger: "For Halloween, I'm considering going as hunky Conan O'Brien—but that might be too farfetched." O'Brien's comeback: "YES—My first twitter war with a former Secretary of State! You're next, George P. Shultz!" My response: "Never get into a word war with a diplomat. We talk even more than comedians." His white flag: "Damn—Whenever I go toe to toe with Madeleine Albright, she always wins." The irony is that by surrendering with grace, O'Brien fought me to a happy draw.

A CHILD OF radio, I did not watch television regularly until my daughters came along and we enjoyed an occasional show together. When I was in government, I was too busy for anything other than news, but in more recent years I developed an affection for a few programs, among them *Army Wives*. The show reminded me of the early months of my marriage, some of which I spent in a converted motel room in Missouri while my husband, on duty in the U.S. Army, was stationed nearby at Fort Leonard Wood. Despite my eagerness for a job, I turned down positions as a carhop and a tattoo parlor come-on girl before landing my one and only stint with a newspaper. Employed by the *Rolla Daily News*, I wrote obituaries, reported on people who were sure they had seen a UFO, and arranged for the placement of such classified advertisements as "Cemetery plot: owner must move; will sell at sacrifice."

Although separated by decades from my own experience, *Army Wives* stirred bittersweet recollections of newlywed bliss, intermittent loneliness, friendships among women, and an episode or two of harassment from men who couldn't seem to see the ring on my finger. One day my car was acting up, so I took it to a garage on the base, where I had to leave it to be repaired. The sergeant in Joe's unit, his superior officer, was there and he offered to give me a lift home. I accepted, and we were soon on our way in his white Thunderbird. "What makes you trust me?" he asked. I said, "Because you have been telling me about your family."

A couple of days later, my own car fixed, I pulled into the motel driveway only to find the Thunderbird outside and the sergeant, too. Not knowing what else to do, and with no way to contact Joe, I rushed inside, locked the door, grabbed a knife, put on my thickest panty girdle, and sat for hours on the bed quaking with fear. There was no window facing the parking lot, so I couldn't check to see whether the white car was still there. Nothing happened, thank God, and the next day, I moved out of the motel and into a guesthouse on the base. When we reported the sergeant's behavior to the authorities, I was accused of leading him on.

IN 2005, THE producers of *Gilmore Girls* asked if they could have an actor appear as Madeleine Albright in an upcoming episode.

"Would you mind?" they inquired.

I answered, "Yes, I do mind. I want to portray myself."

Why not? After all, when young, I had played Mr. Bennet (complete with pasted-on mustache) in a school production of *Pride and Prejudice*. Also, the script for *Gilmore Girls* revolved around the value of education, a cherished topic, and the lines I was given to recite fit my personality. As my daughter Katie would remark later, all I had to do was be myself.

The plot idea was that Rory Gilmore, on her twenty-first birthday, has a dream in which I am her mother. The scene sustains a tradition dating from the show's first season, when Rory's mom awakens her daughter at 4:03 a.m. to recount the moment of the girl's introduction to the world. We used the same dialogue, which required some memorization on my part. Per the script, I come into Rory's bedroom, lie down next to her, wish her happy birthday, and ask what she thinks of her life so far.

"I think it's pretty good," she says.

Then we reminisce a bit about her childhood, and I tell her that she's "a great cool kid and the best friend a girl could have."

She responds immediately, "Back at ya."

Next, I recall the circumstances of her birth "many moons ago," when "I was lying in exactly the same position only I had a huge fat stomach and big fat ankles and I was swearing like a sailor."

Rory adds, "On leave."

"Right, on leave. And there I was . . ."

"In labor"

"And while some have called it the most meaningful experience in life . . ."

"You compare it to doing splits on a crate of dynamite."

"Right."

"I wonder," Rory concludes, "if the Waltons ever did this."

ON THE FIRST season of *Parks and Recreation*, the heroine portrayed by Amy Poehler (Leslie Knope) has a photo of me in her office. In one episode, a suitor (Dave, the policeman) sees the picture and asks, "Is that your grandmother?" Leslie spends the remainder of the half hour trying to decide whether it is okay to date someone so clueless as not to know who Madeleine Albright is. During the show's final year, its production company came to Washington and invited me to take part in a scene set in a diner. Over breakfast, I am frank with Leslie and tell her that she is sometimes so focused on herself that she forgets to account for the feelings of others.

Leslie is indignant. "Name one time I've done that," she huffs.

I reply, "Well, you were so wrapped up in your story that you actually ate my waffle."

Then I ask her to return my eagle pin, which had found its way onto her collar.

This tiny morsel of television history took less than half an hour to film, a contrast to my experience on another program, *Madam Secretary*.

That began when Téa Leoni, also known as Secretary of State Elizabeth McCord, called and asked to meet. She was seeking insights into the job held by her fictional character. Our talk gave the show's writers some ideas, and those, in turn, led to a guest slot.

Filming (at a park in New York) started at around 5:30 a.m. with makeup and hair. The outdoor set had all the bustle of a zoo at feeding time. Production assistants and extras came and went all over the place, the skies threatened to open at any moment, and there were so many cameras I despaired of discerning which were actually on.

Per the script, McCord and I were to chat while sitting and then strolling together along a concrete pathway. Following the first take, the director said, "That was superb. Let's do it again."

I asked, "Why? Did I do something wrong?"

He said, "No—you were perfect. Let's try it one more time."

So, we did it one more time, then two more, then three—a dozen takes in all. After each, I was assured that I was flawless and so was Téa and yet, still, we were sent through our paces again and again. We ended up laboring for six hours to produce what was less than a minute for the screen. I was pleased that I had been allowed to add a line of my own to the script: "There is plenty of room in the world for mediocre men, but there is no room for mediocre women." And I had the chance to relax with Téa and her costar and real-life boyfriend, Tim Daly. That spring, we went on a double date to the White House Correspondents' Association Dinner and shared a laugh when, as we walked the red carpet, onlookers called out, "Madam Secretary," prompting Téa and me to inquire with a single voice, "Which one?"

In July 2018, I taped another episode of the same show, this one a season premiere; joining me were two of my successors, Colin Powell and Hillary Clinton. Once again, we made an early start, and again the set was busier than pigeons with popcorn. Secretary McCord's office, I was bemused to find, is in a warehouse in Brooklyn. Inside are portrait-lined hallways, meeting rooms, and elevators designed to resemble the seventh floor of the Department of State.

As we waited for the filming to begin, Hillary, Colin, and I sat in the makeup room exchanging random stories about hotels. Téa arrived, and after salutations all around, we began rehearsing the script. The former secretaries, including me, sounded robotic at first, but eventually we loosened up until the scene was, as we show business people like to say, "a wrap."

The plot, which centers on a dispute between India and Pakistan, reminded me of why I like the program. It's hard to create fictional narratives about contemporary events without seeming fanciful or getting basic facts wrong. *Madam Secretary* is more credible than most, and I could certainly vouch for the realism of that episode, which is based on the durability of national rivalries, one of diplomacy's bigger headaches. In the late 1940s, my father chaired a UN commission on Kashmir that tried to mediate between claims made by the same pair of South Asian countries. Now he is dead, I am old, and the tensions are more dangerous than ever.

While the morning and the filming wore on, I was struck by how differently people behave depending on circumstances. Hillary, Colin, and I had all held high positions in the executive branch; Téa Leoni is a glamorous television star. We were all accustomed to giving orders, yet spent the whole time doing exactly what we were told by assistant directors, camera operators, audio technicians, cosmeticians, and lighting experts. There were lessons in this—were there not?—about the utility of teamwork, the value of listening, and the need to respect the talents of others.

That afternoon, Colin and I rode together on the train from New York to Washington. Many of our fellow passengers retrieved phones from their pockets and backpacks and requested pictures. When everyone had finally settled in, I asked Colin what he does to avoid being recognized. He said it helps to wear casual clothes and pointed with his thumb to the hat he had on, a well-worn baseball cap that he could pull down over his forehead and that bore the inscription "Lucky Dog." Now that I have told this story and exposed his disguise, I probably owe Colin a new (old) cap.

NOT EVERY OPPORTUNITY works out. In 2010, I was honored to attend the wedding of Chelsea Clinton and Marc Mezvinsky at Astor Courts, a rented estate overlooking the Hudson River in Rhinebeck, New York. At the reception, I was seated at a table with men of roughly my age, none of whom had any interest in dancing; so I got up, crossed the floor and held my arms out to one of the many handsome young guys. As Jim Valli's band played, we swirled, swished, and swung without hurting anybody; I felt like moonlight. In any case, I couldn't have performed too badly, for I was contacted a few days later by a representative of the American Broadcasting Company: would I like to appear on *Dancing with the Stars*? Well, it hasn't happened, not because I am reluctant to risk making a fool of myself; it's just that *Dancing* requires a lot of practice and rehearsals. We couldn't make the network's schedule mesh with mine. This makes me sad. With the right partner—a reincarnated Nureyev, perhaps—I coulda been a contender.

EARLY IN 2017, the Smithsonian's National Portrait Gallery held a fundraising gala featuring five honorees, including me. As part of the occasion, a photograph of each of us was unveiled, in my case, one taken by the brilliant Timothy Greenfield-Sanders. I had chosen the image, which shows me with my dove pin and earrings, for the cover of *The Mighty and the Almighty*, my second book. The honorees were also each presented with a foot-high metal sculpture as a memento of the occasion. To present his, filmmaker Spike Lee turned to former New York Knicks basketball star (and now Georgetown coach) Patrick Ewing. When asked whom I would like to have perform the same task for me, I reached for the sky: "Robert Redford?"

I have known the actor and Oscar-winning director since the 1970s, when I was on the staff of Senator Muskie who, like Redford, was a staunch defender of the environment. In 2005, I suggested to Václav Havel that he invite the movie star to appear at a film festival in the Czech Republic. Havel considered that to be the smartest suggestion I had ever made, and the three of us (who were born within nine months of one another) had a fine time discussing world affairs and gallivanting around Prague. Redford has his own festival in Sundance each year, and I have been there as his guest. The only problem is that every time he calls my office and identifies himself, I have to calm down a hyperventilating receptionist. I had trouble breathing myself when, in my living room one day, he demonstrated the difficulty of shooting dance scenes with costars who insist on being photographed from one side only. When, at the portrait gallery, Redford handed me my award and added a kiss, I doubt I breathed at all.

I ONCE STAYED in a hotel room in Dubai that had enough little bars of soap to scrub my knuckles for a year, a bed sufficient in size to accommodate a pair of amorous giraffes, and an aquarium that covered an entire wall. With little to do before my next meeting, I sampled the soap and then sat on a sofa and studied the fish. My first thought was to look for tiny surveillance cameras strapped to the fins, but there were none that I could detect. After observing for a while, though, I did notice something disquieting. There were many marine species represented in the tank, yet instead of mingling, they swam separately, dividing themselves into groups limited to their own kind. This depressed me. Here I was, a staunch advocate of democracy, sitting in a room in the middle of the desert surrounded by snobby fish.

Upon returning to the United States, I received a call from the Aspen Institute inviting me to head a project on religious pluralism in the United States. Given my recent experience with the unsociable swimmers, I said "sure." My co-chair this time was David Gergen, a journalist, professor, and former adviser to three presidents.

I welcomed the assignment because I was confused. I had seen enough of the world to know that the United States is as open to a variety of spiritual beliefs and practices as any nation. The tone had been set early when, in 1787, George Washington led delegates attending the Constitutional Convention in Philadelphia to a Roman Catholic church for mass. The delegates, like Washington, were Protestant, and this was at a time when most states prohibited Catholics from holding public office. The people's representatives were sending a message that, in the new nation, worshippers of every faith would have a place. Later, the first president explicitly condemned bias against Muslims and Jews. This tradition of inter-religious comity remains strong today, yet there are vexing undercurrents. After 9/11, hate crimes directed at Muslims spiked. Fearmongers have rallied to oppose mosque openings and sought to spark panic about the threat allegedly posed to freedom by Sharia law. Crimes stemming from anti-Semitism have also increased. Beyond the statistics, whole segments of the internet wallow in bigotry: radical Muslims rage against Christians and Jews; extremist Christians against Muslims; Jewish zealots against Muslims and other Jews; atheists versus believers; and so on. The spectacle is dismal, and the emotions behind it dangerous.

Conventional wisdom suggests that ignorance spawns hostility and knowledge breeds tolerance. We are more likely to respect people with whom we socialize or transact business—or so the argument runs. That seems often to be true. Yet familiarity can also be a problem. The residents of culturally mixed neighborhoods, especially those that are *increasingly* mixed, may feel more threatened by diversity than people who live in areas that are homogenous. Sometimes it is easier to think well of people who are not so close.

Whether we believe, and in what, can also influence our attitudes toward others. A devout Christian, for example, may have more in common with a pious Muslim or Jew than with a person, nominally Protestant or Catholic, whose religious commitment is minimal. At the same time, people who care little about religion can still see themselves as ardent champions of their faith. In the Balkans in the 1990s, men who never went to church insisted that they were protecting a Christian Europe by slaughtering Muslims who rarely went to mosque. Before flying to their deaths with God's name on their lips, several of the 9/11 terrorists hung out at strip joints and bars. Racial and religious supremacists may pride themselves in how different they are from those they disdain—yet the similarities are many between a Muslim terrorist and a gunman who opens fire on strangers in defense of the supposed superiority of the white race.

Our task force sought to make sense of such contradictions and to allow representatives from a range of religious and ethical traditions to state their concerns. Many cast blame on social media for contributing to the coarseness of public debate and to the reinforcement of harmful stereotypes. One encouraging anecdote was shared by Eboo Patel, a young American Muslim and task force member. He told the story of a Turkish journalist who visited the U.S. Capitol and was astonished to come across a contingent of Muslim employees at their Friday prayers. The person responsible for setting aside the prayer room was not some liberal do-gooder but, instead, a diehard conservative, the House Speaker at the time, Newt Gingrich.

Our report, *Principled Pluralism*, was released in June 2013 and included a host of recommendations aimed at reinforcing the idea that diversity is a source of cultural richness and strength. To underline our findings, we pointed to America's founding motto, "E Pluribus Unum." We also warned that events overseas were complicating relationships among faith and ethnic communities in the United States; that some groups were intimidating others; and that in the absence of unifying national leadership, there might well be a socially destructive backlash against minorities and immigrants. Implicit in our message: we needed to elect a president in 2016, Republican or Democrat, who would oppose bigotry in all its forms and help bring the American people together.

TWENTY-EIGHT

Midnight

Saturday night in Concord, New Hampshire, three days before the Granite State's 2016 Democratic presidential primary. Outside, the weather is frightful; inside the auditorium, parkas are draped across chairs, mittens dangle from sleeves, and sweaters smell pungently of melted snow. Ruddy-cheeked rallygoers stomp their heavy boots and clap. I look out upon a sea of faces and whisper a prayer of thanks.

Up before dawn, I had survived a hair-raising day hurtling along snowy roads in an oversize SUV driven at high speeds by a volunteer. Happy not to be in a ditch, I had looked forward to the warmth now being generated by this boisterous crowd. A few minutes earlier, I had been asked by a reporter why so many young women preferred Vermont Senator Bernie Sanders to my candidate, Hillary Clinton. In the Iowa caucuses, held the previous week, the reported margin in that demographic had been depressingly lopsided. I didn't have a satisfactory answer to the question but knew that Sanders' call for a "revolution" was exciting starry-eyed Democrats even though a similar summons, coming from Hillary, would have played directly into the hands of the right wing—especially had she conveyed such an appeal, as Sanders did, by bellowing.

Standing on the small stage, I watch as New Jersey's silver-tongued Senator Cory Booker speaks first and gets the voices roaring. When my turn comes, motivating women is at the top of my mind. I point to Hillary's qualifications as the one person who has been a First Lady, a U.S. senator, and secretary of state. I tell stories about our travels together and credit her with mending America's reputation after the dispiriting images and actions of the Bush years. I proclaim how vital it is that the next president nominate progressive justices to the Supreme Court. Finally, I strive to ignite the ardor of my listeners with a question: "People are talking about revolution. What kind of a revolution would it be to have the first woman president of the United States?" This bit of rhetoric is followed by chants of "Hillary, Hillary."

Sitting toward the front, waving signs and cheering, is a platoon of teenage girls. When they catch my eye, I hold the microphone more firmly and think to myself, *This is the constituency we must energize.* Gesturing toward the girls in what I hope is a welcoming way, I tell them how wonderful it is that they are here and say, "You have to help. Hillary will always be there for you." The next words slip from my mouth as reflexively as "Bless you" after a sneeze; I had uttered them so many times: "There is a special place in Hell for women who don't help each other." I then turn to Clinton and add, "Because of all you have done, you are not only going to the White House, but also"—pointing skyward—"To that other place." My comments are greeted with a cascade of chortles and shouts and cause no problem at all—until later that night, when the tweets begin.

Ancient Greek dramatists employed a chorus to comment on folly. In our age, we have social media. Almost before the applause in New Hampshire had quieted, my words became a story, and not a good one. Urging women to help other women? Always appropriate. Telling a woman who votes for a man that she will therefore be ticketed for Hell? Not so smart. Also, not what I meant to imply. Gender has never dictated how I vote and shouldn't be used as a litmus test for candidates, male or female. The whole point of empowering young women is to ensure that they will be free to make up their own minds, a principle I have always supported. Still, Clinton and Sanders were locked in a two-person race. I could understand how people might misinterpret what I had said. In trying to inspire an audience, I had turned to a familiar phrase at the wrong place and time; the mistake earned the ire of our contemporary Greek chorus and quickly crossed over to mainstream news.

It didn't help that a few days earlier, Gloria Steinem had said in an interview that women "get more activist as they grow older. And when you're younger, you think: *Where are the boys? The boys are with Bernie.*" Taken together, her comments and mine caused a brief firestorm. One college student wrote, "A woman can be a feminist and vote for Mr. Sanders, and no amount of tantrum-throwing from powerful women will change that." Added a Bernie booster from Brooklyn, "The cluelessness of these feminist elders is astounding."

The truth is that I hadn't intended to denigrate anyone; my tongue simply moved faster than my brain, and indignant outbursts aside, I doubt very much that any actual human feelings were hurt. The essence of the flare-up was political. I had inadvertently created an opening that Sanders supporters could jump through in the full glory of viral passion, and that is exactly what they did.

In retrospect, the clash between the Clinton and Sanders campaigns, however fraught, was almost irrelevant to the dominant political story of 2016. The rivalry laid bare contrasts in attitude and style, but aside from some of Sanders' more utopian promises, policy differences were modest. The storm that mattered most was raging elsewhere on the political landscape.

THE REPUBLICAN PRIMARY season began with Mitt Romney's decision to bypass the race because he did not think he could defeat Jeb Bush. Next came debates that were divided, due to the bulky field, into the political equivalent of first class and steerage. For months there was an abundance of name-calling as Senator Cruz attacked Governor Christie who attacked Senator Rubio who attacked Mr. Trump who attacked everyone including Governor Bush; Bush didn't attack anyone and soon dropped out. Meanwhile, President Obama was popular, and the economy was in fine shape. For Democrats, all this should have been great news.

There was, however, one ground for concern. Since 1952, voters had allowed a party to remain in power for three consecutive terms just once (the Republicans between 1981 and 1993). The most recent chief executives, Bill Clinton, George W. Bush, and Barack Obama, had campaigned as deliverers of change. Hillary wouldn't be able to do that. She was already clearly defined in the minds of most voters and bore a multitude of scars from her twenty years in the White House, Senate, and State Department. As she later wrote, "Despite being the first woman to have a serious chance at the White House, I was unlikely to be seen as a transformative, revolutionary figure. I had been on the national stage too long for that, and my temperament was too even-keeled."

For these and other reasons, it seemed possible that a Republican candidate with a down-to-earth touch could attract the votes of socially conservative Democrats and independents in the Midwest, possibly tipping the election in favor of the Grand Old Party. But as the field narrowed, this worry eased. The Republicans were about to nominate a thrice-married billionaire real estate developer from New York with no government experience and little in common with heartland voters. It was one thing to crave change; quite another to choose Donald Trump to define it.

TO PREPARE FOR the 2016 balloting, I hosted several dinners to which I invited friends who specialized in world affairs and who supported Clinton. Among them were people likely to be considered for top administration jobs should our effort be successful. Sitting around my living room, we discussed the global and regional issues that we thought voters would care about most: terrorism, trade, Syria, Iran, and climate change. We talked as well about what our own roles in the campaign might be.

Those of us who had been through the process before knew that an international affairs expert is not necessarily a good fit in a presidential race. In 1988, after performing poorly in a general election debate, Mike Dukakis accused me of stuffing his head too full of foreign policy. I love the man, and we laughed about it later, but at

that moment, I could have hit him over the head with a souvlaki platter. Because most elections are decided on domestic issues, the home
front is where political advisers prefer to focus. James Carville's 1992
declaration "It's the economy, stupid" still rings true, yet a president
must also be trusted to keep Americans safe.

Generally, a governor such as Dukakis has to devote more time
to establishing credentials as a potential world leader than a former
vice president or member of Congress. That's why Texas Governor
George W. Bush, when campaigning in 2000, surrounded himself
with such figures as Colin Powell, Stephen Hadley, and Condi Rice.
Hillary Clinton, in 2016, was in a contrasting position: with her résumé already a part of U.S. history, she was in scant need of policy guidance. The imperative for the campaign was to persuade the
public that her past labors should be considered a future asset. To
that end, I traveled the country giving speeches about the high points
of Obama-Clinton diplomacy and about how essential it would be,
given the dangers we faced, to have a president who understood how
to influence foreign states and actors. For a character reference, I
could point to the words of a widely respected Republican and former colleague of hers, Defense Secretary Bob Gates:

> My experience working with Hillary illustrated, once again,
> that you are never too old to learn a lesson in life. Before she
> joined the Obama administration, I had not known her per-
> sonally, and what views I had were shaped almost entirely by
> what I had read in newspapers and seen on television. I quickly
> learned I had been badly misinformed. I found her smart,
> idealistic but pragmatic, tough-minded, indefatigable, funny,
> a very valuable colleague, and a superb representative of the
> United States all over the world.

Throughout the 2016 campaign season, I was convinced that if
voters cast their ballots for the person best prepared to be president,

Clinton would win a plurality. I was right; she did—but as the entire solar system now knows, it wasn't enough.

HILLARY CLINTON BEGAN using email in 2006 when, while a U.S. senator, she acquired a BlackBerry. In 2009 she moved her account to a server set up in their Chappaqua home. In this way she could continue, as secretary of state, to employ a single phone for her email, whether personal or professional. Of Clinton's three most recent predecessors, Condoleezza Rice and I had not used email at all, and Colin Powell had an AOL account that he relied on primarily for personal communications. But the rules were in flux. The State Department sought to tighten security in the face of leaks and the risk of cyber warfare. By 2009, department employees were required to conduct public business solely on official accounts. This standard should have applied to the secretary.

Clinton's error, however, was nowhere near the magnitude that her political opponents and pundits made it out to be. Despite many months of investigation, there is no indication that, as a result of her actions, any information harmful to U.S. security fell into the wrong hands. The email story was a legitimate one, yet relatively minor. The media, egged on by Republican operatives and allies of Russian intelligence, nevertheless made it the most exhaustively reported issue of the entire 2016 campaign.

Notwithstanding the email distraction and other nagging problems, Clinton was maintaining her lead in the polls. The reason was Trump. Whenever he seemed about to gain ground, the Republican nominee would insult a judge or a Gold Star mother and his momentum would stall. By any traditional measure, his general election effort rarely had a good day. During the debates, he appeared tired, showed little command of the issues, and failed to control his body language. When listening to Hillary, he looked like someone swallowing a sour pickle. When hovering close behind her on stage, he seemed creepy. Asked whether he would accept the results of the vote, he said it would depend on whether he won—the kind of implied threat typical of foreign dictators, not U.S. presidential candidates. Then, just a month before the election, release of the notorious *Access Hollywood* tape gave further evidence of Trump's preening ego and goatish attitude toward women.

American politics has always been a contact sport. No serious candidate, especially at the highest level, can survive without a thick skin. Back in 1800, Federalist preachers labeled Thomas Jefferson an atheist for his skepticism about the miracle working and resurrection of Jesus of Nazareth. Homely Abraham Lincoln was accused of being two-faced, causing him to reply, "I leave it to my audience: If I had two faces, would I be wearing this one?" In 1960, John Kennedy was denounced from Protestant pulpits for allegedly taking orders from the Vatican. Barry Goldwater was depicted as a madman intent on nuclear Armageddon. Dukakis was portrayed in incendiary commercials as soft on crime, and Obama's candidacy drew racists out from under rocks across the country. A national election campaign is a test of character and endurance for everyone involved. It is rare, however, for a White House aspirant to personally lead the way down, down, down into the muck.

Donald Trump repeatedly encouraged supporters to use violence against protestors. He has denied this, but such statements as "knock the crap out of them," "punch him in the face," and "maybe he should have been roughed up" are preserved on video. He regularly ridiculed reporters, pointing to them and inviting his fans to shower them with abuse. He also stoked fear against Muslims and immigrants. Many a Trump rally was marred by profanity, with printed signs or T-shirts showing Clinton with a noose around her neck, her head on a stake, or her body riddled with bullets. One saying that went viral on Twitter: "Rope. Tree. Journalist. Some assembly required."

In September, Hillary handed her opposition a gift by saying (at what was supposed to be a private gathering) that "you could put half of Trump's supporters into what I call the basket of deplorables.

Right? The racist, sexist, homophobic, xenophobic, Islamophobic—you name it." The other half, she added, "feel that the government has let them down" and are "desperate for change." The first part of the statement was unfortunate because it smacked of the same kind of facile stereotyping and name-calling that was so characteristic of her adversary. One reason some people are turned off by liberal Democrats and the media is that they are tired of being dismissed—in their minds, unjustifiably—as bigots, gun nuts, or religious zealots. They don't want to be lectured about ethics by politicians, or told how to treat women by admirers of Bill Clinton. They're also weary of allegations that they are privileged when they don't feel that they are, and of claims that everyone is a victim except them. Such are the feelings that prompt Trump admirers to insist that he "tells it like it is," regardless of how often he gets his facts wrong.

I had a humbling reminder of my own shortcomings during a dinner event at St. John's Episcopal Church in Georgetown, my home parish. Mariann Budde, the Bishop of Washington, was there, and the event was hosted by our rector, Gini Gerbasi. We ate lemon chicken with vegetables and talked about politics and God. After the meal, I gave a brief talk and invited questions. Among those who raised his hand was an undergraduate who denounced "East Coast elites"—he was from New Jersey—for supporting big government and for failing to understand and treat seriously the views of average Americans. He was, he said, a proud supporter of Trump and a staunch opponent of racial stereotypes. He was also African American. I told him frankly that his views surprised me, but that he had given me a needed lesson in judging people by appearances. I added that respect was a two-way street, and that I hoped he had as much regard for the opinions of others as he demanded for his own.

ELECTION NIGHT BEGAN for me at the Manhattan abode of the U.S. ambassador to the United Nations, Samantha Power, whose other guests included her female counterparts from nations around the world. Hosting the women ambassadors was a tradition I had started more than two decades before in that very apartment. Samantha's reception was a fitting way to launch what promised to be one of history's more memorable moments. My mind flipped back to 1984, when Democratic women were thrilled that Geraldine Ferraro had been nominated for vice president. I accompanied Gerry throughout that campaign and became convinced that the Mondale-Ferraro ticket would find a way to scale Mount Reagan and come out on top. Win it did, but only in Washington, DC, and Mondale's home state of Minnesota.

This time, the odds seemed tilted heavily in our direction. Despite the unfair media coverage, Clinton's edge in national surveys had remained steady. Pundits who added up the projected Electoral votes said there was no way she could lose. Anticipating what was to come, I had affixed my "shatter-the-glass-ceiling" pin to my jacket. Victory, I felt sure, was but a few hours away.

Eager to make the most of the evening, I left Samantha's when the mood was still merry and made my way south and west to Hell's Kitchen and the glassed-in Javits Center, where the Clinton team's party was under way. Because the front entrance was clogged by half of humanity, I ascended by freight elevator. There was a trinity of rooms set aside, and I felt like Goldilocks as I sampled the contents of each. The first was filled with show business people—Lady Gaga, members of the *Saturday Night Live* cast, Amy Schumer, and Katy Perry wearing a dress so wide that when she sat, it covered three chairs. The scene looked like fun but was too La-La Land for me. The second room swarmed with political figures from New York and across the country: too noisy and crowded. In the third room were longtime members of Hillary's staff and a flock of old friends. Just right. That's where I settled down to revel in the results, but when Florida went wrong, and Virginia wasn't moved to the Clinton column straight away, I started to fret.

At around nine o'clock, I left to do a video feed for students at Wellesley who had gathered—now with increasing nervousness—to cheer on the candidate they had expected to be the first graduate from any women's college to win the presidency. Though on edge myself, I tried to exhibit calm, saying, "Everything is always harder for a woman." Then I went back to the Clinton party and stayed until midnight. By the time I left, staffers were sobbing in the corners.

TWENTY-NINE

A Warning

WHEN DEFENDING THE bundle of compromises agreed to at the 1787 Constitutional Convention, Alexander Hamilton called attention to the link between the survival of freedom and a system of government based on checks and balances. Neither can endure without the other, he writes, and both depend on the willingness of citizens to give their primary allegiance not to any party or faction but to "the evidence of truth." The fact that the good and the wise can be found on opposite sides of many issues, he suggests, should "furnish a lesson of moderation to those who are ever so thoroughly persuaded of their being in the right in any controversy." He goes on to caution that excesses of political zeal can let loose "a torrent of angry and malignant passions." "Of those men who have overturned the liberties of republics," he advises, "the greatest number have begun their career by paying an obsequious court to the people, commencing demagogues and ending tyrants."

FOR MONTHS AFTER the 2016 election, some of my closest friends did little except rearrange furniture, watch television reruns, and, with a pathological glint in their eyes, stalk and murder aphids. Colleagues at work greeted one another with shaking heads and existential sighs. Churchgoers looked to Heaven for an apology. Progressives, old and young, explored real estate opportunities in Canada. More constructively, the day after the inauguration, a million women and friends of women assembled in Washington and other cities to resist. As for me, I commiserated with the staff members who work most closely with me on a daily basis, including confidential assistant Jan Stewart and speechwriter and adviser Jacob Freedman. Then I dipped my pen in sulfur and began to write.

Fascism: A Warning was published in April 2018. My sixth book is addressed to the present and future even when describing past events. The first chapters outline the origins of Fascism and the ill-fated careers of Benito Mussolini and an early admirer of his, Adolf Hitler. In my recounting of their sordid exploits, themes emerge that project a light forward on the tactics of a more contemporary breed of autocratic leaders, including Russia's Vladimir Putin, Turkey's Recep Tayyip Erdoğan, Hungary's Victor Orbán, North Korea's Kim Jong-un, the Philippines' Rodrigo Duterte, and closer to home, Venezuela's Nicolás Maduro and Donald Trump.

Mussolini and Hitler both came along at times when an ornery public was dissatisfied with conventional politicians; each of them gained power through constitutional means, then ruthlessly undermined competing centers of authority. To instill fear, each relied on brutal security forces and, as needed, violent street gangs. Each attracted followers by promising a return to national glory and to the values of what was portrayed as a simpler, happier age. Both equated opposition with treason and blamed every problem on supposed outsiders, including, in Hitler's case, Jews who had for generations fought in wars on Germany's behalf. Through a relentless cascade of propaganda, the despots portrayed themselves as folk heroes whose identities were at one with those of the nations they led. Hitler claimed to be a savior appointed by destiny to rescue *das Vaterland* from the *Schweinehunde* he said had betrayed it. Mussolini recalled the triumphs of ancient Rome and spoke grandly of his own infallible instincts, telling a reporter, "Often I would like to be wrong, but so far it has never happened."

I did not intend, in writing the book, to suggest that twenty-first century autocrats are as depraved as the Fascists who dragged our parents and grandparents into World War II. That's why I included "A Warning" in the title. I did argue that antidemocratic trends were gaining strength in countries that should be among freedom's strongholds and that conditions were ripe for further deterioration. Mussolini had compared the acquisition of dominant political authority to plucking a chicken, proceeding feather by feather, so that few would notice something wrong and raise an alarm. I wasn't worried that a president or prime minister would suddenly offer a Nazi salute and scream, "Sieg Heil!" My dread was that freedom and the institutions that safeguard it would gradually wash away. Democracies are built over time, and so, too, can they erode.

Indeed, in the months surrounding the book's publication, heads of government with an authoritarian bent were reelected in Russia, Hungary, Egypt, Venezuela, Turkey, Azerbaijan, and Cambodia. In each case, those in charge of the process manipulated it to favor the incumbent. These were not fair elections. Elsewhere, in Brazil, voters fed up with corruption, crime, and recession turned to an openly misogynistic right-wing candidate, Jair Bolsonaro, who promised law, order, and prosperity made possible, in part, by a full-scale retreat from environmental stewardship. In Europe, extreme nationalist movements from Scandinavia to the Mediterranean gained ground, becoming prominent in legislatures, shifting the terms of debate, and grabbing for themselves a thicker slice of power. In China, the National People's Congress erased any term limits on the presidency, potentially allowing Xi Jinping to remain in office for life even as his regime suppresses the rights of minorities on the Chinese mainland and, in Hong Kong, of pro-democracy activists.

In Syria, Bashar al-Assad claimed victory in his country's civil war seven years after Obama had urged his removal. Elsewhere in the Middle East, more ugliness ensued due to, among other shocks, the brutal homicide and dismemberment of a journalist, on October 2, 2018, in the Saudi Arabian consulate in Istanbul. Much has been made of the value, to diplomats, of leaving some matters shrouded in "constructive ambiguity." As I remarked to a congressional committee following the murder of Jamal Khashoggi, "There is nothing constructive, ambiguous, or diplomatic about a bone saw."

Worldwide, in this period, we were witnessing a disturbing pattern of retreat from the ideals of democracy and human rights. The defenders of those principles were being pushed back, while the proponents of more cynical objectives were learning from and emboldening one another, becoming steadily more aggressive and confident. Ordinarily, in such an hour, we would have known to which country's leaders we might look for notice of the oncoming peril. Thus alerted, a modern-day Paul Revere could then have spread the alarm to every nation and region, broadcasting "a cry of defiance, and not of fear." However, these weren't ordinary times. America had seemingly nodded off, and instead of lamps shining in its belfry tower, there was only darkness.

THAT YEAR (2018), I embarked on a nationwide tour to highlight the message ingrained in *Fascism: A Warning*. The jaunt was a bracing one—with odd moments. In Las Vegas my appearance coincided with a convention of the wine and spirits industry. Behind the table at which I signed books for both the sober and the sodden, a banner read, "MAKE WHISKEY GREAT AGAIN." Despite all the attention given to the Me Too movement, a gentleman in Miami rose to his feet and said, "I'm ninety years old but haven't lost my eyesight, and you're a good-looking gal." An article in the *Washington Post* referred to me as "a lovable feminist granny." By contrast, a woman in Brooklyn who heard me speak told a reporter later that I was a "ghoul warmonger," this according to a Russian news service. At every stop, when I opened the floor to questions, a hundred hands flew up.

I found many of my fellow citizens bewildered and cranky. It's no wonder. The executive and legislative branches of government were (and remain) at odds over nearly every consequential issue, including the conduct of the president. The major political parties are also at war. Activists from the left are accusing moderates of cowardice, despite the courage required to resist demands for ideological purity and the understanding, central to governing, that services and programs must be paid for by something more tangible than wishes. If I ever write another book, I may title it *Reveille for Moderates*.

Republicans, meanwhile, have undergone a metamorphosis worthy of Kafka. A friend of mine, once a member of that party, compared what is happening to a fable he had read in high school about the hijacking of identity. In the story, a tortoise decides to attend a feast given annually for birds—an aim met with derision throughout the animal kingdom. After all, the festival site is high in the mountains, and everyone knows that a tortoise cannot fly. But this is no ordinary terrapin. He persuades each bird he meets to lend him a single feather until he has enough to make himself a set of wings and become airborne. The birds are astonished to find him among them when flapping their way to the feast. More startling still, he convinces his fellow travelers that, to honor the gala occasion, each should adopt a new name. The tortoise chooses one for himself meaning "all of us." Later, when the birds arrive at the mountaintop and are asked to whom their food should be given, they reply without thinking: "to all of us." In this way, the usurper gains not only a position to which he would ordinarily have no claim, but he does so with help from all the other birds, eats their food, and assumes the identity of the entire species. What once was an avian party now belongs—beak, talon, and feathers—to an imposter.

IS DONALD TRUMP a Fascist? During my book tour, this was the question I was asked most often. To me it was a trap. I could not in good conscience defend the president, but it would have been ridiculous to put him in the same category as such mass murderers as Hitler or Stalin. I replied, "I do not call him a Fascist. I do say that he has the most antidemocratic instincts of any president in modern American history."

Why? Not merely because Trump berates the media, is often at loggerheads with Congress, complains about court decisions, and fired the director of the FBI. Other presidents have done all of those things. Some, too, have been excessively self-absorbed, and throwers of ear-splitting tantrums. What separates this president from his predecessors is a matter of degree. No other president has so thoroughly combined a boorish personality with an incapacity to accept criticism, an utter disregard for the responsibilities of his office, and a tendency to make stuff up worthy of both Guinness's book and Ripley's.

There are those who point to Trump's atrocious spelling and reliance on short words as evidence that he lacks brainpower. I am not so sure. The man has a multitude of blind spots, but he also has an instinct that he has relied on throughout his career: to go on the offensive and claim at the same time to be under attack. Politically, this approach energizes supporters and channels their outrage in whatever direction Trump is pointing his finger. The tactic is deliberate, reflects cunning, and often leaves opponents floundering about in the mud that seems to be the president's favored terrain. The effect on society is correspondingly bog-like. More than six decades ago, the philosopher Eric Hoffer wrote that "rudeness is the weak man's imitation of strength." The observation holds. I am not being an alarmist when I say that we must aim for a more uplifting understanding of what it means to be strong and that we must do so soon if we are to avoid causing grave damage to the foundations of our democracy.

According to a study released in 2019, 42 percent of Americans now believe that people belonging to the opposing political party are "evil." Nearly 20 percent think that their adversaries "lack the traits to be considered fully human," and that the world would be better off if many of those foes didn't just steer clear of politics but were dead. Other surveys show that people often attribute to ideological opponents beliefs (e.g., about race, religion, law enforcement, and illegal migration) that the rivals do not in fact hold. Meanwhile, legislators and commentators who dare to disagree openly with the president are besieged with death threats. Individuals who have served in the administration are harassed in public. Conservative speakers have been barred from sharing their views on college campuses because university authorities say they cannot protect them. Partisans of the left and right increasingly think it clever to direct obscenities and dehumanizing chants toward political enemies. Social media platforms are used systematically, intentionally, and effectively to propagate falsehoods about people and events in public life. And all of this was true even before the polarizing confrontation over impeachment.

These trends are extremely worrisome. They are also out of place in a society that still claims to lead the free world—because what Hamilton referred to as a "torrent of angry and malignant passions" could, if left unchecked, indeed carry us toward Fascism.

A FEW BLOCKS from where I work is a patch of open land that is half park, half blocked-off roadway. The address of the nearest residence, 1600 Pennsylvania Avenue, is familiar to people everywhere, but to grasp the larger meaning of the place, one must explore, as I have many times, the area outside its gates. Cross the street to the square on the northern side and one can enjoy a close-up look at statues honoring a quartet of foreigners who helped make America great the first time: Marquis de Lafayette, Comte de Rochambeau, Tadeusz Kościuszko, and Friedrich Wilhelm von Steuben. A tourist with a guidebook might inform you that von Steuben, a trusted adviser to General Washington and the man responsible for transforming a raw Continental Army into a competent fighting force, was gay. Beneath the statues and among the eclectic array of trees, a visitor will see squirrels with fur of varied pigments (gray, white, and black) playing tag with one another and competing for discarded sandwiches and nuts.

Between the greenery and the White House fence is a stretch of pavement that was closed to vehicular traffic following the 1995 terrorist bombing (by a Christian) of the federal courthouse in Oklahoma City. The shutdown, though an irritant to motorists, makes room for an ever-changing exhibition of performance art. Stroll through on a random afternoon and you might encounter breakdancing buskers, bagpipers in kilts, a black man soliciting funds to help the children of Haiti, a white man proclaiming the cause of clean government, a delegation of Yazidi elders protesting ISIS sex slavery, Jehovah's Witnesses seeking readers for their pamphlets, a five-woman anti-Trump band, and adherents of the Falun Gong spiritual practice denouncing China's persecution of their compatriots.

Winding their way through the scene are the perspiring chaperones of American schoolchildren on field trips and Asian tourists who find space alongside them to snap pictures with the White House fountain in the background. Among the other visitors are adolescent girls in distressed jeans, Middle Eastern men in long robes, African and Latina women in brightly colored dresses, teenage boys wearing MAGA hats, veterans in "Semper Fi" T-shirts, and activists carrying signs that read, "Black Lives Matter"—all laughing or emitting startled oaths as they dodge the scooters and Segways that flit between them. Watching all this from the entrance of their weather-beaten blue and gray tent are the keepers of a peace vigil that began in 1981 and has since continued around the clock and through every season.

The panorama is different every day, yet the same as well. It reflects contemporary political currents but is above them. It is exuberant, varied, inclusive, clamorous, respectful, disrespectful, alive, and above all free. The whole area could be shut down in ten minutes.

THIRTY

Unhinged

JUNE 2018. I am in Versailles for a meeting of the Aspen Ministers Forum. This, I tell my colleagues—other former cabinet officers from around the world—is our most important session. We represent, for better or worse, what might be called the foreign policy establishment in exile. We share a conviction that the foundation for international advancement designed by our forebears was a firm one, based on transatlantic partnership, democratic values, open economies, arms control, and human rights. The familiarity of such concepts has not, in our eyes, ever undermined their worth. Indeed, when the Berlin Wall crumbled, we felt that our beliefs had been vindicated. In the struggle between East and West, the more hopeful side had prevailed, thus enabling us to look forward to a united Europe and to a world where democracy would have an uncontested claim to the high ground. Why, then, was the theme of our gathering "What Went Wrong?"

For starters, both Brexit and Trump's election had taken us by surprise. The first rule of critical thinking is to question one's own assumptions, and I was among the speakers in Versailles to suggest that perhaps we had taken too much for granted. For many in Europe, the ideal of regional integration was losing its luster as radical nationalists, confined previously to the political shorelines, paddled their way into the faster waters of the main stream. Political parties that had shared or controlled power for decades were being crowded out by upstarts with slick slogans, big promises, and no record in government for which they could be held accountable.

One reason for all this: the passage of time. The lessons learned during World War II about the benefits of multilateral cooperation and the dangers of unbridled jingoism are no longer fresh. The majority of people in Europe and North America are too young even to remember the Cold War in any depth. Having nothing to compare, many cannot conceive of a system worse than the imperfect democracies with which they are currently saddled. Lacking patience, they underestimate the difficulty of governing and are quick to find fault when their needs are not swiftly gratified. The resulting gap between desire and reality creates a demand for what no governments can produce: societies that are adapting constantly to change and reassuringly familiar at the same time.

Globalization contributes to this divide. For years, experts have been telling us that most people would gain from liberal rules of trade and the advances wrought by innovative technology. The evidence could be found in a world economy that doubled in size in the first two decades of the twenty-first century and that continues to grow at a rate far in excess of the pre-modern era.

The market, however, is more efficient than fair. The fruits of expansion have been concentrated among the well educated in the major urban centers of the West and among broader segments of the population in the East, where the biggest economies have decentralized and plugged into the global system. Should these trends continue, the size of the middle class will remain stagnant in the United States and Europe while exploding in Asia, where, by 2030, two-thirds of the world's middle class will live. This lopsided pattern is creating large pockets of resentment in traditional manufacturing and farming sectors and among people who lack up-to-date communications skills.

Twenty years ago, we worried about the impact of change on the least developed nations. Today, millions of people see themselves as victims while living in such places as Greece, France, Spain, Italy, the former East Germany, and America's industrial heartland. Their grievances are shaking up politics in these countries and beyond—and have been amplified by the arrival of a record number of illegal immigrants and asylum seekers.

In 2016, the British voted by a narrow margin to leave the European Union out of a desire to reclaim power from the regional bureaucracy in Brussels and to stem the flow of newcomers to their shores. Almost everywhere on the continent, animus toward migrants has grown even more rapidly than the size of immigrant populations. The traditional liberal reflex is to dismiss such feelings as prejudice, but that can boomerang. Hubert Védrine, the former foreign minister of France and the host of our meeting, argued that there are many more French who say they are discomfited by the recently arrived than who identify with the right wing. Yet, if all who show unease are dismissed as bigots, at least some will feel pushed into the arms of extremists.

That is why Hungary's Viktor Orbán and other openly illiberal politicians try to make every trip to the ballot box a referendum on the issue. As they see it, their ticket to power is stamped "fear." Thus they exaggerate the harmful impacts of immigration on jobs, crime, public expenditures, and national identity. These arguments can be effective anywhere, including states where foreign-born populations remain small. Regardless of whether it is so, the perception is spreading that the influx of Africans and Arabs has gone about as far as it should. There are people on the left who have reluctantly come to share this view because of the bias occasionally displayed by some migrants against women, Jews, and gays.

Caught in the middle are millions from the Middle East, Africa, and Central America who, because of violence or repression, cannot live where they were brought up. Their ordeal has caused many to leave behind their every physical belonging; to risk starvation, robbery, and rape; and to flee in quest of a better life. One such family was that of Alan Kurdi, a three-year-old Syrian whose parents, in 2015, paid more than five thousand dollars for four spaces on a small boat without functioning lifejackets; the overcrowded vessel capsized at the start of its intended journey from Turkey to Greece. The boy's corpse washed up on the sand.

My friend Lloyd Axworthy, the former foreign minister of Canada, is chair of the World Refugee Council. He points out that there are some seventy million people displaced by strife today—up from forty-three million a decade ago and more than at any time since the end of World War II. He also notes that throughout history, immigrants have contributed richly to most of the societies they have joined. As a refugee myself, I have always believed in the right of men and women to a safe haven from persecution, a right that extends back to biblical times. I also find it shameful that under Trump, the United States is less welcoming to the international homeless than it has ever been. When I arrived in New York, the Statue of Liberty was there to greet me because a much earlier generation of Americans had sacrificed its nickels and dimes to build a place for her to stand. The last I looked, Lady Liberty was still at her post but, I have imagined, with tears in her eyes.

Whether in Europe or America, a sustainable immigration policy can be implemented without vilifying migrants or professing to see greatness in high walls (or deep moats). All that is required are leaders who will cooperate across borders to minimize the number of people who feel they have no choice but to escape from their countries in the first place. That means building inclusive democracies, fostering peace, strengthening the rule of law, and generating prosperity from the ground up. We must also put out of business the human traffickers who use social media to persuade potential migrants (like the Kurdi family) to pay fees they can't afford to undertake journeys that rarely end well. This agenda is exacting but requires no miracles to advance. It's what many people in authority claim to want.

Sadly, effective high-level leaders are in short supply. Look around. Where are they? The White House? Downing Street? Rome? A France whose last three presidents (Sarkozy, Hollande, Macron) began losing popularity the day they were elected? The best answer is Germany, yet even there, Chancellor Angela Merkel is under fire domestically and preparing to leave office. Among her more recent observations: The U.S.-led global order "has collapsed into many tiny parts. "

During our meeting in Versailles, former German Foreign Minister Joschka Fischer was similarly bleak. "Will the West survive?" he asked rhetorically. "No." The West, he declared, is systematically destroying itself. He reminded us that Germany's postwar transformation into a vibrant, internationally respected democracy had long been seen as one of America's more impressive foreign policy triumphs. So, what was happening? Instead of supporting European integration, a core principle of both U.S. and German policy for decades, Trump has called the EU a "foe" and urged members to leave. Instead of closing ranks with Berlin and other European capitals, the president has picked fights over trade, climate change, Iran, and NATO. No wonder, then, that in the past few years the standing of the United States has dropped more sharply in Europe than in any other region. Looking to the future, how can the West thrive if the governments of its leading nations no longer believe in the same things?

IN MARCH 2019, I went to Central Europe to observe the twentieth anniversary of NATO enlargement, meet with business clients, and promote the Polish- and Czech-language editions of *Fascism: A Warning*.

In Poland, I renewed my acquaintance with Lech Wałęsa, the electrician who in the 1980s exposed the true nature of the communist workers' state by demanding the right to form an independent labor union. Though his handsome mustache long ago turned from a lustrous brown to silver, Wałęsa remains a man of strong opinions. For years, he has feuded with a government in Warsaw that he claims has undermined the constitution by attacking the press and forcing changes to the judiciary. Poland, like Hungary and the Czech Republic, is a democracy strained by tension between hypernationalists and moderates.

Given the charged political climate, I was unsure how I would be received when I showed up at the University of Warsaw to give a speech. The answer was evident well before I reached the auditorium: four thousand people were attempting to squeeze into a hall that seats four hundred. Afterward, I signed books and was reminded that when asked to take their place in a lengthy queue, Americans will do so grudgingly while Europeans pretend not to have heard the instruction; instead, they mill around and use their elbows. The crowd was so large that we decided, when I inscribed books, to use only the first names of the people in line. So, we began. An aide handed a copy of the book to me, and after noting the initial word on the accompanying slip, I wrote, "To Dla." In the second book, I wrote, "To Dla." In the third, "To Dla." Pausing, I looked up. The people whose volumes I had signed appeared puzzled. Belatedly, I remembered that in Polish, *dla* isn't somebody's first name; it means "for."

Our second stop was Prague, city of my birth, where some Czechs treat me as if I were a queen, and others, like an irritating older sister. During one event, the ex-minister of defense grinned, knelt, and kissed my hand, while the incumbent prime minister sat stone-faced, pretending I wasn't there. In fairness, he might have been remembering my description of him in *Fascism: A Warning*, as "cold, detached, uncommunicative, [and] remote." Our failure to connect was too bad, because I had planned to ask him about a meeting he had just had at the White House, where he had given Trump a Czech-made revolver. The obsequious nature of the encounter, and the irony of the inscription on the gun's barrel ("Truth Prevails"), would have fit snugly into one of Václav Havel's plays.

I AM OFTEN asked to assess the Trump administration's approach to foreign policy, but what is there to say that hasn't already been said a thousand times? This president has attracted more commentary in conventional and social media than any public figure in memory. The hubbub is a response, frequently hysterical, to Trump's incessant bullying and to his apparent belief, evident in much of what he says and does, that the Sun rises and sets only as a favor to him. The president has a transparent yearning to be praised as a world leader, yet because of his arrogance, he is instead a source of dismay to many U.S. allies and, behind his back, widely mocked.

The day will come, though, when the furor has quieted, and historians will assess the actual record of his time in office. They will surely separate, if they can, the impact of the chief executive's personal qualities from his influence on the globe and on America's place in it. They will not assume—nor should they—that a leader with deep character flaws must also fail professionally. Nations, as we have learned throughout history, are motivated more by their own interests than by the charm of individual officials. Trump need not win a popularity contest to be a success in the international arena. With that in mind, and granting that no administration's record can be judged fully until long after it is over, what do we see?

Plainly, Trump conceives of foreign policy less as a strategy than as a style. He thinks it clever to offer threats one day and air kisses the next, to zig and zag and feint and bluff on such weighty matters as Iran policy, trade, North Korea's nuclear program, and Middle East peace. He employs the same hot-then-cold manner in key bilateral relationships—for example, those with Mexico, Argentina, Pakistan, India, and Turkey. There is a worthy precedent for this technique. During the Cold War, Henry Kissinger sought to pry concessions out of Soviet rulers by suggesting that Nixon was unhinged and that there was no telling what he might do were he not to get his way. Trump's lack of discipline seems tailor-made for a similar tactic, but only if (as with Nixon) it is part of a coherent plan. Mere unpredictability is a character trait, not a policy.

Ordinarily, the center of any nation's foreign policy is embodied by a set of clear goals. Other than a desire to sell weapons and reduce trade deficits, however, it is far from obvious what the Trump administration seeks to achieve or what it stands for. The president is clearly attracted to leaders abroad in whom he recognizes something of himself, especially the desire to appear strong regardless of democratic considerations and human rights. There is hardly a despot anywhere about whom the president has not expressed admiration, even to the point of trusting their assurances more than the reporting of U.S. analysts. Dictators who silence dissident movements and jail journalists aren't so much criticized by Trump, as envied.

The president also delights in disparaging the global system of international problem solving and law that his predecessors in the White House led in creating. In his view, the United States came out on the short end of just about every negotiation it entered into prior to his taking office. The country, he insists, has been pushed around and repeatedly victimized at the bargaining table by wily foreigners. This assertion is completely at odds with America's status as the world's number one economic and military power. Facts aside, Trump is determined to show that the nation can best succeed not by trying to forge further cooperative arrangements with other countries, but instead by acting unilaterally. How well is that approach working?

In the domain of national security, the president has accomplished little despite his many exaggerated promises. The administration's confrontational approach to Iran has damaged U.S. credibility as a country that keeps its word and has, at times, brought regional tensions to a boiling point without winning any tangible concessions from Tehran. In the broader Middle East, Trump has switched signals constantly, bewildering allies, betraying anti-terrorist Kurdish fighters, and opening the door wide to greater Russian and Chinese influence. Meanwhile, the president's attempt, for domestic political reasons, to extort cooperation from Ukraine was amateurish, unethical, and a poor way to treat one of America's longtime friends. In Asia, North Korea's nuclear arsenal has grown, and its missile testing has continued apace.

On economic issues, Trump's trademark mix of huffing and bluffing has injected immense anxiety into a global system that does not always cope well with stress. "Tariff Man," as he calls himself, brags nonstop regarding his negotiating prowess, yet has produced just a modestly updated agreement on North American trade and a mini-pact with China that fell far short of U.S. goals. Despite his claim that it is easy to "win" a trade war, Trump has not been able to persuade China to reform its policies toward state-owned enterprises, the enforcement of contracts, and intellectual property. The president appears to believe that tariffs are paid for by foreign governments, not consumers, and that trade between countries is a zero-sum game. In fact, the world has never been more interdependent. Manufacturers, farmers, and service providers all rely increasingly on exports—and prosperous countries will buy more from the United States than insolvent ones. I have yet to meet a corporate executive who doesn't understand that America will do better when others do, too; why has our businessman president failed to grasp that?

Managing world affairs, like any serious task, requires preparation and organization. Even many admirers of Trump concede that these are not among the man's strong points. The result has been a lot of churning. By the end of the president's third year in office, he had already had three chiefs of staff and four national security advisors. His original selections for secretary of defense, secretary of state, and ambassador to the United Nations were also gone. Instead of putting his trust in experts, Trump has turned to such diplomatic neophytes as his son-in-law Jared Kushner and the self-interested former mayor of New York, Rudy Giuliani.

The disorder extends to the White House's mode of national security decision-making, a subject I teach in my classes. Normally, that process is designed to bring together as much information as possible in advance of important judgments. Under Trump, the system has often been bypassed by presidential whim. There is no telling whether a policy will be decided after careful analysis, or because the commander in chief saw a suggestion that he liked while watching television. The mixed signals make it hard for America's partners to coordinate their own policies, because what the White House wants keeps changing and those who speak for the administration today may be unemployed tomorrow.

The president's contemptuous attitude toward career professionals, both military and civilian, is without parallel in U.S. history. Trump has an apparently insatiable need to blame others, and public servants are a convenient target. The impact on morale has been significant in the State and Defense departments, our intelligence agencies, and the armed forces. The result is grossly unfair to people who have worked their entire lives on behalf of American interests and ideals. It also weakens our country in the face of its enemies, and further undermines the trust of U.S. citizens in their own institutions. All in all, a textbook example of how not to lead.

Before slipping into hysteria myself, let me explain that I have devoted this much space to Trump only because he is so hard to escape. As an individual, he repels me far more than he interests me, yet every day, I am asked to discuss him on the radio, in newspapers, in my classes, when giving speeches, and in dealing with clients. I tell myself to remain calm, because who wants to spend their final years in a bad mood? What I honestly don't know as I write this (early in 2020) is whether the harm he is causing to America's reputation, interests, and ability to rally others will prove temporary or lasting. The good news—at least, I pray it is good—is that the answer to that question depends far less on him than it does on us.

THIRTY-ONE

Renewal

A FEW WEEKS AFTER the 2018 election, I was invited to historic Williamsburg, the prerevolutionary capital of Virginia, to meet with new members of the U.S. House of Representatives. Our host was the Librarian of Congress, Carla Hayden, the first actual librarian to hold the post in six decades and, as is typical of librarians, a wise and awesome person. The goal of the gathering was to enable the fledgling lawmakers to meet one another and to share with them information about how Congress operates.

In 1974, one of Hayden's predecessors, Daniel Boorstin, wrote a book about democracy in which he observes that "anybody who comes to Washington cannot fail to be cheered by the frequent expressions of respect by legislators for other legislators with whom they disagree." Having lived through that period, I can vouch for the accuracy of Boorstin's seemingly far-fetched description. Courtesy ruled once upon a time, and the era really wasn't so long ago.

What I saw and heard from the bipartisan mix in Williamsburg early in 2019 did not begin to match Boorstin's cheery standard, yet I was heartened nonetheless. Surrounded by restored Colonial buildings and the reminders of America's founding debates, the newcomers focused on how to stitch together the country's ripped social fabric, not on how to tear one another apart. Many had survived bitter campaigns yet craved a return to civility—or so they said. Even their name tags, which revealed the states from which they had come, made no mention of party.

The incoming class of the 116th Congress included a pair of Democratic Socialists, the most women and people of color in the chamber's history, and some two dozen alumni of the U.S. armed forces or CIA. More than a hundred strong, the freshmen have taken up their jobs in the manner of such jumbo-size predecessor classes as the recession Democrats (elected in 1958), the Watergate babies (1974), the acolytes of Ronald Reagan (1980), pro-Gingrich conservatives (1994), and Tea Partiers (circa 2010). Wave after wave, from left, center, and right, these newly empowered bands have descended on Washington with high hopes of cleansing the temple. None has fully succeeded, yet each has left its mark. Every congressional class reflects the mood of its times, but attitudes are not typically the same in Manhattan, Kansas, for example, as on Manhattan Island. Collectively, the legislators represent "We the People" in a country where many of their constituents see a canyon-size gap between "them" and "us." Members have the choice of enlarging that divide, often the easier course politically, or of trying to narrow it through compromise, a process Benjamin Franklin compared to a carpenter fashioning a table out of random pieces of wood: trimming here and cutting there until a good fit is achieved.

In January 2019 in Williamsburg, where discussions were conducted in private, the talk was uniformly positive, and my spirits climbed a notch. However, back in Washington, where microphones are everywhere, tempers soon flared. Ideological purists in both parties spoke loudest, while moderates were derided, even threatened; instead of assembling planks into new tables, there was much pounding on old ones. This is worrisome, because Congress could be America's last best hope. Our current president is hardly a unifying force, and the judiciary, by design, is more a responsive institution than a proactive one. For the United States to emerge from its present funk, Congress cannot allow itself to be paralyzed; in both the House and the Senate, and on both sides of the political aisle, it must do its job.

To highlight this point, many months ago I began running around the country proclaiming, "It's Article One time!" to people who have no clue what I mean. I explain that Article I is where the U.S.

Constitution spells out the privileges and obligations of the legislative branch. I argue that—lest it be steamrollered by whoever is in
the White House—Congress must reassert itself as a coequal partner
in government. How? Lawmakers have the right to hear testimony
from executive branch officials, demand information from agencies,
investigate cases of wrongdoing for referral to the courts, and evaluate the integrity and competence of persons nominated for positions
of trust. They have a duty, as well, to help set the nation's agenda so
that urgent economic, social, and security needs are not lost amid
political posturing. Internationally, they have a chance to reassure
allies that America will stand with them in moments of stress; they
can also set an example for democracies worldwide by collaborating
with one another for the common good.

Admittedly, Congress isn't easy to love. There is hardly a humorist from Mark Twain on who has not milked laughs from its shortcomings. As an executive branch official, I found that dealing with
Capitol Hill and its many committees was often painful; but when
invited by Congress to testify, I did. When asked questions, I answered.
When prevailed on to submit documents, my office complied. When
laws were enacted, my team implemented them regardless of what we
thought about each provision. In so doing, I didn't win any prizes;
nor did I expect to. This is how our system is supposed to operate.

Legislators can be wrong and still merit esteem. In my career, I
have worked both for them and with them and have found most to be
earnest, hardworking, well intentioned, and exhausted. Every couple
of years, they allow themselves to be judged in the most visible way
imaginable—that takes guts. When I was in the executive branch, I
accompanied many lawmakers to their home states and districts for
joint appearances. They spoke, then I did, and whether we agreed or
not, we clasped hands and meant at least some of the nice things we
said about each other. The relationships so forged paid off when the
time came to negotiate on budgets, gain consent for nominations, and
win support for such measures as NATO enlargement and a treaty
to ban chemical weapons. The constitution has been described as an

invitation to struggle between the White House and Congress for influence over foreign policy, but a struggle, when honorably contested, can strengthen both sides. In my experience, debates involving the two were often conducted at a high pitch, but few officials in either the executive or legislative branch questioned the motives of the other; neither did we accuse one another of lying, for there was no cause.

An observer of the contemporary clash between Trump and Capitol Hill might think that one party has traditionally favored, and the other opposed, an imperial presidency. This isn't so. The checks and balances that are woven into our democratic system are without ideological tint. They prevented left-leaning presidents from packing the Supreme Court in the 1930s and nationalizing the steel industry in 1952. They imposed accountability on the Nixon administration's wrongdoings in the 1970s and the Reagan White House's bizarre scheme to trade arms for hostages with Iran a decade later. Liberal or conservative, the principle is plain: no one, including the president, is above the law and everyone is entitled to due process under it. Both parties have ample reason to uphold those propositions.

In any showdown with a president, Congress will be handicapped by its chronic inefficiency and by its Babel-like tendency to speak in many tongues. The Constitution, however, has its back. A president's powers are limited to those cited in that document or in laws approved by Congress. That's it. A commander in chief who tries to circumvent the Constitution should be restrained by the legislature and judiciary. That may not happen, however, if the public fails to weigh in. Democracy frays when citizens fail to show interest in preserving the integrity of its institutions or are complicit in the fraying.

I may be naïve to think that in the social media age, we might yet return to a time when observers of U.S. politics are astonished by the mutual respect shown by rivals. Part of the cost of freedom is that we are all allowed to speak our minds; yet, there is no requirement that we be lucid, courteous, or fair. Inevitably, some of us will fall short of those standards. But societies aren't expected to be perfect; they are measured by their overall values and by the distinctions most citizens make between what is or is not reasonable. Hitler, had he begun his career in a time and place other than interwar Germany, might well have spent his entire adulthood peddling his ideas before tiny groups of drunks and Dobermans. Instead, he found millions of listeners who were so angry that they had stopped thinking and so bitter they needed but a quick shove to set sail as vessels of hate. What kind of listeners are we?

The answer to that question is ever changing, and impressions are less scientific than anecdotal. There is no denying that combustible emotions are abroad in our land. However, I have been encouraged by conversations I have had with people, young and old, of every political affiliation. There is, I believe, a dawning realization that we cannot continue on the present course without lasting harm. Within the past few years, a flock of civic-minded organizations has either sprung up or intensified efforts to defend our democracy from attacks both external and internal. Books on the subject have attracted a wide readership. The same surveys that reveal stark divisions among some segments of the electorate also indicate a yearning for the animosity to end. Awareness is also growing, thankfully, that the choices we make at the polls are important not only to individual candidates but also to the country's social viability in the near future and beyond.

Amid World War II's grimmest days, when the Nazis appeared invincible, the British radio broadcasts that brought real news to Europe were introduced by the sound of a kettledrum playing the first notes of Beethoven's fifth symphony: dah-dah-dah-dum. The notes equated, in Morse Code, to the letter V (dot-dot-dot-dash), the Allies' symbol for victory. The triumph then envisioned was not one of conquest or of the type that glorifies emperors and kings. It was instead a victory of the democratic spirit, a way of living and thinking that, in 1943, the essayist E. B. White captured by means of a prosaic list: "the line that forms on the right," the "don't" in "don't shove," the hole in a stuffed shirt, the dent in a high hat, the sense of sharing in a library, the confidence of privacy in the voting booth, the letter to the editor, the idea that hasn't been disproved yet, and the "feeling of vitality everywhere." During the Cold War, my father offered a companion idea in three words: "every individual counts." A community bound together by that conviction will not have time to sort itself into the categories beloved by chauvinists, zealots, and bigots. My parents' generation found meaning in the letter *V* and all it represented. Does the *U* in USA still have the ability to inspire us? If so, we must prove it.

The dilemma for citizens today is whether to sit back and permit the loudest voices to speak for us, or to promote our ideals as best we can despite the uproar those sowers of discord generate. As a cause, civility is not usually of the type that prompts one to lace up boots, grab a water bottle, and march, yet we can't accept the current "lie, deny, and defy" approach to executive leadership as some sort of new normal. It is neither normal nor okay. For the past several years, my exhortation to audiences has been "See something, say something, do something." Exactly what we are able to say and do will depend on our circumstances. There are no guarantees that any particular action will make a difference; there never are. But that doesn't let us off the hook.

Whoever we are, we each have our opportunities and choices. And at the risk of sounding like Judge Judy or Dr. Phil, we each have the capacity to show fairness toward others and to probe in our relations with contemporaries for what is sincere and good. None of us is so caught up in the fever of daily life (or in the throes of political rivalry) that we cannot at least ask ourselves some basic questions.

If we are members of Congress, what principles will inform our actions and words? If we are parents or teachers, what kind of example will we set, and what values will we seek to nurture in the young? If students, what lessons will we take from class? If involved in business or the professions, what standards will guide our practice? If religious leaders, how will we define what is moral? Regardless of our station or calling, how can we most wisely allocate the time and skills we have been given?

Finally, if one is a former secretary of state of a certain age, to whom might she look as an example for how to make something meaningful of the opportunities in life that she still has?

ON THE MORNING of October 23, 1837, an old man opened a newspaper and saw an advertisement offering for sale Dorcas Allen and her two daughters, ages nine and seven. He had never heard of the woman and had not been contacted by anyone on her behalf. Nevertheless, the notice upset him, and he inquired into the details. Allen, once a slave, had been living in the District of Columbia but without a legal document to prove her emancipation. After more than a decade of freedom, during which she bore four children, she was suddenly claimed as property by the second husband of the second wife of the widower of the woman who had once owned her and, before dying, sought to release her from bondage. Due to the claimant's greed, Allen and her offspring were separated from Nathan, Allen's spouse, and sold to slave traders for seven hundred dollars, then jailed to await public auction. The first night after this perversion of inheritance law was engineered, the woman killed her two youngest children and tried to slit her own throat before being stopped. Pressed to explain, she said she had hoped to send her family to Heaven. Now, she was to be sold. The old man with the newspaper, a former U.S. secretary of state, had no desire to become involved in this tangled and sordid case, but he could not outrun the tentacles of conscience.

John Quincy Adams was America's chief diplomat from 1817 to 1825 and president for four years thereafter. Rather than retire, he was elected to the House of Representatives beginning in 1830. A decade later, he asked of his diary, "What can I, upon the verge of my seventy-fourth birthday, with a shaking hand, a darkening eye, a drowsy brain, and with all my faculties dropping from me, one by one, as the teeth are dropping from my head, what can I do for the cause of God and Man?"

The manner in which he answered his own question is why he is among the ex-secretaries of state I admire most. After consulting with the district attorney of Washington (Francis Scott Key) and sorting through the legal issues, Adams helped raise enough money to reunite the family of Dorcas Allen. On the floor of Congress, he presented so many petitions to limit or abolish slavery that his colleagues voted to bar his entreaties—thus inaugurating the original "gag rule." He refused to be silenced; instead, he lured pro-slavery representatives into debates on the very matter they wished to avoid, reminding them of "great resemblances between the progeny of the colored people and the white men who claim possession of them." In 1841, he spoke for nine hours in front of the Supreme Court to secure the freedom of a group of Africans who had mutinied against the officers of a Spanish-owned slave ship, the *Amistad*. By his persistence, he won that case and eventually turned Congress around, too, when in 1844 the gag rule was lifted.

During his final years of service, Adams advocated on behalf of Native Americans, argued that women had the right to petition Congress, and was one of only fourteen in the House of Representatives to oppose declaring a war of aggression against Mexico. He even took up the cause of booksellers who sought to protect their intellectual property through a global copyright law. Every New Year's Day, he held an open house during which he received visits from "some of the bitterest political enemies, North and South, that I have in the world." Diligent in his duties, Adams believed that "Article One time" came every day.

Asked why he chose to remain active in public life for so long, he said that he would not otherwise be good for anything. "This," he wrote, "is the weakness of my nature, which I have intellect enough to perceive but not energy to control. And thus while a remnant of physical power is left me to write and speak, the world will retire from me before I shall retire from the world."

On February 21, 1848, Adams collapsed at his desk in the House of Representatives—until the last, good as his word.

THIRTY-TWO

Shadows and Light

IN AN EARLIER chapter, I recorded my pleasure at attending the annual dinner parties hosted by my friends Fred and Marlene Malek. In 2018, the Maleks' daughter, Michelle, invited me to a Halloween celebration. Although I had returned from giving a speech that day in Nebraska, I love the family and decided to go. Mindful of Conan O'Brien's tweet from several years before, I went costumed as a decidedly non-slutty Madeleine Albright.

To get to Michelle's house, I had to navigate Georgetown Pike, the kind of curvy, too-busy, too-narrow thoroughfare one often encounters in Northern Virginia. My GPS wasn't working so, to be sure I wouldn't get lost, I wrote Michelle's address on a pad of paper that I placed beside me on the car seat. A good plan, except that the road has a paucity of streetlights, which meant that I couldn't read the mailbox numbers as I drove by. Fearing that I had traveled too far west, I pulled into a driveway, turned around, went too far east, then did another U-turn, and called Fred's cell; he didn't pick up. Finally, I found a spot to park, knocked on the nearest door, and was greeted by a man, six and a half feet tall, wearing a clown suit. I had arrived.

Clown man guided me to a buffet, then offered to me and other guests a platter of what appeared to be crispy human fingers and, in a translucent jar, brains. There were martinis with olives masquerading as eyeballs. On the dinner table, surrounded by cold cuts, was a red-splashed axe planted in a life-size leg. Urged to explore the basement, I felt a faux snake slither up my ankle and, though fully on guard by that point, still jumped when a scary face popped out of the blackness screaming, "Boo!" Dinner was accompanied by the wailing of ghosts whose gloomy chorus, I supposed, might testify to the fate of moderate Democrats and principled Republicans. As I was preparing to leave, Michelle insisted that I first have dessert—delicious despite the very real human head (nobody I knew) sticking up from beneath the middle of the table. A memorable evening, but I reflected on my way home that it might not be smart for a travel-weary octogenarian to drive around Virginia late at night along twisty roads in the dark.

There have been other causes for reflection.

Years ago, when late for a dinner appointment with Condoleezza Rice, I tripped in my backyard and, in considerable pain, was driven by my brother to the nearest emergency room. When I finally got through to the doctors, I was diagnosed with a torn rotator cuff. "When will you operate?" I asked. The physicians said surgery would probably be unnecessary. Instead, I was given a sling, some drugs, exercises to do, and advice: don't put too much strain on your shoulder. The formula worked. After a few weeks, the discomfort went away, and I shifted my mind to other matters.

Not long ago, the malady returned. The rotator cuff never fully healed. This means that I can't raise my right hand for more than a short period. Ordinarily, this would not be a great hardship, but there is one problem. I am often asked by strangers who recognize me to stand next to them and pose for a picture. If the person is a man, he will almost always be taller. Attempting to please, I smile, place my hand on his back, and then try not to grimace as the shoulder weakens and the hand falls. In this age when sexual harassment is constantly in the news, I have been photographed a hundred times with my palm (thankfully unseen) hovering around some poor guy's butt.

Then there was the phone call.

In January 2019, I returned from an exhilarating but hectic trip to the West and South to mark the publication in soft cover of *Fascism: A Warning*. The events went well, but the days were long, and by the time I returned to my house, the hour was late and I was spent. After unlocking the door and collapsing on a sofa, I thought to myself, *I feel like I'm dead*. Off to sleep, I vowed, but first one final peek at the phone. A voicemail:

> Hello, my name is Robert McFadden. M-C-F-A-D-D-E-N. I write for the *New York Times*. My assignment, er, uh, is to write what we call an advance obituary. I expect that will give you a chuckle. Anyhow, I really need to speak to you, not so much about your career as about the early years and to verify a few facts. Also, I need to establish a contact, perhaps one of your daughters, to make sure that the *Times* will be notified when you, uh, die. Again, that's McFadden, M-C-F-A-D-D-E-N.

I'M NOT IMMUNE to nature's dictates; I know that. Dark roads, a torn rotator cuff, and a reporter whose assignment did *not* give me a chuckle are hard to ignore. Also, my hair is thinning to the point where I have taken at times to wearing a wig. If that weren't enough, when walking on a street near my home, I came across what looked like a child's castoff picture book. The cover showed a brontosaurus looking sad; its title: *All My Friends Are Dead*. The message was clear: I need to go faster.

In the spring of 2017, I reached the milestone age of 70 years and 120 months. Over my objections, we had an over-the-top party. Friends and family requisitioned a hall in the U.S. Institute of Peace, passed around hors d'oeuvres, and sliced up a cake with enough candles on it to start a wax museum. In addition to three generations of my family, the fête attracted co-conspirators from every phase of my life, including Wini Freund, Bill and Janet Cohen, Barbara Mikulski, Susan Rice, a sampling of ex-foreign ministers, former colleagues, esteemed journalists, and the Clintons, surprise guests, both of whom were funny and gracious in their remarks. As is often the case these days, I was startled to see people whom I had first met when they were riding around in strollers now toting offspring of their own. I thanked everyone for being there and mentioned that my father, to avoid being depressed by his next birthday, had always claimed to be a year older than he was. That way he would already be accustomed to whatever age he became.

I have never known a woman (above the legal drinking age) to mimic my father's ploy, and I am no exception. My remedy to the passage of time is to proceed ardently and headlong with what I care about. I don't pretend to be another John Quincy Adams, who in addition to his political and diplomatic exploits, published an epic poem, rewrote the Psalms to suit his fancy, maintained a diary for nearly seventy years, and greeted many a dawn by swimming naked in the Potomac. I can, however, identify with his frame of mind. In the month I turned eighty, I taught my course at Georgetown, chaired business meetings, testified before a U.S. Senate committee, participated in the search for a new CEO of the Aspen Institute, worked on my latest book, delivered the commencement address to my grandson Daniel's high school class, hosted a dinner of foreign policy experts, presented an award bearing my name to a group of women activists from the Central African Republic, made a speech on diplomacy and faith, lobbied members of Congress to support NDI's budget, and spoke at one conference convened in Dallas by the George W. Bush Presidential Library and another in Lisbon by the government of Portugal.

The activities are varied but the dots representing them are connected and form a single coherent pattern. Each involves using my voice for a cause in which I believe or, ideally, several causes. I compare the method to one of those conveyor belt–style food displays we see in some restaurants, but instead of Jell-O or sushi, I pluck a slice of information in one place that could prove valuable in another; or home in on a person at a business meeting whom I might later ask to teach at the Albright Institute, co-chair a think tank project, or join NDI's board of directors. John-Paul Sartre, who must have been fun at parties, described Hell as "other people." I, by contrast, am never happier than when adding to my inventory of acquaintances and enlisting new recruits for purposes that are worth both my while and theirs.

Yet, because of my age, people persist in asking why I do all this. Here, too, I find an affinity with Adams. I don't know of another lifestyle I would enjoy as much. Maybe that's neurotic, but who cares? I think of the legendary water sprites of Prague who, when separated from their duties on the river, would pine and waste away. Isn't it better to love what one does than to spend every afternoon counting the hours to retirement? Yes, I agree, a person should know how to relax; that's why I so often "stop and smell the roses"—before stooping to pull weeds.

We all, in our own way, search for fulfillment, happiness, or a general sense of well-being. In that pursuit, some buy books and others the next round; some go shopping while others go hunting; some occupy themselves with children while still others seek the company of cats, yoga instructors, or a therapist. Many—by far the majority—are too busy coping with life's complications to allocate to this quest more than a series of passing thoughts; we measure our serenity in coffee spoons. Perhaps we hope to find time in the future to sit on a mountaintop or recline beneath a banyan tree and figure everything out. I once experimented with meditation, cleared my mind, and immediately remembered a phone call I had to make; that was that. Sadly, I see no evidence that enlightenment comes with age. A four-year-old slurping ice cream knows as much about contentment as any elder. I envy those among us who have full faith in Heaven and their prospective place in it. I tell myself that I, too, believe, but if the conviction were implanted deeply enough to leave no space for doubt, I wouldn't be afraid of death, and I am.

My health issues to this point (back and shoulder notwithstanding) haven't severely restricted either my movements or my mind. To that I attribute good fortune, regular workouts, my lifelong disinterest in smoking, and the fact that I knock on wood a minimum of three times a day.

Although determined to resist aging as best I can, I find it easier to accept that natural process than the risk of being blindsided by disease. Getting older is less unfair and arbitrary than just about anything else in life, though life is not where it leads. Whether billionaire or pauper, we are all, despite Botox and Viagra, bound by time. While disease is a mugger, age is a cat burglar who steals but a single day each night; and the thief has learned patience. Medical advances have made it possible for us to function far longer than earlier generations. The most recent rounds of U.S. presidential politics, with viable candidates in their mid-seventies, is evidence of that. So was the 2019 alumni parade during my sixtieth college reunion at Wellesley, where we all marched behind a still-upright member of the Class of '39. I think back to my final weeks as secretary of state and how I wished the clock hands would slow. In a sense, they have, and yet I am greedy for more. Sum up my life? Not yet; I am still counting. Until I am carried out, I will carry on.

IN 2018, I began co-chairing an initiative, sponsored by the Atlantic Council, to promote a new international Declaration of Principles for Freedom, Prosperity, and Peace. The project aims to remind us that democracy is more than a word or even a system; it is a way of life that both trusts human nature and makes demands on it. The declaration is offered as a rallying point, a timely successor to the 1941 Atlantic Charter proclaimed by Franklin Roosevelt and Winston Churchill. That charter denounced the immorality of wars fought for territorial gain, underlined the right of people to choose their own leaders, advocated global economic cooperation, and was designed to persuade wavering populations across the globe to support the allies in their confrontation with Nazism.

The list of public rights and responsibilities in the 2018 declaration goes beyond the familiar quintet of freedoms (religion, speech, assembly, petition, and the press) to emphasize protections for those who build democracy or attempt to defend it. Admittedly, the world is not threatened in the same manner now as it was in 1941. There are no massed armies intent on blitzkrieg or demented dictators vowing to conquer whole continents and, in the process, murder millions of people. However, the crisis of confidence we face is undeniable.

The Declaration of Principles evinces faith in what amounts to the old-time religion: freedom, human rights, law, and a commitment to peace—but those concepts will be under constant trial in an era when realities are changing more rapidly than institutions can keep up and when people everywhere are unsure of so much. A century has passed since Czech author Karel Čapek first wrote of a society ruled by robots. (*Rabota* is a medieval Slavonic term meaning "forced labor.") We are embarking now on a future in which machines teach machines, and artificial intelligence, aided by large data sets, is opening new frontiers in communication, transportation, medicine, recreation—and war. How relevant will the old rules be in a world that is moving faster each year despite spongy brakes, an out-of-kilter compass, and leaders who remind no one of Roosevelt or Churchill?

Perhaps I am incorrigible, but I am optimistic, nonetheless. Times change, pendulums swing, and warnings, if they are on target, have a way (if not always immediately) of being heeded. It also helps to have friends with whom to talk issues out.

Some of those involved in the Atlantic Council project are members of the Aspen Ministers Forum that, in May 2019, met again, this time in Kansas City. The setting was a stark contrast to that of our previous gathering in Versailles. Compared to that elegant city in France, the architecture is plainer, the decorative gardens humbler, and the art displays, though impressive, less renowned. One of Kansas City's many nicknames is "Cowtown." It was, I felt, a more appropriate environment to discuss democracy's future than the former hunting quarters of French royalty. At the same time, one of Kansas City's other aliases is "Paris of the Plains." Only the French capital has more boulevards.

I arrived for our meeting with a story to tell. "Once upon a time," I began, "a former secretary of state took the train from Paris to London. She had a seat on the aisle, just across from a handsome gentleman who was engaged in conversation with a friend. Our heroine is not the type to eavesdrop; however, she found that by tilting her head just so, she could not help but overhear. When the man started talking about the merits of Kansas City, she interrupted, politely introduced herself, and explained all about the ministers' group and its plan to convene in the man's hometown. 'Just think,' she said, '2019 is the one hundredth anniversary of the treaty that ended World War I, the seventieth anniversary of NATO's founding, and the twentieth anniversary of the entry into the alliance of the Czech Republic, Hungary, and Poland. Isn't that interesting?'"

Fortunately, the traveler whose journey I had interrupted was a patient fellow and, it turned out, also a generous one. Sandy Kemper is a financial expert, entrepreneur, and philanthropist who both loves Kansas City and is beloved by it. That day on the train, he agreed to help underwrite the ministers' meeting—and not just because I was blocking the exit.

Our conclave in 2019 was more upbeat than it had been the previous year. Why? What difference did a few months make? Perhaps it was wishful thinking, but there seemed a hint of something positive in the air. Enough alarm bells had sounded to make complacency less of a problem. From the streets of Hong Kong to Budapest, Warsaw, and even Moscow, pro-democracy forces were rallying, and mainstream political parties were showing signs of recovery in Italy and Greece. Elsewhere in Europe, environmental parties were making gains, and the Brexit imbroglio was quashing talk that other nations would soon follow the British out of the European Union. In Syria, the scope of the war was diminishing and so, too, the outflow of refugees and migrants, depriving demagogues of the fodder they need to exploit fear and pursue power. In Ethiopia, a bold young prime minister had brought peace to the Horn of Africa and was wagering that democracy could succeed in a country historically divided along ethnic and regional lines. In the United States, elections were on the horizon and with them a precious chance to ease partisan gridlock. Worldwide, the danger of political subversion via the misuse of social media platforms remained, but users had become more attuned to the risk. Overall, surveys showed that most people hadn't given up on democracy; they just wanted better results.

One highlight of our sessions was a trip to the nearby city of Independence and the house where Harry Truman once lived with his wife, Bess. Our tour guide was Clifton Daniel, Truman's eldest grandson. Here again, the contrast to our previous meeting, in the Palace of Versailles, was evident: chandeliers and intricately designed parquet floors had given way to worn-out linoleum. Daniel noted how remarkable it was that a man of his grandfather's modest background could rise to the nation's highest office; indeed, Truman is the sole president in the past one hundred years not to have graduated from college. Originally dismissed as nothing more than a machine politician, he was expected to fail—yet his legacy includes the United Nations, the Marshall Plan, NATO, the Berlin Airlift, and memorable examples of plain speaking: "I never gave anybody hell," he said. "I just told the truth and they thought it was hell."

In between our discussions and side trips, Sandy Kemper's wife, Christine, invited me to drop by a girls' school that she had helped to found. I always enjoy such visits but was especially moved this time because most of the students I met were eleven years old—the age I was when Truman was president and I first came to the United States.

As I talked with the students, I wondered, looking at their faces and braces, how big a portion of the little girl I once was still survives. Obviously, my gall bladder is gone and so, too, my ability to jump rope, but much of the young me remains—or at least that is what I tell myself. I still believe in trying to make the best of things, still want people to think highly of me, still love my clubs, still give thanks each day (especially for my family), and still want to involve myself in the world at its widest.

I have to admit that the budding scholars, with their reservoirs of energy and thousand-megawatt smiles, evince a luminescence I can no longer muster and that I envy. If wishes were horses, I would have my own cavalry. In thrall to the youngsters, I can't help wondering what fate has in store for them. What astonishing changes will they witness? Where will they find disappointment and joy? What destinations will they aim for, and how far will they go? Above all, what will they do to take control of their lives and, in solidarity with those of like character and spirit, act to brighten the futures of eleven-year-olds half a century from now?

Grand questions all, but to be answered another day. I say "goodbye" to the girls and "farewell" to Kansas City, then turn to my aide with but one thought on my mind, "Liza, that was terrific. Now, what's next?"

Journal of Růžena Spieglová

1 January 1942

Dear Andulko!

Because I cannot write to you so that I can tell you all the events of my life, and because I don't know whether we will meet at some point again so that I can describe to you how we lived here during your absence, I want to note daily events for you every day and to describe the past life of our most beloved dead Maruška—I know that in case we never see each other, I would like you to know how your mother and sister lived through the war and nobody would be here who could tell you everything. Maybe Honza (Maruška's ex-husband) is the closest person. Perhaps you will meet with him and he will be able to answer your questions. On the eighth of February, it will be a year since Maruška died . . .

From your departure to the declaration of war, we wrote to each other fairly often . . . Maruška sometime in May got divorced. She did not make too much of that. We were in Poděbrady, we rented then an apartment to summer guests and M (Maruška) was for the most part the landlord and I was the hidden housekeeper. She was quite healthy. Honza used to come here and we lived quite peacefully. We talked about Madlenka. M remembered her and all the cute things she used to say. The first of January 1940 we rented an apartment in Prague Zitna 42. It was a pleasant small apartment and we liked it very much. It was however a new building and Honza blames it because M's illness got worse there. I think however it didn't hurt because we did not live there that long and went often to P (Poděbrady).

You can understand that the people already feel the third year of the war. It doesn't concern me that much especially because I don't have my dear daughter here anymore. So I don't really worry about too much. I only pray that dear God gives you health and peace and also to M after her suffering. We here are waiting as we hear everywhere that we will be moved to a camp—about ten transports left from Prague already and that seven will go to Poland, the rest to T (Terezín), and now there is a break, and that it will be short and then it will begin again. We are all here getting ready, and the first concern has already passed, people, that is Jews, have partially gotten used to it because it is said, that it is terrible in those camps. You know me dear Andulko, and you must be able to imagine that what concerns me personally you should not have great worries about. We all our whole life were preparing for this kind of sadness and bad time but up till now nothing has been happening. I am living still in our villa in those two rooms, I have heat and I have food. So physically I am fine and spiritually I am calm, especially when I think how our M would be suffering with this and she would die from these worries. And so I thank dear God, and that you two are in good hands and that Madlenka our dear gift is probably healthy and happy. People here are sad and everyone is taking the war with difficulty. This includes Aryans and non-Aryans, to use this rather peculiar naming into which God's creation are now divided. We wear stars as you know, some proudly, some hide them even though you are not allowed to . . . Today, I celebrated the New Year and went for a walk to some field not too far away, since Jews cannot leave town and cannot go into any village. And if I had to write all the things that can't be done, it would take too long so again, some other time. Now I am sitting in that small room under the eaves. I am warm, and I am waiting for a visit from some ladies who visit me sometimes. I forgot to note that President Haha (Emil Hácha, president of the occupied Czech Protectorate) announced a few days ago a statement that people should give warm underclothes and fur coats to the German military.

2 January 1942

Although there is nothing exceptional that I would write down today, I would still like to write down a few lines because I think in this current time every day is historic . . . From the window of my little room I can see the fields and once in a while a train. Today, one went by after another, and then another full of military train cars. There were many such trains during the summer of 1941. In the morning, I sorted through the potatoes, which I take care of every day because I know in the spring, they will be rare. Sometimes, I hear that they are already rare. I still have enough food, only there is not enough fat. You get 10.5 dkg (2.83 dekagrams are equal to one ounce) of butter a month. Before Christmas, they added 6 dkg. That is the only thing that they gave Jews before Christmas. For the others, they get 5 dkg of raisins, one lemon, and some kind of cheese. Jews, however, cannot buy cheese but the others almost never find any, only rarely. You get 1/8 liter of milk daily per person. . . . The Jews have all their goods inventoried including footwear and underwear.

3 January 1942

Today, I practically didn't see anybody, only an old lady whose son had rented our apartment. They are Czechs but the son became a German and he is a clerk of the city government. I don't know why he did it. They are, despite that, good people and I regret if they will someday have a problem with this. In this very difficult time, a person stops being normal and doesn't know where to go. . . .

Mainly I thought about our dear M, and I want every day to write some memory of her. What she used to do and talk about at the time when you, dear one, were already abroad. When she wanted to go somewhere to the movies or theater (that was, of course, early after your departure, because later that was all forbidden to Jews). She said: Aninka says that as soon as I feel better, I should go and amuse myself. You really did used to say that, you dear good daughter. In 1940, in the summer, M began to draw and she drew very well. We did not even know about this talent. Maybe I will save her drawings for you and Madlenka. She wanted afterwards to enroll in some course but because of her illness it was not possible—you know how sweet she was, sometimes even with her sickness, we laughed a lot because she really really was very amusing . . . so today I will end, since I don't know any new events. To listen to foreign radio is the death sentence, so I think people are listening less. Jews do not have radios and they took them away from others.

4 January 1942: not notable.

5 January 1942: It is said that soon Jews will be moved from Plzeň.

6 January 1942: In the store windows, you are mostly only able to see vinegar and things to polish shoes with. In stores with fabrics, the same story, with hardly anything for sale. Everything is on ration points, which Jews do not get . . . I am not hungry since I don't like to eat meat of which there isn't any anyway. I like to eat some kind of dumpling and soup and buchta (small roll, usually sweetened) and I have things for that . . . There is almost no fruit, a lemon is a big luxury, there is also a scarcity of any kind of alcohol, vegetable, marmalade, eggs, milk, cheese, cigarettes. That is what there is—in Prague, it is supposed to be even worse. They say that in these days they will move the Jews out of Plzeň. Tomorrow, I will go to the Jewish Center so I will learn something more certain. In the morning, I will go to the bank for money, there, Jews can only go 8–9 o'clock. On the street, Jews are not allowed to talk to non-Jews, not even to greet them. As far as the yellow stars are concerned,

nobody notices, only German boys when they were here called "Jew, Jew." They were probably told to do it, because they didn't do it at the beginning, only later.

8 January 1942—Today there is a decree that there is now an understanding that all warm clothes and underwear will be taken away from Jews. We will get specific instructions tomorrow . . . It's now almost two years since Jews have been able to buy anything except scarves. There is a ration coupon to buy materials, which Jews didn't get, they therefore only have what they had before.

10 January 1942—Today, they are taking away fur coats, hosiery, and wool underwear. I don't have a lot, so it doesn't cause me great worries . . . And what will they want in a while? From Jews not much more because they already took from them everything when they sent them to the camps. Yesterday, our tenant from the basement, Mr. Trybal, from Plzeň, came and said that the Jews . . . on Tuesday they will go to a camp somewhere . . . they are cutting women's hair, they leave 4 centimeters, they get injections against disease . . .

11 January 1942—Just now I had a fright, someone called. It is evening around 8 o'clock; I thought that it's some kind of official because it is constantly being promised that there will be some kind of inspection. I quickly stopped my writing and hid it and went downstairs. It was nothing like that. What it was, however, I cannot write here. It could harm somebody, but it was nothing important. Now I have taken this little book out of its hiding place which always gives me a little bit of work—a person lives all the time with one foot in the grave. And for every day we have to thank God. Our sad lady neighbor, beautiful young mother of three children has probably been arrested. How long will we still be in Poděbrady in our nice warm room. Yesterday, I heard how they are talking to Jewish men, that is how the German officers are talking to them. I

heard this indirectly. They say "ty Jew" (you Jew). M would bear this with great difficulty, thank God that she has calmness and peace.

14 January 1942: We don't learn a lot. I don't read the newspapers because I don't believe them and otherwise it is hard for a person to learn anything. We are not allowed to listen to foreign radio, so people are afraid. They already took a lot of radios away from Jews, about two years ago.

15 January 1942: Today, we were again called to the Jewish Center . . . they are going to take everything. In front of the Jewish Center, a moving car stood that they are probably going to load with fur coats and warm underwear tomorrow. There will be ten Jewish men loading up the truck and the Gestapo will come tomorrow to take it over. They are saying that there will be inspections of homes. I don't know where I will be able to hide this book. Weather: frost.

15/1: addendum: I forgot to write that Jews are forbidden from buying and reading Czech newspapers and magazines. Also, the coupons they gave us for food were cut in half.

16 January 1942—My friend, Mrs. F, who comes to visit me almost every day, was not here. She probably went for meat, which is sold once a week and that only several dkg per person. I don't even know how much, since I don't eat meat myself. I want to also write here that I want to systematically remember what has already happened to the Jews. I am the only woman in P who lives in her own house. The others have been moved out and they are afraid that even where they are now they will not be able to stay. I am here maybe because my apartment doesn't have any accessories.

18 January 1942: Today I have not said one word to anybody and did not see anybody . . . Today, again German children came

who were not here during the winter. I think that Jews heard something from them. Otherwise, Czechs don't make comments if they meet Jews; at least, it's never happened to me. Of course, from others I've heard that some old lady says something. I realize that we live in strange times and are viewed by some as members of a less valuable race. Of course, blacks are also underrated and yet the world is quiet about that, even Jews. When God enlightens our brains and we understand that we are all equal before God, it will be better. I do not hope that Jews can be recognized while other peoples are underestimated because of their race. Maybe this big war will bring justice. Today, there is again a great frost, there are poor people who have no protection from it. Apparently three transports are leaving Plzeň. The men, where they are taking them, sleep on wooden boards, women are always three on two straw mattresses, without comforters and only one pillow and two or three blankets.

20 January 1942—I heard that Jews are leaving for T, then further, many of them are dying. There is supposed to be a new government in the Protectorate. Mr. President stayed. Apparently not from here, two foreign parachutists landed. Parachutes were found.

21 January 1942—Today, a new government was started in the Protectorate. Why are they acting so strangely? I think that nothing works according to plan and some ideas are just spur of the moment—what will be tomorrow? Today, I also heard that Jews are no longer allowed to go to stores for their bread and their groceries where they used to go, they can go only to two specific stores.

8 February 1942—I didn't write for a longer time because there was nothing. The days pass the same and no special events take place. Today, it is a year that our lovely Maruška , my dear daughter,

left forever. I want today, dear Andulko, to describe to you her sickness, if for some reason I am not able to tell you this in person, certainly everything about us will interest you. As I already wrote, her sickness got worse in the summer of 1940. We were planning after the vacation, again moving to Prague and M wanted to attend a course in drawing that was given for Jews. That, however, did not happen because of her sickness. We, therefore, let the Prague apartment go, also because of great anti-Semitism that was in the building. It was a modern building occupied primarily by Jews. Later, Germans moved in and it was said that Jews would anyway have to leave soon—M's disease kept getting worse and so we then went at the end of October in Prague to Dr. Klein . . . At the end of November, somebody drove us by car to Poděbrady and we tried to get by without a doctor for a while. It was not possible, and we got Dr. Bodala who came almost every day and gave M an injection. She became very thin and could barely get beyond the bed. But nevertheless, the poor woman was able to sometimes enjoy herself with me. There were days when she felt a bit better and we ordered a wheel chair for sick people and we were looking forward to the spring when we could take her in the wheel chair for walks. About the 2nd or 3rd of February she got the flu, which somebody brought to her (I got it also). The doctor gave her an injection against the flu and that also probably hurt her. She then felt worse. About a week before the flu, I gave her a piece of meat that had a bit of fat with it. She ate and had big pains. That whole week that she had the flu she didn't eat anything and the last day before her death she had some kind of seizure, then a morphine shot, she went to sleep and in her sleep about 4 hours she died. She took her last breath from Friday to Saturday at 3 am in the morning. I sat with her and with old Mrs. Pardubska, mother of Lidusky Frybak, our tenant. Honza came as soon as I sent news, also Aunt Pavla. I do not know whether I can write anymore because it is getting dangerous when they examine the house.

22 April 1942: We were taken for departure and categorized for work. There were 4 health gradations. I was in the second category which means that my health is pretty good. Now they are saying that we will soon be moved out of Poděbrady and that is why all Jews are leaving by train to Kolín for registration. For me, it is not anything upsetting, on the contrary, it is calming me down because I see that for my dear child M, that she would not have lived for anything pleasant. I myself am pretty hardy, it is possible that the troubles, which await us, I will survive. Perhaps, we will see each other, dear ones, who are abroad. May God give you health. When I come back (I hope I will today, a person never knows), I will write down what it was like in Kolín. There is here a lot of arrests and the persecution of Aryans and non-Aryans.

[Journal ends]

Afterword

MARSHALING MY THOUGHTS for this postscript, I can see that the 2021 calendar on my desk has reached its final page. Tomorrow will mark the beginning of a new year. Optimistic by nature, I am looking forward to what the future will bring. My purpose here, though, is to reflect on the events of the recent past. I do so with mixed feelings for, as we all know, the road we have been traveling has been a rough one.

Little did I expect when selecting a title for this book, for example, that the months following its April 2020 publication in hardcover would feel as if Hell had arrived on Earth. The COVID-19 pandemic was the most lethal public health catastrophe since the outbreak of HIV/AIDS and, due to its intensity and global reach, already serves as a common reference point for people everywhere. Decades from now, today's teenagers will be telling tales to their grandchildren about the virus that came, spread, and for too long conquered. Centuries of innovation in medical technology could not shield us from a modern-day variant of the bubonic plague.

Because of the timing, plans for this book's unveiling—a nationwide series of events in meeting halls and shops—had to be put on ice. Instead, I engaged in online interviews during which I touted the memoir's themes: dreams aren't confined to the young, each stage of life can be made more exciting than the last, and by remaining active, men and women of advanced age can contribute much to the common good. This was my message to readers at precisely the moment a deadly disease was forcing much of the senior generation (myself included) to live behind closed doors. The words of encouragement sounded, even to me, as if they were coming from another universe.

Early in 2020, when the virus had not yet fully invaded our minds, endangered our bodies, and crashed our schedules, I read cautionary tales about travelers making their way back from China or from an ill-fated cruise and being compelled to enter quarantine for two weeks or more. I told friends how horrified I would be if required to undergo such an ordeal. As the pages of this book attest, I am an extrovert.

Once the virus established its grip, and restrictions were imposed, I took them personally. Being an elder, and therefore particularly vulnerable, I felt singled out for punishment. No one among my family and friends thought they could approach me safely or I them. Mutual protection was our motive, of course, but that didn't stop me from feeling that I had been transformed overnight into a creature both radioactive and decrepit. I had always viewed birthdays with skepticism, thinking that I could not possibly have been around as long as the candles impaling frosting atop my cakes testified. On the best days, I saw myself as forever young. Now, when looking in the mirror, I saw Methuselah's grandmother.

We all learn that life is finite, but our minds tend to swat away the knowledge of our own mortality as if it were a menacing wasp. When we grow older, that wasp comes flying back more often and with reinforcements. Thus did COVID-19 prey psychologically even on seniors who escaped physical harm. By isolating us, the virus was stealing a larger percentage of the "normal" days we had remaining than it was for those who were younger. As the possible consequence of a single misdirected sneeze, it threatened to devour *all* our remaining days. A child's life is full of "first times"—a person of age must confront the looming reality of "last times." Throughout the pandemic's early weeks, I wondered whether I would ever hug my daughters and grandchildren again, or share a meal with old friends, or referee a student discussion, or give a speech to a live audience, or journey to a place I had never before seen.

My gloominess was out of character and didn't endure. I soon told myself to heed the same advice I was doling out to friends: focus on what can be controlled and make the best of what cannot. What other choice had we? I was fully aware, too, that most were dealing with trials far more severe than mine. Globally, approximately five million people died, many of them taking their final breath while in mandated separation from their families. For the majority in poor countries, there was no realistic means of self-defense. How could one maintain a socially safe distance while living in an overcrowded tenement? How could people wash their hands regularly in a region where water was costly and scarce?

Although time and vaccines have brought with them the promise of relief, today's memories of those grim yesterdays remain fresh in our minds. Each morning, beginning in mid-March of 2020, I scanned the front page of my newspaper (as others did their phones) searching for the little chart that showed how many among us had tested positive since the day before. For months, the tidings were bad, then worse. Economically, the pandemic was dire for anyone whose income depended on thriving downtowns, tourism, international travel, or any form of direct human contact. Socially, we had no houses of worship we could go to in person, nor museums, sporting events, parades, movies, plays, picnics, weddings, or reunions.

Instead, people discovered jigsaw puzzles and solitaire, exhausted the limits of Netflix, lavished attention on pets, and developed a thing for Dr. Fauci. We sent online messages to one another, asking how everybody was and urging all on our contacts lists to remain patient and to keep safe. But not everybody was safe. While the disease was causing sickness and death, fear of it was contributing to increased domestic abuse, mental illness, lost educational opportunities, a rise in shootings and thefts, and an ever-widening gap between rich and poor. The full cost in lives, income, anguish, and delayed learning can never be accurately tabulated.

All the disruption reminded me of my earliest years as a wartime refugee in London, when my family cloaked our windows with blackout curtains, hoarded household supplies, exchanged ration coupons for food, and lived in constant danger of external attack. I have never understood how my parents coped with the anxiety. Every night before I went to bed, we prayed for a return to ordinary times, though I was too young to recall what those might be.

ALTHOUGH MY AGE put me in the high-risk category, my daughters were fully grown and my father and mother had long since passed away. This exempted me from the familial responsibilities that weighed heavily on the parents of young children and on adults whose parents were confined to hospitals, assisted-care facilities, or nursing homes. Because of my occasional grumpiness, I did not always feel fortunate, but I had eyes to see what was going on around me and knew that I was extraordinarily lucky. Despite the virus, I had plenty of opportunity to move ahead with my many activities, albeit in changed ways. I still gave speeches, but less often and via Zoom or Webex. I still participated in a cross-Atlantic dialogue with former colleagues in the Aspen Ministers Forum. I still taught, but instead of meeting with my class at Georgetown, I sat in front of my home computer, surrounded by piles of assigned papers and lecture notes. I still pursued my duties as chair of the National Democratic Institute. All this left me, nevertheless, with more than my accustomed allotment of spare moments.

Marooned in my house, I methodically sorted the contents of every closet and drawer, many more than once. I sent still-serviceable clothes to be recycled and finally liberated myself from high heels because I had no social events to totter around in and had become convinced that, should I wear heels again, I would inevitably lose my balance. Watching television, I grew fond of the Hallmark Channel, not because the stories were exciting but because I knew the endings would be upbeat.

To mitigate my sense of claustrophobia, I was grateful to have in the back of my house a garden through which I could safely wander, gulping cool air in spring and liquid heat during the inferno of a Washington summer. Each day, I faced the choice of whether to stroll clockwise or counterclockwise around the colorful flowers and fragrant herbs. One morning, I spied a female cardinal gathering seeds in her beak and dropping them into the open mouth of her indolent mate, a gesture I found to be simultaneously romantic, unhygienic, and sexist.

Throughout the pandemic's first year, I had virtual meetings with coworkers, students, and friends. I found, unsurprisingly, that young people were better able to adjust to the new way of operating because of their comfort with the technology. In the early weeks, I frequently had to call fresh-faced aides for navigational help with log-ons, downloads, cryptic icons, tracked changes, and balky printers. It took much experimenting before I was able to participate in meetings without having the top of my head cut off by a bad camera angle, or finding myself stranded in front of a blank screen. I wasn't embarrassed to ask elementary questions because I discovered long ago that it is wiser to speak up and learn than to remain both silent and clueless. Eventually I felt confident enough to start giving advice to others. I even had the idea of crafting a needlepoint pillow with the lettering "Unmute Yourself" to display when necessary.

I also learned to adjust to the hazards of online interviews. In the pre-pandemic era, one simply drove to a television studio, then went to a room with a lot of mirrors for hair care and makeup, before joining the host in front of a camera. Experts were always on hand to help. Now my home office was the studio, and I had to do everything myself. In the beginning, because of harsh lighting, I often looked as if I had the eyes of a raccoon or the pallor of a ghost. In addition, the delay in back-and-forth audio transmissions, although brief, was nevertheless long enough to make conversations sound stilted. It was difficult, in any case, to develop a sense of rapport with a person sitting far off in another city, perhaps, or country.

Whether for meetings or interviews, the world of Zoom is better than no contact at all, but it doesn't generate the same energy as a face-to-face encounter. With everyone staring at a screen, there is no unspoken "feel" in the room and no reliable way to gauge from body language or from the exchange of meaningful glances what other people are thinking. That makes it harder to inspire a sense of camaraderie, enliven the discussion, and guarantee that everyone feels included.

Despite the adjustments required for social distancing, my consultancy business survived 2020 in good shape. Of course, a lot of the advice we shared with clients involved coping with the disease. This experience brought home to me how different the crisis looked in various parts of the world at various times, as infection rates surged, receded, then jumped once more when the Delta and other pernicious permutations kicked in. I couldn't help noting that governments headed by women (including those of Germany, Iceland, New Zealand, Taiwan, and several Nordic states) generally fared better than those led by men.

During this period, my partners at Albright Stonebridge Group and I were approached about becoming part of a new strategic advisory company affiliated with Dentons, the world's largest law firm. After lengthy negotiations, we agreed to become a founding member of Dentons Global Advisors, launched in June 2021. DGA, as we call it, meets the needs of clients who want ideas that cover every aspect of their operations and that can be tailored to reflect perspectives ranging from local to global. I view the venture (now well under way) as an exciting chance for further growth and as a means to sharpen the talents of our professional staff by enabling them to work closely with many other accomplished men and women. I am convinced that the key to success in business, as in most aspects of life, is to stay one step ahead of whomever or whatever may be gaining on you.

With that caution in mind, I tried to maintain my physical health by exercising regularly at home. As to my mental well-being, I stayed in close communication with my family. We had a virtual Mother's Day celebration, regular Sunday evening sessions online, and small gatherings to enjoy the holidays. Less happily, for one of the few times in my adult life, there was no end-of-the-year family trip to snowy Colorado. Hoping for a white Christmas amid the unrelenting grayness of Washington, DC, we were teased on December 24 by faintly falling flurries, then pelted by rain and forty-mile-an-hour wind.

The arrival of cold weather put me in the mood to resume the tedious yet addictive task of archiving my old papers for donation to the Library of Congress. Much of the material is now of purely academic interest, but I occasionally come across special items. For example, I retrieved a letter written by a woman from Georgia shortly before Halloween in 1994. The correspondent shared with me her low opinion of my performance in the State Department and sent along a broom she thought I might like to ride. In my return note, I congratulated her on the quality of the broom and promised to use it, which I have; it is still on duty, ever ready to sweep the floors at my farm.

AS THE PANDEMIC dragged on, I had more than enough opportunity to try and reinvent myself as an introvert. The attempt flopped. Rather than trudge in bafflement around the inner workings of my consciousness, I have always preferred to gaze outward at the daily drama of national and world events. That is where my mind finds its stimulation. In 2020, however, what I saw when looking outward—and what the world saw—was appalling.

Consider this historic parallel. The time is the summer of 64 A.D. and the place Rome. The head of the West's most powerful government is confronted by an unprecedented popular outcry. Three-quarters of his capital is on fire, with flames spreading rapidly through the wooden structures framing the city's narrow streets. Survivors mourn their inability to rescue loved ones from the falling timbers and thick smoke. Several times the blaze kindles false hope by appearing to burn itself out, only to flare up again. Angry citizens demand action and answers. Emperor Nero, a man known for his love of spectacle, tries desperately to save his reputation by finding a scapegoat. "The Christian God fearers are responsible," he declares. "It is a Christian fire." He accepts no blame.

Though Nero was not guilty of fiddling while Rome burned (the ancient world had no violins), it is incontrovertible that President Trump failed to do his job while hundreds of thousands of Americans died from COVID-19. Much has been written about Trump's imperfections when faced with his sternest test, and I mention the subject only because he continues to boast falsely that his handling of the crisis saved many lives. It is certainly true that the virus would have challenged the skills and temperament of the most diligent chief executive, but Trump didn't even try. We will never know how many deaths might have been prevented had our leaders put in place an urgent, clearly explained, scientifically based, and nationally coordinated strategy. The president's refusal to tell the truth about the virus, his dismissal of warnings from public health experts, and his contempt for state and local containment efforts rendered impossible a coherent nationwide response. Equally disturbing was his utter lack of concern for the victims. As with Nero, empathy was not among his gifts.

The pandemic was a test for leaders, but also for followers; Americans, overall, should have come through far better than we did. Sadly, the president's unwillingness to treat the virus seriously was mirrored in the cavalier attitude of many citizens. We had no excuse. We couldn't claim ignorance, poverty, or a shortage of health care facilities. Americans had an opportunity to be a model for the world. Instead, our rate of infections in 2020 was higher than in most other countries and, with barely five percent of the globe's population, we accounted for more than a fifth of the fatalities attributed to the disease. Why? Too many among us ignored expert advice regarding social distancing, the wearing of masks, and later the need for vaccinations, thus endangering the lives of others, prolonging economic hardships, and casting discredit on the entire country. More perverse still, some equated this callous stupidity with a love of freedom.

ON MAY 25, 2020, America's character was tested in a different way when George Floyd, a forty-six-year-old Black man, was killed while in the custody of the Minneapolis police. The tragedy—which was both preceded and succeeded by other outrages committed by law enforcement personnel against Black citizens—ignited a summer of protests and prayer meetings in hundreds of cities within and beyond the nation's borders. As the movement gained steam, the slogan "Black Lives Matter" proliferated on lawn signs, T-shirts, and athletic wear. In many urban areas, police tactics came under renewed scrutiny while statues were removed and a smattering of parks, military bases, schools, and streets renamed to terminate their association with America's slaveholding past. Thousands of op-eds and dozens of hurriedly written books promised (and occasionally delivered) novel insights into the oft-explored topic of racial injustice.

My own reaction to the episodes of unwarranted police violence was profound disgust. Fifty-seven years had passed since the 1963 March on Washington, led by the Rev. Dr. Martin Luther King, Jr. Substantial progress in civil rights had been made since then, culminating in the election and reelection of a Black president. The murder of George Floyd and other grim cases, however, provided evidence of how deeply ingrained bias was and how complacent our country had become in settling for incremental change. After centuries of suffering and sacrifice, racism continues to place a heavy burden on our society.

President Trump, predictably, offered the wrong answer to the questions posed. Instead of seeking to mend the country's social fabric through informed dialogue and reform, he sought to rip it further apart. In his view, the problem was less racism than protests against racism. Intentionally stoking the fears of his political base, he called on authorities to "dominate the streets," and claimed inaccurately that most of the demonstrations were violent.

A week after George Floyd's death, on the first of June, Trump's signature blend of hypocrisy and moral rot was on full display when federal commanders ordered a composite armed force to push aside civilians protesting peacefully in Lafayette Square. As I mention in chapter twenty-nine, this area near the White House is a traditional haven for free speech, though easy to block off and clear. The federal directive that Monday evening opened a path for the president to walk across the square and pose for cameras in front of a historic church while holding somebody else's Bible. The Rev. Mariann Budde, Episcopal bishop of Washington, commented: "My major outrage was the abuse of sacred symbols and sacred texts. There was no acknowledgement of grief, no acknowledgement of wounds. There was no attempt to heal. The Bible calls us to our highest aspirations, and he treated it as a prop."

Trump's grandstanding on June 1 intensified the public's focus on a second date: November 3, Election Day.

I DOUBT THAT any Hollywood producer intent on dramatizing an epic showdown would have selected as his leads the septuagenarians Joe Biden and Donald Trump. Nevertheless, it was their duel, waged largely with costly media advertisements and unflattering adjectives, that commanded our attention as 2020 lurched into its final months.

The campaign was a study of contrasting approaches. In deference to the pandemic, Biden spoke to voters most often from the basement of his Delaware home. His tone was earnest and his message both plain and shrewd: *I am not Donald Trump.* His opponent meanwhile tried to recapture the energy of his 2016 race via boisterous rallies during which he denounced Biden as a criminal, a threat to the flag, a danger to the suburbs, an enemy of freedom, a tool of China, a socialist, anti-God, and sleepy. Trump hoped that his mudslinging would besmirch the public's generally favorable view of Biden, but the challenger proved impervious. To many voters, the man from Delaware resembled a kindly uncle who always meant well even when uttering awkward remarks or grinning too broadly at his own jokes. Unlike 2016, when Democrats controlled the White House and were identified with the status quo, Biden could cast himself as the candidate of positive change. This helped because we Americans are rarely quite as happy as we think we should be.

Never before in my memory had a national election in America been conducted amid so many doubts concerning the process. These were prompted by the difficulty of voting safely during a pandemic, the logistical hurdle of counting a record number of absentee ballots, and the likelihood that cyber demagogues, whether foreign or domestic, would spread falsehoods about the candidates. It didn't help that the president in his daily tirades was describing the polling place—America's most sacred secular spot—as a den inhabited by scalawags and thieves.

Anxious to contribute what I could to avert a meltdown, I joined the newly formed bipartisan National Council on Election Integrity, a group of more than forty former somebodies (ex-cabinet members, elected officials, and military leaders). Together, we affirmed our faith in America's ability to conduct an honest vote despite the health crisis and warned against attempts to discredit or disrupt the proceedings. We also counseled patience. State and local officials would take longer than in previous years to scrutinize every ballot, we advised; such a delay would be a symptom of diligence, not fraud.

MY HABIT ON Election Day evenings is to party. Every four years, I join friends, family members, and coworkers to celebrate or mourn depending on the voters' decision. In 2020, because of the virus veto, I was stuck at home accompanied only by the television remote, a glass of wine, and a dangerously elevated heart rate. When Trump leapt to an early lead in key states, I felt as if rabid gerbils were devouring my innards. I started to recover when analysts noted that most of the ballots received by mail were still to be counted and were thought to favor Biden. As many had predicted, election night provided neither final answers nor restful sleep. Not until Saturday morning, when Pennsylvania was finally called for Biden, did I exhale. At that moment, through the miraculous alchemy of democracy, "Good old Joe" was reborn as president-elect of the United States.

From a civics perspective, the Trump presidency went low more often than a limbo champion, but it truly scraped bottom in the weeks that followed. That is when the incumbent refused to concede defeat and sought instead to bully state officials and the courts into overturning the results. A bumbling legal team and platoons of pusillanimous Republican legislators aided him in this doomed and degrading effort. The nadir, of course, came on January 6, 2021, when a pro-Trump mob forced its way into the US Capitol. At that moment, I happened to be on the phone with former president Jimmy Carter. We each had our television sets on and so shared our reactions, which consisted of such penetrating insights as "Oh my God!" "Unbelievable!" "Outrageous" and "Where are the police?"

American history is speckled with disputed elections and bitter protests marred by criminal acts. The events of January 6, however, were especially shocking because of the violent intent of some of the instigators, the threats of harm directed at members of Congress and the vice president, the injuries suffered by law enforcement personnel, and the inexcusable behavior of the chief executive, who incited the rioters, then cheered them on, before finally urging them—late in the day—to stand down. The insurgent ringleaders sought to substitute their own will for that of the voters by achieving through mayhem what their hero had failed to earn at the polls—a second term. That is the very definition of an attempted coup, and it conjured images in my mind reminiscent of the Fascist gangs of 1930s Europe and of the Communist thugs who subverted postwar governments in, among other lands, my native Czechoslovakia.

Among the essential ingredients of a healthy democracy is the willingness of electoral losers to accept defeat, secure in the knowledge that they can regroup and try again—a right not available in dictatorships. I fear there are some in America, an increasing number it would seem, who no longer respect those rules. All who cherish our system must strive to contain the danger created by this development and we must do so continually and regardless of party loyalty. Whether we will succeed remains to be seen, but I find heartening the fact that the scheme to undermine free institutions on January 6 was ultimately thwarted by the same principles and practices the agitators sought to weaken: the rule of law, judicial due process, and measures to establish the truth through criminal investigations and legislative oversight. The doors of the Capitol were breached on that day, but the American Constitution emerged intact. That is reassuring news, but the risk remains that future attempts will be undertaken to rip the document to shreds.

AFTER DECADES OF trying, Joe Biden finally reached the pinnacle of American politics, pulling himself slowly upward by dint of his ebullience and decency. The win came on his third bid, thirty-two years having elapsed since his initial effort to gain the nation's highest office; no other successful candidate persisted so long.

As secretary of state in the late 1990s, I often joined forces with Biden, then the senior Democrat on the Senate Foreign Relations Committee. The two of us saw eye to eye on the need to oppose ethnic cleansing and terror in the Balkans and, more generally, on the importance of America's role as a leading partner in solving international problems. When testifying before his committee, I was impressed by the senator's ability to expound knowledgeably (and at length) on almost any topic. The man from Delaware entered the Oval Office with a host of well-earned friends and more foreign policy experience than any predecessor since another former vice president, George H. W. Bush, in 1989.

Every new chief executive inherits headaches. A dozen years earlier, I said of President-elect Obama that he was being put in charge of an entire emergency room. Biden, in 2021, was heir to the whole hospital. Domestically, he was confronted by a pandemic at its height, a divided country, a dormant economy, and a depleted treasury. Internationally, he had to breathe new life into our alliances, check the darker impulses of China, Russia, and Iran, and remind people of America's identity as a champion of democratic practices.

Because of Biden's savvy and my familiarity with his team, I had lofty hopes for his foreign policy. Aside from his well-intentioned but inadequately prepared decision to withdraw US troops from Afghanistan, I have not been disappointed. After an absence of four years, it is refreshing to see the United States once again acting in concert with others to address a long list of global ills. It is reassuring, as well, to have an administration that honors the dignity of its own professional diplomats. This explains why, after dipping sharply under Trump, the number of young Americans planning careers in the Foreign Service has rebounded.

In substance and symbol, Biden's core message is the opposite of his predecessor's. Instead of shunning international cooperation, he embraced it by reentering the Paris climate change agreement, rejoining the World Health Organization, and revisiting the Iran nuclear deal. The forty-sixth president knows what the forty-fifth apparently did not: the modern world is interdependent, a long word for a plain fact. Countries are linked together in myriad ways and will generally be more peaceful, healthy, and prosperous when their neighbors (and nations farther away) are also doing well. To foster cooperation, leaders must help states to identify and act on their shared interests, a process that requires a dash of faith mixed with sound judgment and what the president refers to as *relentless diplomacy.*

While paying due attention to other regions, Biden's chosen focus thus far has been Asia. Why? The continent is home to India, the world's largest democracy; North Korea, a nuclear state headed by a regime as ruthless as it is stubborn; and China, still referred to by foreign policy experts as "a rising power," but now a *risen* power, fully capable of competing with any country, and no longer to be underestimated, coddled, or patronized.

The US-China relationship is a big deal and thus essential to get right. The government in Beijing's principal objective and trickiest task is to maintain control over a sprawling, diverse, aging, and far from docile population. It does this by a mix of repression, propaganda, and hypernationalism that shows itself internationally in a determination to resist external direction. The Chinese people, similar to those of any major power, feel they are entitled to respect. To avoid seeming timorous, Chinese officials refuse under any circumstances to admit fault. In pursuit of their own ambitions, they have launched projects to modernize the military, dominate the South China Sea, intimidate Taiwan, engage in digital espionage, become an internationally preeminent commercial force, and compete for global leadership on technology. At the same time, they show no eagerness to spark a major military confrontation with the West. Historically, China has not been an overly aggressive state and its current diplomatic leverage stems almost entirely from its economic clout, which is substantial. Ideologically—and here is the regime's weakness—the Communist leadership does little to attract admirers, offering only an unsavory stew of single-party rule and crony capitalism.

Given all this, the Biden team has responded with an appropriate blend of blunt talk on human rights and cyber issues, invitations to China to work in harmony where possible, and enhanced security collaboration with regional allies—especially Australia, Japan, and India. The administration has also sought, with bipartisan congressional help, to keep pace with China on high tech by investing large sums in research. In contrast to his predecessor, Biden has maintained a steady course toward China rather than jumping back and forth between expressions of undying affection for its leaders and racially tinged allegations of perfidy. The US-China competition, like so much else in foreign policy, is not an equation to be solved, but rather an unfolding drama to be managed.

Biden's unflashy style of handling international affairs is unlikely to set the world on fire, but then that goal (not setting the world on fire) is precisely its point. Presidents earn their pay by keeping diplomatic relations as routine as possible. While Trump's secretary of state boasted of his "swagger," Biden's chief diplomat, Tony Blinken, advertises "humility and confidence." Bland though the slogan may be, it reflects the mood of an era in which US leadership is most likely to be productive when both widely felt and modestly presented.

IF, AFTER LEAVING public office in 2001, I had assumed the identity of Madeleine Van Winkle and laid myself down for a twenty-year nap, what would my reaction have been upon awakening? Provided you have been around long enough, you might ask yourself the same question. Over the past twenty years, what has disturbed you most? For me, possible answers include the rise of domestic terrorism, the persistence of economic and racial divides, the mind-numbing horror of mass shootings in a gun-besotted America, and the nagging feeling I have acquired that the whole universe could be brought down by a mischievous teenage hacker from Hyderabad, Chongqing, Yekaterinburg, or Hoboken. As scary as these developments are, I am most dismayed by the deteriorating condition of democracy across the globe. This is a subject I touch on regularly, but feel obligated to cite again before closing because it is related to everything I do.

When completing my term as secretary of state, I saw no reason why momentum toward free government should not continue to accelerate. After all, democracy had already whupped Communism, turned the Berlin Wall into rock-sized souvenirs, and booted despots out of office everywhere from Central Europe and Latin America to large swaths of Africa and Asia. With the Cold War done, dictators were on the run and even those whose instincts mirrored George III were eager to portray themselves as latter-day Thomas Jeffersons. Unfortunately, the euphoria surrounding democracy did not extend more than a few years into the new millennium. The century now under way has brought backsliding, or at best stagnation, in dozens of countries. The reason hasn't been a revival of Marxism, which remains comatose, but rather a raft of unrealized public expectations and a boatload of amoral politicians who, after attaining power, decided that keeping it was worth the price of a tarnished reputation.

In Russia, Vladimir Putin's first year as prime minister (2000) coincided with my final one as secretary of state. In the more than two decades since, he might have steered his country toward a beneficial partnership with the West and shown people everywhere how a totalitarian government could be remolded into a thriving democratic one. Had Putin done so, the world would be a less edgy place, and Russia better liked by its neighbors—and happier. Instead, the former KGB operative chose Stalin for his model and has employed the authority of the state to co-opt, silence, marginalize, and (many suspect) assassinate opponents. Putin set out to restore Russia's glory, but his efforts have come at the cost of his country's freedom and good name.

Similar stories, different in detail but comparable in results, can be found in such disparate nations as Venezuela, Nicaragua, El Salvador, Uganda, Rwanda, Hungary, Turkey, Poland, the Philippines, Myanmar, and Belarus. This trend received a boost from Donald Trump, whose contempt for democratic institutions is a defining characteristic, and further help from the COVID-19 pandemic, which provided autocrats with a convenient excuse to postpone elections and lock up critics.

As the century progresses, we can expect to witness an ongoing competition between democrats and despots. The struggle is likely to be long, waged in every region, and without clearly delineated front lines. It will resemble neither war exactly nor peace exactly, but rather a state of constant tension. Some governments will align themselves with one side or the other, but many leaders will slide back and forth, taking advantage of the fact that in this confrontation there will be no rigid membership lists and few climactic moments. Progress in either direction will be gradual, fragmentary, and reversible. It's going to be a hell of a fight.

Over time, I do see an opportunity to reverse freedom's decline provided democratic regimes help one another in responding to social divisions, economic hurdles, security threats, and the destructive downsides of advanced technology. Dictators will work together when convenient; democrats must do so whether it is convenient or not. In what promises to be a relatively even match, freedom's advantage is its ability to inspire collective effort and, when necessary, painful yet willing sacrifice. Solidarity to this degree of intensity is hard to envision without America in a senior mobilizing role. The United States is where modern democracy was invented. No other country so firmly linked to human liberty has the resources and power to withstand the obstacles placed in its path. Joe Biden apparently gets this; so must his successors.

ON OCTOBER 18, 2021, Colin Powell died of COVID-19. Although fully vaccinated, his immune system had been compromised by multiple myeloma, rendering him more vulnerable to the virus's deadly effects. I had spoken to Colin by phone a couple of days earlier, finding him in excellent spirits and hopeful that he would soon recover. His passing saddened me because he was my successor as secretary of state and, more important, one of the kindest and most decent people I have ever met. Our friendship had blossomed in recent years as we came to know each other better when occupying the same stage at public events, occasionally traveling together, exchanging birthday greetings, and—as recounted in chapter twenty-seven—making a joint television appearance on *Madam Secretary*.

Powell's funeral drew an overflow crowd of mourners—including presidents Biden, Obama, and George W. Bush—to Washington, DC's National Cathedral. In a eulogy, I praised my friend for his "Homeric" virtues of honesty, dignity, loyalty, and an unshakable commitment to duty. These were the same traits he sought to instill in the soldiers under his command, the colleagues with whom he worked, and the many young people who benefitted from the causes he championed.

I am an immigrant and Colin was the son of immigrant parents. In our conversations, we talked often about how lucky we had been to grow up in America and about how proud we were of our families. We also commiserated about the debilitating effects of aging. Neither of us welcomed the prospect of slowing down but neither could we deny the reality. The last time I saw him he suggested that, to reduce the risk of stumbling, I should count the steps when descending my stairway at home. Following that advice ever since, I think with each step of Colin.

MY HOME CITY, Washington, DC, is not yet a state and is therefore without U.S. senators. We do, however, have some very old cemeteries. Wracked by weather and time, their headstones typically resemble the teeth of an outpunched boxer: some still upright, some crooked or broken, some clumped together, and others separated by irregular gaps. Study closely enough the barely legible birth and death dates inscribed on their well-worn surfaces and it becomes hard to hold back tears. A large portion of the interred are children.

As this evidence attests, through much of the past, life has been a gamble that many lost without ever being given a fair chance to succeed. For centuries, families routinely bore half a dozen offspring or more and, shortly after, on average, buried several of them. In some countries this is still the case. Billions who began life never reached the age at which it was possible to appreciate any but the most basic appetites of existence, let alone explore the liberties, big and small, that many of us now take for granted. Add in the multitudes of young men and women whose tenure on Earth ended abruptly due to war, genocide, mishap, or plague, and it is shaming to see how frivolously we who still draw breath use many of the hours God gives us.

This is something I have thought about more and more in recent years and it is why I have always preferred doers to idlers, whiners, and excuse makers. As I have written, introspection is hardly my strong point, but as the author now of three memoirs I have had numerous chances to reflect on what I have seen, felt, thought, and done. In assessing myself, I have tried to be honest without overdoing it. People intent on finding fault with me can do their own research. I have, however, admitted to an array of shortcomings including pride, ambition, fits of hot temper, occasional bouts of insecurity, and an affinity for sweets. In foreign policy, my area of expertise, I have been compelled at regular intervals to modify my views in light of new information without abandoning certain basic principles. Genius is often defined as the ability to be right the first time; unable to meet that standard consistently, I still strive to be right eventually. My parents taught me what the best teachers tell us all: that it is no sin to make a mistake, but unpardonable not to try and make the most of our talents.

To me, resilience of spirit (far more than brilliance of intellect) is the essential ingredient of a full life. No matter how smart we are, we can allow sorrows and grievances to overwhelm us or we can respond positively to setbacks—be they caused by our own misjudgments or by forces beyond our control. This choice has rarely been starker than in the past two years. As individuals, we have had to adapt to the shock of unwelcome and unexpected circumstances. Collectively, we have had to bounce back not only from the pandemic but also from doubts about our willingness to pursue social justice, our power to make self-government succeed, and our capacity to prevent advanced technology from causing more harm than good. Worldwide, we have undergone a period of trial that has changed us in ways not yet fully revealed. Clearly, our future leaders will have to be gutsy and resourceful and so, each in our own way, will we.

To those who despair of that possibility, I have a measure of sympathy but little patience. There is no shortage of worthwhile work to be done and, as those broken headstones remind us, no surplus of seasons in which to achieve our goals. So let us buckle our boots, grab a cane if we need one, and march.

WASHINGTON, DC, DECEMBER 31, 2021

Acknowledgments

"A new book by Madeleine has just arrived in my hermitage, and I'm bowled over: I simply don't understand how she can fulfill all her many public responsibilities and simultaneously write two thick and interesting books." So, in 2005, Václav Havel exclaimed to his journal upon receiving a copy of my second work of nonfiction (*The Mighty and the Almighty*). "Of course," he went on, "she certainly has assistants."

I certainly do—and they are the full answer to Havel's implied question. I am an insatiable devourer of help. Books are team efforts, and this is now my seventh, six more than I had originally envisioned. Plainly, I am not good at stopping, but for that, I blame my enablers. These include Bill Woodward, my adviser Elaine Shocas, my ever-patient editor Richard Cohen, and my matchless counselors Bob Barnett and Deneen Howell. The marriage between a publisher and an author can be a rocky one, but mine (with HarperCollins) has been an extended honeymoon. For that I am in debt to the estimable Jonathan Burnham, the sure-handed Jonathan Jao, and their cadre of professionals, including Tina Andreadis, Janice Suguitan, Kate D'Esmond, Sarah Haugen, Brian Murray, Juliette Shapland, and Leah Carlson-Stanisic.

On the way to its final destination, what we referred to affectionately as "the Hell book" went through numerous drafts, as we sought to get our facts straight and to reflect on what incidents to include or leave out. I am grateful to everyone who took time to recall events or to review various chapters, including especially my brother, John, and sister, Kathy, both of whom eyeballed the entire text and offered many valuable suggestions, corrections, and comments. I am grateful, as well, for the contributions of my daughters (Anne, Alice, and Katie), former Secretary of the Treasury Hank Paulson, the multitalented Lissa Muscatine, and my current and former colleagues Wendy Sherman, Carol Browner, Jim O'Brien, Suzy George, Melissa Estok, Greg Bowes, Alexis Krieg, Fariba Yassaee, and Nate Tibbits. Jacob Freedman, Liza Romanow, and Jan Stewart, three crucial aides of the type Havel referred to, provided essential feedback throughout the process, and Liza was critical in planning for the book tour as well. Thanks are due also to Mica Carmio, Nancy Sefko, Kirby Neuner, Robert Claure, Denson Terry, Audrey Waldrop (who furnished rigorous editing and research assistance), and many, many others.

Selecting and gaining permission to use photographs is a vital but time-consuming part of assembling any book in which they are to be used. To that end, I was delighted that we were able to lure Lauren Hadley away from her young family long enough to do for us on this book what she had accomplished previously with an earlier volume, *Prague Winter*. Hadley, who is meticulous and has a good eye, also devoted much effort to research and fact-checking. I appreciate, as well, the many who worked with Lauren and other members of our team to make images available. As for the photograph on the cover, that is the work of the supremely talented Platon, who did the best anyone could with the material at hand.

This book, to the extent that it has virtues, owes them to the many who share in the love, labor, and laughs that fill the best parts of my days. That cast begins with my siblings; my sister-in-law, Pam; two wonderful nephews; three "perfect" daughters; an equal number (conveniently) of sons-in-law; and half a dozen flawless grandchildren. Without them I would be lost; with them, I find something new to be excited about every day.

This dependence extends to my partners in every endeavor: personal friends (especially Wini Freund, who also provided helpful edits to this volume, and Susan Terris), associates at the Albright Stonebridge Group, students and fellow professors at the Edmund A.

Walsh School of Foreign Service, and what my British pals might call "mates" from the National Democratic Institute, Wellesley College, the Aspen Institute, the Aspen Ministers Forum, the United States Institute of Peace, the 34th Street Group, the Harry S. Truman Scholarship Foundation, the Herbie Hancock Institute of Jazz, the Washington Speakers Bureau, and an assortment of other organizations and think tanks spanning, alphabetically, from the Atlantic Council to the Wilson Center.

The truth is that virtually every project I have taken on since leaving government has been a group endeavor, and that has made those activities both interesting and fun. The central theme of this book is about how people of all descriptions can work together for common goals against a background of accelerating history. It is about trying to make sense of the world we have while attempting to contribute in small ways (though, as large as we can make them) to something better. To all who are present in these pages, whether in name or spirit, may all your destinations be happy ones and thanks for being part of the tales I tell.

Notes

PREFACE

ix It is also the name of a town: Hell is an unincorporated community in Livingston County, Michigan, about twenty miles from Ann Arbor. It boasts a housing development called "Satan's Hills" and an annual auto show that consists entirely of hearses.

ONE: AFTERLIFE

6 "by the working men, the tradesmen": Joseph Pulitzer, article in the *New York World*, March 16, 1885, https://www.nps.gov/stli/learn/historyculture /joseph-pulitzer.htm.

TWO: VOICE LESSONS

10 Diplomatic Security Service: The Diplomatic Security Service traces back to 1916, when Secretary of State Robert Lansing formed a small team to ferret out German and Austrian spies who were using false identity papers. The DSS in its current form was founded in 1985 following the 1983 terrorist bombing of the U.S. embassy in Lebanon.

11 I identify more with Bashful, Doc, and Sneezy: Three characters from Walt Disney's 1937 movie *Snow White and the Seven Dwarfs*. The original story of *Snow White*, published by the Grimm Brothers in 1812, did not name the dwarfs. A 1912 Broadway stage production did, calling them Blick, Flick, Click, Snick, Plick, Whick, and Quee. Among the names considered but rejected by the Disney studio were Flabby, Gabby, Snoopy, Weepy, and Biggo-ego.

THREE: FROM THE GROUND UP

19 the person generally credited: John Watson Foster was also a scholar who wrote several books on diplomatic history; the father-in-law of another secretary of state, Robert Lansing; and the grandfather of yet another, John Foster Dulles.

21 Among the principals: TAG's original group of partners also included a lawyer, Ed Lieberman. When he left, he was replaced as a partner by Suzy George.

22 the American-based pharmaceuticals firm: TAG's contract was with Merck and Co., known outside the United States and Canada as Merck Sharp and Dohme (or MSD). Merck and Co. is not to be confused with the German firm Merck KGaA.

23 "We face no less than extinction": Festus Mogae, president of Botswana, quoted in Elizabeth Farnsworth, "The Botswana Battle," *NewsHour with Jim Lehrer*, PBS, May 15, 2001.

24 the level of mortality: Botswana National Aids Coordinating Agency, "HIV/AIDS in Botswana: Estimated Trends and Implications Based on Surveillance and Monitoring," July 2008, Data.unaids.org/pub/report/2008 /20080701_botswana_nationalestimate2007_en.pdf.

24 By the following spring: I do not mean to imply that Merck was solely responsible for easing the HIV/AIDS crisis in either Botswana or Romania. Other pharmaceutical companies also played a role, as did such philanthropic organizations as the Gates Foundation. The public health community, and especially the Baylor College of Medicine, provided critical resources and expertise. The establishment of the President's Emergency Plan for AIDS Relief (PEPFAR) by the U.S. government and the UN-sponsored Global Fund were milestones in the worldwide campaign to curb the epidemic.

25 The battle against HIV/AIDS: As of 2018, approximately 38 million people were living with HIV. Of these, 26 million were Africans, of whom about 16 million were receiving drug therapy.

FOUR: "DO NOT BE ANGRY"

29 I could not take many of my official files: Although the government retains most official documents, I have accumulated plenty of material on my own. In an ongoing process, I am donating my personal and professional papers to the Library of Congress, and my undergraduate papers and memorabilia to Wellesley College. My sister, brother, and I have donated our father's papers to the Josef Korbel School of International Studies at the University of Denver.

33 "Two years after finishing with college": Author's essay, unpublished, 1961.

34 I had also come to dislike: See Monroe's *A View of the Conduct of the Executive in Foreign Affairs* (1798) and, for example, *All Too Human* (1999), by George Stephanopoulos.

36 the author of *Time to Pee!*: Mo Willems, in 2003, was just setting out on a prolific writing career that includes three Caldecott Honor–winning books and volumes with such intriguing titles as *Naked Mole Rat Gets Dressed*.

FIVE: QUICKSAND

41 "born with a birth defect": Condoleezza Rice, interview, CBS News, May 7, 2017, https://www.cbsnews.com/news/condoleezza-rice-on-russia-putin-and-trump/?ftag=CNM-00-10aab8c&linkId=37312666.

43 "no doubt": Richard Cheney, quoted in Scott McClellan, *What Happened: Inside the Bush White House and Washington's Culture of Deception* (New York: Public Affairs, 2008), 137.

43 "mushroom cloud": Rice, interview with CNN's Wolf Blitzer, September 8, 2002. "There will always be some uncertainty about how quickly he can acquire nuclear weapons. But we don't want the smoking gun to be a mushroom cloud." http://transcripts.cnn.com/TRANSCRIPTS/0209/08/le.00.html.

44 "It isn't just a simple matter": Colin Powell, interview with Jason M. Breslow, "Colin Powell: U.N. Speech 'Was a Great Intelligence Failure,'" PBS *Frontline*, May 17, 2016, https://www.pbs.org/wgbh/frontline/article/colin-powell-u-n-speech-was-a-great-intelligence-failure/.

44 the reintroduction of weapons inspectors: An earlier team of inspectors had been withdrawn in 1998 due to Iraq's unwillingness to cooperate.

45 "factories on wheels": Powell, UN Security Council, February 5, 2003.

45 "every statement I make today": Powell, UN Security Council. Powell's statements reflected accurately the overall view of the intelligence community at the time of his speech. However, the State Department's own Bureau of Intelligence and Research had warned that the information supporting several key points was weak.

46 "I'm gonna make a prediction": Bush, speaking at a meeting of Republican governors, September 20, 2002, quoted in McClellan, *What Happened*, 140.

47 "In the military, your superiors": Colin Powell, with Tony Koltz, *It Worked for Me: In Life and Leadership* (New York: HarperCollins, 2012), 35.

SIX: CLUBBING

50 colleagues from Barbados and Liechtenstein: Andrea Willi was the foreign minister of Liechtenstein (1993–2001), and Dame Billie Miller, of Barbados (1994–2008). The only country represented in both clubs was Liechtenstein, whose ambassador to the United Nations from 1990 to 2002 was Claudia Fritsche.

57 "the Democratic wing of the Democratic Party": Howard Dean, address to the California State Democratic Convention, Sacramento, CA, March 15, 2003. In his remarks, Dean acknowledges that the originator of the phrase was Senator Paul Wellstone of Minnesota.

SEVEN: PROFESSOR MADDY

61 But just to be clear: That was then. I no longer do leg presses.

66 "Now when I am old": Robert Frost, "What Fifty Said."

68 "Professor Korbel was always hoping": James Bruce, quoted in preface to *Czechoslovakia: The Heritage of Ages Past; Essays in Memory of Josef Korbel*, ed. Hans Brisch and Ivan Volgyes (New York: East European Quarterly, Columbia University Press, 1979), 7.

68 "was never anecdotal or trivial": Charlotte Read, quoted in Brisch and Volgyes, eds., *Czechoslovakia*, 7.

69 "History becomes more and more": H. G. Wells, *The Outline of History* (Garden City, NY: Garden City Publishing Company Inc., 1920), 1100.

EIGHT: BULLS

70 "You can render a valuable public service": The statements attributed to U.S. Senator Paul Sarbanes in this paragraph reflect the author's best memory of the conversation cited. The quotations may not be exact.

71 "Many a rapid fortune": Charles Dickens, *American Notes: A Journey* (New York: Fromm International Publishing Corporation, 1985), 81.

73 To implement the new policy: Until that time, the CEO of Home Depot, Kenneth Langone, had been chair of the NYSE Compensation Committee, while Grasso was on a comparable committee, setting Langone's compensation, on the board of Home Depot. This was, in the minds of many, too cozy an arrangement.

77 "Grasso's Jackpot": Jenny Anderson, "Grasso's Jackpot: NYSE Ok's Special 140M Payout, Extends Contract," *New York Post*, August 28, 2003.

77 "In my view, the approval": Letter from William Donaldson, chairman of the U.S. Securities and Exchange Commission, to Carl McCall, chair of the Compensation Committee of the New York Stock Exchange Board of Directors, September 2, 2003. Donaldson, it might be noted, was Grasso's predecessor at the NYSE. The two men had their differences.

78 "grossly excessive": Dan K. Webb, Winston and Strawn LLP, *Report to the New York Stock Exchange on Investigation Relating to the Compensation of Richard A. Grasso*, December 15, 2003, 2, https://www.concernedsharehold ers.com/CCS_NYSE_WebbReportFull.pdf.

NINE: DEMOCRATS WITH A SMALL *d*

80 I was offered the chair: At NDI, I have worked closely and benefited immensely from the organization's senior staff, which was headed from 1993 until the summer of 2018 by Ken Wollack and since then by his successor, Derek Mitchell. I also enjoy the counsel of a superb board of directors, with whom I have traveled on educational visits to such intriguing capitals as Tbilisi, Kyiv, Amman, Bogotá, Nairobi, and Tunis.

80 NDI is one of four organizations: The others are the International Republican Institute, the American Center for International Labor Solidarity, and the Center for International Private Enterprise.

80 Having just written a study: The study was sponsored by the Woodrow Wilson International Center for Scholars, where I was a fellow.

86 "Behold," said a spokesman: Not an exact quote. Incident based on an interview with Melissa Estok, former NDI staffer, September 8, 2018.

87 "Lord, make me pure": Augustine of Hippo, *Confessions*, book 8, chapter 7.

87 "the policy of the United States": President George W. Bush, Second Inaugural Address, Washington, DC, January 20, 2009.

87 "mission inebriation": Peggy Noonan, "Way Too Much God," *Wall Street Journal*, January 21, 2005.

90 "I would give it a failing grade": In the years since 2007, Nigeria has continued to hold regular parliamentary and presidential elections. Although there have been improvements in voter registration and vote-counting procedures, there continue to be instances of vote buying and problems in distributing election materials and in ensuring that polling stations operate smoothly. The major political parties have also done a poor job of incorporating women and youth into their hierarchies. Nigeria has the lowest percentage of women serving in parliament in sub-Saharan Africa.

TEN: A FOOTHOLD

95 "monetize their assets": This and succeeding quotes from Dr. de Soto do not reflect a word-for-word transcription of a particular conversation but are consistent with the tenor of our discussions over time.

98 "I know that in a matter of hours": Joseph Muturi, quoted in *Making the Law Work for Everyone*, final report of the Commission on Legal Empowerment of the Poor (Commission on Legal Empowerment of the Poor and United Nations Development Program, 2008), 13.

99 "We have gone back in time": Letter from Muturi, cited in *Making the Law Work for Everyone*, 4.

99 "legal identity is not a privilege": Madeleine Albright, May 25, 2009, The Hague, European launch of *Making the Law Work for Everyone*.

100 "rational persuasion": Stephen Golub, "The Commission on Legal Empowerment of the Poor: One Big Step Forward and a Few Steps Back for Development Policy and Practice," *Hague Journal of the Rule of Law* 1, no. 1 (March 2009).

100 Global Legal Empowerment Initiative: The initiative is a partnership between George Soros's Open Society Foundations and Namati, a movement of legal advocates that includes more than three hundred groups worldwide.

ELEVEN: THINGS UNSEEN

102 In a fourth-grade classroom: Joke borrowed from a sermon on holy humor by Rev. Cara Spaccarelli, Christ Church + Washington Parish, Washington, DC, April 8, 2018.

102 In popular entertainments: Freeman played God in *Bruce Almighty* (2003) and *Evan Almighty* (2007); Sheen, in an episode of *Insight*, a syndicated television show (1974); Burns, in *Oh, God!* (1977); Morissette, in *Dogma* (1999); and Goldberg, in *A Little Bit of Heaven* (2011).

104 The 9/11 attacks sparked: Among those who influenced me at this stage were Douglas Johnston, coeditor of *Religion, the Missing Dimension of Statecraft* (Washington, DC: Center for Strategic and International Studies, 2004); and Robert Seiple, who served as the first U.S. ambassador-at-large for international religious freedom.

105 "Good people do good things,": I suspect my friends, whether they knew it or not, were quoting American physicist Steven Weinberg. In April 1999, during an address to the Conference on Cosmic Design, American Association for the Advancement of Science, in Washington, DC, Weinberg said, "Religion is an insult to human dignity. With or without it you would have good people doing good things and evil people doing evil things. But for good people to do evil things, that takes religion."

105 A Baptist minister, a rabbi: The quotations cited in the account of this dinner are not exact but do reflect contemporaneous notes. More than fifteen years have passed since that gathering in my home. In 2009, Imam Rauf sought permission to build an Islamic Cultural Center at a location in Manhattan, two blocks from where the World Trade Center had been. Even though the site was already being used for Muslim worship, the imam's proposal elicited vicious verbal attacks from anti-Muslim activists. The imam expressed regret for the pain that had been caused and, in 2011, withdrew his plan. Since 2013, Dr. Land has been president of the Southern Evangelical Seminary in Charlotte, North Carolina. He is the author of *The Divided States of America: What Liberals and Conservatives Get Wrong About Faith and Politics*. In 2014, President Obama appointed Rabbi Saperstein to serve as U.S. ambassador-at-large for international religious freedom, the first non-Christian to hold the post. I have been a regular guest of David and his wife, Ellen, for Passover dinner.

107 take the lead in providing debt relief: Many religious advocates linked the issue to a reference in Leviticus (25:8–13) regarding the semicentennial "Year of Jubilee" during which ancient Israelites were instructed to forgive debts and "return every man unto his possession."

107 "foreign policy as social work": Michael Mandelbaum, "Foreign Policy as Social Work," *Foreign Affairs*, January–February 1996.

107 "must move humbly and wisely": Sam Brownback, quoted in Peter Waldman, "Evangelicals Give U.S. Foreign Policy an Activist Tinge," *Wall Street Journal*, May 26, 2004.

108 The outcome was a conference: Brownback and I had hoped to use the bipartisan conference as a platform for more ambitious projects, but the senator chose to run for president in 2008 (unsuccessfully) and then for governor of his home state, where he served from 2011 to 2018. He left that

job to succeed Rabbi David Saperstein as America's ambassador-at-large for international religious freedom.

110 "January 9, 1966": Author's journal (unpublished) for that date.

112 I'm reminded of a story: I owe this anecdote, as well, to Rev. Cara Spaccarelli, former rector of Christ Church + Washington Parish, Washington, DC.

113 John Unger: As of this writing, early in 2020, Unger is coping with serious health problems and St. John's is without a regular pastor.

TWELVE: ADVISE AND DISSENT

115 "War criminal or role model?": Rosanna Xia, "War Criminal or Role Model? Madeleine Albright as Scripps College Commencement Speaker Hits a Nerve," *Los Angeles Times*, May 9, 2016.

115 "We have heard": Leslie Stahl, *60 Minutes*, CBS, May 12, 1996.

115 "I think that is a very hard choice": Madeleine Albright, *60 Minutes*.

116 "were rigged to show": Tim Dyson and Valeria Cetorelli, "Changing Views on Child Mortality and Economic Sanctions in Iraq: A History of Lies, Damned Lies, and Statistics," *British Medical Journal of Global Health* 2, no. 2 (July 24, 2017), Gh.bmj.com/content/2/2/e000311.

117 "More than 600,000 Iraqi children": Osama bin Laden, quoted in Michael Paget, "The Iraq Sanctions Myth," *Pacific Standard*, April 26, 2013, https://psmag.com/news/the-iraq-sanctions-myth-56433.

117 who later cited this cleverly manufactured lie: Bin Laden, videotape broadcast, Al-Jazeera, November 1, 2004.

119 "disorder and profaneness": Increase Mather, quoted in Marvin Hightower, "The Spirit and Spectacle of Harvard Commencement," https://www./commencement.harvard.edu/background/spirit.html.

119 "evils of the church": Ralph Waldo Emerson, address to the graduates of Harvard Divinity School, Cambridge, MA, July 15, 1838.

123 "I'm deeply disgusted": Kinzie Mabon, quoted in Xia, "War Criminal or Role Model?"

123 "there is a special place in Heaven": Madeleine Albright, commencement address, Scripps College, Claremont, California, May 14, 2016.

123 "all shall be well": T.S. Eliot, "Little Gidding." Eliot's phrase, repeated three times in the last of his *Four Quartets*, is originally from Julian of Norwich (1342–1416), author of *Revelations of Divine Love*, the earliest surviving book written by a woman in the English language.

THIRTEEN: COMPANIONS

125 "poisonous bunch-backed toad": William Shakespeare, *Richard III*, act 1, scene 3.

126 a secretary's final duty: In March 2018, Congress approved a law banning the

use of federal funds to paint the portraits of cabinet secretaries. Although I do see value in the portraits, I agree with the ban on public funds.

133   "newspapers, books, shoes": Susan Terris, "Getting Naked with the Secretary of State," essay, 2001, www.webdelsol.com/InPosse/Terris15.htm.

FOURTEEN: DIGGING OUT

135   "Military history is rife": Steve Coll, *Directorate S: The C.I.A. and America's Secret Wars in Afghanistan and Pakistan* (New York: Penguin Press, 2018), 102–3.

135   "summer of 2006": George W. Bush, *Decision Points* (New York: Crown Publishers, 2010), 367.

136   "we had repair work to do": Condoleezza Rice, *No Higher Honor: A Memoir of My Years in Washington* (New York: Crown Publishers, 2011), 292.

138   "I know we've made tactical errors": Rice, *No Higher Honor*, 456.

140   "Papa says I may offer you": Ulysses S. Grant, *Ulysses S. Grant: Personal Memoirs and Selected Letters* (New York: Library of America, 1990), 26. Grant insists in his autobiography that this story is exaggerated; he admits to being overeager, not stupid. He says that the tale was widely told nonetheless and that it "caused me great heart-burning [when it] . . . got out among the boys in the village and it was a long time before I heard the last of it."

141   "outlining, for example, a federal agency's new policy": Madeleine Albright, *Memo to the President Elect: How We Can Restore America's Reputation and Leadership* (New York: HarperCollins, 2008), 4.

FIFTEEN: MAKING OF THE PRESIDENT 2008

143   "fulfill the responsibility you have": King Hussein quoted in Madeleine Albright, *Madam Secretary: A Memoir* (New York: HarperCollins, 2003), 315.

144   "I can play with the boys": Hillary Rodham Clinton, *Living History* (New York: Simon and Schuster, 2003), 12.

144   voter fraud in Chicago: By coincidence, my first vote in a presidential election was in Chicago in 1960. I cast my ballot, emphatically and legally, for JFK.

146   "a congenital liar": William Safire quoted in Clinton, *Living History*, 329.

147   According to the Book of Revelation: To be clear, the Book of Revelation includes neither any mention of the Antichrist nor of a man in his forties and was written centuries before the Islamic faith was founded.

149   "It's not easy, and I couldn't do it": Hillary Clinton, quoted in Anne E. Kornblut, "It's Not Easy, an Emotional Clinton Says," *Washington Post*, January 8, 2008.

151   "Although we weren't able to shatter": Hillary Clinton, remarks, National Building Museum, Washington, DC, June 7, 2008.

153 "There's no indication that ideology": Andrew Kohut, quoted in James W. Ceaser, Andrew E. Busch, and John J. Pitney Jr., *Epic Journey: The 2008 Elections and American Politics* (Lanham, MD: Rowman & Littlefield Publishers, Inc., 2009), 14.

SIXTEEN: FIRST LIGHT

154 "We know that our patchwork heritage": Barack Obama, inaugural address, Washington, DC, January 20, 2009.

155 "Help us work for that day": Rev. Joseph Lowery, benediction, inauguration of President Barack Obama, Washington, DC, January 20, 2009.

155 a faith tradition dating back to 1789: Following George Washington's inauguration as first president of the United States, in Manhattan on April 30, 1789, the official party adjourned to St. Paul's Episcopal Church on Broadway for prayers and hymns led by a U.S. Senate chaplain.

159 I have friends: Thanks to Karl "Rick" Inderfurth for bringing this faux application to my attention. Ambassador Inderfurth served with me on the National Security Council staff under Carter and Brzezinski, at the United Nations during Bill Clinton's first term, and as assistant secretary of state for South Asian affairs during Clinton's second term. He is also a board member of the National Democratic Institute.

160 "Madeleine, dear, how are you?": This is a description from memory, not a verbatim transcript. The husband's name is not "Herman."

160 Fred and Marlene Malek: Fred Malek died on March 24, 2019. RIP.

SEVENTEEN: THOUGHT AND PURPOSE

163 In the late 1980s and early 1990s: In 2013, the Center for National Policy began working in partnership with the Truman Project and has since merged to form the Truman Center for National Policy.

168 "Words are grown so false": William Shakespeare, *Twelfth Night*, act 3, scene 1.

169 I was interested to learn: Dr. Seuss (Theodor Geisel) was a vigorous foe of Nazism and isolationists who opposed the Allied effort in World War II. Less happily, he supported the internment of Japanese Americans during the war and drew racist cartoons implying that all Japanese Americans were disloyal. For this, he later apologized.

169 a task force on the prevention of genocide: Sponsorship of the study was split among three nonpartisan research organizations: the U.S. Holocaust Memorial Museum, the American Academy of Diplomacy, and the U.S. Institute of Peace.

171 "The Holocaust is a lie": Notebook of James von Brunn, quoted in Matthew Stabley, Jim Iovino, and Andrew Greiner, "Slain Museum Guard's Kindness Repaid with Bullets," NBC4 TV Washington online, July 13, 2009.

174 "Secretary Clough, thank you very much": Madeleine Albright, remarks, Smithsonian Institution Castle building, June 15, 2010.

175 Per medieval superstition: See, for example, "blood-consuming sighs," a reference to the superstition in Shakespeare's *Henry VI, Part II* (act 3, scene 2).

175 "Albright, Albright, all right, all right": Excerpt from poem "To Madeleine Albright, Without Greetings," exact source unknown but reported as appearing in the Iraqi press in a cable to the State Department from a U.S. embassy in Europe, September 1994.

179 The museum tour: Between 2009 to 2018, the pins were displayed in the following venues: Museum of Arts and Design; William J. Clinton Presidential Library and Museum; Smithsonian Institution; Indianapolis Museum of Art; Miami Dade College, Freedom Tower; New Orleans Museum of Art; Jimmy Carter Presidential Library and Museum; Carnegie Museum of Natural History; Denver Art Museum; Mint Museum; Bowers Museum; Gerald R. Ford Presidential Museum; National Czech and Slovak Museum and Library; Phoenix Art Museum; Wellesley College, Davis Museum; Franklin D. Roosevelt Presidential Library and Museum; Harry S. Truman Presidential Library and Museum; Bellevue Arts Museum; Richard Nixon Presidential Library and Museum; Fine Arts Museums of San Francisco, Legion of Honor; Ronald Reagan Presidential Library and Museum; Lyndon Baines Johnson Presidential Library and Museum.

181 "Albright has done": Robin Givhan, "Madeleine Albright's Pins Were Mightier than the Sword," *Washington Post*, November 8, 2009.

NINETEEN: MUSCLES IN BRUSSELS

183 "I had assumed": Secretary of State James Byrnes, quoted in Norman A. Graebner, ed., *An Uncertain Tradition: American Secretaries of State in the Twentieth Century* (New York: McGraw-Hill Book Company, 1961), 229.

184 "refuge and strength": Dean Acheson, quoted in James Reston, "Atlantic Nations Sign Defense Pact," *New York Times*, April 5, 1949.

184 the peculiarity of the military band selections: The band also played "Bess, You Is My Woman Now," an apparent tribute to the First Lady, Bess Truman, who was seated in the front row. James Frederick Green, the State Department officer responsible for logistics at the event, later recalled, "Immediately after it was decided to hold a ceremony for the signing in Washington, I was assigned responsibility for making all the arrangements. I engaged the National Theater [*sic*] for the morning of April 4; borrowed 12 flags of the NATO members, to be set across the back of the stage; arranged for 12 chairs to be placed below the flags; placed a large, overstuffed chair, stage right, for President Truman, and set a small table, stage center, to hold

the treaty. I also arranged for State Department officers to escort the foreign ministers from their limousines into the theater and out again after the ceremony. The only item I forgot to check was the music to be played by the Marine Band at the end of the ceremony. So, immediately after Secretary of State Dean Acheson, in the presence of President Truman, signed the first entangling Alliance in our history, the band struck up a medley from 'Porgy and Bess,' beginning with 'It Ain't Necessarily So.' Seated in the front row of the balcony, I almost fell overboard." "What the Band Played at NATO's Birth," *New York Times*, June 2, 1989, https://www.nytimes.com/1989/06/02 /opinion/l-what-the-band-played-at-nato-s-birth-832889.html.

184 "an armed attack against one": Article V, North Atlantic Treaty, signed in Washington, DC, April 4, 1949.

187 "pathological hatred of Slavs": Boris Ratnikov, cited in Brian Whitmore, "Russia's Ministry of Mind Reading," RadioFreeEurope/RadioLiberty, June 23, 2015, https://www.rferl.org/a/russias-ministry-of-mind-reading/27087718.html.

190 "No one should doubt": *NATO 2020: Assured Security; Dynamic Engagement: Analysis and Recommendations of the Group of Experts on a New Strategic Concept for NATO*, May 17, 2010, https://www.nato.int/cps/en /natolive/official_texts_63654.htm.

192 "iron curtain": The three quotations in this paragraph are from the John Findley Green Foundation Lecture given by Winston Churchill at Westminster College in Fulton, Missouri, on March 5, 1946.

TWENTY: A BIGGER SEA

195 substantial gains were made: Under the Taliban, approximately 3 percent of Afghan girls attended school; the figure in 2018 was approximately 37 percent.

195 "If you don't have no schooling": the character Rooster Cogburn in Charles Portis, *True Grit* (New York: Simon and Schuster, 1968), 82.

198 "In the world today": Katharine Graham, *Personal History* (New York: Vintage Books, 1997), 418.

198 "unabashedly careerist": Hailey Huget, "The Problem with The Albright Institute," *Wellesley Underground*, July 11, 2012, Wellesleyunderground.com /post/26971604058/the-problem-with-the-albright-institute.

TWENTY-ONE: PUZZLES

202 "Greed is good": from the film *Wall Street* (1987), directed by Oliver Stone, co-written by Stone and Stanley Weiser, distributed by 20th Century Fox. The line spoken by the character Gordon Gekko (played by Michael Douglas) is "Greed, for lack of a better word, is good." The sentiment was reportedly derived from a commencement speech by the investor Ivan Boesky,

who, in 1986, told graduates of the University of California at Berkeley School of Business Administration that "Greed is right."

205 I have met few men: In 2005, Sandy Berger was convicted of a misdemeanor charge of unauthorized removal and retention of classified material from the National Archives Reading Room. He was fined fifty thousand dollars and performed one hundred hours of community service. By mutual agreement, we never discussed the incident.

TWENTY-TWO: INFERNO

211 "I will try to catch a show": George H. W. Bush, letter to Richard Allen, March 17, 1990. Thanks to Derek Chollet for coming across this note and sharing it with me.

212 "although every new American president": Madeleine Albright, remarks, Georgetown University, March 24, 2009.

213 "No system of government": Barack Obama, address to Cairo University, Cairo, Egypt, June 4, 2009.

218 Perhaps our second run-in: Early in 2016, I visited Egypt for a project on behalf of the Atlantic Council. Among the many items on my agenda, I had to meet with Fayza Mohamed Abul Naga, who was by then the country's national security advisor. I remained upset with her because of the accusations she had lodged against NDI. When I walked into a meeting room in Cairo that February, I anticipated a hostile reception. This is my memory of our exchange:

> She: Dr. Albright, how wonderful to you see you again (big hug).
> Me: Fayza, how great to see you (big hug returned).
> She: Boutros-Ghali wanted me to extend to you his very best wishes.
> Me: Please tell him how much I appreciate that; and I hope you will
>   give him by best wishes as well.

Maybe Fayza cast a spell on me, but all my vinegar turned to sugar. A few days later, I had reason to be grateful for the alchemy when word reached me that Boutros-Ghali had died. A confrontation would have left a bitter taste and solved nothing. There is an Arab proverb: "The best answer will come from the person who is not angry."

218 "cockroaches": Muammar Gaddafi, quoted in "Libya Protests: Defiant Gaddafi Refuses to Quit," BBC News, February 22, 2011.

<?> "all necessary measures": UN Security Council Resolution 1973, approved March 17, 2011, by a vote of 10 in favor, zero opposed, 5 abstentions, including China and Russia.

219 "responsibility to protect": The sponsoring organizations for the report on the responsibility to protect were the U.S. Holocaust Memorial Museum, the U.S. Institute for Peace, and the Brookings Institution. My co-chair was Richard Williamson, who had served as special envoy to Sudan under President George W. Bush.

223 the president told stories: During his speech, President Obama inadvertently made the wrong kind of news. Among the Medal of Freedom recipients in 2012 was Jan Karski, a tall, thin man with a hawklike face, an almost photographic memory, and a fierce commitment to truth. These traits had led him in 1942 to venture inside the Jewish ghetto in Warsaw, where he observed whole families being crammed onto train cars for transport to Nazi gas chambers. After an eventful escape to the West, Karski conveyed the horror of what he had seen to Allied officials in London, which led to one of the first high-level public denunciations of the Holocaust. The presidential recognition of Karski, though posthumous, was highly appropriate and had special meaning for me because I had known Karski as a fellow professor at Georgetown and had written the foreword to his memoir. Sadly, in praising Karski, Obama said that the atrocities Jan had witnessed took place in a "Polish death camp." The implication was that Poles were to blame. This led, understandably, to protests from Poland and the Polish American community. The White House took the rare step of amending the official transcript to note the error and to say that the president should have referred instead to "Nazi death camps in German-occupied Poland."

223 He has two: Powell and diplomat Ellsworth Bunker are the only individuals who have received two Presidential Medals of Freedom. Powell received his in 1991, from President George H. W. Bush, and in 1993, from Bill Clinton. The second included the designation "with Distinction."

225 Herbie Hancock Institute of Jazz: Until 2018, the event was called the Thelonious Monk International Jazz Competition.

232 I had never doubted: In 2013, I was a guest at an event at Princeton University. The school's president, Christopher Eisgruber, told me that he had never believed my claim of ignorance regarding my family's heritage until the same thing happened to him. Like me, Eisgruber was raised a Roman Catholic and married an Episcopalian. In the process of helping his nine-year-old son with a school project, he learned that his mother, who had been born in Berlin, was Jewish and had arrived in the United States as a refugee. In 2004, when Senator John Kerry was preparing to run for president, he discovered from reporters that his paternal grandfather was an Austro-Hungarian Jew. Since learning the truth about my own family's past, I have heard many comparable stories.

232 "Not to transmit an experience": Elie Wiesel, "Why I Write: Making No Become Yes," https://www.rjuhsd.us/cms/lib05/ca01001478/Centricity/Domain/351/Why I Write elie wiesel.pdf.

233 "I have to get used to": Olga Körbelová, letter to Greta Deimlová, July 22, 1942, Author's files.

235 "The past was to be deaf": Josef Korbel, unpublished manuscript, in possession of the author's family.

<?> I was also in contact: In a coincidence, I discovered that I had known the sister of the woman in Austria. Before her death in 2007, Irena Neumann was the wife of Lane Kirkland, president of the AFL-CIO, and someone with whom I had worked on many projects in support of labor rights and democracy.

238 What was this?: Not long after this discovery, I began the job of translating the journal. Most of the work was done, oddly enough, while sitting in a hospital waiting room. My sister-in-law Pam Korbel was having an operation, so my brother John and I made productive use of the time by translating and transcribing what our grandmother had written.

238 "and all the cute things": Journal of Růžena Spieglová, entry for January 1, 1942, in possession of the author's family.

239 "I want to systematically remember": Journal of Růžena Spieglová, entry for January 16, 1942.

239 "is possible": Journal of Růžena Spieglová, entry for April 22, 1942.

TWENTY-FIVE: LEAVING

242 "Mr. President, Mr. Prime Minister": Madeleine Albright, remarks at the funeral of Václav Havel, Prague, Czech Republic, December 23, 2011.

242 his reputation was magnified: Havel wrote of a dinner at the White House on February 20, 2005, "I tried to explain to several of the guests that if I seem to be a hero it's certainly not because I ever set out to be one. It was only a long series of events, circumstances, or dilemmas that provided the setting in which I had to make certain decisions . . . I used that explanation to mask my embarrassment." Václav Havel, *To the Castle and Back*, trans. Paul Wilson (New York: Vintage, 2008), 86.

244 "For forty years": Havel, New Year's address to the Czechoslovak people, Prague, January 1, 1990.

245 "You can't spend your whole life criticizing": Havel, *To the Castle and Back*, 5.

246 "Mafia capitalism": Ibid., 151.

246 "Even a poet has teeth": Havel, quoted in Dennis O'Driscoll, "Recent Poetry Pickings," Poetry Ireland, https://www.poetryireland.ie/publications /poetry-ireland . . . /recent-poetry-pickings5.

246 "Washington is populated": Havel, *To the Castle and Back,* 101.

247 "herds of useless horses": Ibid., 63.

247 "endearing": Ibid., 86.

248 Michael Žantovský: For anyone interested in Havel, I highly recommend Žantovský's insightful and beautifully written *Havel: A Life*, published by Grove Press (2014).

248 "He cast light into places": Albright, remarks at Havel funeral.

250 "trousers hung like an accordion": Josef Korbel, unpublished manuscript.

253 On it are twenty-six names: On the side of my paternal grandparents—in addition to their daughter, Greta; son-in-law, Rudolf; and granddaughter, Milena—are the names of three of my grandfather Arnošt's six siblings, a sister-in-law, a brother-in-law, two of his nieces, and a nephew. From our mother's side of the family, in addition to our grandmother Růžena, are Růžena's sister, brother-in-law, and nephew. Grandfather Alfred's brother, sister-in-law, two nephews, a niece and her husband and two children also died during the Holocaust.

253 Among the poems: refers to "May" by Hanuš Hachenburg. A typewritten copy of the poem was found among papers left at Terezín. The poem is unsigned, but the author was identified by O. Klein, a former teacher at Terezín, as Hachenburg. The young poet was born in Prague on July 12, 1929, and sent to Terezín on October 24, 1942. He died in Auschwitz on December 18, 1943.

254 "even the most ordinary": Havel, *To the Castle and Back*, 90.

TWENTY-SIX: CRADLE OF CIVILIZATION

255 "wicked problem": Hillary Rodham Clinton, *Hard Choices* (New York: Simon and Schuster, 2014), chapter heading.

256 "change my calculations significantly": Obama, remarks to White House Press Corps, Washington, DC, August 20, 2012.

256 "You take the victories": Barack Obama, "Obama: The Vox Conversation—Part One: Domestic Policy," *Foreign Policy*, January 2015, https://www .vox.com/a/barack-obama-interview-vox-conversation/obama-foreign-policy -transcript.

257 "ending tyranny in our world": George W. Bush, Second Inaugural Address, Washington, DC, January 20, 2005.

257 "vast and feverish": Benjamin Netanyahu, remarks at the United Nations General Assembly, October 1, 2013.

258 "a manipulative liar": Author's notebook, unpublished.

259 "America's first Pacific president": Obama, speech in Tokyo, Japan, November 13, 2009.

261 half the Syrian population: Amid the crisis, I was proud once again of NDI. Working with the local population in areas controlled by the opposition, the organization assisted in the formation of dozens of democratically elected administrative councils to assume government functions and meet public needs. These councils competed directly with more radical groups and created a basis for hope that, should Assad be removed, Syria could develop a government that reflected fairly the aspirations of its people.

263 My Republican co-chair was Stephen Hadley: I didn't yet know Hadley well but was aware of his reputation. On a single page of his memoir, Bush refers to him as scholarly, thoughtful, steady, kind, selfless, cerebral, a

"reluctant public figure," and someone who "listened, synthesized, and pondered without brooding."

264 "aerial policing": Winston Churchill, quoted in Marek Pruszewicz, "The 1920s British Air Bombing Campaign in Iraq," BBC News, October 7, 2014, https://www.bbc.com/news/magazine-29441383.

TWENTY-SEVEN: BREATHLESS

274 Redford has his own festival: After the 2006 gathering in Sundance, Redford sent me a thank-you note with a curious compliment: "You move like someone escaping from a crime or chasing someone committing one—so is your energy for travel and engagement."

TWENTY-EIGHT: MIDNIGHT

279 "People are talking about revolution": Madeleine Albright, rally for Hillary Clinton, Concord, NH, February 6, 2008.

280 "get more activist": Gloria Steinem, *Real Time with Bill Maher*, HBO, February 5, 2016.

280 "A woman can be a feminist": Letter to the editor from Natalie Beam, *New York Times*, February 8, 2016.

280 "The cluelessness of these feminist elders": Letter to the editor from Joan Grossman, *New York Times*, February 8, 2016.

281 "Despite being the first woman": Hillary Rodham Clinton, *What Happened* (New York: Simon and Schuster, 2017), 77.

282 "My experience working with Hillary": Robert M. Gates, *Duty: Memoirs of a Secretary at War* (New York: Alfred A. Knopf, 2014), 290.

284 "I leave it to my audience": Abraham Lincoln, quoted in Richard Lederer, "Lincoln as Jokester," *Saturday Evening Post*, June 25, 2013.

284 "knock the crap out of them": Donald Trump, remarks, Cedar Rapids, IA, February 1, 2016.

284 "punch him in the face": Trump, remarks, Las Vegas, NV, February 23, 2016.

284 "maybe he should have been roughed up": Trump, remarks, Birmingham, AL, November 22, 2015.

284 Many a Trump rally: For a photographic review of the Trump campaign, see Paul Sherman, *Look Away: Documenting the Crude and Sexist Items from the Trump Campaign Trail* (Washington, DC: X Park Press, 2017). After the campaign, on December 16, 2016, Trump told a crowd in Orlando, Florida, "You people were vicious, violent, screaming, 'Where's the Wall? We want the Wall.' Screaming, 'Prison! Lock her up!' I mean, you are going crazy. I mean, you were nasty and mean and vicious, and you wanted to win, right?"

284 "you could put half": Hillary Clinton, remarks at a campaign fund-raiser, New York, September 9, 2016.

285 the Manhattan abode: From 1947 to 2016, the U.S. permanent representa-

tive to the United Nations was housed in an apartment on the forty-second floor of the Waldorf Astoria Hotel in Midtown Manhattan. The arrangement was terminated for security reasons about a year after a Chinese insurance company purchased the Waldorf.

TWENTY-NINE: A WARNING

288 "the evidence of truth": The four quotations in this paragraph are from Alexander Hamilton, No. 1, *The Federalist Papers* (New York: New American Library, 1961), 34–35.

289 "Often I would like to be wrong": Benito Mussolini, quoted in Denis Mack Smith, *Mussolini* (London: Phoenix Press, 1981), 110.

290 "There is nothing constructive": Author's testimony, Committee on Foreign Affairs, U.S. House of Representatives, Washington, DC, February 27, 2019.

<?> "a cry of defiance": Henry Wadsworth Longfellow, "Paul Revere's Ride."

291 "a lovable feminist granny": Jessica Contera, "Madeleine Albright Has Ascended from Historic Diplomat to Yas Queen Feminist Icon," *Washington Post*, April 19, 2018.

291 "ghoul warmonger": Taryn Fivek, quoted in "'You're a Murderer': Protestors Disrupt Madeleine Albright's 'Fascism' Book Tour," Sputnik News Service, April 12, 2018, https://sputniknews.com/us/201804121063464437 -Protesters-Disrupt-Madeleine-Albrights-Fascism-Book-Tour.

292 a fable he had read in high school: The story is drawn from the 1958 novel *Things Fall Apart*, by the renowned Nigerian author Chinua Achebe.

293 "rudeness is the weak man's": Eric Hoffer, quoted in George Will, "The Constant Ubiquity of Trump," *Washington Post*, August 6, 2019. The observation is from Hoffer's *The Passionate State of Mind and Other Aphorisms* (1955), section 241.

293 According to a study: Data cited in David Brooks, "Cory Booker Finds His Moment," *New York Times*, March 18, 2019, A27.

295 keepers of a peace vigil: The originators of the protest were Thomas and Concepción Picciotto.

THIRTY: UNHINGED

300 "has collapsed into many tiny parts": Angela Merkel, remarks, Munich Security Conference, Munich, Germany, February 16, 2019.

300 Trump has called the EU a "foe": Trump, quoted in Maegan Vazquez, "Trump Calls the European Union a 'Foe' of the United States," CNN Politics, July 16, 2018, https://edition.cnn.com/2018/07/15/politics/donald -trump-european-union-foe/index.html.

301 "cold, detached, uncommunicative, [and] remote": Madeleine Albright, *Fascism: A Warning* (New York: HarperCollins, 2018), 184.

303 "Tariff Man": Trump tweet, 7:03 a.m., December 4, 2018.

THIRTY-ONE: RENEWAL

306 "anybody who comes to Washington": Daniel J. Boorstin, *Democracy and Its Discontents: Reflections on Everyday America* (New York: Vintage Books, 1975), 7.

308 There is hardly a humorist: For example, Twain: "There is no distinctly native American criminal class except Congress," and "Suppose you were an idiot, and suppose you were a member of Congress, but I repeat myself." Will Rogers: "This country has come to feel the same when Congress is in session as when the baby gets hold of a hammer."

310 a flock of civic-minded organizations: One list, offered by *Washington Post* columnist Max Boot (April 26, 2018) includes the Protect Democracy Project, R Street Institute, Citizens for Responsibility and Ethics in Washington, Issue One; Project on Government Oversight, Common Cause, Public Citizen, the Committee to Investigate Russia, Stand Up Republic, Republicans for the Rule of Law.

<?> "the line that forms on the right": E. B. White, "Notes and Comments," *The New Yorker*, July 3, 1943.

312 "What can I,": John Quincy Adams, *Diaries (1821–1848)* (New York: Library of America, 2017), entry for March 29, 1841, 504.

313 reunite the family of Dorcas Allen: Nathan and Dorcas Allen moved with their surviving children to Rhode Island.

313 "great resemblances": Adams, quoted in *Diaries*, chronology for 1837, 653.

313 "some of the bitterest political enemies": Adams, *Diaries*, entry for January 1, 1844, 581.

313 "This," he wrote, "is the weakness": Adams, *Diaries*, entry for April 23, 1841, 504.

THIRTY-TWO: SHADOWS AND LIGHT

317 "other people": Jean-Paul Sartre, from his play *No Exit* (1944). The drama describes three ill-matched people, recently deceased, who are trapped in a drawing room and come gradually to understand the full nature of their predicament. Toward the end, one character exclaims, "What? Only two of you? I thought there were more; many more. So this is hell. I'd never have believed it. You remember all we were told about the torture-chambers, the fire and brimstone, the 'burning marl.' Old wives' tales! There's no need for red-hot pokers. HELL IS OTHER PEOPLE!"

322 "I never gave anybody hell": Harry Truman, quoted in *Look*, April 3, 1956.

Index

Page numbers followed by n indicate notes.

Abdullah, king of Jordan, 261
Abul Naga, Fayza Mohamed, 217, 350n217
Acheson, Dean, 29–30, 184, 349n184
Adams, John, 81
Adams, John Quincy, 312–313, 317, 318
Afghanistan, 51, 98
    education of women in, 194, 195
    G. W. Bush administration and, 42–43, 46, 87, 135
    NATO and, 186, 192
    see also Taliban
Albright, Alice Patterson (daughter), 8, 127, 128–129, 130
Albright, Anne Korbel (daughter), 8, 127, 128, 130, 182
Albright, Joe, 3–4, 33, 127, 198, 269, 270
Albright, Katharine "Katie" Medill (daughter), 8, 129, 130, 178, 267, 270
Albright, Madeleine
    as ambassador to United Nations, 5, 21, 40, 44, 49–50, 115, 159, 175, 217
    asked for information for "advance obituary," 316
    Atlantic Council and, 263–265, 319–320
    birth name of, 2, 237
    CIA and, 225–229

Columbia University and graduate education, 55, 61, 68, 127
commencement addresses and, 117–123
consulting firm of, *see* The Albright Group (TAG) and Albright Stonebridge Group (ASG)
continued interest in foreign policy and current affairs, 49–54, 319–323
daughters and grandchildren of, 127–130
drum playing and, 223–226
early interest in politics, 54–55
e-mail and social media and, 267–269
exercise and, 60–61
extended family of, 130
with family in England during World War II, 12, 19, 37–38, 201, 208, 231, 233–236, 238, 250
Fascism: A Warning, author of, 291, 300–301, 315
friends of, 130–133
G20 conference in 2009 and, 159
Georgetown University teaching and, 4, 61, 63–69, 165, 168, 170, 220, 237
Harry S. Truman Scholarship Foundation and, 138

Albright, Madeleine (*continued*)
 health and age of, 124–126,
  266–267, 315–319
 imposter syndrome and, 26–27
 involvement in Democratic party
  politics, 55–59
 jewelry of, *see* pins, of Albright
 learns of Jewish ancestry, 231–232,
  351n232
 loss of child at birth, 32
 Madam Secretary, author of, xiii,
  28–37, 139
 marriage and divorce of, 3–4, 32–33
 *Memo to the President Elect: How
  We Can Restore America's
  Reputation and Leadership*,
  author of, 139–141
 mentioned in grandmother's
  journal, 325, 326, 328
 *Mighty and the Almighty:
  Reflections on America, God, and
  World Affairs*, author of, 105,
  108–109, 110, 139, 147
 mistaken for Mother Teresa, 204
 myth of anti-Russia attitude of,
  187–188
 National Democratic Institute and,
  4–5, 80–82, 85–87, 342n80, 350n217
 on staff of National Security
  Council, 4, 57, 159
 as New York Stock Exchange board
  member, 70–79
 optimism of, 320–323
 Partners for a New Beginning and,
  213–214
 personality of, 49–50, 93
 portraits of, 126–127, 274
 poverty elimination and, 94–101
 public opinion about, 115–119, 123
 recognized in public, 13–14
 as secretary of state, *see* secretary of
  state, of U.S.
 support for Hillary Clinton in
  2008 election primaries, 142–144

 television and, 211–212, 269–274
 think tanks and, 163–165, 169–172
 on unpredictability of life, 37–38
 Washington Speakers Bureau and,
  10–16
 Wellesley College and
  undergraduate education, 4, 13,
  40, 43, 63, 68, 110, 120, 130–131,
  144
 Westminster College address of,
  191–192
 on women's roles, 33, 194–196
Albright Capital Management, 204
The Albright Group (TAG), 17, 58, 158
 becomes Albright Stonebridge
  Group (ASG), 205–207
 consulting work of, 21–27, 201–204
 growth of, 204–205
Albright Institute, at Wellesley
  College, 196–200, 317
Albright Stonebridge Group (ASG),
  206–207
 consulting work of, 207–209
Algeria, 264–265
Allen, Dorcas and family, 311–312
Allen, Richard, 211
al-Qaeda, 42–43, 45, 71, 135, 186, 212,
  257
Amanpour, Christiane, 212
American Friends of the Czech
  Republic, 160
Amistad, 313
antidemocratic trends, in 21st century,
  289–295
anti-Semitism, 171–172, 276. *See also*
  Holocaust
Arab Spring, difficulties of Middle East
  diplomacy and, 214–221, 255–265
Arabs, democracy and, 87–88
Army Wives (television program), 269
Article I, of U.S. Constitution,
  307–308, 313
Aspen Institute, 51, 129, 164–165, 182, 317
 religious pluralism and, 275–277

Aspen Ministers Forum, 51–52, 296,
    320–321
Assad, Bashir al-, 218–219, 256,
    259–261, 263, 264, 290, 353n261
Atlantic Charter, 319
Atlantic Council, 319–320
    Albright's report to, 263–265
Atrocities Prevention Board (APB),
    171, 219–220
Augustine of Hippo, 87, 110
Axworthy, Lloyd, 299
Azerbaijan, 290

Baker, James A., 17, 174, 180
Balkans, 17, 50, 104, 128, 185, 190, 276.
    See also Bosnia; Kosovo
Barbados, 50, 341n50
Barnett, Bob, 29–31, 71
Bashir, Omar al-, 265
Ben Ali, 215
Berger, Sandy, 34, 52, 53, 205, 206,
    350n205
Biden, Joe, 132, 156
bin Laden, Osama, 42–43, 87, 117,
    257
Bismarck, Otto von, 165
Bolsonaro, Jair, 290
Booker, Cory, 278
Boorstin, Daniel, 306
Bosnia, 40, 104, 130, 185
Botswana, 23–24
Botti, Chris, 223–225
Bottomly, Kim, 196
Bouazizi, Tarek al-Tayeb Mohamed,
    214, 220–1
Bouteflika, Abdelaziz, 265
Boutros-Ghali, Boutros, 217, 350n217
Bowes, Daniel (grandson), 129, 317
Bowes, David (grandson), 129
Bowes, Gregory (son-in-law), 129, 204
Brazil, 290
Brexit, 296–297, 298, 321
British Medical Journal of Global
    Health, 116

Brookings, Robert, 166
Brookings Institution, 166
Brown, Tina, 31, 37
Brownback, Sam, 107–108, 344n108
Browner, Carol, 21, 202, 204
Bryan, William Jennings, 5
Brzezinski, Zbigniew, 68, 132, 187
Buchanan, James, 5
Budde, Mariann, 285
Burma. *See* Myanmar
Burnett, Tom, 121–122
Burnham, Jonathan, 31, 37
Bush, George H. W., 40, 164, 211,
    351n223
Bush, George W., 57, 104, 139, 212,
    280, 281
    democracy in Iraq and, 87–89
    foreign policy and, 134–139, 257,
        263, 353n263
    NATO and Afghanistan, 186
    post-9/11 invasion of Iraq and, 39,
        42–48, 117
    on Powell, 48
Bush, Jeb, 161, 280

Cambodia, 220, 290
Campbell, Caroline, 224
Čapek, Karel, 320
Carnegie Endowment for
    International Peace, 165–166
Carper, Margo, 60, 61
Carter, Jimmy, 67, 161, 205, 222
    Albright and National Security
        Council of, 4, 57, 68, 208
    fake application for employment
        in administration of, 159,
        347n159
Carville, James, 282
Cathedral Church of St. Peter and
    St. Paul (Washington National
    Cathedral), 155–156
Cecil, William, 165
Center for National Policy (CNP),
    163–164, 347n163

Central Intelligence Agency (CIA)
    Albright on External Advisory
        Board of, 225–229
    women and leadership and, 228
Charter 77 movement, Havel and,
    243–244
Cheney, Richard, 43, 46, 136–137, 139,
    161
Chile, 85
China, 16, 19, 202, 257, 303
    antidemocratic trends in, 290, 295
Christie, Chris, 280
Christo, *See* Javacheff, Christo
    Vladimirov
Churchill, Winston, 191–192, 193, 264,
    319
Cisco Systems, 213
Clark, Wesley, 57
climate change (or global warming),
    212, 257
Clinton, Bill, 2, 3, 34, 41, 132, 137, 159,
    164, 281, 316
    Council on Foreign Relations and,
        167
    democracy and, 91
    foundation of, 17
    G. W. Bush and, 139
    Hillary Clinton and, 145–146
    NATO and, 184–185
    Obama's postinaugural prayer
        service and, 156
Clinton, Chelsea, wedding of,
    273–274
Clinton, Hillary Rodham, 59, 125, 132,
    143, 180, 268, 316
    Bill Clinton and, 145–146
    email and, 283
    as First Lady, 143, 146, 147
    Obama's postinaugural prayer
        service and, 156
    as secretary of state, 157–158, 183,
        216, 255
    as senator from New York, 108,
        146–147

stereotypes and, 145–146
    on television, 272–273
    2008 presidential election primaries
        and, 142–144, 147–152
    2016 presidential election campaign
        and, 278–280
    youth and education of, 144–146
Coca-Cola, 213
Cohen, Bill, 34, 169, 170, 171, 219, 316
Cohen, Emily (MacFarquhar), 131–132
Cohen, Janet Langhart, 171, 316
Cohen, Richard, 35–36
Coll, Steve, 135
Colombia, 257
Columbia University, Albright's
        graduate education at, 55, 61, 68,
        127
commencement ceremonies and
        addresses, Albright on, 117–123
Commission on Legal Empowerment
        of the Poor (CLEP), 96–101
Communism
    Czechoslovakia and, 38, 183
    NATO and, 183–184
Congress, U.S.
    Article I on legislative obligations,
        307–308, 313
    citizens and democratic spirit and,
        309–311
    clash with Trump, 309
    composition of 116th, 306–307
Constitution, of U.S., Article I,
        307–308, 313
Constitutional Convention (1787), 20,
        275–276, 288
consulting firms
    history of, 19
    women and, 18
    see also The Albright Group (TAG),
        Albright Stonebridge Group
        (ASG)
Cook, Robin, 50, 51
Council on Foreign Relations (CFR),
        166–167

Crimea, 64, 257
Cruz, Ted, 280
Cuba, 257
Cuban Missile Crisis, 140–141
cultural diplomacy, jazz and, 223–225
Cunningham, Stacey, 79
cyber warfare, 65, 190, 191, 228, 283
Czech Republic
    Albright's family's visits to, 232,
        249, 252–254
    Havel and, 5, 244, 245–246
    NATO and, 2, 185, 321
Czechoslovakia
    Albright visits in 1987, 226–227
    Albright's ancestry and, 2, 160, 188
    Albright's family flight from in
        World War II, 12, 19, 37–38, 208,
        231, 233–236, 238, 250
    Albright's parents' youth in,
        249–250
    Albright's youth in, 230–231, 233
    Communism and, 38, 183
    democracy movement in, 82–84
    legends of, 249, 251–252

Dancing with the Stars (television
    program), 274
Daniel, Clifton, 322
Dante (Alighieri), xiii
Darrow, Clarence, 5–6
de Soto Polar, Hernando, 95–97, 101,
    220
Dean, Howard, 57–58, 341n57
Declaration of Principles for Freedom,
    Prosperity, and Peace, of Atlantic
    Council, 319–320
Deiml, Rudolf (uncle), 234
Deimlová, Markéta "Greta" (aunt),
    233
Deimlová, Milena (cousin), 234, 236
democratic ideals, 3, 321
    citizens and legislatures, 309–311
    NATO and, 192
    post-Cold War popularity of, 19–21

Democratic National Conventions
    1948, 81
    1952, 54
    1984, 80–81
    2004, 58–59, 147
    2012, 81–82
Dickens, Charles, 71
Dienstbier, Jiří, 82–83
DiGioia, John, 68
Dini, Lamberto, 50
Diplomatic Security Service, 10, 237,
    339n10
Dollars for Democrats, 55
Dubinsky, Susan. *See* Terris, Susan
    Dubinsky
Dubler, Dianne, 179
Dukakis, Michael, 134, 205, 281–282,
    284
Durant, Henry and Pauline, 200
Duterte, Rodrigo, 289

Ebadi, Shirin, 98
economics
    Trump and, 303
    U.S. foreign policy and, 297–298
Edelman, Marian Wright, 132
education, of women
    Albright Institute at Wellesley and,
        196–200, 317
    importance of, to any country's
        development, 194–196
Edwards, John, 57, 59
Egypt, 16, 215–217, 264, 290,
    350n217
election of 1952, U.S. presidential, 54
election of 1972, 55–57, 149
election of 1984, 29, 286
election of 1992, 164, 282
election of 2000, 41, 282
election of 2004, 54, 57–59, 103
election of 2008, 140, 152–153
    primaries, 142–144, 147–152
election of 2016
    campaign, 281–285

election of 2016 (*continued*)
  Democratic primaries and, 278–280
  election night, 285–287
  political climate after, 288–289,
    291–292
  Republican primaries and, 280–281
Emerson, Ralph Waldo, 119, 120
England, Brexit and, 296–297, 298,
  321
Enron, 72
Erdoğan, Recep Tayyip, 192, 289
Ethiopia, 94, 321
Evarts, William Maxwell, 6
Everett, Edward, 5
Ewing, Patrick, 274
ExxonMobil, 213

Farrell, Christine, 13
Fascism: A Warning (Albright), 291,
  300–301, 315
Ferraro, Geraldine, 29, 125–126, 132,
  286
Fiorina, Carly, 26
Fischer, Joschka, 50, 300
Ford, Gerald, 161
foreign policy, U.S.
  Albright's continued interest in,
    49–54, 319–323
  G.W. Bush and, 39, 42–48; 135–139,
    257, 263, 353n263
  Obama and, 171, 212–221, 255–265,
    290
  Trump and, 300–305
  see also secretary of state, of U.S.
Foster, John Watson, 19, 339n19
Foster, Vince, 146
France, 191, 299–300
Franklin, Aretha, 155, 225
Franklin, Benjamin, 125, 307
Freedman, Jacob, 289
Freund, Wini Shore, 130–131, 133, 196,
  316
Frost, Robert, 66
Fuerth, Leon, 52

Gaddafi, Muammar, 215, 218
Gates, Robert, 137, 282
Gates Foundation, 23, 340n24
Geisel, Theodor Seuss, 169, 347n169
genocide, task force on prevention of,
  169–172
George, Suzy, 17, 22, 59, 204, 205, 206,
  340n21
Georgetown University
  Albright as professor at, 4, 61,
    63–69, 165, 168, 170, 220, 237
  origin of "Hoyas" designation,
    62–63
  Qatar and, 182–183
  slavery and, 63
Gephardt, Richard, 57
Gerbasi, Gini, 285
Gergen, David, 275
Germany, in 21st century, 299–300.
  See also World War II
Ghani, Ashraf, 98
Gilmore Girls (television program),
  270–271
Gingrich, Newt, 277
Gittleman, Ann Louise, 60
Giuliani, Rudy, 280, 303
Givhan, Robin, 181
Global Legal Empowerment
  Initiative, 100–101, 343n100
Global Partnership for Education, 128
globalization, changes in U.S. foreign
  policy and, 297
Globus, Dorothy, 180
Goldwater, Barry, 284
Goodwin, Doris Kearns, 158
Gorbachev, Mikhail, 16
Gore, Al, 43, 52, 58, 151, 152
Graham, Bob, 58
Graham, Katherine, 30, 32, 198
Grant, Ulysses, 140, 346n140
Grasso, Richard, 70–71, 72, 342n73
  NYSE compensation issues and,
    74–79
Great Decisions (PBS program), 211

Greenfield-Sanders, Timothy, 274
Greenspan, Alan, 161, 162
Guantanamo, prison at, 137, 213, 214
Gutierrez, Carlos, 206

Hácha, Emil, mentioned in
  Spieglová's journal, 326–327, 331
Hachenburg, Hanuš, 253, 353n253
Hadley, Stephen, 263–265, 282,
  353n263
Hamilton, Alexander, 288, 294
Hancock, Herbie, 225
Harrington, Tony, 205
Harry S. Truman Scholarship
  Foundation, 138
Harvard University, 119
Havel, Václav, 5, 143, 227, 254, 274
  Albright on character of, 242–245
  Albright's eulogy of, 242, 248
  as author, 243, 244, 247
  democracy movement and, 82
  funeral of, 242, 246, 247–248
  as president of Czechoslovakia and
    Czech Republic, 244, 245–246
  on Washington D.C., 246–247
Hay, John, 165
Hayden, Carla, 306
Healy, Patrick Francis, 63
Hell, Michigan, xiii, 339n
Hellman, Joel, 68
Herbie Hancock Institute of Jazz, 225,
  351n225
Heydrich, Reinhard, 240
Hills, Carla, 18
Hitler, Adolf, 32, 172, 236, 240, 253,
  289, 292, 310
HIV/AIDS, 23–26, 94, 139, 340n24
Hoffer, Eric, 293
Holocaust
  Albright's family and, 231–232,
    236–241, 325–333
  memorial museums, 169, 171, 219
  see also Terezín
Holocaust Museum, in Houston, 169

Howell, Deneen, 29
Hubbell, Webb, 146
Hungary, 290, 298, 300
  NATO and, 2, 185, 192, 321
Hurricane Katrina, 135
Hussein, king of Jordan, 2, 143
Hussein, Saddam, 43, 45, 115–117, 135,
  175, 215

Iliescu, Ion, 24
imposter syndrome, 26–27
Indonesia, 16, 213
Institute for Government Research
  (later Brookings Institution), 166
Intel, 213
International Republican Institute
  (IRI), 83, 84, 217
Iran, 46, 88, 117, 189, 208, 281
  nuclear pact with, 17, 150, 257–258
  Trump and, 284, 300, 304
Iraq
  Albright questioned about, 115–117
  bombed in 1920 and 1930s, 264
  democracy and, 87–89
  G. W. Bush foreign policy and, 39,
    42–48, 135–139
  Obama and, 148
  poem about Albright from, 175,
    348n175
Isaacson, Walter, 164, 182, 213
ISIS, 261–263
Israel, 107, 143, 177, 257, 258
Ivanov, Igor, 50

Javacheff, Christo Vladimirov,
  209–210
jazz, cultural diplomacy and, 223–225
Jazz Section (of Czechoslovak
  Musicians Union), 227
Jefferson, Thomas, 5, 284
John Paul II, (Karol Józef Wojtyła), 63
Johns, Stephen Tyrone, 171
Johnson, Lyndon, 222
Johnson, Paula, 197

Joint Comprehensive Plan of Action
(JCPOA), 258
Jordan, 261, 264
Joseph (son of Jacob and Rachel),
165

Kempe, Fred, 263
Kemper, Alexander (Sandy), 320–321
Kemper, Christine, 322
Kennedy, Anthony, 98, 100
Kennedy, Caroline, 151
Kennedy, John F., 15, 30, 55, 121,
140–141, 145, 222, 284
Kennedy, Edward (Ted), 151, 173
Kennedy, Robert, 30, 145
Kent, Muhtar, 213
Kenya, CLEP and Toi Market in,
98–99
Kerry, John, 57–59, 151, 180, 255, 257,
263, 351n232
Keslinke, Alexis, 268
Key, Francis Scott, 312
Khashoggi, Jamal, 290
Kilson, Billy, 224
Kim Jong-un, 65, 289
King, Larry, 212
King, Martin Luther Jr., 145, 156
Kissinger, Henry, 5, 174, 180, 302
Klaus, Václav, 246
Kohut, Andrew, 132, 153, 182
Kōno, Tarō, 68
Korbel, Anna Spieglová "Mandula"
(mother), 12–13, 37–38, 61, 109,
227
in London during WII, 234–235,
238
personality of, 231
youth in Czechoslovakia, 232,
249–250
Körbel, Arnošt (paternal grandfather),
233–234, 235
Körbel, Gert (father's cousin), 234
Körbel, Jan "Honza" (uncle), 19
Korbel, Joe (nephew), 130

Korbel, John (brother), 8, 39, 130, 231,
253, 315
Jewish ancestry and, 232, 237,
352n238
Korbel, Josef (father), 31, 109
death of, 230
as diplomat, 12, 83
family papers of, 237–238
personality of, 19, 109, 231, 244, 314
short novel of, 235
United Nations and, 273
University of Denver and, 61, 68,
134, 164, 237
World War II and, 208, 234–235,
236, 238
youth in Czechoslovakia, 232,
249–250
Körbel, Karel (great uncle), 234
Korbel, Kathy (sister). *See* Silva, Kathy
Korbel
Korbel, Magdelena "Magda" (niece-in-
law), 130
Korbel, Pam (sister-in-law), 8, 130,
352n238
Korbel, Peter (nephew), 130
Körbelová, Olga (paternal
grandmother), 233–234, 235, 236
Kościuszko, Tadeusz, 294
Kosovo, 2, 90–92, 130, 185, 220
Krieg, Alexis. *See* Keslinke, Alexis
Kurdi, Alan, 298–299
Kushner, Jared, 303

Lafayette, Marquis de (Marie-Joseph
Paul Yves Roch Gilbert du
Motier), 294
Land, Richard, 106, 107, 108, 344n105
Laurel and Hardy (comedy team), 255
Lavrov, Sergey, 188–189
Leaving (Havel), 247
Lee, Spike, 274
legal empowerment. *See* Commission
of Legal Empowerment (CLEP)
Leoni, Téa, 271–273

Lewis, Mary Jane Durnford, 196
Liberia, 16
Libya, 217–218
Lieberman, Evelyn, 132
Lieberman, Joe, 57, 58
Liechtenstein, 50, 341n50
Lincoln, Abraham, 5, 158, 284
Living History (Hillary Clinton), 144
Locke, Gary, 117, 118
Los Angeles Times, 123
Love in the Time of Cholera
　　(Márquez), 34
Lowery, Joseph, 155

Madam Secretary (Albright), xiii, 139
　　publicity and book tour for, 36–37
　　writing and editing of, 28–36
Madam Secretary (television
　　program), 271–273
Madoff, Bernie, 71
Maduro, Nicolás, 289
Making the Law Work for Everyone
　　(CLEP report), 99–101
Malek, Fred, 160–161, 314, 347n160
Malek, Marlene, 160–161, 314
Malek, Michelle, *See* Olson, Michelle
Mandela, Nelson, 74, 85
Marcos, Ferdinand, 85
Márquez, Gabriel García, 34
Marshall, George, 67, 158
Martin, Judith, 40
"May" (Hachenburg), 253, 353n253
Mayhew, Elston, 38
McCain, John, 83–84, 152–153, 161
McCall, Carl, 73, 75–77, 78
McConnell, Mitch, 161
McFadden, David, 180
McFadden, Robert, 316
McGovern, George, 57
McKinley, William, 28
*Memo to the President Elect: How We
　　Can Restore America's Reputation
　　and Leadership* (Albright),
　　139–141

Merck and Co., 22–26, 340n22
Merkel, Angela, 300
Meyer, Eugene, 30
Mezvinsky, Marc, 273
Microsoft, 213
Middle East
　　democracy and, 87–88
　　difficulties of diplomacy and,
　　　214–221, 255–265
　　Trump and, 304
　　see also specific countries
*Mighty and the Almighty: Reflections
　　on America, God, and World
　　Affairs, The* (Albright), 105,
　　108–109, 110, 139, 147, 274
Mikulski, Barbara, 125–126, 316
Miller, Emma Guffey, 81
Miramax, 30–31, 35
Mitchell, Derek, 91, 342n80
Mitchell, George, 214
Mkapa, Benjamin, 100
Mondale, Walter, 29, 286
Monroe, James, 34
Morocco, 264
Mubarak, Hosni, 215–217
Muskie, Edmund, 55–57, 149, 203, 274
Mussolini, Benito, 289–290
Muturi, Joseph, 98, 99
Myanmar, 16

Nasser, Gamal Abdel, 215
National Collegiate Athletic
　　Association (NCAA), 182
National Democratic Institute (NDI)
　　Albright and, 4–5, 80–82, 85–87,
　　　342n80, 350n217
　　Bush and Iraq and, 87–89
　　Czechoslovakia and, 82–84
　　democratic culture and, 86, 92
　　Kenya and, 98
　　Kosovo and, 90–92
　　Nigeria and, 89–90, 343n90
　　Syria and, 353n261
National Endowment for Democracy, 80

National Museum of American Diplomacy, 180–181

National Public Radio (NPR), commencement speeches and, 120

National School Boards Association, 11–12

national security, Trump and, 303, 304

National Security Council, 4, 57, 159

NATO
Albright and expert group of, 183, 186–191
Albright on future and challenges of, 190, 191–193
obligations of members, 190–191, 193
origins and aspirations of, 183–184, 348n184
post-Cold War members of, 2, 90–91, 183, 184–186, 189, 321

NATO 2020, 190–191

Netanyahu, Bibi, 257–258

New York Post, 77

New York Stock Exchange (NYSE)
Albright on board of, 70–79
Grasso's compensation issues and, 74–79
history of, 71–72

New York Times, 43, 262
asks Albright for information for her "advance obituary," 316

Nigeria, 89–90, 343n90

Nixon, Richard, 55–57, 302, 309

Noonan, Peggy, 87

Noor, queen of Jordan, 143

Obama, Barack, 157, 161, 280, 281, 284, 344n105
Albright and G20 conference, 159
foreign policy and, 171, 212–221, 255–265, 290
inauguration events and, 154–156
NATO and, 183, 186–191

Presidential Medal of Freedom and, 222–223, 351n223
2008 presidential election campaign and, 142, 147–152

Obama, Michelle, 150, 156

Obasanjo, Olusegun, 89–90

O'Brien, Conan, 268–269, 314

O'Brien, Jim, 17, 21, 22, 204, 205, 206

Olson, Michelle, 314–315

Orbán, Victor, 289, 298

Pakistan, 194, 302

Palin, Sarah, 152–153, 161

Panetta, Leon, 71, 73, 226

Parks and Recreation (television program), 271

partisanship
after election of 2016, 293–294
think tanks and, 167–168

Partners for a New Beginning (PNB), 213–214

Patel, Eboo, 277

Patterson, Cissy, 30

Paulson, Hank, 78, 79

PBS, Albright and *Great Decisions* program, 211

Personal History (Graham), 30

Peru, 95–96

Petraeus, David, 228

Philippines, 16, 85

Pinochet, Augusto, 85

pins, of Albright, 223, 271, 274, 286
book about, 173–175, 178–180
history of wearing of, 175–178, 188
museum tour of, 180–181, 348n180

Plastic People of the Universe, 227, 248

Podesta, John, 52, 71

Poehler, Amy, 271

Poland, 24–25, 240, 300–301
NATO and, 2, 185, 189, 191, 192, 321
Solidarity movement in, 80

Polson, Steve, 126

Pompeo, Mike, 229

Porterfield, Daniel, 165

poverty, 94–96
  CLEP and, 96–101
  history and, 96–97
Powell, Colin, 180
  Albright's note to, 3
  anonymity and, 273
  Bush's invasion of Iraq and, 43–45,
    46–48, 341n45
  Presidential Medal of Freedom and,
    223, 351n223
  as public speaker, 10–11
  as secretary of state, 39–41, 282, 283
  on television, 272–273
Power, Samantha, 285–286
Power of the Powerless (Havel), 243
Prague Winter (Albright), xiii,
  230–237, 241, 250, 253
Present at the Creation (Acheson),
  29–30
Presidential Medal of Freedom, 222,
  351n223
  Albright as recipient of, 222–223
Principled Pluralism (report), 277
Pritzker, Penny, 213
Pulitzer, Joseph, 6
Putin, Vladimir, 64, 187, 188, 189, 191,
  289

Qatar, 60, 162, 182–183, 264

Rabin, Leah, 177–178
Rasmussen, Anders Fogh, 186
Rasputin, Grigori Yefimovich, 165
Rauf, Feisal Abdul, 106, 107, 344n105
Rayburn, Sam, 81
Read My Pins (Albright), 173–175,
  178–180, 182
Reagan, Ronald, 80, 163, 309
Redford, Robert, 274–275, 354n274
Reed, John, 78
religion
  Albright and, 109–114
  Albright's "God book," 105,
    108–109, 110

foreign policy and, 103–108
importance of religious pluralism,
  275–277
prayer and, 112–113
responsibility to protect (R2P) doctrine,
  of UN, 219–220, 260, 350n219
Rente, Lucia, 54
Revere, Paul, 291
Rhoads, Harry, 13
Rice, Condoleezza, 268, 282, 315
  as national security advisor, 39,
    40–41, 43, 47, 282
  as secretary of state, 43, 47, 126–127,
    134, 136–137, 138, 283
Rice, Susan, 316
Rice University, 17
Robinson, Mary, 100
Rochambeau, Comte de (Jean-
  Baptiste Donatien de Vimeur),
  294
Rolla Daily News, 269
Romania, 24
Romanow, Liza, 16, 323
Romney, Mitt, 280
Roosevelt, Franklin, 319
Root, Elihu, 166
Rouhani, Hassan, 257–258
Rudman, Warren, 205, 206, 226
Rumsfeld, Donald, 137
Russia
  antidemocratic trends in, 290
  NATO's role after Cold War and,
    184–186, 187–189, 191
  Syria and, 263
  see also Putin, Vladimir; Soviet
    Union
Rwanda, 169

Sadat, Anwar, 16
Safe & Sound, 129
Safire, William, 146
Salter, Kate, 13
Sanders, Bernie, 278–280
Saperstein, David, 106, 108, 344n105

Sarbanes, Paul, 70–71, 342n70
Sartre, John-Paul, 317, 356n317
Saudi Arabia, 117, 259, 290
Schatz, Benjamin (grandson), 128,
    129, 253
Schatz, Eleanor "Ellie"
    (granddaughter), 127, 129, 253
Schatz, Jack (son-in-law), 129
Schiff, Vera, 235
Schrempp, Jürgen, 77
Scopes, John T., 6
Scripps College, 122–123
secretary of state, of U.S., 17, 28
    after-office activities of, 5–6, 28
    Albright as, 1–3, 5, 6–7, 9–10,
        20–21, 33–34, 42, 50, 89, 94,
        104, 112, 138, 164, 194, 201–202,
        259–260, 267–268
    Albright's life after service as, xiv, 5,
        6, 7–10, 17–18
    Albright's swearing in as, 176–177
    Hillary Clinton as, 157–158, 183,
        216, 255
    National Museum of American
        Diplomacy and, 180–181
    Powell as, 39–41, 283
    Rice as, 43, 47, 126–127, 134,
        136–137, 138, 283
Securities and Exchange Commission
    (SEC), 72, 77
Segretti, Donald, 56
September 11, 2001 terrorist attacks,
    41–42, 104, 117, 121–122
Sherman, John, 28
Sherman, Wendy, 17, 21, 22, 52, 204
Sherman, William Tecumseh, 28
Shocas, Elaine, 173–174, 178–180
Shore, Wini. *See* Freund, Wini Shore
Silva, Kathy Korbel (sister), 8, 130, 231,
    232, 252, 267
Simon, Bren, 179
Šimová, Dagmar "Dáša" Deimlová
    (cousin), 233

60 Minutes (television program), Iraq
    sanctions and, 115–119
Skorton, David, 132
Smith College, 121
Smithsonian Institution's National
    Portrait Gallery, 274
social media
    after election of 2016, 293–294
    Albright and, 60–61, 115, 268–269,
        279
    ASG and, 207–209
    governments and, 89
    immigrants and, 299
    Middle East and, 214, 262
    politics and, 293–294, 309, 321
    religious tolerance and, 277
    Trump and, 301
    young people and, 66
Solana, Javier, 50
Solidarity movement, in Poland, 80
South Africa, 85
Soviet Union, as nuclear power,
    184. *See also* Putin, Vladimir;
    Russia
Spiegel, Alfred (maternal
    grandfather), 237
Spieglová, Klara (great grandmother),
    250
Spieglová, Marie "Máňa" "Maruška,"
    (aunt), 237, 238, 239
    mentioned in her mother's
        journal, 325–326, 327–328, 330,
        331–332
Spieglová, Růžena (maternal
    grandmother)
    Albright and journal of, 236–241
    journal of, 325–333
Spitzer, Eliot, 72
St. John Knits, 179
St. John's Episcopal Church,
    Georgetown, 113, 285
St. John's Episcopal Church, Harpers
    Ferry, 113–114

Stahl, Leslie, 115–116
Starbucks, xiii
State Department
    portraits and named rooms at,
        126–127
    see also secretary of state, of U.S.
Statue of Liberty, 6, 299
Steinem, Gloria, 280
Steuben, Friedrich Wilhelm von,
    294
Stevenson, Adlai, 52–53
Stewart, Jan, 289
Stewart, Martha, 72
Stonebridge International, 205
Stránská, Hana, 236
Sudan, 93, 169, 265
Summers, Larry, 100
Syria, 218–219, 255–256, 259–261, 263,
    353n261
    see also Assad, Bashir al-

Taliban, 42–43, 46, 135, 186, 194–195,
    349n195
Taylor, John Bigelow, 179
Team of Rivals (Goodwin), 158
Terezín
    Albright family's visit to, in 2015,
        252–254
    Albright's contacts with survivors
        of, 235–236
    Albright's relatives sent to, 233–236,
        240
    Family plaque at, 253, 352–3n253
Terris, Susan Dubinsky, 131, 133
Theodore Roosevelt Award, of
    NCAA, 182
think tanks
    Albright and, 163–165, 169–172
    history of, 165–167
    partisanship of, 167–168
34th Street Group, 52–54, 58, 182
Tibbits, Nate, 22
Time to Pee! (Willems), 36, 340n36

"To Madeleine Albright, Without
    Greetings" (Iraqi poem), 175,
    348n175
Trawniki (Nazi forced labor camp),
    240
True Grit (Portis), 195
Truman, Harry, 81, 138, 183, 322,
    348n184
Trump, Donald
    and NATO, 192
    antidemocratic tendencies of, 289,
        292–293
    clash with Congress, 309
    election of 2016 and, 280–281,
        283–285
    foreign policy and, 300–305
    immigration and, 299
Tuggle, Clyde, 104
Tunisia, 86, 213, 214–215, 220–221,
    264
Turkey, 192, 213, 218, 262, 289–290,
    302
Tutu, Desmond, 110
Twain, Mark, xiii, 308, 356n308
Twelfth Night (Shakespeare), 168
Twentieth-Century Czechoslovakia
    (Korbel), 83
Tyco, 72

Ukraine, 64, 84, 101, 191
Uncommon Leadership for Common
    Values conference, 108
Unger, John, 113–114
United Arab Emirates, 209–210, 264
United Nations
    Albright as ambassador to, 5, 21, 40,
        44, 49–50, 115, 159, 175, 217
    Josef Korbel and, 273
    Millennium Development Goals
        of, 195
    post-war security and, 183
    responsibility to protect (R2P) and,
        219–220, 260, 350n219

University of Arizona, 121
University of Denver
    Albright's father as professor at, 61,
        68, 134, 164, 237
    Josef Korbel School of
        International Studies at, 182
University of Warsaw, 301
University of Washington, 117–119
U.S. Institute of Peace, 316
U.S.-Islamic World Forum, 162

van Aartsen, Jozias, 51
Védrine, Hubert, 50, 298
Venezuela, antidemocratic trends in,
    290
Vietnam, 16
von Steuben, Wilhelm, 294

Wałęsa, Lech, 300–301
Walsh, Diana Chapman, 196
Warren, Michael, 205
Washington, George, 34, 81, 275–276,
    347n155
Washington Post, 30, 181, 198, 231, 291
Washington Speakers Bureau (WSB)
    Albright and, 10–14
    Powell and, 10–11
Washington Times-Herald, 30
Watson, Geoffrey (son-in-law), 128
Watson, John "Jack" (grandson),
    128
Watson, Madeleine "Maddie"
    (granddaughter), 128
Weinstein, Harvey, 30–31
Wellesley College
    Albright as alumna of, 143,
        286–287, 317, 319
    Albright as student at, 4, 13, 40, 43,
        63, 68, 110, 120, 130–131, 144
    Albright Institute at, 196–200, 317

Hillary Clinton and, 143, 145
    hoop-rolling tradition at, 197–199
Wells, H. G., 69
Westminster College, 191–192
White, E. B., 310
Wiesel, Elie, 232
Williams, Rowan, 110–111
Wilson, Woodrow, 166
Winfrey, Oprah, 151
Wisner, Frank, 216
Wold-Olsen, Per, 24
Wolf, Frank, 108
Wollack, Ken, 91, 342n80
women
    Albright Institute at Wellesley and,
        196–200, 317
    Hillary Clinton's campaign and,
        279–280
    importance of education of to a
        country's development, 194–196
    work-life balance and, 199–200
Woodward, Bill, 31–32
World Conference on Women (1995),
    143, 197
World War II
    Albright's family flees to England
        during, 12, 19, 37–38, 208, 231,
        233–236, 238, 250
    Havel and, 243
    NATO's creation after, 232–235
    see also Holocaust
WorldCom, 72

Yale Divinity School, Albright's
    speech at, 104–105
Yeltsin, Boris, 16
Yonemoto, John, 204
Yugoslavia, 12, 169

Žantovský, Michael, 248, 353n248

About the Author

MADELEINE ALBRIGHT served as America's sixty-fourth secretary of state from 1997 to 2001. Her distinguished career also includes positions on Capitol Hill, on the National Security Council, and as U.S. ambassador to the United Nations. She is a resident of Washington, DC, and Virginia.

ALSO BY
MADELEINE ALBRIGHT

"[Albright] witnessed the evils of *Fascism* firsthand.... And she effectively makes the case: pay more attention to the signals, subtle and strong. A lot more."

—*The New Yorker*

"A gripping account of World War II. . . . Albright weaves a powerful narrative that wraps her family's story into the larger political drama unfolding in Europe."

—*The Philadelphia Inquirer*

"Lively and evocative. . . . The result is a book that creates a sense of policy made by real people."

—*The New Yorker*

"An engrossing, important read."

—*People* (4 stars)

"Affairs from which our next president, and of course the electorate, might profit."

—*Seattle Times*

"Tells the compelling story of how these small objects became part of her 'personal diplomatic arsenal."

—*Chicago Tribune*

HARPER ⬤ PERENNIAL

📕 HarperCollins*Publishers*